ROME AND THE COUNTER-REFORMATION IN ENGLAND

Reginald Pole
(1500–1558)
Archbishop of Canterbury
Cardinal of S. Maria in Cosmedin

ROME

AND THE

COUNTER - REFORMATION

IN

ENGLAND

By

PHILIP HUGHES

BURNS OATES

1944

First published, 1942
Reprinted May, 1944

NIHIL OBSTAT:
Thomas E. Bird, S.T.D.,
Censor Deputatus.

IMPRIMATUR:
✠ Thomas,
Archiepiscopus Birmingamiensis.

Birmingamiae,
die 3a Martii, 1941.

MADE AND PRINTED IN GREAT BRITAIN
FOR
BURNS OATES & WASHBOURNE LTD

M.A.
A.M.
K.M.L.

CARISSIMIS

CONTENTS

Book I

CARDINAL POLE

Book II

CARDINAL ALLEN

vii

LIST OF ILLUSTRATIONS

BOOK I

CARDINAL POLE

CHAPTER I

THE REFORMATION IN ENGLAND, 1531–1553

LET it first of all be clear what this book intends. It does not offer itself as a history of the fortunes of the Catholic Church in England during the period of which it treats. Nor is it a history of the Counter-Reformation. It is simply an attempt to describe the measures which the Catholic Church adopted to counter the Reformation in England. The subject of the book is Catholic Action in England three and four hundred years ago ; to say what Catholics did in reply to militant anti-Catholicism, in what spirit these Catholics acted, who the men were that led them, and how their endeavour fared.

The heart of this long drama, played through a period of a hundred years or so (1553–1640), is the reign of Queen Elizabeth. The reign of Queen Mary is a kind of prologue to the story. The reigns of James I and Charles I are its epilogue.

The form the book takes is due to its genesis, a paper, read, by invitation of His Grace the Archbishop-Bishop of Southwark, to the Catholic Truth Society Conference at Brighton in September, 1938. It seemed an easy way out of the difficulty of covering this vast subject, of putting it before an audience of a thousand people in the space of an hour, to associate the chief events and the forces that shaped them with the men who were the chief actors on the Catholic side ; namely, for the reign of Mary, Cardinal Pole ; for the reign of Elizabeth, Cardinal Allen and Fr. Robert Persons, S.J. ; for the early-seventeenth century, Dr. Richard Smith, Bishop of Chalcedon.

It is only in the period I have called the prologue that the story of the Counter-Reformation in England follows the general lines of that movement throughout Europe ; that is to say, only in this period is it the story of the co-

3

operation of a Catholic prince with the Holy See to restore
the status of the Catholic religion in a country which has
been partially protestantised by previous heretical princes.

In the next period, the reign of Elizabeth, we are faced
with the new, and peculiarly English, situation, of a vigorous
attack on the Reformation in possession, in possession, that
is to say, of the means of government and of every organ
of the national life. England is the one country in Europe
where the Reformation victory is violently disputed, and
where a long, concerted attempt is made to reverse that
victory.

As the Elizabethan age passes into that of the first two
Stewarts, and throughout their reigns, the objective of the
Catholic Church in England begins to change somewhat.
The aim now is rather to obtain toleration for Catholics,
liberty for them to practise their religion, than to dislodge
the heretics who had possessed themselves of the government
of England.

Some explanation why the attempt to counter the
Reformation in England failed, must be implicit in any
book that professes to tell the story of the movement, and
any such book should contain some indication, some hint,
as to the reasons why Catholicism almost disappeared from
this country during the early-eighteenth century. It should
also offer some clue as to the origin of some, at least, of
those anti-Catholic prejudices which still so actively hinder
the development of the Catholic Church among the English
people.

It is a very English story that is to be told, of action
English on both sides ; a story in which the characteristic
strength, and weakness, of the race is displayed very fully.
And through it all, the same forces work, to the very end.
There is the interest of the English generally in religious
conflict, if not in religion. There is the memory of the
Protestant martyrs as presented by the never-to-be-forgotten
book of John Foxe. There is the small but ever active group
of bitterly anti-Catholic theologians, and the politicians
with whom, from 1559, they are in alliance. The genius of
Cecil—in one thing fierce at least and savage, namely, his
opposition to the renascent English Catholicism—contributes
a permanent element that is of first importance to the
struggle, and just as permanent and as unchanging and as
important is the mentality of the Catholic exiles. Rome,

almost to the end, has a double anxiety; to supply the English with priests and spiritual succour, and also to free them from their heretical rulers. There is a further permanent feature of the history in the failure of the Holy See to provide any effective ecclesiastical government in England after 1559, and in the resultant chaos of Catholic life, its feuds, and its scandals. There are the glorious minority of the confessors and martyrs, who gave gladly their property, their liberty, and their life rather than surrender their religion, and whose sacrifice is all the more glorious when it is seen against the background of the general ecclesiastical life of the time. And, finally, there is the *Ordo Doctorum*, that array of controversialists, theologians, historians, spiritual writers, and poets, who from tiny new Englands beyond the seas, at Antwerp and Louvain and Douay, strove hard to rebuild Sion and, incidentally, added to the continuity of English literature a new, and as yet scarcely recorded, chapter.

The attitude of the Crown to this great stir among its Catholic subjects varies from one period to another. In Mary's reign the Crown and all its forces are at the service of the Counter-Reformation. For the next sixty years they are just as whole-heartedly anti-Catholic. Then comes a period of political and cultural alliances with those states abroad where the Counter-Reformation flourishes, and a consequent slackening of hostility to Catholics at home; even a certain protection and patronage of them.

And if the relation of the Crown to the Counter-Reformation varies so largely, so do those four chief personages differ around whose activity I should like to group the events. Cardinal Pole is the Archbishop of Canterbury; Cardinal Allen an attainted exile with a price on his head. Fr. Persons is a man with powerful friends at Rome and at Madrid, the twin centres of the Counter-Reformation activity; Richard Smith has little beyond his own abilities to assist him in the increasingly laborious task. All these four men are scholars, as well as men of action, true Renaissance types, learned, thinkers, writers—Allen and Persons, indeed, deserving of high place in the story of their country's literature.

Part of what this book tells will be new to the general reader. Some of its chapters hint at a story never told as yet. The sketch of the work of Cardinal Pole is wholly indebted to sources and works long in print and within every student's reach. But the life of Pole still remains to be written, an extraordinary fact to record of the most international Englishman of his day, one who was an English force shaping the course of such international affairs as the papal reform of the Catholic Church and the Council of Trent. Even the beginnings of any really adequate life of Pole can hardly be attempted so long as his letters remain uncollected and unedited. The two best modern lives are in foreign tongues, and neither has as yet found an English translator —not even the life, in German, by Fr. Alphonsus Zimmerman, S.J., which is the only really scholarly study, and which appeared now nearly fifty years ago. This may be taken to argue a curious indifference on the part of the nation generally to one of the greatest English churchmen of all time. The next two lacunæ are to the particular discredit of the Catholic body, the missing lives of Allen and of Persons. It is fifty years and more since Fr. Knox of the London Oratory collected and edited the great edition of Allen's letters. But in all that time no one has come forward to provide either the wanted life or the means by which some writer might be encouraged to take on the task of writing it. Possibly the hesitation which, time and again, holds back all those who are faced with a task whose achievement can scarcely bring popularity, has had something to do with this, and a related fearfulness may be responsible for the lengthy, the too, too lengthy silence, about his fellow-hero, Fr. Persons, an Elizabethan of the Elizabethans. Fr. Pollen's masterly work, *The English Catholics in the Reign of Elizabeth*, is an indispensable guide for the first twenty years of the queen's reign, and Arnold Oscar Meyer's *England and the Catholic Church under Queen Elizabeth*, for the whole of it. Various publications of the Catholic Record Society and the valuable papers which historically minded fathers of the Society of Jesus have, these forty years past and more, contributed to *The Month* are equally useful and, for the present, very often the sole assistance of the general historian.

And now we come to the point of greatest hesitation, certain chapters of the story which can so easily make the telling of it seem little else but an extensive public washing of domestic linen that is none too clean. These are the chapters which describe the origin and progress of the great feuds between the various sections of the clergy, and the influence of these feuds on the general Catholic life of the time. These are the chapters which deal with the extraordinary fact that for almost the whole of this period Rome left the English Catholics without that episcopal government which is a normal feature of Catholic life, and they must deal to some extent with the vexed question as to how this came about. They must deal, too, with the no less inconvenient fact of chronic weaknesses in the Catholic life of the time, weaknesses that resulted, directly and inevitably, from this lack of a local episcopate.

In much of the exposition of this last difficult period this book is something of a pioneer. The first to attempt to tell this story was Hugh Tootell, otherwise Charles Dodd, a secular priest who published his famous church history in 1737. How biased he was against the Society of Jesus is, I suppose, matter of fairly common knowledge. A hundred years later another secular priest took up the matter again. This was Mark Aloysius Tierney, librarian to the Duke of Norfolk, who in 1837 began to bring out a new edition of Dodd, with new chapters and a copious appendix of original documents. Tierney's fifth volume, which ends with the death of James I, was his last. So much opposition, it is said, had been aroused by what he had already written about these controversies that, as he approached the bitterest of them all, the bishops prayed him to hold his hand. They were less than thirty years away from the ravages of the various Cisalpine quarrels ; new difficulties, due to the twin influence of the Oxford Movement and the Irish immigration, were upon them ; it was well within living memory that the Society of Jesus had been restored in England in the teeth of their passive hostility ; and to allow the peace of Sion to be further troubled by what perhaps appeared to them archæology, would be an act of wanton carelessness. So, while Lingard fumed, the great work came to an end.

We live in happier times than those of Dodd and Tierney. The hierarchy is no longer under a present suspicion of desiring the destruction of the Society or of working against its full restoration. In every part of England to-day Jesuits work with seculars, their fellow-labourers in parishes as well as in colleges. And since, a hundred years ago now, fears on all sides brought Tierney's work to so abrupt an end, much has come to light which he never knew and much of this has been published, and not least by Jesuit writers in their own reviews. Archives where, in Tierney's day, the dust of two centuries lay undisturbed, are now open to all who are interested to study these matters. It is only a matter of time before everything is published. And, as Cardinal Ehrle, S.J., said to the writer, about these very quarrels and feuds : ' As a mere matter of policy it is better that the story makes its first appearance under Catholic auspices,' a dictum that holds true, surely, of the history of all ecclesiastical scandals. He also said to me in the course of a memorable conversation : ' When you tell the story leave nothing out and print the documents in full, or you will be responsible for the greater scandal still of giving new cause to the anti-Catholic prejudice that no Catholic dares to tell the truth where Catholic interests are affected.'

Almost nothing new has been written for two hundred years about the internal condition of Catholicism in England during the early seventeenth century, and here I make use of manuscripts in the Vatican Library and the Vatican Archives, open, since Leo XIII's great gesture, to all the scholars of the world. But still more important for this purpose are the archives of the Roman Congregation *De Propaganda Fide*. This is the body which, founded in 1622, controls all that relates to the Foreign Missions, and it was to this Congregation that, from its foundation down to 1908, Catholic affairs in this country were subject. It was to the late Prefect of Propaganda, H.E. Cardinal Van Rossum, C.SS.R., that the writer owed the privilege of working for twelve months in these archives. He feels that he ought here, when for the first time he is making use of what he then discovered, to express his appreciation of that privilege. At the same time he owes much also to the, present Abbot General of the Canons Regular of Prémontré Mgr. Hubert Noots, to whose friendly influence with the Cardinal Prefect the coveted permission was entirely due.

If, from one point of view, whoever for the first time ventilates this story risks the accusation of what has been expressively termed ' muck-raking,' he has also before him the delicate task of indicating an early instance of the tragedy that eternally threatens Catholic Action, namely, that it can be fatally compromised by the activities of political Catholics—of Catholics, that is to say, who are not merely politicians (which all Catholics have a right to be, and even sometimes a duty to be), but who identify their politics with their Catholicism.

I hope there is no need for me to say that I nowhere offer a judgement on what was done in this long drama nor on the men who were the actors. We cannot but judge the policies of the past—for it is of their effects that all history is made up. But it is often foolish to spend time sitting in judgement on the men who devised the policies. For we to-day can see results which they could not have been expected ever to foresee, and, knowing only a part of their difficulties, while yet we see where their policies led, we risk judging rashly, and of straying even from probability. To the immense complexity of any historical subject there is always added this very real difficulty that we are prone to judge the men of past ages as though their lives were set in our own age—simply because they happen to share our human nature. It is a tendency akin to that which moves us to judge the way foreigners conduct their domestic affairs by the ideals which—often in quite other circumstances—guide our life here in England. The French, the Germans, the Americans are not English. The seventeenth and the sixteenth centuries are not the twentieth—still less, if one may risk saying it, were they the nineteenth. And our historical prejudgement only too often, still reeks of Victorianism. The Moral Law, nevertheless, is eternal.

We have then first to remember, to force our minds to accept the fact, and then to labour with our minds until they really understand all this implies—processes none too easy—that, in the period of which this book treats, a conception of what human society ought to be, to which all men, for a thousand years, have unhesitatingly subscribed, is in its death agony. Throughout every province of Christendom, something of the threshing of those mighty limbs is felt, as the stricken thing writhes in its throes. The whole of Western civilisation heaves, strains, pants, gasps, and at times roars and screams, with rage, with anger, or with terror. There is nothing academic about the central activity of the Reformation century. And while the opponents of the old ideal are everywhere most active, everywhere too, in like devoted activity, there are to be found its defenders, who cling to it passionately, desperately, because its defeat is, for them, the defeat of civilisation. So it is that they make a great fight, not merely for certain special Catholic doctrines, not merely for such endangered fundamentals as the Roman Primacy and the Sacrifice of the Mass, but for the whole medieval Catholic ideal of a religion-inspired civilisation built up of states whose strong arm is at religion's service, to protect it against attack, and for the offensive, too, whenever new, hostile ideals—heresy—menace the established order.

This medieval ideal had in the sixteenth century reached its term, but that generation of Catholics could not foretell the future, any more than can our own. The ideal for which Catholics then fought would one day cease to be, except as an ideal and—what could hardly have seemed possible to those who agonised in its defence—Catholicism has survived its disappearance. We Catholics to-day are witnesses to this. Let us beware, in our security and comfort, of judging that bygone generation, the desperate anxiety of those men—and the desperate measures to which they resorted—as though they had known then, what none could possibly know for a further three hundred years.

One hot August day, in the year 1553, two messengers, travelling post-haste on business of the utmost importance, met at Bologna. The one was proceeding from Pope Julius III. at Rome to His Most Reverend Lordship Cardinal Reginald Pole at the abbey of Maguzzano by the side of Lake Como. The other was Vincenzo Parpaglia, the Abbot of Maguzzano, who, sent by that very cardinal, was on his way for Rome and the Pope. The news each carried was the same good tidings, that the Catholic heir to the throne of England, the Princess Mary, had really reached the throne at last. Just one month before, her brother, the sixteen-year-old King Edward VI, had died, and now, after weeks filled with conspiracy, the plot to enthrone in her place her young Protestant cousin, Lady Jane Grey, had miscarried and the Princess Mary was really queen.

The news had reached Rome on August 5 and Pole the day following. The cardinal was writing to Rome to offer his services in the work of restoring the Church in England, and the courier of Pope Julius whom his own messenger now met, actually carried in his wallet Pole's commission as Legate and remarkably ample powers to deal with the hundred anomalies which, to the theologian and the canonist, the English situation must present.

At the moment, however, that situation appeared, both to the Pope and to the cardinal, a thing essentially simple. The Pope was prepared to meet the case with the utmost benevolence—as these first despatches to Pole prove—and, with a generous bestowal of absolutions, to receive back into the household of the Faith this prodigal nation that had for so long been wasting its substance and, more recently, living on husks. Pole would arrive and the waiting people be reconciled.

But things were by no means so simple as this, and within a very short time the Holy See was made aware that only the most careful handling of the situation would preserve the nascent restoration from a premature end.

It was now something like nineteen years, in August, 1553, since the breach between England and the Holy See had been consummated. Between the days when Rome and England were in constant touch with each other, —through the relations of the English bishops with the Curia and the intercourse of nuncios in London and English diplomatic agents in Rome—and this year of grace 1553, there stretched nearly twenty years of almost complete isolation, a whole generation during which neither government had first-hand information about the other. And for the whole of that period Reginald Pole, who was now to play the great part of the Holy See's principal agent, had been an exile from England, cut off, no less really than the Holy See, from any vital contact with the national life. During those years a new England had grown up, and this the cardinal only knew as men know a land and a race they have never seen, but of which and of whom travellers tell strange tales. A revolution in the religious life of the English had been accomplished, a revolution clad in all the forms of English legality, rooted in a host of acts of parliament, of royal proclamations, of synodal decrees, of bishop's injunctions. There had, of course, been some resistance to the change. The new laws expected this, and provided penalties in anticipation. There had, then, been martyrs and confessors, risings, executions, imprisonments and, for some years, a reign of terror. And the whole drama had gone on against the background of that general European struggle between Catholicism and the new heresies which began many years before the English breach with Rome, and in this struggle the English king had continued, in many instances, to be an anti-heretical champion even after the breach.

The Church of England, that *Ecclesia Anglicana* whose liberties were specifically declared by the English State in the most famous of all English charters, the Metropolitans of the two ecclesiastical provinces of Canterbury and York, their suffragans, with the clergy and the faithful people organised under them in the twenty-one dioceses of England and Wales, had bowed before the storm. Individuals had resisted, made their protest, and paid its price. But the general body had yielded, and yielded in all the solemnity of official form. The *Ecclesia Anglicana* pledged itself never for the future to enact any ecclesiastical laws except with the king's consent, and it petitioned the king to examine the whole body of church law then existing, and to abrogate and annul as it pleased him. Nor for the future would the bishops and clergy so much as assemble unless the king's writ called them together.[1]

The ancient subordination of this *Ecclesia Anglicana* to that *Ecclesia Romana* which, in the dawn of the Middle Ages, had called it into being, had been sapped by yet further enactments and surrenders. Appeals in matrimonial causes, matters of probate and cases concerning ecclesiastical properties, carried for centuries now to Rome from the decisions of the local English church courts, were henceforward to be given their ultimate decision in England. Roman citations, sentences, excommunications, and interdicts are henceforth to be ignored. Clergy who take any account of such papal action, and because of it refuse the sacraments to those excommunicated or, because of an interdict, refuse to say Mass, are to be punished. As far as English members of the Catholic Church are concerned, the Roman jurisdiction ceases.[2]

The metropolitans and the bishops of this *Ecclesia Anglicana* had, originally, been directly nominated by that *Ecclesia Romana* which created their sees. Then, for centuries, they were elected by the chapters of their cathedral churches, the Roman Church intervening to settle disputed elections, and even, at times, to make its own nominations over the

---

[1] 25 Henry VIII, c. 19—1534 ; G. and H., LI.
[2] 24 Henry VIII, c. 12—1533 ; G. and H., L.

heads of the electors. Next it had come to be the rule, in these provinces of Canterbury and York as in the other provinces that made up the Catholic Church, that the archbishops and bishops were ' provided ' by the direct act of the Pope. But in all this time, whatever the diversity of the system by which the Catholic Church in England secured the succession of bishops, one thing remained fairly constant, namely, the influence of the Crown. Whether by influence lawfully used at elections, or by influence directly brought to bear on the popes, the kings of England had generally been able to secure that no man was made a bishop but such as they willed. There were indeed famous occasions when pope and king failed to agree in the matter. There are such dramatic incidents as Innocent III's imposition of Cardinal Langton as Archbishop of Canterbury. But the usual thing was agreement, and especially was this the case once the system of appointment by ' provision ' was established. Although it was the papal bull which made the candidate the bishop, the bull was generally issued to the candidate of the king's choice. The subordination of the Church in England to Rome, which was the foundation of this system, was now brought to an end.[1] From henceforward when the royal permission was sent to a cathedral chapter to elect a new bishop or archbishop, there was sent also the name of the candidate whom they must elect. The election thus made, the metropolitan must confirm it, and consecrate the elect. The English episcopate henceforward would owe nothing of its jurisdiction, of its right to rule men in spiritual matters, to any act on the part of the Pope. As a ruling body in spiritual matters the *Ecclesia Anglicana*, the provinces of Canterbury and York of the Catholic Church, is now, by an Act of Parliament, autonomous. And a hint is given as to the source whence its jurisdiction is held to derive, in the act's provision that shall the chapter delay to elect above twelve days after receipt of the royal commands, the king shall himself, by letters patent under the great seal, appoint the new bishop.

The Roman Church's financial claims on its daughter the *Ecclesia Anglicana* were also swept away, the payment by new bishops of their first year's revenue as a tribute money (which henceforward went to the king), the popular tribute called Peter's Pence, and all that elaborate financial system

[1] 25 Henry VIII, c. 20—1534 ; G. and H., LII.

by which, for some three centuries now, the popes had raised revenues from the possessions of the Church in England.

To complete the breach—legislative, financial, judicial —between Rome and the Church in England, there was now only needed some provision for that immense traffic of dispensations, licences, and ecclesiastical faculties of every kind which, at every turn, the administration of a huge system of law touching men's personal lives makes necessary. Some of this traffic had been between the individual suppliant and his diocesan bishop. But the most important part of it, by far, had been with the Pope, either directly with the Roman Court or indirectly with its agents in this country, and among these last with the English bishops acting as the Pope's delegates or commissioners. All the Roman share in this system was now terminated. All such dispensations, grants, licences, and so forth, are, from now on, to be granted and obtained within this realm and not elsewhere. The supreme source of such favours and powers is henceforth, for the English king's subjects, the Archbishop of Canterbury. The more important grants made by the archbishop in virtue of this Act of Parliament [1] require the royal confirmation before they go into act. And if the archbishop unnecessarily deny the favour sought, the petitioner's remedy is through the king's writ compelling the archbishop to make the grant or to show cause for his refusal in the king's courts.

The climax of this religious revolution was the Act of 1534 [2] which proclaimed the Royal Supremacy, and enforced acceptance of this new doctrine on all the king's subjects. The king of England—it is now declared—is the only Supreme Head in earth of the Church of England. He alone has full power to reform abuses, to correct heresies, and generally exercise spiritual jurisdiction. Nearly four years before this date the *Ecclesia Anglicana* had already recognised the king as its Supreme Head on earth, with the saving clause ' as far as, by the law of Christ, this is allowed,' and in the early part of this year, 1534, it had declared that the Roman pontiff has no greater jurisdiction bestowed on him by God in the Holy Scriptures over this realm of England than any other foreign bishop. This was in March and

[1] 25 Henry VIII, c. 21—1534 ; G. and H., LIII.
[2] 26 Henry VIII, c. 1 ; G. and H., LV.

May and the king followed up the declaration by a proclamation in June ' abolishing the usurped power of the Pope.' Then came the Act of Supremacy itself, that annexes to the king's imperial crown the dignity of supreme head and the jurisdiction belonging to it, and finally, in the same month of November, 1534, an act [1] regulating the succession to the crown which sets out the prescribed oath which all the king's subjects are to take. In this oath they swear, not only to be loyal to the king and to his issue by Anne Boleyn, but also ' to defend the said Act of Succession [2] and all the effects and contents thereof.' Among such ' contents ' is the declaration that the marriage with Katherine was invalid, and that with Anne ' good and consonant to the laws of Almighty God ' and also the declaration that the Pope's power of dispensation is but usurped.

The religious life of the English people was thus organised as a thing in every way distinct from the Roman Church, something which enjoyed a complete autonomy, under the supreme control of the English king. Within the boundaries of this new ecclesiastical autonomy the power which had called it into being—the Parliament—and the power thus called into being—the Royal Supremacy—began, each in its own sphere, to make additional innovations. By two successive acts of parliament the whole monastic life of the country was destroyed, and by implication, the value of the contemplative life consecrated to God through vows of religion, reputed nil. Christianity in England, that had so lately abjured the Pope, stripped itself now of monasticism. In these two features it agreed with the new heresies, for which, nevertheless, it still professed the greatest abhorrence and whose adepts it still continued fitfully to persecute.

But the position of the English doctrinal innovator, once the English king had definitely broken with the Pope, was very different indeed from what it had been in the earlier half of the reign. Then, to propose any modification of doctrine or such liturgical changes as might imply new doctrine, was to court a heresy trial and death as its penalty. But it was naturally among these already bitter foes of Catholicism that the king found his most zealous supporters in his first desire of breaking with the Roman Church.

[1] 26 Henry VIII, c. 2 ; G. and H., LVI.
[2] *I.e.* the preceding Act (25 Henry VIII, c. 22 ; G. and H., LIV) passed in the spring.

That once accomplished, it was just as natural that these innovators should make the most of their new chance to influence English Christianity in a heretical sense, to protestantise it, if the convenient expression be permitted. How the degree of that chance varied with the king's moods and the needs of his foreign policy is matter of history, and the gradual, steady growth, in the royal councils, in the hierarchy and in all the places of influence, of this element of what, before 1529, would universally in England have been called heresy, is matter of history too.

To what extent all this innovation had succeeded by the time the founder of the Royal Supremacy died, in January, 1547—that is to say the progress of the religious revolution in the first thirteen years during which the Supremacy was operative—can easily be ascertained by anyone who will read the Injunctions issued to the clergy by the various bishops and by the Supreme Head of the Church himself.[1] Many of the old feasts, ' certain superfluous holidays,' had been abolished and their fasting vigils with them,[2] and the ancient devotion to the saints had received another blow when the clergy were bidden to take down images that were the centre of pilgrimages, to which offerings were made, or before which lights were burned.[3] When the clergy were commanded to teach their people that any use of images, except as remembrances of the lives of holy persons, ' books of unlearned men,' [4] was idolatry, the royal injunction passed from the reform of discipline to innovation in doctrine. It again invaded the realm of doctrinal change when it bade all parish priests preach once a quarter, not only an exhortation to the works of charity, mercy, and faith commanded in Holy Scripture, but also a condemnation of such practices as ' pilgrimages, offerings of money, candles and tapers to images or relics, or kissing or licking the same, saying over a number of beads, not understood or minded on ' since Holy Scripture far from promising any reward to those who practise these things denounces them as idolatry and superstition, ' which of all other offences God Almighty does most detest and abhor.' [5]

---

[1] Cf. Visitation Articles and Injunctions of the Period of the Reformation, Vol. II, 1536–1558, by W. H. Frere and W. McC. Kennedy, pp. 1–102.

[2] First Injunctions of Henry VIII, 3 ; F. and K., p. 5 ; G. and H., p. 271.

[3] Second Injunctions of Henry VIII, 7 ; F. and K., p. 38 ; G. and H., p. 277.

[4] Ibid.   [5] Ibid., 6 ; F. and K., p. 37 ; G. and H., p. 277.

Again a whole chapter of the popular, traditional, daily practice of religion disappeared when such ' superstitions ' were proscribed as ' casting holy water upon their beads, or other places, bearing about holy bread, blessing with the holy candle, thinking thereby to put away sins, drive away devils, dreams, or fantasies ; or putting trust and confidence of salvation in the same ceremonies. . . . Whereas they be ordained only to put us in remembrance of the benefits which we have received by Christ.' [1] Here in this last sentence is implicit the new heresy that good works do nothing towards man's salvation, that ceremonies are ' only outward signs and no workers of salvation.' [2] And the same heresy is apparent in the abolition of the prayer called to-day the Angelus, ' lest the people do henceforth trust to have pardon for saying their Aves between the said knelling, as they have done in times past.' [3]

It was a great innovation when not only was the choice of the English tongue in preference to Latin officially ordered for private prayers, but priests, in hearing the Lenten confessions, were bidden to interrogate the penitent whether he knew the Pater, Ave, and Creed in English and the Ten Commandments too, and, should he fall below this standard of knowledge, warn him to better his ignorance before the next Lent, on pain of being refused his Easter Communion.[4] The old Litany of the Saints was first discouraged [5] and then replaced by a new Litany in English from which the saints had disappeared.[6]

The outstanding novelty of the new order of things however, was the popularising of the whole text of Holy Scripture, in a fashion hitherto quite unknown. An English translation of the Bible had lately (1535) for the first time been printed, and now a copy of the new translation specially made was ordered to be set up in every parish church, ' one book of the whole Bible of the largest volume, in English, and the same set up in some convenient place within the said church that you have cure of, whereas your parishioners may most commodiously resort to the same, and

---

[1] Articles of Edward VI (1547), 51 ; F. and K., p. 110.
[2] Royal Proclamation of February 26, 1539, in WILKINS, Concilia, III, p. 862.
[3] Second Injunctions of Henry VIII, 16 ; F. and K., p. 42 ; G. and H. p. 280.
[4] Ibid., 5 ; F. and K., p. 37 ; G. and H., p. 272.
[5] Ibid., 17 ; F. and K., p. 42 ; G. and H., p. 280.   [6] In 1544.

read it ; . . . you shall discourage no man privily or openly
from the reading or hearing of the said Bible, but shall
expressly provoke, stir, and exhort every person to read
the same. . . . ' [1]

One leading feature of the most of these Injunctions is
their insistence on the parish priest's duty to preach, a
topic which is indeed a commonplace of most ecclesiastical
legislation. But this legislation, in two matters, provides
new subjects for the parish priests' sermons, topics to rouse
the most hardened of somnolent back-benchers. For in the
first place priests who had ever extolled pilgrimages, the cult
of relics, images, ' or any such superstition ' were now
commanded, not only to ' recant and reprove the same,'
but to show their parishioners ' that you did the same
upon no ground of Scripture, but as one being led and
seduced by a common error and abuse crept into the
Church, through the sufferance and avarice of such as felt
profit by the same.' [2]

The second new, and universally prescribed, topic was
the Royal Supremacy and the Pope in relation to it. The
clergy are, of course, ' to keep and observe, and as far as
in them may lie to cause to be observed and kept of other,
all and singular laws and statutes . . . made for the
abolishing and extirpation of the Bishop of Rome's pretended
and usurped power and jurisdiction, within this realm, and
for the establishment and confirmation of the king's
authority and jurisdiction within the same, as of the supreme
head of the Church of England.' Also, every Sunday for
the three months following this injunction, and thenceforward twice a quarter every year, they are to preach on
this topic, and to set forth how ' the Bishop of Rome's
usurped power and jurisdiction, having no establishment
nor ground by the law of God, was of most just causes taken
away and abolished, and therefore they owe unto him no
manner of obedience or subjection, and that the king's
power is within his dominion the highest power and potentate under God, to whom all men within the same dominion
by God's commandment owe most loyalty and obedience,
apart and above all other powers and potentates in earth.' [3]

[1] Second Injunctions of Henry VIII, 2, 3 ; F. and K., pp. 35–6 ; G. and H.
pp. 275–6. (The First Injunctions, two years earlier, made like provision,
but the Bible was to be ' both in Latin, and also in English.')
[2] *Ibid.*, 10 ; F. and K., p. 39 ; G. and H., p. 278.
[3] First Injunctions of Henry VIII, 1 ; F. and K., p. 3 ; G. and H.,
pp. 269–270.

And the cleric had before him, also, the king's express command ' To cause all prayers, rubrics, canon of the Mass books, etc., wherein the Bishop of Rome is named, or his presumptuous and proud pomp mentioned, to be utterly abolished and rased out ; and his very name and memory to be never more remembered, except to his contumely and reproach.' [1] Finally, in order that this fundamental article of the new religious system should be understood of even the meanest intelligence, in supplement to the eight annual diatribes, a new petition was added to the Litany and, Sunday by Sunday, before the High Mass, the Englishman henceforth publicly prayed ' From the tyranny of the Bishop of Rome and all his detestable enormities, Good Lord deliver us.'

Of all the activities of the reign none was to be more lastingly effective than this skilfully organised, far-reaching, anti-papal propaganda. After twenty years of it, actively to hate the Pope and all things papal had become part of the normal English mentality. In this matter, at least, there was an apparent agreement and unity of belief among the spiritual leaders of the people, while in other matters the fight continued, more or less openly, and to the very end of Henry's reign, between those who favoured and those who opposed the doctrinal novelties of the continental reformers.

In the last period of the reign the king's position in this matter was conservative, and although the chief of the supporters of heresy—Thomas Cranmer, Archbishop of Canterbury—never lost Henry's personal confidence, the official creed and discipline of the newly organised *Ecclesia Anglicana* remained as before in such matters as belief in the Real Presence, in the sacrificial nature of the Holy Eucharist, in the necessity for auricular confession, in the

---

[1] Letters General of Henry VIII to the bishops, June 1, 1535 ; quoted in Frere and Kennedy, II, p. 109, note 2. How these one-time Catholic bishops understood the Royal Supremacy, once they had accepted it and repudiated their obedience to the Pope, is illustrated by such a detail as the ' style ' adopted by Longland, Bishop of Lincoln, in the preface to his injunctions for Oriel College, Oxford. It runs as follows : ' Safeguarded lawfully for the exercise of ecclesiastical jurisdiction within our diocese and jurisdiction by the supreme ecclesiastical authority of the most illustrious prince in Christ, our lord Henry VIII, by the Grace of God King of England, France and Ireland, Defender of the Faith, and Supreme Head on earth of the Church of England and of Ireland, John, by the divine permission, Bishop of Lincoln to our beloved Provost, Dean, Fellows and scholars of Oriel College . . .' (*ibid.*, II, p. 99).

binding force of vows of chastity, or again in the belief
that communion under one kind suffices for the sacrament
and that clerical celibacy is a thing willed by God. These
were the points determined by the famous Act of the Six
Articles,[1] passed in June, 1539, and the penalties for any
breach of the law were terrifying indeed. Not only the
heretic with unorthodox views about the Holy Eucharist,
but, henceforward, the priest who persisted in his so-called
marriage and the layman who persisted in his neglect of
the law of Easter Communion did so at the peril of their lives.
This summary code of belief and discipline has won for
Henry VIII the curious reputation of being an admirable
Catholic, save for the detail of his anti-papal heresy, though
a theologian would hesitate before admitting the orthodoxy
of all the positions he adopted. But for the *Ecclesia Anglicana*
it was orthodoxy, because it was orthodoxy for its Supreme
Head, and the Supreme Head remaining in this orthodoxy
for the rest of his life, the progress of heresy in the Church's
official formulæ during that period of eight years went no
further.

Henry's death—January 28, 1547—brought to the throne
the son of his marriage with Jane Seymour, Edward VI,
a child of nine. The government of the realm fell to his
mother's brother, Edward Seymour, now Earl of Hertford,
and Duke of Somerset shortly to be. Seymour was a whole-
hearted reformer in the continental sense. The eight years'
dogmatic truce came to an end, and the party led by
Cranmer had now a free hand to protestantise the national
religion. We can trace the process in various acts of Parliament, and, more vividly, in the Injunctions set forth by the
new Supreme Head and by the various bishops under his
authority. As in the earlier stage of the revolution, so,
again, there were protestations, and Bishops Gardiner and
Bonner now went to prison as Bishop Fisher had gone under
Henry. There was the great insurrection in the west of
England in 1549 as, in Henry's time, there had been the
Pilgrimage of Grace. And as, in the earlier reign, there had
been the Dissolution of the Monasteries to create an immense
reserve of wealth whereby to call into being a vested interest
both in the actual change, and in the new doctrine it
implied, namely that the contemplative life is a waste of
time, a thing displeasing to God, so now in the new reign

[1] 31 Henry VIII, c. 14—1539; G. and H., LXV.

the Dissolution of the Chantries Act created a like vested interest in the opposition to the traditional belief that the Mass is a really efficacious sacrifice, profitable to the dead as to the living.

The first hint of the coming revolution in the official conception of what the central act of the national worship was meant to be, was given in the very first law enacted in the new reign. This is called *An Act against Revilers and for Receiving in Both Kinds*.[1] Its object is stated as being to end unseemly language about the Blessed Sacrament, used by many of the controversialists of the day, and the first novelty to strike the reader of the act is a definition of the Holy Eucharist that reduces its role to a mere receiving of Holy Communion. Of its primary importance as a sacrifice there is not a word, nor does the act make it a punishable offence to revile the Mass. The act dissolving the Chantries,[2] passed in this same session of Parliament, completes the teaching of the first act, for it definitely states that the belief ' in purgatory and masses satisfactory, to be done for them which be departed ' is an empty theory, and one great cause of the superstitious errors that have crept into the Christian religion. It is indeed because the custom of bequeathing legacies—either to maintain priests to say masses for the dead, or to provide other memorials (such as lights) by which to provoke the piety of the living into like remembrance of the dead—is the chief reason why this belief —this ' doctrine and vain opinion '—survives, that the act now proposes to confiscate all such legacies.

Despite this official condemnation, however, the liturgical service called the Mass, as it had been celebrated from time immemorial, remained written in a thousand missals in all the parish churches of the realm, a silent witness, in every prayer and every line, of the older belief, the belief still of all but a tiny minority, a belief obligatory indeed, under King Henry's ferocious law, even upon those now planning the change. No doctrine so radically hostile to the traditional conception of the Eucharistic liturgy could hope for success, so long as that liturgy continued to be celebrated in terms which proclaimed the older conception. That there should be a new Eucharistic liturgy was a logical consequence of the reformation of doctrine, and within little

[1] 1 Edward VI, c. 1—1547 ; G. and H., LXVII.
[2] 1 Edward VI, c. 14—1547 ; G. and H., LXVIII.

more than twelve months after the passing of the Chantries
Act this new liturgy appeared. It was not, of course, any
mere translation of the Mass into English. Such a proceeding would have advertised only the more loudly the conflict
between the newly imposed doctrine and the older belief.
The new service was indeed in English, and in better English
almost than any man before or since has ever devised, but
it was also a careful re-modelling of the service and a re-
writing of its prayers such that every sign or hint that this
rite ever was, or was ever meant to be, a sacrifice itself
efficacious for the living and the dead, was entirely and
completely removed. Between the Eucharistic Liturgy as
The Book of Common Prayer rewrote it, and the new legally
established dogma there was no contradiction.[1]

Compared with this great change in the central act of the
Christian's relations with God, all others are indeed small.
But the setting of general change in which it was situated
shows how, by the end of the six years' reign of Edward VI,
the whole religious practice and discipline of the *Ecclesia
Anglicana* had been entirely transformed. The ancient
rites for Candlemas, Ash Wednesday, Palm Sunday, and
the last three days of Holy Week were now abolished.[2]
The midnight office disappeared. The Office of Our Lady
and the Lady Mass, in places where it was customary
to have them, were replaced by sermons. The Divine Office,
first of all reduced, when, instead of Prime and the other
Little Hours, a sermon was allowed, was replaced by the
Morning Prayer and Evening Prayer of the new rite.
The multitude of masses said daily for centuries in the great
cathedrals and the principal churches of the country gave
place to a single celebration of the new Communion Service.
Cranmer, in his diocese of Canterbury, proscribed Mass
legacies as ' a blind devotion,' [3] and while Ridley, Bishop of
London, warned his clergy using the new rite, ' that no
minister do counterfeit the popish mass,' [4] Hooper, Bishop
of Worcester and of Gloucester, made careful inquisition
' Whether the Communion be used in such place and after

---

[1] This liturgical revolution went through three stages : (i) the issue of a
new rite for administering Holy Communion ; (ii) the Book of Common
Prayer imposed by the Act 2 & 3 Edward VI, c. 1, in 1549 (G. and H.,
LXIX) ; (iii) the Second Book of Common Prayer, imposed by the Act
5 & 6 Edward VI, in 1552 (G. and H., LXXI).

[2] Order in Council of Jan. 18, 1548 ; royal proclamation, Feb., 1548.

[3] F. and K., II, p. 182.   [4] *Ibid.*, p. 241.

such sort as most varieth and is distant from the popish
mass.' [1] And another inquisition [2] sought out ' any that keep
in their houses undefaced, any abused or feigned images,
any tables, pictures, idolatry, or superstition.' Finally, to
complete this summary of the changes, the prohibitions
against the marriage of the clergy were declared null, the
penalties abrogated,[3] and an act [4] was passed legitimating
the children of the married clergy. For the ordination of
the clergy a new service was devised. Here again the idea
that guided those who wrote this service was the new,
heretical conception of the Holy Eucharist as merely a rite
by means of which the Christian receives Holy Communion
and as in no way a sacrifice of propitiation and satisfaction,
efficacious for the living and the dead. The new ordination
service is not a translation into English of the service by
which deacons, priests, and bishops had been ordained in
England, as throughout Western Christendom, for centuries
past, but a new, carefully compiled rite from which all
reference, in word or gesture, to such spiritual power as
that of offering a propitiatory sacrifice, or of transmitting
that power to others, has been carefully cut out. The new
ordinal does no more than institute and set apart, with
special blessings, those who are to preach the re-discovered
primitive religion of the Gospel and to administer Holy
Communion through the new Communion Service.

All bishops and priests are henceforward bound by law
to make use of these new rites, in place of the old. All the
faithful people are ' diligently and faithfully . . . to resort
to their parish church ' on Sundays and other days to assist
at them, and no one is to use, or to be present at, any other
form of common prayer, or administration of the sacraments,
under penalties that rise in severity to life imprisonment.[5]

Of all this elaborate change in the religion of her country,
the new queen, Mary, had been a close witness, and the
great drama had, more than once, involved her intimately.
Like all her family she had a first-rate intelligence, and she
shared the Tudor good fortune of the best education her

---

[1] *Ibid.*, p. 296.   [2] Cranmer at Canterbury, *ibid.*, p. 189.
[3] 2 & 3 Edward VI, c. 21—1549 ; G. and H., LXX.
[4] 5 & 6 Edward VI, c. 12—1552.
[5] 5 & 6 Edward VI, c. 1—1552 (the Second Edwardine Act of Uniformity) ; G. and H., LXXI.

century could give her. She was now, at the moment of
her accession, a woman half-way through her thirty-eighth
year. And for a good two-thirds of her life she had known
all the misery and unhappiness that were the inevitable lot
of whoever stood in the way of her father's policies.

Her childhood had been of the utmost brilliance, when,
heiress to the throne, she had been betrothed, now to the
Dauphin, now to the Emperor, and, as Princess of Wales,
had had her Court at Ludlow. But Mary was no more than
eleven when the first slow movements of the long divorce
suit began, and from that moment, through the next nine
years, her fortunes experienced a steady decline that
brought her humiliation, disgrace, and even danger of
death. She saw her father install his mistress at Court, in
equal honour with the queen, her mother. Then her
mother was repudiated and Mary separated from her.
Next the mistress was married, then crowned as queen,
after the king's bishops had pronounced the marriage
between Henry and Mary's mother null and void. Four
months after this annulment, in September 1533, the child
of Henry and Anne Boleyn was born, the Princess Elizabeth, and Mary—now seventeen—straightway lost all her
status, was ordered to admit her own illegitimacy and to
serve in the household of her baby sister, now proclaimed
heir to the throne.

Against consenting to such a final triumph of her mother's
rival, Mary steadfastly set her face. So the next year, 1534,
saw her little better than a prisoner, and in such a state of
destitution that she had to petition the Secretary of State
for even the necessities of clothing. Finally, under protests
to save her rights drawn up for her by the skilled ambassador
of Charles V, her mother's nephew, Mary took her place in
a kind of attendance on her baby sister, though further than
this she still refused to go. Next began a siege, that ended
only with Anne Boleyn's fall, to bring her to acknowledge
that her father's marriage to her mother was no marriage,
and also to accept the new doctrine of the Royal Supremacy.
The long strain brought on a severe illness, and it was not
expected that she would recover. Anne now began, it is
thought, to plot her death, and Mary, after the death of her
mother Katharine of Aragon—January 7, 1536—was thought
to be in greater danger than ever, for her disinheritance
was the one surviving obstacle to a good understanding with

the emperor, and her popularity in the country seemed a lasting bar to any general acceptance of the new marriage. To avert the catastrophe which Mary's death at this moment would have been, Charles V's ambassador, Chapuys, began to work for a reconciliation between Henry and his daughter. Anne's fall and execution (May, 1536) removed the greatest obstacle to this, for Anne had been as personally hostile to Mary as to her mother, and had been jealous of what love for Mary still survived in the king. Also the new queen, Jane Seymour, whom Henry married ten days after Anne's execution, was very friendly to Mary, and, of course, she was, what Anne had never been, Henry's lawful wife.

The manœuvres to reconcile Mary with her father began with a letter from her to the all-powerful Cromwell in May, 1536. They ended just a month later in Mary's complete surrender, her explicit acknowledgment of her own illegitimacy and of her father's Supremacy over the Church. The correspondence that filled the intervening weeks is an illuminating example of the way in which Henry, through Cromwell, gradually wore down his daughter's spirit and strove to break her will. The factor which determined her assent to this tragic deed was, however, not her father's violence, but the advice of Chapuys, who believed her life to be now really in danger. He bade her think of the future of England and of the Faith, and explained that since all men knew under what duress she signed, and since she had already protested that she was the victim of violence, no one would believe she had really surrendered, and such a nominal surrender would not stain her conscience. And so, on June 26, 1536, after a week of crisis during which the Council met daily to consider her fate, Mary, without so much as looking at the papers, signed what was placed before her. But through Chapuys she besought the emperor to procure her an absolution from the Pope, 'otherwise,' she told him, 'her conscience could not be at perfect ease.'

Two years later her life was once more in some peril when Henry arrested his Yorkist cousins, the countess of Salisbury, her son Lord Montague, and the marquis of Exeter,[1] for one of the alleged plans of these 'conspirators' was the marriage of Mary with Reginald Pole. But the last years of her father's reign passed quietly for Mary. She was on friendly terms with Katharine Parr, the last of Henry's

---

[1] Reginald Pole's mother, brother, and cousin.

queens, and from her retirement, at her manors of Hunsden and New Hall, she collaborated with this lady in a translation of the Paraphrases of Erasmus.

But, with the death of Henry VIII, Mary's troubles began anew. The accession of her little brother, and godson, Edward VI—nine years of age—was followed by the further religious changes, already described, and when Mary was bidden to forgo the Mass and to accept the new services of the Book of Common Prayer, she resisted with an obstinacy nothing could shake. ' Her soul was God's, she told the Council in 1551, ' and her faith she would not change, nor dissemble her opinion with contrary doings.' Her cousin the emperor intervened and threatened war if she were disturbed, and for a few months there was peace. Then, in August of that same year, the assault was renewed. Some of her friends were imprisoned for the offence of hearing Mass in her house, and a deputation from the Council was sent down to her to enforce conformity. Once again she defied them. ' Rather than she will agree to use any other service than was used at the death of the late king her father,' so runs the report they made to the Council of what Mary said, ' she would lay her head on the block and suffer death ; but (said she) I am unworthy to suffer death in so good a quarrel.' They next proposed to order her chaplains to leave the Mass, to which she replied : ' My priests . . . may do therein as they will, but none of this new service shall be used in my house, and if any be said in it I will not tarry in the house.' Nor was this attachment to spiritual values inspired by any imperial diplomacy : ' As for the emperor . . . if he would give me now other advice, I would not follow it.'

For the short remainder of Edward's reign the Government left her alone. The fall of Somerset in December, 1551, was something of a gain, but it was the bolder villainy of his successor, Northumberland, which, in the last month of the reign, plotted to deprive her of the succession. When that crisis came it was Mary's personal decision to fight and Mary's own determination which alone saved her inheritance for her. The emperor had hardly counted on her victory. He was indeed prepared to fight for her against the new government should they endeavour to harass her as in 1551, but prepared for no more than this. Her success was to him unexpected, but, prepared for anything, Charles

turned immediately to extract from it all that it promised
of profit to his own imperialist policies.

From the very beginning two things played into his hands.
He had, of course, been Mary's sole reliable friend for nearly
twenty years. Despite the trials of those years she still
remained ' easy, good, and ill-experienced in affairs of the
world and of state . . . a novice in everything.' [1] Then her
very council was unreliable, its loyalty more than doubtful.
' Those here are so governed by avarice,' Charles V's
ambassador informed Granvelle,[2] ' that if you would talk
them over and buy them with presents and promises, you
would convert them to whatever you liked by one single
method.' [3] And the queen, some three weeks later, begging
the imperial ambassadors to delay their going, could
explain that ' owing to the objections people took to the
Mass, and the conspiracy of ill-willers, she knew not what
course to take without their help, as she could not entirely
trust any of her own Council.' [4]

What was the state of English opinion regarding the
religious controversies when, in July, 1553, the defeat of the
partisans of Lady Jane Grey brought to the throne so sincere,
instructed, and tested a Catholic as Henry VIII's eldest
daughter ? ' The population of London is treacherous, and
obstinate in heresy,' one of his correspondents in London, a
Frenchman, informed the Papal Legate at Brussels, Cardinal
Girolamo Dandino, ' but in the rest of the country this is not
true to the same degree.' [5] There was, he thought, a strong
anti-Roman *bloc*, composed of those who had made fortunes
out of Church plunder, and of doctrinal enthusiasts—an
academic type these last, many of them foreigners. That
there were indeed many foreign heretics in London we know
on the authority of one of the most famous of them all,
Henry Bullinger, who in the same month of August, 1553,
writing to Calvin, set down their numbers as fifteen
thousand.[6] Two months later another of Dandino's

---

[1] The imperial ambassadors at London to Granvelle, cited in GAIRDNER :
Lollardy, IV, pp. 99, 100.
[2] The emperor's principal minister in the Netherlands.
[3] GAIRDNER, *ibid.*
[4] Mary to the ambassadors. Text *ibid.*, IV, p. 37.
[5] Dandino to Del Monte, Aug. 20, 1553, cited ANCEL 774, from *Vat.
Archiv. Fiandra*, I, f. 159.
[6] The population of London at this time was about 120,000 : Bullinger's
letter is in Calvin's Works (edid. Baum), Vol. 14, p. 598.

correspondents reported that 'The devil has gained great power in this realm ; he has committed it so deeply to heresy that, in the end, many are come to this that they no longer believe in the immortality of the soul, have no knowledge of God and pay Him no worship.'[1] The queen herself, writing to Pole just a fortnight later than this last correspondent wrote to Dandino, speaks in just as grave a tone and goes to the heart of the most thorny question of all.[2] After a packed three months of observation from the very centre of things, with, it must be supposed, full information from men of all parties, and the opinions of the most experienced advisers, she writes : 'As the discussions in parliament proceed, we are becoming well aware that the recognition of the Holy See has to face infinitely greater difficulties than the re-establishment of Catholic worship, so great has been the success in planting false ideas about the Pope.'[3]

How much of this did Reginald Pole know ? How much of it was he able to grasp as a reality, once the knowledge of it was sent to him ? What kind of a man was he, this slight, bearded ecclesiastic, whose kindly melancholy face, with its intelligent brow and lively eyes, looks out at us from del Piombo's celebrated portrait ?

[1] Vimercato–Dandino, Oct. 13, 1553 ; in ANCEL 755.
[2] Letter of Oct. 28, 1553, in QUIRINI, IV, p. 119–121, also TIERNEY, II, App., p. ci.
[3] Compare with this the remark of the Venetian ambassador in London two years earlier, that ' detestation of the Pope was now so confirmed that no one either of the old or new religion could bear to hear him mentioned.' *Venetian Calendar*, V, p. 346.

CHAPTER II

REGINALD POLE, THE CATHOLIC REFORMER, 1500–1553

REGINALD POLE, Cardinal Deacon of the title of Sta. Maria in Cosmedin, was, at the time of Queen Mary's accession, a man fifty-three years of age, for he was born in the Castle of Stourton, in Staffordshire, on March 3, 1500. He was the third—and in 1553 the eldest surviving—son of Sir Richard Pole K.G., a personage of high importance in 1500, for his mother and the mother of the reigning king, Henry VII, were half-sisters.[1] Sir Richard Pole was, in fact, one of those many people whom the Lancastrian revolution of 1485 transformed overnight from being almost no one at all to being a leading figure in the national life. One important charge after another was heaped upon him, and it was to his care that the new king confided the upbringing of his eldest son Arthur, and the general supervision of the court at Ludlow where the young Prince of Wales resided, as a kind of Viceroy for Wales, after his marriage to Katharine of Aragon. Henry VII, a somewhat obscure Welshman, save for descent from various illegitimate royalties, had bettered the condition of the family he proposed to found, by marrying the eldest daughter, and, by her survival of her brothers, the heiress of King Edward IV. He did a similar good office for the son of his own mother's half-sister when, in 1491, he gave Richard Pole in marriage one of

---

[1] The common ancestor of Henry VII and Sir Richard Pole was their grandmother, Margaret Beauchamp.

John, Duke of=Margaret Beauchamp=Sir Oliver St. John
Somerset
† 1444

Edmund Tudor=Margaret Beaufort   Edith St. John=Sir Geoffrey Pole
Earl of Richmond
† 1456

HENRY VII   SIR RICHARD POLE

the greatest heiresses in the land, the Lady Margaret Plantagenet. For this lady, the mother of Cardinal Pole, was the daughter of George, duke of Clarence. She was therefore niece to the king reigning at the time of her birth, Edward IV, first cousin to his successor, Edward V, and to that successor's brother, Richard, duke of York—the ill-fated princes murdered in the Tower—and niece to King Richard III, and first cousin to Elizabeth, the queen of Henry VII. Her own father, the ' false, fleeting, perjured Clarence ' of Shakespeare's tragedy, had been attainted in 1478, prior to that mysterious death ' in a butt of Malmsey wine.' His son and heir, the young earl of Warwick, a prisoner from his babyhood almost, was still in the Tower at the time of Margaret's marriage to Pole.

Alas, Margaret Pole stood too near the throne for her happiness to continue unalloyed.[1] The House of York, defeated at Bosworth only a matter of fifteen years before, still had its partisans, and in an England where no woman had ever been allowed to rule as sovereign, the prisoner earl of Warwick, Margaret's brother, was an obvious centre around which a Yorkist revenge might gather, and should this party succeed, the future king. Ferdinand of Aragon, about to marry his daughter to Henry VII's heir, suggested that while Warwick lived there was no assurance that the Tudor line would continue in possession. And so, on a trumped-up charge of treason, the young earl was put to death in 1499, four months only before his sister gave birth to the boy who was to be Cardinal Pole.

Years later Henry VIII restored her state and her possessions, creating her in her own right countess of Salisbury, the title borne by her great-grandfather, the famous fighter of the Wars of the Roses and father of the still more famous

---

[1] A summary and simplified genealogical table will illustrate the relationship.

Richard, duke of York, d. 1460

	EDWARD IV, 1461–1483	RICHARD III, 1483–1485	George, duke of Clarence, d. 1478	
HENRY VII = Elizabeth 1485–1509		Katharine	Edward, earl of Warwick	Margaret Pole

earl of Warwick, called the King-Maker, Lytton's 'Last of the Barons,' who was himself the father of Margaret Pole's mother.

Katherine of Aragon never forgot the bloody setting of her espousals. In a spirit of restitution she did all in her power to forward the interests of Margaret Pole, who became indeed her intimate friend and the governess of the one child of Katharine's marriage to live beyond its cradle days, that future queen Mary Tudor to whom, in 1553, Reginald Pole was commissioned as legate. Katharine of Aragon, when her own matrimonial troubles came upon her, recalled the murder of Margaret Pole's brother, that had been her father-in-law's guarantee to her father that she should one day reign as queen, and it had been one of her deep desires that reparation should be made for the crime by a marriage between her daughter Mary and the youthful Reginald Pole.

Reginald Pole's formation, in things spiritual and things intellectual, was of quite unusual quality. The time in which he was born was, as is known, a time of general religious decay, when bad priests, bad bishops, and bad popes too, were almost part of the accepted order. But this child, born when Rodrigo Borgia reigned as Pope Alexander VI, was put to school with the Carthusian monks of Sheen. After six years of this sheltered, holy life he passed to Oxford and to William Waynflete's college of Magdalen, then still in the first fervour of its foundation, and the premier seminary of England. Here also he remained for six years, and then, in 1519, with the retinue his rank demanded, and with liberal assistance from his kinsman King Henry VIII, he crossed the sea to the wonderland of Italy, and to that university of Padua where the flower of the English intelligence, for a whole generation now, had sought its rich maturity.

Letters that still survive from his teachers, the famous humanists with whom he studied, and from Pole himself, give us an attractive picture of the early manhood of this studious princeling. He reads Aristotle with Leonicus, or again he is mentioned as preparing a critical edition of Cicero.[1] Leonicus notes his acute mind, the elegance of his learning, and, in a letter to William Latimer, ' his most cultured manners.' [2]   Poggio is told that Pole has few

---

[1] Gasquet, p. 91.   [2] *Ibid.*, p. 34.

equals, and is outstanding in all literary studies.[1] Bembo, who a quarter of a century hence will rejoin Pole in the Sacred College, but whose life so far suggests nothing so little as church reforms, praises him too, and between the complimentary generalities of his letter we can read an evidence that they are meant literally in the reference to a trait which distinguished Reginald Pole throughout his life, his seriousness. He is, says Bembo in 1522, ' perhaps the most virtuous, erudite . . . grave young man in Italy at the present time.' [2] Another of the group of humanists, de Longueil, who was to die presently, and leave his library to Pole, laughs—ruefully perhaps—in his turn at the youthful gravity. 'I find myself transported to distant England,' he writes to Sauli, ' I miss your delightful company, and all our happy talks. For Reginald Pole, though of excellent parts and learned, as well as being a youth of fine discernment, cares little for our kind of discussions ; and while he is endowed with marvellous modesty, he is also prodigiously taciturn,' [3]

Like all young men Pole had his heroes, and two of them, his fellow-countrymen, find mention in these Italian letters. One is Cuthbert Tunstal, who twenty years earlier, in these very schools of Padua, had laid the foundations of that knowledge of law which made him, to his own contemporaries, another Ulpian.[4] Now, after ten years of rapid ascent in the twin spheres of law and diplomacy, after service to church and king, as judge and as ambassador, he had recently (1522) been named Bishop of London and Lord Privy Seal. ' Reginald Pole,' Leonicus writes to him, ' is your great admirer.' [5] The second of these English heroes is he who was to become St. Thomas More, and it is a letter from Leonicus to More himself which tells us of Pole's admiration for the future Lord Chancellor and martyr. He constantly speaks about you, no less plainly than with truth, and he declares that you may truly and rightly be accounted one of the most learned men alive, deeply versed in the study of all the true arts.' [6]

So for eight years, the happiest years of Pole's life, the

[1] Gasquet, p. 64.   [2] Ibid., p. 32.   [3] Ibid., pp. 29–30.
[4] Campeggio at the Blackfriars trial of Henry VIII's marriage suit, July, 1529. ' Cum Tunstallum lego, videor mihi ipsum Ulpianum audire.' Cf. The Earliest Life of St. John Fisher, ed. PHILIP HUGHES (1935), p. 100.
[5] June 8, 1523, ibid., p. 48.
[6] Jan. 19, 1524, ibid., pp. 58–9.

only entirely happy years one is tempted to think, the royal humanist grew more and more akin to what he studied at Padua, his beloved classics, the fathers, the New Testament, until there arose to compel his return to England that ' King's matter ' which was to drag him, like his admired More, into reluctant, if inevitable, opposition to his kinsman and signal benefactor, King Henry VIII. With Pole's return to England in 1527 the first chapter in his life was closed. The Catholic Christendom in which, in England as in Italy, he had been bred was about to break up. The king would apostatise and Tunstal too. Sheen would become a waste, its holy monks be scattered, imprisoned, martyred, and More martyred with them.

The ten years which followed Pole's return from Italy are the critical years when the world to which he belonged, Catholic England, is destroyed. Pole, inevitably, is at the heart of the crisis. Despite himself the taciturn learns to speak ; despite his best endeavour, the student, the bibliophile and humanist is forced into action. That action, like the action of almost all these early Tudor Catholics, save the simplest of all, the Reformed Franciscans, is reluctant, if never hesitant ; it shrinks from anything that can savour of defiance, or of disloyalty, and only at the inevitable last moment will it risk even the appearance of ungrateful disrespect.

For the first two years after his return (1527–1529), the years while the king's business, as one of those major causes reserved to the Holy See, was being pleaded in the Curia at Rome, Pole lived at Sheen, in the house which Colet had built for himself within the area of the Carthusian priory. Thence the royal will in October, 1529, hauled him forth. Dr. Cranmer, of the University of Cambridge, had made his famous suggestion that the king should sound the universities of Europe on this question whether popes could validly grant such dispensations as that through which Henry had come to marry Katharine. With a unanimity of theological opinion favourable to his case he could then the better confront and argue with the Roman officials. Reginald Pole, granted his rank, his learning, his familiarity with the personages and the ways of the world of learning, would be an ideal canvasser of university opinion. Despite his resistance, his pleas, his excuses, the commission was forced upon him. With him was joined, a much more

efficient agent, Edward Fox, the future Bishop of Hereford.
But Pole, once out of England, managed to keep himself
clear of any share in the work, and even to secure from the
king permission to leave the whole business to Fox. In
July, 1530, he came home, his family begging him to put
an end to the rumours that he was opposed to the king's
policy, and once more it was to Sheen he went and to
retirement, a retirement brusquely interrupted within a
matter of months.

Now came the great crisis of Pole's life and an event which
must have appeared to him ever afterwards a direct intervention from heaven upon his action. On November 29,
1530, Cardinal Wolsey died, disgraced and actually under
arrest for high treason, at Leicester Abbey. A few days
later the duke of Norfolk waited on Pole with the offer from
the king of the vacant archbishopric of York. But Henry
needed some kind of assurance that Pole would favour the
divorce. For the young man of thirty, no less than for his
family, the offer marked the very peak of the royal goodwill.
Norfolk, seeing Pole's embarrassment, refused to take an
immediate answer, and it was agreed that Pole should have
a month to think out a means of satisfying the king without
doing violence to his conscience. Thereupon there began
a real siege of Pole, in which friends and relations plied
him with arguments and pleas and excuses ' until I could
resist no more.' To the next of Henry's messengers—his
own brother Lord Montague, and Edward Fox his late
colleague in Paris—he declared that he had found a
solution, and the king straightway sent for him to set it
forth.

The meeting of the two kinsmen took place privately
at Whitehall. But when Pole came to speak, though his
tongue was not held, he found himself delivered of quite
other sentiments than those he had so carefully prepared.
He argued plainly the wrong of the divorce and the blunder
it was, if only as a matter of national policy. Confused and
trembling, he heard himself stammering forth his real
opinion, and saw the king grow pale with temper and
finally put his hand to his dagger. For a moment Pole
thought his end was come, but Henry mastered himself,
and, as Pole began to put forth some excuse, said only :
' I shall consider your opinion,' and, slamming the door,
withdrew, leaving the unhappy young man in tears.

When Pole now proposed to put his case in writing, his friends and his family opposed the suggestion violently, and it was through Sir John Russell, one of the king's gentlemen-in-waiting, that he sent the paper to Henry. The paper has not survived, but we know something of its contents from a letter to the earl of Wiltshire written by his chaplain, Dr. Thomas Cranmer. And we know that Pole put the case well, the political case that, once doubts begin to be expressed about royal marriages and the legitimacy of heirs to the throne, after an acknowledgment that has lasted a whole generation, no man can say where the questioning will cease : less than fifty years after Bosworth, is it wise to proceed with an action that may revive the feuds of York and Lancaster ? The leisured meditation of Pole's argument seems to have brought the king back to all his old friendliness. He admitted to Montague the truth of what Pole had to say, and also that though the argument went contrary to what he had determined to do, Pole's real affection in setting it forth was so manifest that he could not continue in anger against him.

During these critical days at the New Year of 1530–1531, Henry's mind was, in fact, a battle-field in which strove for mastery Reginald Pole and Thomas Cromwell. It was now, so Pole wrote later, that Cromwell made his great suggestion, to cut the gordian knot of the divorce suit by the device of the Royal Supremacy. And it is Pole's opinion, too, that it was only by a hairsbreadth that Cromwell won. Henry all but resolved to abandon the divorce. What finally happened was, of course, the legal manœuvring which, in the January (1531), brought the clergy in Convocation to the first steps towards schism, their acknowledgment of the king as Head of the Church. Pole was present on the occasion when they made their famous offer of £100,000 to buy themselves free of the general indictment for præmunire. He was not present in the session when they voted the king his new title and status.

And in the autumn of that year, 1531, he asked leave to go abroad. The king refused, and continued to refuse until, in the first days of 1532, Pole made it clear that should he still be in England when the parliamentary session began— Parliament had not sat in 1531—he would have no choice but to speak as his conscience moved him. The royal permission was now granted, and sometime in 1532 Pole,

for the third time, made his way over the sea, to Paris,
and Avignon, and thence to Padua.

Pole's courageous stand had left him an isolated figure,
as a still greater refusal left St. Thomas More isolated two
years later. His family were in despair and it was in a kind
of universal disgrace that he had left England, for Padua
and the congenial employment of its scholarly occupations.
And in some such retreat, half forgetting, and indeed
wholly evading, the violent troubles that rocked his country,
drugged with the heavy laudanum of letters, Pole, left to
himself, would possibly have drifted through all the best years
of his life. From such a fate he was saved by the appreciation
two stronger men than himself possessed of the possibilities
latent in his rare combination of rank, talent, and innocency
of life. Henry VIII could not be indifferent to the fact that
Pole was not among his supporters, any more than he could,
as a politician, suffer More to remain neutral and alive.
And the new Pope, Paul III,[1] planning a radical reformation
of Catholicism and looking for such learned, disinterested
service as Pole could furnish, could not be indifferent either.
From both sides efforts were made to decide the reluctant
scholar. To Henry's overtures he made no sign, save, finally,
to draw up for the king's information the famous treatise
Pro Ecclesiasticæ Unitatis Defensione. Paul III he never indeed
resisted, but his surrender was slow, and only determined
finally by a peremptory reminder from the Pope that there
are times when conscience must enforce acceptance of an
active mission in the Church. Pole consented, came to
Rome, and, in the consistory of 1536, was created cardinal.
The acceptance of this dignity brought a hail of bitter letters
from all his English friends; and from his own family, upon
whose loyalty to the new Supreme Head this clamant
support of the Bishop of Rome's primacy cast suspicions
that nothing ever cleared away from the royal mind.
There was, from this moment, no surer indication of hidden
traitorousness than kinship with the English cardinal,
kinsman of the king and counsellor of the king's chief
enemy. And it was their own close kinship with the cardinal
which, in the next two years, reversed all that the royal
favour had done in forty years to restore these last Plan-
tagenets, and brought them to the scaffold : Lord Exeter,
the grandson of King Edward IV, the cardinal's eldest

[1] Elected Oct. 10, 1534.

brother, Lord Montague, and his aged mother, the countess
of Salisbury.[1]

The headsman of Henry VIII completed that divorce
of Reginald Pole from England which his own exile had
begun. Henceforth he was simply the servant of the Church.
Paul III began by employing him as Legate in the political
business of building up an alliance of Christian princes
that would deliver England from the tyranny of its king
and restore the *Ecclesia Anglicana* to the unity of Christendom.
For two years Pole, in all the state of a Legate *a Latere*
travelled Europe, to Toledo and Charles V, to Paris and
Francis I. From all he gained good words, and everywhere
his innocency of life made an impression men never forgot.
But the diplomatic mission failed and always failed. Whatever the needs of England, and the views of the Christian
princes concerning their apostate brother, neither Charles
nor Francis could trust each other enough ever to combine
in this punitive crusade. And neither of them trusted the
Pope. Had Reginald Pole possessed the diplomatic gifts
of such great contemporaries as Morone and Commendone,
or, as great as any of these, of the Farnese Pope he served,
it would still have availed nothing with this generation.
The long half-century of the papal effort to reverse English
history through armed intervention from the continent,
failed in the moment that gave it birth.

And, of course, it has to be allowed—and here is the
place to make a first mention of the important fact—Pole
was no diplomatist. He was a learned man and a holy man,
cultured, travelled, experienced. But he lacked initiative,

----

[1] It should be remembered that, in 1536, Exeter and Montague were,
after the King of Scotland, Henry's nearest male relatives : *e.g.*

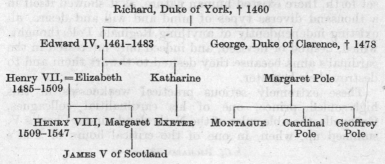

Richard, Duke of York, † 1460

Edward IV, 1461–1483   George, Duke of Clarence, † 1478

Henry VII, = Elizabeth   Katharine   Margaret Pole
1485–1509

HENRY VIII, Margaret EXETER   MONTAGUE   Cardinal   Geoffrey
1509–1547.   Pole   Pole

JAMES V of Scotland

he was no leader, and once his instructions terminated he was feeble in action. He constantly gives the impression that he had never the strength to get his own way ; he seems to have lacked the force to impose his views, or even to force a hearing for his views, upon those who needed to consider them. Perhaps he hardly, really, ever wanted his own way. His detachment from self had become a new means through which his natural diffidence functioned. Once he sensed in higher authority a contrary indication to what his own mind was working out, his own wishes shrank to mere velleity, at any rate in his exposition of them. He shrank from putting his own informed case against authority inclining in another direction, and his own good case, when put, was often put too late. There comes a moment in the lives of all those whose lot is cast in stormy times, and indeed in the lives of all who have to co-operate in the taking of joint decisions of any importance, when if they do not actually storm and violently assault all within their reach, they convey the impression that only by strong mastery are they holding back the lion that stirs within them. Of such a quality as this Pole's nature was entirely bereft. He had no audacity, and was incapable of anger.

Such a lack of irascible passion—the attitude, habitual with him, of a victim ready to be sacrificed [1]—was an almost fatal defect in a public personage of the sixteenth century. Pole was further handicapped by a temperament that instinctively turned from the hard, unpleasant, unchangeable realities of a problem to the ideal way in which it ought to be solved. Time and again he failed to make allowance for the fact that, outside his own desires and his own will, and beyond that perfectly planned scheme of a better church and world which his books and his despatches set forth, there existed human nature, as it showed itself in a thousand diverse types of mind and will and desire, all existing independently of anything Reginald Pole thought, willed, desired or devised, and indeed only interested in the cardinal's aims because they desired to thwart them and to destroy their begetter.

These extremely serious practical weaknesses in this high-souled prince, one of his cardinalitial colleagues, Granvelle, the able ruler of the Netherlands under Charles V, summed up, when, in one of the critical hours of Pole's

[1] *Cf.* RICHARD, 73.

career, he wrote to the one-time Spanish Ambassador in England, Mendoza, in June, 1554. ' Speaking between ourselves [Pole] is truly a learned prelate, very virtuous and indeed of holy life. But he does not understand the first thing about the conduct of affairs. I suspect he would be glad to stay here [*i.e.* in Brussels] and not busy himself with the affairs of England, of which he knows very little and about which he can do even less. And so, with all the good zeal that he can put forth, far from improving matters he would more likely compromise them.' [1]

Was his original formation at the court of despots who had all but destroyed his family, and by the mere chance of whose favour it continued to survive, the cause ? or was it the succession of family tragedies he himself witnessed, and, following upon this, the repeated failure of one effort after another—in which he had been a leading actor—to defeat the policies of Henry VIII ? Whatever the cause, as the years went by, a certain melancholy began to colour the sensitive soul of the cardinal, who somehow remained, in a workaday world, and amid very workaday ecclesiastical officials, as expectant of the ideal as in the hey-day of his studious youth, and who remained, too, as easily the captive of his desires and aspirations. Certainly the catalogue of violent deaths in Pole's own family must give it a place of its own in the history of blood. Henry VIII put to death his mother ; his brother ; his cousin, Lord Exeter ; his cousin, Edmund de la Pole ; and the great duke of Buckingham who was so close a connection by marriage. Henry VII had beheaded his uncle Warwick ; Warwick's two cousins, the princes in the tower, had been murdered by their; and his uncle—the cardinal's great-uncle—Richard III, and, of Richard III's brothers, Rutland had been murdered during the Wars of the Roses and Clarence—the cardinal's grandfather—by order of his eldest brother, King Edward IV : while the head of all this clan, Richard, duke of York, the cardinal's great-grandfather, had been executed after the battle of Wakefield. To the catalogue of violence must be added Richard III himself, slain at Bosworth, John de la Pole, his heir, slain at Stoke, and Richard de la Pole, the last hope of this branch of the family, killed at Pavia in 1525. Small wonder if, in his distrust of princes, Reginald Pole had come to write almost as though human causality could

---

[1] Quoted in ANGEL, p. 766.

not produce any good act, and as though good men must
begin by refusing to consider secondary causalities at all,
there being no human prudence that is not, by the fact,
treason to the divine.[1]

In 1541 Pole's employment changed, and he was sent
to govern the province of Viterbo in the Papal States.
Here he spent some very happy years. He administered
his little domain in a fashion that would have well contented
the critic who penned the *Utopia*. He resumed his studies,
and busied himself with the Academy he founded. He
developed his idealistic friendship with Vittoria Colonna ;
and, with his friend Contarini, a Venetian Thomas More
whom Paul III had made a cardinal, he worked out theories
to reconcile the Lutherans in the great debate on Justification.

During these years of his legateship at Viterbo, Pole was
by no means a stranger to Roman affairs. At every turn
Paul III continued to make use of his really deep, theological scholarship and to rely on his unshakable loyalty to
the ideal of a thorough reformation of Catholic life. When
at last, after eleven years of patient diplomatic persistence,
the Pope, in 1545, summoned the long-desired general
council to meet at Trent, Pole's nomination as one of the
three legates who would act as its presidents was thus
very much in the natural order of things. If, so far, in his
life the cardinal had never had the kind of experience that
makes a good committee-man, nor any opportunity to

The tragedy of the family is shown by the accompanying table

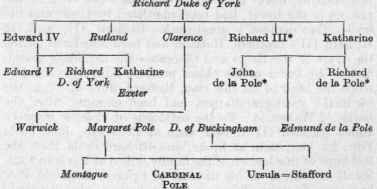

The executions and murders are denoted by italics : the deaths in battle
by asterisks.

discover such talents as would make a successful chairman of an international assembly, Pole, as the council proceeded, showed himself possessed of the supremely useful gifts of a calm, unhurried, imperturbable manner, a patient and conciliatory disposition, and a never-failing sense of the essentially spiritual character of the work that brought the bishops together. He was indeed the ideal arbitrator, whether between bishops hotly opposed and driven in the stress of debate to picturesque and cutting personalities, or between the gouty and somewhat choleric senior legate, the Cardinal Del Monte, and the many eager critics of the Curia and its ways among the *patres concilii*. Pole was the junior legate, and as such somewhat in the background always, so long as the assembly's course ran smooth. But let there be need of reconciliation, or of any recall to realities —whether of the abuses that called for reform or of the spiritual world in which all this business was, by hypothesis, transacted—it was Pole on all these occasions who intervened, easily, naturally, as gifted with some special authority and always he intervened with immediate effect. When his health finally broke down, after eighteen months of the terrible daily grind of the council, and, threatened with a stroke, he had to leave the singularly insalubrious city where the council was lodged, it was immediately made very clear what his presence had achieved, for, thenceonwards, the 'scenes' were more frequent and more violent.

It was on March 13, 1545, that Pole arrived at Trent. The first solemn session of the council took place nine months later, December 13. Pole's last appearance was on June 28, 1546.

His first notable intervention was the great *Admonitio ad Patres*,[1] composed by him and read at the opening of the second solemn session, January 7, 1546. In the preliminary discussions on the canon of Sacred Scripture Pole was a strong supporter of the view that the council should re-examine the claim to canonicity of each separate book, lest a new excuse be given to the hostile Lutherans to argue that Catholics dared not examine their own origins. In a later discussion, on the adoption of an official version of the Bible, Pole made the interesting suggestion that to the Vulgate

---

[1] Translated in *Dublin Review*, Jan., 1936 (also published separately, *Causes of Christian Disunion*) by Fr. Vincent McNabb, O.P.

there be added also the Hebrew and the Greek texts, lest Catholicism should seem to limit itself to that more particular thing, the Latin culture. Again, however, he was in a minority.

When Pole left Trent he did not cease to be legate, and for the next five months—until Paul III recalled him to Rome in October, 1546—by systematic and regular correspondence from his residence near Padua—only sixty miles away from the council—he kept in close touch with all that passed, and his learning continued actively to influence the shaping of the various decrees and canons. At the moment when Pole retired, five solemn sessions had been held, and the dogmatic work of the council had proceeded as far as the definition on Original Sin. It was perhaps not without effect on his later career that he was absent from the long six months of discussion in which the decree on Justification was built up. Ever since Luther, nearly twenty years before this, set forth his revolutionary theory on Justification, Catholic theologians had given themselves whole-heartedly to a re-examination of the subject. In all this general endeavour to state Catholic teaching anew in the light of the Lutheran controversy, and in the effort so to state it that Catholics who had gone over to Lutheranism might be brought back, it was inevitable that mistakes should be made, and explanations given which, to some extent, explained the truth away. ' Truth is wrought out by many minds working together,' it has been well said,[1] and the preliminary working out of Catholic truth by individual Catholic thinkers has always been exposed to those chances of error from which scientific investigation can never wholly be free. So it was that Pole's great friend, Contarini, the greatest of all the Catholic reformers, constructed a theory to explain Justification which, once the council met, was very soon shown to be inconsistent with Catholic teaching. And it is matter of history that Pole 'undoubtedly had shared certain opinions of his friend Contarini which were afterwards reprobated by the council.' [2] But no Catholic is a heretic until he begins to hold to his own theory after it has been officially declared to be incompatible with Catholic teaching. And even before the Council of Trent had published its definition, Pole had come round to the teaching

[1] Newman to Ornsby, 1863, in WARD, *Life of Newman*, II, p. 49.
[2] H. THURSTON, S.J., in *Catholic Encyclopædia*, art. *Pole*, v, pp. 335–7.

there stated. But had Pole been able to express his mind
during the debates at Trent he would have cleared himself,
in advance, of the suspicion which, in the minds of some of
his fellow-reformers—sometimes more zealous to correct
heretics than skilled to discern where heresy lay [1]—had never
ceased to hang around his orthodoxy since the days of
his first association with Contarini.

For the next three years after his return from Trent
Pole's time was divided between the government of his
province and assistance at the cabinets of Paul III during
the last crises of his eventful reign. Once again there was
a serious conflict between the Pope and Charles V on the
subject of the council, and Pole continued to show himself
one of the staunchest supporters of the Pope in the Sacred
College. Then, November 10, 1549, Paul III died, and
unexpectedly, for all that he was in his eighty-second year.
Pole was about to touch the very summit of any earthly
career.

There were, at this moment, fifty-four cardinals in the
Sacred College and fifty-one of them ultimately appeared
for the conclave—a greater number than had ever been
known before. Twenty-two were reckoned as favourable
to the policies of Charles V, King of Spain and Emperor ;
twenty-four were pro-French ; and the rest neutral. When
the conclave opened, there were only forty-two cardinals
present, so that, by the two-thirds rule, twenty-eight votes
were needed for the election.

Pole's name was on all men's lips, and he had the strong
support of the Emperor. The late Pope, in the instructions
he left behind for his grandson, Cardinal Alessandro
Farnese, praised him as ' superior to all others, in his birth,
his character, and his learning.' The only thing likely to
be an obstacle to his election was his known determination
to press forward the reform of abuses. The conclave opened
then with Pole's chances decidedly good, but with a party
determined, for political and personal reasons, to oppose
him to the utmost. Among his opponents must be reckoned
the Cardinal Gian Pietro Carafa, who as Grand Inquisitor
—he was practically the founder of the Roman Inquisition
—had developed such a hatred of heresy that he now
saw heretics everywhere, and among the rest suspected
Pole.

[1] RICHARD, 73.

The cardinals went into conclave November 30, 1549. The first plan of the 'imperialist' cardinals was to secure Pole's election by the method, then lawful, called *per adorazione*. This could only be practised if the candidate was already certain of almost the whole of the needed two-thirds of the votes. It consisted in his supporters standing round him, and the votes were counted, whereupon the half-dozen needed votes would be gained from waverers whom the spectacle and the excitement of the moment might win over. The imperialists, to carry out their plans, demanded a voting session for the evening of the day the conclave opened. But the anti-Pole party guessed their intentions, and managed to secure a decision that the usual practice be followed, of taking the first ballot on the first morning after the entry into the conclave.

It was not, however, until three days later, December 3, that the voting began. In the first ballot Pole received twenty-one votes. If he did as well in the next ballot, the rule allowed the practice known as the *accessus*. That is to say, the result of the ballot being declared it was open to any cardinal to transfer his vote to the candidate at the head of the list, using the phrase : 'I accede to Cardinal X.' Pole's opponents realised, only too well for his success, what his chances were in the *accessus*, and so after this first ballot they raised a new storm in the conclave by calling in question the validity of this method of election. The discussion ended in a compromise. The *accessus* would not be allowed until the third ballot. But, to the consternation of Pole's foes, he increased his vote, on the second ballot (December 4) to twenty-four. He lacked only four votes of the required two-thirds. What would the next ballot not achieve for him ?

The French cardinals, in their consternation, called in the aid of the French ambassador. He, equal to the occasion, announced that the remaining French cardinals—there were twelve in all—had got as far as Corsica. The conclave should await their arrival before proceeding further. Unless the cardinals waited, the King of France would refuse to recognise the Pope they elected. The story about Corsica was a lie, but the threat of schism threw the conclave back into a fury of debates. The imperialists returned to their plan of carrying the election *per adorazione*, and managed their canvass of the waverers so well that Pole was warned

to hold himself in readiness for the coming visit of all the
majority to his cell to acknowledge him as Pope.

Pole, alone of the Sacred College, seems to have kept his
head. He had carefully avoided all contact with the
manœuvres and private discussions which for days had
centred round him. He had sat unmoved through the
exciting hours of the first two ballots, steadily refusing to
make any comment, whether to supporters or to opponents,
keeping faithfully to his principle that he could only be Pope
by the will of God if, so far as he was concerned, the whole
business was left entirely to the divine action. And now,
to the two cardinals who came with the news about the
proposed *adorazione*, Pole simply refused. He must go in, he
said, through the door, not climb through a window. The
cardinals remonstrated that the method they proposed was,
nevertheless, lawful. Pole could not but agree, and for a
moment they won him round. But it was only for a moment,
and he sent after them to withdraw his consent.

The managers of the ' imperialist ' group had failed with
their candidate, but returning to the task of arranging for
the next ballot they had a promise of three votes in the
accessus, provided Pole reached twenty-six.

All that night and all the early morning of December 5
the negotiations and discussions continued. It was everywhere taken for granted that the election would take place,
and that Pole would be Pope. The cardinals had their cells
dismantled and their goods packed. The troops were ready
outside St. Peter's to control the crowds who assembled
for the new Pope's blessing. The sacristans had ready the
papal vestments adjusted to Pole's slight figure, and Pole
had his speech of acceptance prepared.

The third ballot gave him twenty-three votes. Then
Carpi acceded, and then Alessandro Farnese. This brought
up the total to twenty-five. If one more would accede,
the three promised votes, of Morone, Cesi, and Gaddi,
would be given, and Pole, with twenty-nine votes, would be
Pope. An inhuman silence followed Farnese's vote, and
across the chapel from throne to throne there were signs and
nods and beckonings. The cardinal who presided finally
broke the silence to ask did anyone else accede ? Silence
again, and then the president declared the session at an end.

It was the end of Pole's chances. The relaxed cardinals
did not want so whole-hearted a reformer. The Italians

fought shy of a non-Italian Pope. The French were fixed in their objections to any whom the emperor supported, and after the amazing scene of the third ballot it was not hard for the saying to gain credence that God could not really want as Pope one whom He had allowed to come so near and to fail.

As to Pole, he continued to be his reserved, unmoved. prayerful self. When the two cardinals had entered his cell on their fateful errand, so he later wrote to a friend, it brought to his mind the two disciples whom Our Lord despatched to seek the ass on which He meant to ride into Jerusalem. ' And, as the event proved,' the letter ends, ' the Lord did not require this particular ass.'

It was a matter of nearly three months before the conclave ended. The Pope it elected—Julius III—was Pole's old colleague at Trent, the Cardinal Gian Maria Del Monte. And presently Pole, by his leave and favour, disappeared altogether from Rome and the public life of the Church. He retired to the abbey of Maguzzano, belonging to the Cassinese Benedictines of the Strict Observance, whose cardinal protector he was. Here in the solitude by the lovely Lago di Garda the cardinal returned to his life of study and prayer, and it was in these congenial employments that the Pope's messenger found him who brought his nomination as legate to Mary Tudor.

CHAPTER III

THE SHADOW OF POLITICAL NECESSITY

POLE'S commission as legate was made out and despatched to him on August 5, 1553. But it was not until November 24, 1554, that he arrived in London. The story of that long fifteen months' delay, in the critical first phase of the Catholic restoration, reveals at once how complex were the realities of the situation in England, how diversely the Pope's choice of Pole met the different problems that awaited the legate, and how it came about that the religious restoration was fatally compromised, from the beginning, by its political associations. The Counter-Reformation in England is tragically mishandled at its very outset, and in the sole period when it had, humanly speaking, any real chance of success.

While the Pope and the cardinal of England were exchanging their first felicitous budgets of news and of augury, another high official of the Curia was already at work in a very practical way. This was the papal legate at the court at Brussels, Cardinal Enrico Dandino. Dandino was at this moment the most influential of the cardinals of Pope Julius III.[1] He was, practically, the Secretary of State, and his business in Flanders was to negotiate a peace between the Emperor Charles V and the King of France, Henry II. He had the news of the events in England some days before it reached Rome, and realising the importance for the Holy See of a first-hand report on the situation in London, he immediately sent over one of his secretaries, the young Gian Francesco Commendone, whom he thus provided with a first chance of showing those superb talents that were rapidly to make him the leading diplomatist of the Curia for the next quarter of a century. Commendone was still in London when there arrived in Brussels Henry

[1] PASTOR, Vol. 13, p. 75.

Penning, the bearer of a letter from Pole to Queen Mary, and Dandino stayed Penning until, from Commendone's report, he could be certain not only of the kind of reception Penning would receive, but also whether the tone of Pole's message would not conflict with the English queen's own view of things.

Dandino had one very great advantage, over both Pole and Julius III. He realised from the beginning not only that Charles V would strive to play the decisive role in the initial stages of the new régime in England, but this also that, for the emperor, the chief importance of the change was not the chance it seemed to offer of restoring the Catholicism of the *Ecclesia Anglicana*, but the fact that now his aunt's daughter, and his own protégée of so many years, had really come to the throne, and that by keeping her there and strengthening her position in England he was assured of a most faithful ally in his war against the French.[1]

Commendone's task in London was to find out what were Mary's own real dispositions, and what were Pole's chances of bringing about that restoration to which he was commissioned. He stayed in London a month, and during that time he had audience with the queen, and he made the most of his opportunity to discuss the actual situation with the leaders of the presumably pro-Catholic party. Dandino, while he awaited his envoy's return, had an important conference with Charles' experienced chief minister. It was Granvelle's opinion that the queen would need to go very slowly ; that she must be left to go her own way, and, at all costs, must not be pushed into any restoration of Catholicism, nor indeed too much encouraged. It was rather restraint she needed. And he explained to Dandino how the emperor had heard with great disapproval of the Requiem Mass she had had sung for her brother the late king, on the day of his funeral,[2] and at which she had assisted.[3] Mendoza, another of the emperor's diplomatists, and a Spaniard, who had spent two years as ambassador in London, had also added a word of counsel, to the effect that the English had, all of them, drunk very deeply of the delights of the liberty of living in heresy.[4]

[1] *Cf.* Dandino to Cardinal Del Monte, Aug. 2, 1553, in ANCEL, p. 529.
[2] August 8, 1553.
[3] Dandino to Del Monte, Aug. 15 1553, in ANCEL, p. 530.
[4] *Ibid.*, p. 531.

Thus, already, before Commendone returned, all the information Dandino could gather about English affairs seemed to point the same way, and to this he added, for Rome's enlightenment, that current talk among the people who knew these kind of things, credited the emperor with the design of incorporating England in the vast political entity of which he was the head, and this through a marriage between Mary and his own heir Philip. This was within a month of Mary's triumph over the faction of Northumberland.

Dandino came to the conclusion that the restoration of Catholicism was not a matter of immediate practicability. For it could not be achieved without the aid of Charles V, and at the moment Charles was interested in one thing only, the matter of Mary's marriage. Until that was settled he would not so much as hear of any innovations in England that might rouse new opposition to the scarcely established queen.[1]

How far these judgements about opinion in England at this moment were correct, it is not easy to say. But there is no doubt that Dandino gauged the emperor's mind perfectly, and Charles' immediate hostility to Pole's mission is clearly shown in a letter which about this time (August 27, 1553) he sent to Granvelle for Dandino. In this letter the emperor stated that the rumour of Pole's return was causing great resentment in England, and that the French were making the most of this disturbance. Pole, if indeed he leaves Italy at all, must not for the present come any nearer to England than Trent. Charles, at the same time, wrote to the queen in the same sense, and in reply to Pole's own letter to him— a moving piece of eloquence indeed, in which he invited Charles to take up the great role Providence had assigned him and restore the English nation to the fold of Christ— the emperor[2] bade him mark time and suggested that, for the time being, it would be better to drop the whole idea of his legacy and of a Catholic restoration.

All this was in the greatest possible contrast with the mentality of the Pope and of Pole, and with the plan they were preparing. Their common, first idea was that no time should be lost. Whence Rome's immediate despatch of Pole's commission, his ample faculties for the work of

[1] Dandino's letter of Aug. 15 ; *ibid.*, p. 531.
[2] Letter of Sept. 6.

reconciliation and his credentials to Charles V. Pole was
to have a free hand. 'Your Lordship knows better than
anyone what is best to do,' so his instructions ran ; 'we
leave the whole affair to your learning, to your charity,
to your zeal.' [1] It was thus with the glad assurance that the
Pope was at one with him in the matter of English affairs,
and that he possessed the full confidence of the Holy See,
that Pole wrote his first letter to Mary August 13, 1553.[2]
This was the letter sent through Penning, a composition of
great beauty, on a high spiritual plane, a work of great
simplicity and tender piety, the habitual character, indeed,
of all Pole's writing, full of scriptural allusions, and pointing
out both Mary's present graces and her conscientious duty
by reference to scriptural heroines and their history. And
it was now, also, that he wrote (August 21) his first solemnly
joyous letter to Charles V.[3] In this he naturally insists that
the principal matter is the return of the English to their
spiritual obedience to Rome, and by his earnest pleading the
cardinal shows that one illusion at least was spared him.
He knew very well, both from those personal contacts
years before at Toledo and from the contests at Trent,
what manner of man the emperor was, and how he would
need to be brought round to this religious point of view.

And now, too, there appears the first hint of Pole's own
plan of campaign. Parliament was soon to meet (in the
coming October), and the cardinal most earnestly desired
to be in England beforehand, that the case might be put to
Parliament and the reconciliation settled at the very outset
of the reign. The scheme shows immediately how little
Pole was in touch with the realities of English politics, and
in this first contact of the long-exiled Englishman with his
native land the question looms up that is to recur so often
and so tragically in this story, how far could it be reasonably
expected of these exiles that they should succeed in tasks
that called for the most complete understanding of the
spirit of the day, and the closest real contact with every phase
of the mind of the time. A triple disillusionment awaited
the cardinal. The realities of the English situation formed
one element, the extent to which the hostility of the emperor

---

[1] Julius III to Pole, Aug. 6, 1553, in QUIRINI, IV, p. 109, TIERNEY, II,
App. p. xciii.
[2] *Venetian Calendar*, V, pp. 384–387 ; also in TIERNEY, II, App. p. xciv.
[3] *Ven. Cal.*, pp. 389–390.

was to go was a second. The third was the inevitable reaction on English affairs of the complex international situation. In the last matter Pole was speedily to show that he was out of his depth entirely.

The cardinal's first shock, if that be not too strong a word to use, was the picture of the London situation which Commendone painted for him on September 7, for, this diplomatist once returned to Brussels, his chief sent him on immediately to Rome, with instructions to break his journey and report to Pole, still at Maguzzano. The private message of goodwill which Commendone brought from Mary was reassuring, but the rest bore out only too plainly the advice of Dandino to delay his departure.

Four days later Commendone was at Rome, and reporting the whole matter to the Pope. The result was the issue, on September 20, of a new set of instructions for the cardinal legate. The new directions note, as a feature of the English scene, the pride, obstinacy, and boldness of the heretics, the militant quality of their anti-Catholicism. The queen, Pole is now told, is in a sense the prisoner of her subjects,[1] who, almost all of them, hate the Pope. Another leading feature of the prevailing state of mind in London is the general fear that Rome will insist on the restitution of all the wealth looted from the dissolved abbeys and priories. Finally there is the problem of the queen's younger sister, the heiress-presumptive to the throne, Elizabeth, who hates Mary and who ' to-day is in every man's heart and her name on every man's lips.' The queen herself has begged Rome to go slowly, and it is of the utmost importance that it must not even be suspected in England that negotiations with Rome are in progress.[2]

Here begins the first contrast between Pole and his Roman superiors. They have yielded to this evidence. Pole is unmoved by it, probably not believing it, or not interpreting, as Commendone had interpreted them, the talk of London and the violent gestures of its citizens against a new government. And no doubt already there filled the mind of this typical Englishman a deep resentment that

[1] *Cf.* the comment of Dr. Gairdner (who, however, makes no reference to this correspondence). ' She was never mistress in her own house.' *Lollardy and the Reformation in England*, IV, p. 373.

[2] Julius III to Pole, Sept. 20, 1553, in QUIRINI, IV, p. 111 ; TIERNEY, II, p. xcvii.

foreigners were to have such a say in the destiny of his country, and a discernment of what he afterwards plainly told the Pope, namely, that the emperor's hostility to his mission had one cause only, his understanding that Pole would hardly be a party to making England over to the rule of the foreigner.[1]

Julius III did not so far give in to the emperor that he cancelled Pole's mission. But, to mask it somewhat, the cardinal was commissioned as legate, in place of Dandino, now returning to Rome, to negotiate a peace between Charles and Henry II—a mission which Pole's inexperience was to take seriously, with unfortunate consequences. He was given leave to move nearer to England, but bidden henceforward to consult the queen at every step and to do nothing against her wishes.[2] That this was the only way out of an awkward situation, or the only way in which England could gradually be made safe for the reconciliation, is perhaps true. But all the solutions adopted from now had this disadvantage that they definitely decided that the moment of the restoration of England to Catholic unity must depend on the political situation. The restoration cannot, henceforward, wholly escape being confounded with the movements of continental politics. Its opponents will have no difficulty in attacking it as largely a political move, and Catholicism can definitely be opposed as a foreign, un-English thing.

Within a few days of these new instructions reaching him, Pole left Maguzzano (September 29, 1553), to move by slow stages to Trent and through the Tyrol into Bavaria, to Dillingen where the Bishop of Augsburg, Cardinal Otto Truchsess—the great patron of St. Peter Canisius—would give him hospitality.

On the very day of his departure the cardinal received, at last, the Queen of England's reply to his letter of six weeks earlier. It had been sent on by Penning, and with it Penning wrote an account of his three hours' audience with the queen on September 19. Mary was full of gratitude to God and of joy at the news of Pole's appointment. She genuinely looked forward to his coming and desired to have

---

[1] Pole to Julius III, Oct. 27, 1553, in *Venetian Calendar*, V, p. 437.
[2] ANCEL, pp. 535–6 ; Julius III–Pole, Sept. 20, 1553, in TIERNEY II, App, p. xcvii *seq.*, from QUIRINI iv, 111.

him in London as legate. But the heretics were really dangerous, through the degree of their desperation. Moderation and prudence were the only possible ideals to aim at. There must be no needless provocation of the opposition. Finally the queen expressed her anxiety as to her own position *vis-à-vis* the Holy See. Did she fall under all or any of the censures lavished on her excommunicated father and his supporters ? [1]

Meanwhile in England the skilled agents of Charles V moved slowly and surely to the appointed goal. The campaign to achieve the marriage of the queen with Prince Philip really opened with the appointment of Simon Renard as ambassador to London, September 14, 1553. Seven weeks later Mary, kneeling before the Blessed Sacrament, pledged herself, in the ambassador's presence, to marry the prince. For two months the engagement remained a well-kept secret and then, January 12, 1554, the contract was signed and a few days later published in Parliament. From the point of view of the fortunes of the coming attempt to reunite Canterbury and York with Rome, a second mischief was preparing, for in yet another way Catholicism was apparently identifiable with the foreigner.

The eight weeks that passed between Mary's pledge and the Parliamentary acceptance of the contract were full of anxiety for the emperor. The French envoy in London did not cease to work against the plan which, by this time, the whole town suspected was in preparation. And now Pole fell into still greater disfavour than before with the emperor, for since the beginning of October he had been in close contact with the King of France, in pursuance of his mission as peacemaker. The cardinal was already an unwelcome figure in that world where the Spanish marriage was being arranged, as being almost the only Englishman who was of the queen's blood.* There had even been a suggestion in some quarters that he should himself become her husband. The emperor did not at all take seriously the report that Pole himself had ambitions of this sort,[2]

---

[1] ANCEL, p. 745, from the official copies of the letters in *Vat. Archiv. Nunziature) Inghilterra*, III, 66–67 ; *cf.* also Pole–Muzzarelli, Sept. 8, in *Venetian Calendar*, V, pp. 408–409.

[2] *Cf.* Charles V–Renard, Sept. 20, 1553, in *Papiers d'Etat du Cardinal de Granvelle*, IV, p. 109.

* For footnote above see page 54.

but his determination grew to keep the legate out of England until the match was definitely arranged, and he worked to bring Julius III also to his way of thinking. As the next round of the battle drew on in Rome between the emperor and the cardinal, the emperor's animosity heightened.

It was indeed a very battle that filled the last weeks of October, 1553, and its issue was the third set of instructions for Pole, dated October 28 of that year.

On the one side there was Pole, with his ' mystical ' view as to how he should proceed, disregarding all human considerations, simply going forward to England *in nomine Domini*, trusting in God to make his venture fruitful. On the other side there was, besides Charles V—the embodiment of that *prudentia carnis* from which Pole's spirituality turned with unconcealed loathing—the balanced opinion of the papal diplomats, in which is to be discerned the fruit of that virtuous prudence which, before a man performs his act of virtue, bids him survey the circumstances, collect

* The accompanying table will illustrate this, and will show also Mary's relationship (1) to Courtney, whom Gardiner preferred as her husband, (2) to Charles V, and (3) to Philip whom she married.

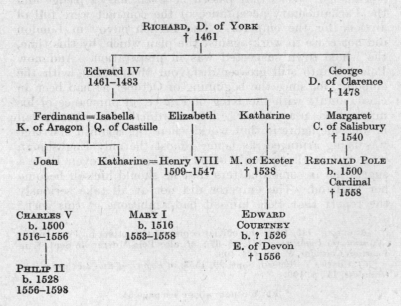

RICHARD, D. of YORK
† 1461

Edward IV
1461–1483

George
D. of Clarence
† 1478

Ferdinand = Isabella
K. of Aragon | Q. of Castille

Elizabeth

Katharine

Margaret
C. of Salisbury
† 1540

Joan

Katharine = Henry VIII
1509–1547

M. of Exeter
† 1538

REGINALD POLE
b. 1500
Cardinal
† 1558

CHARLES V
b. 1500
1516–1556

MARY I
b. 1516
1553–1558

EDWARD
COURTNEY
b. ? 1526
E. of Devon
† 1556

PHILIP II
b. 1528
1556–1598

judgements, and make his choice of the best of the good means available for what he proposes.

This school had Dandino for its chief representative, in the matter of English affairs, and by the middle of October Dandino had returned to Rome, having met Pole, as he passed by Dillingen, on October 16. Before leaving Brussels the emperor had given Dandino a last warning. He was, he frankly declared, opposed to Pole's journey. For his arrival in England would be an excuse for riots and rebellion. The cardinal should make no move until the queen's position was really secure, and until there had been some chance to work the Parliament round.[1]

Also, before leaving Brussels, Dandino had despatched a second envoy to London, the Venetian, Vimercato, who, after a week of enquiries on the spot (September 29–October 5), reported that the project to restore the Pope's authority was regarded with horror by most people in London. Rumours about Pole's mission were getting about and causing lively irritation, and it was Vimercato's opinion that the legate must not be over-eager, but wait for the appropriate moment and leave the choice of this to the judgement of the queen. 'After all I have seen and heard,' he wrote to Dandino, October 13, 1553, ' I consider that the coming of Cardinal Pole will be harmful to religion rather than advantageous. There are two things that people here dread above all : that the queen will marry a foreigner and that she is thinking of making her submission to the Apostolic See.'[2]

Against all this Pole could set his suspicion of the emperor's motives, his own instinct to trust to his appearance in London and to the influence which only an Englishman can really secure over the English. He had realised from the beginning what a part would be played by the general fear that reconciliation with the Holy See would mean the surrender of the properties taken from the Church. Though he felt absolutely sure of the queen's dispositions and good-will, he was none the less well alive to the fact that for nearly twenty years English acquiescence in the schism had been universal, and that all protests against it had long since ceased. All this was part of that message Pole sent to Rome

[1] ANCEL, pp. 752–3.
[2] ANCEL (using Vimercato's letters in *Vat. Archiv. Misc.*, IV, t. 45, ff.), 589–94.

by Parpaglia [1] even before he knew that Rome itself had received the news of Mary's victory. And Pole was sufficiently aware of the lack of knowledge at Rome about the realities of the English situation to suggest, just a week later, that Dandino should be consulted before any definite policy was adopted.[2] Now, two months later, he had before him the opinion of Dandino, and the information on which it was based. He had also the information sent by his own messenger, Penning, and the two reports differed as much as might be, when they touched on the expediency of the legate's appearing in London. From Penning Pole learnt that it was indeed at Mary's request that the emperor was putting obstacles in the way of his mission. Mary herself had told him this. But Penning also stated that if Mary was now showing herself super-cautious about Pole's immediate coming, this was due to the pressure put upon her by the emperor's ambassadors. Mary was in reality as much their prisoner, though she might not know it—nor Julius III either—as she was the prisoner of her subjects. Penning reported conversations with various members of Parliament, the substance of which was that the legate's coming would be generally welcomed, and that the one and only difficulty about his reception lay in the fear that it would entail a general restitution of church properties.[3] And—though Pole may not have known this—the French ambassador in London was, at this very time, writing to his own sovereign in much the same sense, that even the Protestants would be glad to see Pole in London,[4] feeling that in him national interests would have a protector against the manœuvres of Mary's present advisers, the ambassadors of Charles V.

Pole had, also, his view of the way the providence of God must work whenever His servants trust none but Him. Against the eternal repetition on the part of the diplomatists, of ' This alone is possible at the moment,' he never ceased to oppose ' This is the way it ought to be done.' Was he right ? Should he have been supported ? Would it have been better had he travelled express and made his way into

---

[1] *Cf.* PASTOR, Vol. 13, p. 249, quoting Parpaglia's report.
[2] *Venetian Calendar*, V, p. 387.
[3] *Cf.* PASTOR, *ibid.* p. 258, quoting Penning's Report of Nov. 30, 1553.
[4] LINGARD (edit. 1855), V, 200, quoting the dispatches of the French Ambassador Noailles, Vol. II, p. 271, ' Y est-il plus demandé que je n'eusse jamais pensé, le desirans maintenant tant les protestants que Catholiques.'

England—supposing this were possible—before the emperor
had the time to place these reasonable obstacles in his path ?
Who can say what the influence of Pole would have been in
Mary's government in the first few months of the reign ?
Certainly there would never have been a Spanish marriage,
and if the reconciliation with Rome had been a hundred
times more difficult to bring about, it would not have
appeared to the nation as a thing linked with the hated
marriage of the queen to a foreigner.

It was the emperor's Spanish policies, so Pole believed,
and rightly, that were the cause of his being delayed. But
Julius III put faith in Charles, and in the third set of
instructions Pole [1] was told this, and warned not to embarrass
Mary by over-persuasions. More, the matter of his arrival
in England was now left to the emperor's discretion. This
was written on October 28. Four days earlier Pole had left
Dillingen, en route for England. He had travelled no farther
than Heidenheim when there met him one of the emperor's
chief diplomatists, Juan di Mendoza. He had a message
from his master. The cardinal was to remain at Dillingen.
Pole's indignant protests, to the emperor, to Mary, and to
the Pope, may still be read. It was while he still smarted
under this affront that these latest instructions of the Pope
reached him, and a letter from Mary to the same effect.
A fortnight later she wrote, still more urgently, that were
Pole to come over she could not even guarantee his personal
safety.

So at Dillingen, by the Danube, Pole remained for the
best part of two months while, in London, Parliament
de-Calvinised the national religion, and, suspicious of what
was afoot, besought the queen to marry and not to marry a
foreigner. What thoughts passed through the mind of the
cardinal legate it needs no great effort to imagine, as he
meditated on the emperor's victory at Rome and on the
peremptory terms of the Pope's last instructions. A few
days before the New Year he was given fresh evidence of the
degree to which the Pope had yielded, and evidence that
must have been most unwelcome of Rome's utter inability
to understand that the English will rather be lost despite
their own efforts than be saved by the victorious arms of the
foreigner. The letter from Cardinal Morone to Pole, of

---

[1] Julius III to Pole, Oct. 28, 1533, in QUIRINI, IV, p. 115 ; TIERNEY, II,
p. cvii.

December 21, 1553, strikes a note, singularly out of tune
with any in the English scale, but a note destined to echo
and re-echo through all the crises of the next hundred years
and more.[1] The subject of the letter is the Spanish marriage
and Pole's known disapproval of the scheme. The legate
is told that the Pope holds it as certain, for many reasons,
that Mary ought to marry Philip of Spain. The marriage
will be highly advantageous to England and will bring back
the country entirely to the true religion, and to union with
the Church. Unmarried the queen would be too weak an
instrument to be able to rule very long a race that is
by nature so ferocious, so fickle, and so accustomed to
novelties.[2] To this must be added the problems arising from
internal dissension and the intrigues of foreign powers.
No native king, the Pope believes, would, for the reasons
set out, be suited for the task of bringing England back to its
obedience to Rome. The most likely policy of a native king
would be compromise all round in order to establish himself
firmly. But, on the contrary, with regard to the Spanish
prince, the Pope has every confidence that since Philip is a
Catholic born and bred, and possessed of great forces
in the neighbouring countries of Flanders and Spain, he
will be able to introduce the union with the Church with
greater authority and better defend the queen from all her
foes, whether within the realm or from without.

Pole, therefore, is to make this point of view his own,
that to put obstacles in the way of the marriage would be
dangerous and harmful both to religion and to the interests
of the Holy See. At the court at Brussels he is to let this be
clearly known, by his words and his actions, lest the emperor
be displeased, and possibly find some excuse for continuing
the schism once the marriage is accomplished.

What the emotions were of this son of the last Plantagenet,
this princely cardinal of whom even Mary herself had thought
as a native consort, as he read this papal review of his own
people, their characteristics and the remedies opportune
to meet their case, is not recorded. The rest of the letter
testifies to the lively anxiety of the Pope lest Pole should
take a line of his own, and to the papal judgement that there
is no folly to which the legate's idealism, unless he be
restrained, is not able to lead him.

[1] The text in full in PASTOR, Vol. 13, App. no. 21B, pp. 448-9.
[2] ' Quei popoli di natura feroci et instabili et assuefatti alle novità.'

But by the time Pole received this letter, Charles had the English marriage 'in the bag,' and on the day he wrote the good news to Rome he sent Pole his passports to come as far as Brussels. On January 25, 1554, Pole made his solemn entry into the Flemish capital.

And now, all unwittingly, Pole turned to an activity that lost him whatever still remained of the emperor's goodwill towards him. Realising that the Pope preferred now not to know his views about the problem of England, and that he wanted to believe the emperor was right, Pole resigned himself, and prepared to conduct that other business formally entrusted to him of making peace between Charles and the King of France. He made his way to France in the March of 1554, was gratefully received by Henry II, and arrived back in Brussels with nothing achieved save an immense misunderstanding with the emperor. This commission had been given to Pole simply to mask his journey from Italy towards England. But the cardinal read it literally and executed it in such a fashion, taking the words of the French king at their face value, that now it could only appear to the world that the one hindrance to European peace was Charles V. Pole had put himself into the position of a peacemaker who listens sympathetically to one side and wonders why, in the face of such reasonableness, the other side still holds out.

What made the matter worse was that January and February (1554) had seen in England the dangerous rebellion of Sir Thomas Wyatt. In this business the French were strongly suspected to have had a share, and suspicions began to spread about Pole also, that he had been a party to the conspiracy and, even, that he was himself aiming at the throne. The suspicions may to-day seem ludicrous, but their existence then, and the credence they gained, serve to show in what a powder-magazine the legate's simple good faith moved, and to explain how easily his goodwill could lead him into enormous diplomatic gaffes.

Pole's return to Brussels was the occasion of a stormy interview with the emperor, and it was about this time that Granvelle wrote to Mendoza that the legate, though a good and learned man, had still to learn the elements of how to manage affairs. It was generally assumed that the Pope must now recall Pole, held to have compromised his mission irretrievably by antagonising the potentate whose goodwill was all-important. Charles V seems to have taken this for granted, and he angrily demanded why Pole still lingered at Brussels. But Julius III, to his everlasting credit, stood by his old colleague of Trent. Through Cardinal Morone, one of Pole's intimates, he wrote to reassure the unhappy legate, whose thoughts turned only on retirement from public life. He bade Pole [1] make his peace with the emperor by adopting a different attitude towards the now decided marriage. Pole must not seem publicly to disapprove of it, through a silence which, on all hands, was being mischievously misconstrued. The legate replied [2] that his attitude had been wilfully misrepresented. He acknowledged that the task set him was beyond his powers, and, until further order was taken, he proposed to return to his accustomed refuge, his studies, in the library of the great abbey where he was dwelling. Here, the guest of the Premonstratensian Canons of Dilighem, he passed the summer months of 1554, still corresponding with the queen, and attending to the ecclesiastical affairs of England, what time the more practised hand of the nuncio at Brussels dealt with the subtle impero-papal diplomacy.

The marriage of the queen took place on St. James's Day, the patronal feast of Spain, July 25, 1554, and, the main cause for his being kept at a distance now ceasing, the legate once more approached the emperor. But Charles still maintained his reserve and would not move from his position that the appropriate moment for Pole's journey to England was still far off. A new question, in fact, had arisen, and Charles and the legate were once more at cross purposes. This was the question of Pole's attitude towards the owners of the property, valuables, and lands, of the dissolved monasteries.

The first rumbling of storm in this very practical business was the bill, introduced into Parliament, in April, 1554, to prevent any demand for the restoration of the abbey lands. Whatever surprise this may have held for the legate, who anticipating, as ever, the best in those with whom he dealt, seems to have expected an offer, of some kind, to restore some of the loot, Rome, from the very first, had envisaged the possibility of this general resolve to hold on

[1] Morone-Pole, May 6, 1554; ANCEL, p. 767, quoting original in Morone's own hand, Archiv. Vaticano, arm. 64, t. 32, f. 199–200.
[2] *Venetian Calendar*, V, p. 492.

to what had been gained. In the faculties sent to Pole
with his first commission, August 5, 1553, he is given the
power ' To make a final binding agreement with the holders
of church property regarding revenues unlawfully received
by them and goods already used up, and of freeing them
[from any obligations] and setting their consciences at rest
—provided, if it should seem expedient to Your Lordship,
that they first make restitution of any real property which
they still unlawfully detain.' [1]

While this concession showed a realist view of the situation
on the part of Julius III and his advisers, the parliamentary
incident of April, 1554, showed that a still more generous
spirit of renunciation would be needed, a renunciation that
would go as far as the real property so extensively looted.
From England, through Penning, Pole was informed that
at every audience the queen touched on this question.[2]
He asked for more ample powers, and they were sent to him.
Everything, seemingly, would turn on security here. Pole
had, from the beginning, anticipated this difficulty, and
had been just as keenly alive to the gravity of this problem.
In his very first message to Rome about the restoration of
Catholicism in England, the message sent through Parpaglia,
August 6, 1553, along with the news of Mary's victory
over Northumberland, the cardinal spoke of this as the
one real difficulty of the situation.[3] But, attached to the
ideal solution, he found himself once more in conflict
both with the English demands and with the Curia's
scheme to meet them. It was Pole's desire that, at all
costs, things should be so ordered that it could never be
said that the reconciliation was the fruit of a bargain
between the Holy See and the wealthy men who had
made their fortunes out of the plunder of the Church. He
was not opposed to the idea that a general condonation
should be granted, but he thought that this should follow
the reconciliation. Let the English fall on their knees,
confess their apostasy, and ask pardon of God. The Vicar
of Christ would not show himself tyrannical or harsh ; the
papal generosity would be equal to the occasion. The
question of the abbey lands, he thought, would best be
settled as a free act of the Pope's clemency, and therefore

[1] TIERNEY, II, App., p. cxiii.   [2] ANCEL, p. 780, note 3.
[3] Cf. PASTOR, Vol. 13, pp. 248–9, who prints an important passage from
Parpaglia's own (unpublished) Informatione.

the question had best not even be discussed—between England and Rome—until the reconciliation was complete.[1]

The nuncio at Brussels, Girolamo Muzzarelli, the Dominican Archbishop of Consa, was more of a realist; and ready to be more accommodating. He understood, and said this plainly to Rome,[2] that if the question were not settled now, and clearly settled, there would never be any chance of the reconciliation. The suggestion that a settlement prior to the reconciliation would be taken as bargaining, he scouted. There was, as all men agreed, only one way out of the impasse. Then let the Pope take the initiative. Let the first move come from Rome, before any requests were made or the public discussion began. Let the only possible solution make its first appearance as the papal solution. This seems wisdom itself, and Mary asking the simple, unconditional confirmation of the present possession, a new brief was made out [3] giving Pole all the necessary powers.

Everything seemingly was now in order. The Spanish marriage took place on July 25, and four days later Pole received his new powers to settle the question of the abbey lands in the sense desired by Mary. But Charles V still hung back, making his excuse to Pole that Philip and Mary must be first consulted. The weeks went by and then Pole took the matter into his own hands and wrote both to Philip and to Mary, September 21, 1554. Their replies were all that he could desire and now the detail of the journey began to be arranged. On October 11, 1554, Pole had an audience with the emperor, who counselled him to go very slowly, and, when Pole ironically remarked that he seemed now not so much to be taking his leave as to be making the emperor's acquaintance—for in the nine months Pole had been at Brussels they had scarcely met—Charles replied only with a smile. As to the heretics Pole was now to meet among the English ruling class, the emperor, with an experience of the type no man in Europe could better, offered to the scholarly cardinal this seasonable word that doctrinal questions interested them but little; it was property that was all important.

---

[1] Muzzarelli-Del Monte, May 19, 1554, in ANCEL, p. 779.

[2] ANCEL, p. 780.

[3] June 28, 1554 : text in WILKINS' *Concilia*, IV, p. 102 ; also TIERNEY, II, App., p. cxix.

Why did Charles continue, almost to the last, so opposed to Pole's going to England ? Apparently, in the final instance because he still feared Pole was not the man for the delicate task that lay ahead. Pole, we know, still clung to the idea that some return of the landed property, or some compensation for losses, might be expected from the penitent thieves, who would presently be kneeling before him for absolution. He was more than loath to be so ' easy ' in the matter that the expressed regrets might seem mere formality. And he dreaded still that this English settlement might seem to give the world proof that if Catholics turn to plunder the Church, Rome will ultimately be brought round to condone it.[1]

The emperor may well have guessed the English tenacity with which Pole held to his views, the deep-seated aversion from any idea of compromise with successful and sacrilegious rascality, and he may have wondered how much of this would show in the legate's daily traffic with these men. And, it must finally be said, Pole's determination to avoid even the appearance of bargaining had led him to keep to himself, to the very last, the detail of the large concessions made by the Holy See not only in the brief of June 28, but in the previous secret bull of August 5, 1553,[2] that covered all possible cases. Not until the eve of his departure did he make these known to Charles. It was not the least of the nuncio's good services that he won Pole over to be less reserved with Charles, pointing out that his attitude was giving rise to a suspicion of the Pope's good faith.[3] There was some warrant for the emperor's complaint to Muzzarelli : ' If the cardinal is not yet in England let him blame himself.'

The blame lay partly, he thought, in Pole's choice of advisers. ' He is a great man, and will do much good, but in his entourage he has certain servants who lead him to commit these mistakes.'[4] In the sixteenth century Englishmen were already English. Even after twenty years of living amongst foreigners they did not like the foreigners, nor ever wholly trust them, and the foreigners realised this well.

The last anxieties were now over. London was certified that Pole was not coming to whip the repentant with scor-

---

[1] *Cf.* Ormanetto's letter of Jan. 27, 1555, to Francesco Stella, and his remarks on Pole's faculties, quoted ANCEL, p. 784, note 2.
[2] *Cum Nos Hodie*, text in TIERNEY, II, App., p. cxvi.
[3] ANCEL, p. 785 ; PASTOR, Vol. 13, p. 280.   [4] ANCEL, p. 788.

pions, and that there would be no question of demands to restore the monastic property. The Council consented to Pole's admission as papal legate and to make formal petition for absolution and reconciliation with the Holy See. On November 11, 1554, the embassy of notables sent with this news waited on Pole at Brussels. While the legate took his leave of the emperor, November 12, the Parliament at Westminster, in its opening session, passed an act reversing the eighteen-years-old attainder that had for so long barred his native country to Pole. On the 13th he left Brussels and, travelling by Ghent and Bruges, came on the 19th to English territory at Calais. The next day he landed at Dover, declining as yet to appear as legate and already reversing a hundred prejudices by his evidently genuine and deep simplicity. He passed through Canterbury and Rochester to Gravesend, and everywhere rejoicing crowds hailed him. And then, with the legate's cross at the prow of his barge, he came, on the full tide, to London, to the steps of the royal palace at Whitehall, and there to meet him was the king, November 24, 1554.

The next few days were spent in private conferences with Gardiner, Bishop of Winchester—now Lord Chancellor— and the sovereigns and an order of procedure was agreed upon. The reconciliation was to be effected in three successive sessions of Parliament. In the first—November 28 —Pole, to a joint session of both Houses, made clear the nature of his mission in a speech that is a model of tact and of simple English patriotism. He explained what it was that needed to be done and how he proposed to go about it, and he dispelled any fears that his mission had any but a spiritual character. He then withdrew and the Houses, separating, discussed his speech. On the 29th they met once more, to discuss and vote the text of the petition for reconciliation and the terms of the act of submission. The final scene came on St. Andrew's Day, a day whose glory, for Pole, must far have outstripped even that brilliant hour when five years before, the papacy was his for the taking. The proceedings began with the Lord Chancellor reading out the minutes of the parliamentary session of the day before, the Act of Submission, the request for absolution and reconciliation. After which, in the name of the Lords and Commons he prayed the king and queen to present their petition to the legate. Pole's faculties were read out.

He made a second address, and then, all except himself kneeling, he pronounced the formula which lifted the excommunications and restored the English people to the membership of the Catholic Church of Christ. The lengthy ceremonial had filled the whole day, and it was by the light of torches that king and queen, Lords and Commons, made their way to the chapel of the palace for the *Te Deum*.

Two days later Pole made his solemn entry into London. There was a High Mass at St. Paul's—where the members of the legate's suite noted how Bonner pontificated in such fashion as though he had somewhat lost the habit thereof. And on December 6 Pole, at Lambeth, absolved Convocation.

CHAPTER IV

THE RESTORATION OF RELIGION, 1553–1558

§ i THE LEGAL BAN LIFTED

MARY had begun her reign with two very deeply rooted resolves. She would restore the Catholic religion to its former place in English life and she would not coerce any man's religious beliefs. The queen was, from the very first, the most enthusiastic of Counter-Reformers, and she did not wait for the arrival of the legate, eighteen months after her victory over Northumberland, before setting her hand to the task.

Mary's first public pronouncement was the proclamation of August 18, 1553, just ten days after the double funeral of her brother, Edward VI, whom Cranmer buried with the new Edwardine rites while, in the chapel of the Tower, Gardiner, in the presence of the queen, sang a Requiem Mass. Within the next few days the Mass was revived in one or two of the London churches, and on the Sunday between the funeral and this proclamation Dr. Gilbert Bourne, preaching a Catholic sermon at St. Paul's Cross, had a dagger thrown at him and saw his congregation marvellously transformed into a riotous assembly. The proclamation, nevertheless, although it relates that the queen greatly desires that all her subjects were of the religion she professes, declares that she has no intention to compel any man to adopt it unless Parliament shall so decide. Pending the action of Parliament she enjoins a religious truce, forbids brawling and sedition and the use of ' those new-found devilish terms of papist or heretic.' All doctrinal sermons or discussions, except in the schools of the Universities, are forbidden, and it is also forbidden to publish any kind of religious writing without the queen's special licence.

In the seven weeks between this proclamation and the meeting of Parliament (October 5, 1553) many things

66

happened ; the leaders of the Northumberland conspiracy
were tried and some of them executed—Mary here showing
herself incredibly merciful ; Cranmer's manifesto denouncing the Mass as blasphemous and idolatry was published
and the archbishop thereupon committed to the Tower ;
the bishops of Exeter, Durham, Winchester, London and,
Chichester, deprived by Edward VI, were reinstated, their
deprivation being held null and void ; and gradually but
still very slowly, the Mass began to be revived in some more
of the London churches and also at Oxford and Cambridge.[1]
And the French ambassador—inevitably hostile to the half-
Spanish queen whose principal counsellor, it was already
evident, was the emperor's envoy—was initiated into the
anti-Catholic publicity campaign which the Edwardines
were preparing as a setting for the coming parliamentary
session.[2]

The main business of this first Parliament of the reign
was an act [3] which, repealing nine acts of King Edward VI,
restored the religious status of England to what it had
been at that king's accession (January 28, 1547). That is
to say the new liturgy of the Book of Common Prayer was
abolished and the Mass was made the sole, lawful Eucharistic Service.[4] The Catholic ordination service was likewise
restored, with the rest of the Catholic sacramental ritual.
The laws abolishing certain Holy Days and Fasting Days
were repealed, and with them the law ' for abolishing and
putting away of divers books, and images.' Bishops were
no longer to be appointed by letters patent and clerical
marriages were stripped of all legal standing. It took some
time to get this first repealing statute through the House of
Commons, and it was only after eight days of stormy and
persistent opposition that it passed its third reading,
November 8, 1553, by 270 votes to 80.[5]

The House of Commons was then by no means unanimously Catholic-minded in its sacramental views, or in its
notions about clerical discipline. And it showed itself
definitely anti-Roman when it refused in the discussions on
the new Treason Bill, to allow any explicit reference in the
act to the Pope or the papal authority. And the crown

---

[1] GAIRDNER, Lollardy, IV, p. 22.   [2] Ibid., p. 34.
[3] 1 Mary, Statute 2, c. 2 ; G. and H., LXXII.
[4] As from Dec. 20, 1553.
[5] GAIRDNER, Lollardy, IV, pp. 123, 125, 154, 155.

strove in vain for the insertion of the papal sentence in the act which declared valid the marriage of Henry VIII and Katharine of Aragon.

The new year, 1554, had barely begun when the rebellion of Sir Thomas Wyatt broke out, and Mary found herself, directly, in as great danger of losing her throne as ever happened to any Tudor. Only when the rising was suppressed, and justice done—somewhat more rigorously than nine months earlier—to the conspirators, could the government turn to the enforcement of the discipline restored by the first repealing statute. Commissions were issued by the crown and seven of the bishops were deprived of their sees, Bush of Bristol, Bird of Chester, Ferrar of St. David's, and Holgate of York on March 13 ; Harley of Hereford, Hooper of Gloucester, and Taylor of Lincoln two days later. And on April 1, in the one-time abbey church of St. Mary Overy, Southwark, Bonner consecrated new Catholic, reconciled bishops to fill four of these vacancies and the vacancies at Rochester and Bath and Wells.

The episcopate, purged now of married and heretical elements, turned to rid the Church of the clergy who had availed themselves of the Edwardine legislation and married. It seems to be generally allowed that there were in all England about 8000 benefices, and in the seventeen dioceses where any records at all survive [1] we can trace 1057 deprivations for marriage. Usually, where the priest was willing to live apart from the woman with whom he had gone through the marriage ceremony, he was, after penance, given a living in some other part of the diocese.

When Pole at last arrived, in the November of this same year, to begin his legatine task, he thus found an episcopate and clergy wholly Catholic, in profession of faith and acceptance of discipline, and he found the Mass and the Catholic sacraments in legal possession. But ecclesiastical jurisdiction still lay fettered by the Submission of the Clergy Act, and, in English law, the head of this *Ecclesia Anglicana*, now purged of sacramental heretics, was not the Pope but the queen. The next stage of the restoration was the most delicate of all, as everyone but Pole had realised for months. It was, however, accomplished within a few weeks of the great ceremony of reconciliation, by a second statute of repeals,[2]

---

[1] *Cf.* FRERE, *Marian Reaction*, Ch. III, The Deprivations.
[2] 1 & 2 Philip and Mary, c. 8 ; G. and H., LXXVI.

and thus, in the words of a far from sympathetic historian :
' The papacy recovered its rights as absolute sovereign of
the church.' [1]

This very lengthy Act of Parliament [2] repeals, in whole or
in part, eighteen acts of Henry VIII and one of Edward VI,
and, after these particulars, it repeals in general everything
enacted since 1529 ' against the supreme authority of the
Pope's holiness or See Apostolic of Rome.' The Royal
Supremacy was, by this act, abolished, and the Pope again
acknowledged as the head of the Church. All hindrances
to the exercise of his authority were removed. Bishops
would once more be appointed by him and appeals from
their courts be taken to his courts. Once more when the
king's subjects were cited to the Pope's courts they could
obey that citation, and once more they could approach the
Pope for all manner of licences and dispensations. Once
more they were free to pay him the tribute of Peter Pence or
the first fruits of what ecclesiastical benefices they might
hold. And by the repeal of the Submission of the Clergy
Act, the Church recovered its power to make laws independently of the State, and the ecclesiastical courts—with
their jurisdiction, in ecclesiastical matters, over all the
king's subjects—were restored to life. The new ecclesiastical
foundations—the five new sees of Oxford, Bristol, Gloucester,
Peterborough, and Chester created by Henry VIII—were
confirmed. The marriages made during the breach without
dispensation from Rome were validated. All ecclesiastical
appointments made by the crown in the time when it
claimed a supremacy in religious matters were confirmed
also, and all censures, excommunications for example, on
the present holders of monastic property were utterly
removed and taken away. Not only were these holders of
monastic property not required to make any restitution, but
the act specifically confirmed their possession and set out the
text of the legate's decision that they could retain what they
held, and, furthermore, it enacted that suits regarding such
property were not triable in any court save the courts of
common law.

So far as an Act of Parliament could do it, the Catholic
Church was re-established as though Henry VIII had never
been. But the course of history can never be wholly reversed.

[1] A. F. POLLARD, p. 131.
[2] Thirty-one pages in G. and H.

What no act of any parliament or Pope could do was to destroy the new mentality towards the respective roles of cleric and layman in the Church, the mentality which had become part of the English character in the twenty-five years between 1529 and 1554 ; or to obliterate the memory of that long period when the layman was emancipated wholly from clerical control, and the cleric no more than his servant *in spiritualibus*. And no act could fully restore the Church's influence which consecrated the *fait accompli* of its material spoliation. An impoverished church would ultimately be no match, left to itself, for the laymen whose fortunes were built on church plunder. The spirit of the once victorious, and, until lately, wholly triumphant laity, is evident in more than one place in this foundation charter of the restoration ; and nowhere more than in the care of parliament that the reconciled Catholic's title to abbey lands shall not be the papal dispensation simply, but that dispensation as part of a statute, a thing to be discussed not in any bishop's court or legate's court, but in the court of the king. It is also worth noting that the statute does not repeal the law which was the first beginning of all Henry VIII's anti-Catholic revolution, the statute against excessive fees to the clergy for spiritual and quasi-spiritual services.

Nevertheless, this second statute of repeals was a great achievement. It met with no difficulty in the Lords, where it was introduced on December 20, 1554, and it was during the four days' debate in the Commons, apparently, that those amendments made their appearance which so effectively demonstrated that if Englishmen were once more to be Catholics, they had no mind to submit themselves unreservedly to ecclesiastical jurisdiction. The form of the statute and its preamble are important, too, in their witness not only to the presence of this ' lay ' spirit, and to the nature of Pole's reconciling act, but also to the status, in the eyes of a contemporary Catholic, of that unreconciled *Ecclesia Anglicana*, that first attempt to set up a non-papal, merely national and parliamentary Church of England.

' Whereas,' the statute begins, ' since the twentieth year of King Henry VIII [1] ... much false and erroneous doctrine has been taught . . . partiy by divers the natural born subjects of this realm, and partly being brought in hither from sundry other foreign countries . . . by reason whereof,

as well the spiritualty as the temporalty . . . have swerved
from the obedience of the See Apostolic, and declined from
the unity of Christ's Church, and so had continued, until
. . . the Pope's holiness and the See Apostolic sent hither
. . . the most reverend father in God, the Lord Cardinal
Pole, legate *de Latere*, to call us home again into the right
way from whence we have all this long while wandered and
strayed abroad. . . .'

This wandering has not been without ' sundry long and
grievous plagues and calamities,' but the grace of God has
brought the nation to realise its errors and to acknowledge
them to the legate. In proof of repentance and submission,
promise has been made to him to repeal and abrogate all
acts made since 1529 ' against the supremacy of the See
Apostolic,' and the statute sets out the text of the submission
made to the legate through the king and queen on November
29, 1554. This submission is stated to be the act of ' the
Lords spiritual and temporal, and of the Commons,
assembled in this present Parliament, representing the whole
body of the realm of England.' In it Lords and Commons
' do declare ourselves very sorry and repentant of the schism
and disobedience committed in this realm . . .' and they make
the promise demanded to repeal all the anti-papal laws,
' that we may as children repentant be received into the
bosom and unity of Christ's Church. . . .'

Then follows the long list of the acts proposed to be
repealed and two petitions to the legate. The first petition
is for the ratification of certain acts done during the schism,
and amongst these that most important class of acts by
means of which ' the right and dominion of certain lands
and hereditaments, goods, and chattels ' belonging to sees,
monasteries, chantries, colleges is now ' dispersed abroad,
and come to the hands and possessions of divers and sundry
persons, who . . . according to the orders of the laws and
statutes of this realm for the time being, have the same.'
The second petition, next recited, is from the bishops and
clergy of the province of Canterbury. This, in the first
place, supports the layman's plea for condonation of the
looting, for ' we freely confess ourselves to know well how
difficult and almost impossible would be the recovery.' Any
attempt to recover would, indeed, mean such a disturbance
as would speedily end the new religious unity. This concession made, the clergy next petition for the full restoration

of ' our jurisdiction and ecclesiastical liberty ' and the
repeal of all the laws that hinder it.

These petitions the legate has granted, says the next
paragraph of the statute, and it goes on to recite the text
of his dispensation to which, finally, it proceeds to give force
of law, that ' all and singular articles and clauses contained
in the said dispensation . . . shall remain and be reputed and
taken to all intents and constrcution in the laws of this realm,
lawful, good, and effectual.'

The legate was now free to proceed with the rebuilding of
Sion. Although none knew it, the time before the builder
was short. Less than four years indeed was the allotted
span, and then the Catholic queen would die, to be succeeded by her heretic half-sister, and on that same day
Reginald Pole, too, would pass from this life. But two
features of the short-lived reconstruction must be described,
the plan by which it was to proceed, contained in the
elaborate decrees of the great synod of 1555–1556 and the
personalities of the men chosen to be the legate's chief
collaborators, the new Catholic hierarchy of 1554–1558.
And something must be said, too, of those who actively
opposed the reconstruction, the heretics whom it was one of
the legate's principal duties to remove from out the vineyard of the Lord, and whose removal is, indeed, almost
the only feature of this chapter of Counter-Reformation
history to remain fixed in the national memory of the
English.

§ ii. THE LEGASTINE SYNOD

The general movement to de-protestantise the religion of
England, legally authorised by the first great repealing
statute of December, 1553, did not, as has been noted,
really begin until Wyatt's insurrection had been suppressed.
The earliest administrative action, in fact, is Mary's despatch
to all the bishops, on March 4, 1554, of a series of directions [1]
touching on almost every point of ecclesiastical discipline
and of liturgical practice. The queen, whatever her
personal desires, was still, by an English Act of Parliament
not yet repealed, Supreme Head of the Church, and whatever action might be taken by the bishops without the
prescribed reference to the crown's spiritual jurisdiction,

[1] G. and H., LXXIV.

could no doubt be challenged by the Reform Party as illegal and void of effect. Until the act which set up the Royal Supremacy was repealed, the only way to give the Catholic restoration force of law was to take note of the Supremacy at the very outset ; and almost the first thing these instructions from the crown effect is to prevent all further spread of the crown's spiritual jurisdiction, for, by the second article of the series bishops are forbidden for the future to insert in their ecclesiastical sentences and rulings the accustomed phrase ' sustained by the king's authority ' [1] and by the third article any further administration of the Oath of Supremacy is forbidden too.

These royal Injunctions of 1554 are, in fact, no more than a warranty from the crown that the bishop will not suffer any legal consequences for what he does to re-Catholicise his diocese, and they set out in detail some of the chief matters that call for change.

The Canon Law is restored as it existed before the clergy's surrender to Henry VIII. The Royal Supremacy is, as much as the queen can do this, suspended. Catholic belief in matters of sacramental doctrine is to be required of all candidates for ordination and of all appointed to any benefice or ecclesiastical office. Heresy is to be repressed, especially among the clergy, and a strict watch is to be kept of the printing and publishing of ' unlawful books, ballads and other pernicious and naughty devices engendering hatred . . . and discord.' And the bishop, in this particular, is to supervise schoolmasters as carefully as preachers.

' With all celerity and speed ' married clerics are to be deprived, greater leniency being shown to those who are willing to live single lives, and everywhere the one-time monks who have married are to be separated from their wives.

The traditional procession before the High Mass on Sundays and Feast Days is to be restored, and the old Litany of the Saints in Latin is to replace the new litany of the Book of Common Prayer. All the fasting days and the holy days abolished in the reign of King Edward are to be revived, and also the ancient ritual celebrations of Ash Wednesday and Palm Sunday and the last three days of Holy Week. In Baptism and Confirmation the Catholic rite alone is to be used. As for Holy Orders, ' touching such

[1] Regia auctoritate fulcitus.

persons as were heretofore promoted to any orders after
the new sort and fashion of order, *considering they were not
ordered in very deed*,[1] the bishop of the diocese finding otherwise sufficiency and ability in these men, may supply that
thing which wanted in them before, and then, according to
his discretion, admit them to minister.'

Finally, the bishop is to provide a uniform system of
homilies for the instruction of his people ; he is to compel
them to come to church ; he is to remove all schoolmasters
whose faith is suspect and care is to be taken that every
child is taught to serve the priest's Mass.

Six months later than the issue of these articles, there took
place a great visitation of the diocese of London by its
bishop, Edmund Bonner (September 3 to October 8, 1554),
whose record is the elaborate series first of articles, asking
questions, and next of injunctions laying down rules for the
future, which is printed in Frere and Kennedy.[2] Here we
can see the bishop making his own the recommendations of
the earlier, royal injunction of Queen Mary, and restoring
all the religious customs as well as the Catholic sacramental
liturgy and the clerical discipline. These are the most
detailed provisions for the replacement of vestments, service
books, and church furniture, presumably destroyed in the
late reign. Pyxes, oil stocks, crucifixes, statues, rood lofts
with their calvaries, and ' altars of fair stone '—we are given
glimpses of a general restoration that must have filled the
London churches for days and months with busy craftsmen
of every kind. For the use of the ill-instructed—and, not
least among these, of his clergy—the bishop composed
*A profitable and necessary doctrine, with certain homilies ad-
joined thereto.* It is a simple explanation of the creed, the
sacraments, the commandments, the *Our Father, Hail
Mary,* seven capital sins, and the Beatitudes. This the
clergy were to study, and to set forth systematically, Sunday
by Sunday at Mass.

Two details of Bishop Bonner's injunctions sound oddly to
modern ears. The first is the age—fourteen—at which he
makes it obligatory to assist at Mass. The second throws
a strong light on the infrequency with which the sacrament
of the Holy Eucharist was received, and also on the Bishop
as a conservative in this matter, and as in no way touched by
the new habits which, for a generation now, had been

---

[1] Italics *not* in the original.   [2] Vol. II., pp. 331–72.

fostered in Spain and in Italy. From all the vast spiritual
revival of continental Catholicism these English bishops had
been most effectively cut off once they renounced the
Roman jurisdiction. And so the Bishop of London, striving
to restore Catholicism after years of devastation, can note
the infrequency of Holy Communion among his people
and fail utterly to exhort them to any better habit. True
he is, in this particular injunction, explaining the reasonableness of the custom he is restoring, namely that bread is
blessed at the Mass and given to the parishioners, who eat it
as a sacramental. But his incidental reference to that other
Bread, which, in his time apparently, the priest alone usually
received, seems singularly inadequate, '. . . the giving of
holy bread is to put us in remembrance of unity, and that
all Christian people be one mystical body of Christ, like as
the bread is made of many grains, and yet but one loaf '—
a comparison taken from St. Paul indeed, but not used here
as St. Paul used it, to teach a doctrine about the relation
between the mystical body of Christ and the receiving of
Holy Communion—' and that the said holy bread is to put
us also in remembrance of the housel, and the receiving
of the most Blessed Body and Blood of our Saviour Jesus
Christ, which the people in the beginning of Christ's church
did oftener receive than they do use now in these days to do.'
The only reference to more frequent communion is purely
historical, an archæological reminiscence to explain and
justify a new, modern custom! The Council of Trent,
proclaiming the Catholic tradition just three years earlier
than Bishop Bonner's visitation, strikes a very different
note : ' This holy synod, with fatherly concern, warns
exhorts, begs, and beseeches by the loving heart of our God,
that all and singular, who count themselves of the Christian
name, come together in harmony now at any rate, in this
sign of unity, this bond of love, this symbol of agreement,
and that, mindful of the great majesty and the outstanding
love of Our Lord Jesus Christ who gave His beloved life
as the price of our salvation, and His flesh for our eating, all
Christians will believe and reverence these sacred mysteries
of His body and blood with a faith so constant and so firm,
with such devotedness of spirit, with such dutiful worship,
that they may be able frequently to receive this super-
substantial bread, and that it may truly be to them the life
of their soul, and an everlasting health of mind, made

strong by whose strength they may be qualified to arrive, from the journeying of this woeful pilgrimage, at our fatherland which is heaven.' [1]

Repeatedly we need to recall that the Marian restoration never got beyond the stage of first plans and a marking out of sites. In what might have been, in what was to have been, it was Pole that would have made the difference, and in nothing so much as in this all-important matter of infusing into the renascent Catholicism of his native land the rich new life that had warmed his own soul at Padua and Rome and Trent. Something of that great synod's fruitful return to principles and to starting-places, and of the power of far-seeping reform which contact with origins bred in the great churchmen of his generation, marks the whole of that fragment of constructive work which was all he was spared to accomplish, the decrees of the National Council which, as papal legate, he summoned and over which he presided in the winter of 1555-1556.[2]

These decrees [3] are much more than any merely formal addition to the immense mass of ecclesiastical legislation. They reveal the soul of the legislator and all the spirit of hope in which his work was done. They bear in every line the impress of a truly apostolic soul, whose only real interest was the salvation of men, and the first care of the synod is to put on record the great thing done in the reconciliation of St. Andrew's Day, 1554, and to ensure that it shall never fade from English minds. ' The cause of all the deformation of the church in this kingdom ' was, very simply, ' that we, withdrawing from the unity and teaching of faith of the Catholic Church, deserted the authority and obedience of the Roman Pontiff, the Vicar of Christ and the successor of St. Peter, for whose faith, lest it might fail, Christ Himself prayed. . . .' Lest the great mercy of England's return ' after many vagaries of opinions and a long travail.' be ever in danger of being forgotten, special prayers of thanksgiving are to be said in the Mass, in every church, on every Sunday, and on all lesser feasts. On the actual anniversary of the great day there is likewise to be, in every church,

---

[1] Oct. 11, 1551 ; Sess. XIII, *Decretum*, c. viii, De usu admirabilis huius sacramenti.

[2] Nov. 4, 1555–February 10, 1556.

[3] Published as *Reformatio Angliæ ex decretis Reginaldi Poli*, etc., Rome, 1562 (*cf.* Bibliographical Note).

a special celebration, namely a solemn procession and a sermon explaining the reason for the festival.

The root, from which all the troubles had grown, the decrees declare, was the separation of the English Church from the divinely instituted centre, Rome ; and the destruction of all the Roman machinery—and in the first place of the Canon Law itself—had been a well-adapted first step towards the heretical building of the new religious thing. It is with this fundamental matter that the legate's legislation really begins, in the second decree of the synod. The preamble is a succinct description of the achievement of Henry VIII from the point of view of a well-placed Catholic observer. ' After the obedience to the Roman Pontiff and the Apostolic See had been thrown aside, the authority of the ecclesiastical law was taken away, and as a consequence false teachers were admitted and given a hearing, and books of corrupt teaching began everywhere to be read. By such means the populace was infected with various errors in matters of faith, and especially with regard to the doctrine of the sacraments, which are the chief foundations of the Christian religion. At the same time the standard of decent living, both of the clergy and of the laity, and all that belongs to the right discipline of the Church, was plainly depraved.' So the synod goes on to declare that all the old Canon Law, of the general and provincial councils, as the Apostolic See recognises it, is restored. All the constitutions of the Popes, all the ecclesiastical laws canonically enacted, are brought back to life. Moreover, ' we command that the Canon Law itself shall be publicly taught as in former times.' New editions of the old books are to be prepared—in which the legislation of this present synod shall find a place—and every one with cure of souls shall possess a copy, along with his Bible, ' of the old edition in Latin,' and the other books necessary for his office.

As a corollary to this submissive return to the one sure source of true teaching, the authority of the Roman See, the decree proceeds to accept the Roman condemnation of heretical books, and to excommunicate whoever prints, imports, or sells them or in any way defends or praises them. And here, in the provision that no book is to be printed without the bishop's *imprimatur*, the legislation of Trent makes its first appearance in England.

Then follows a singularly clear and explicit declaration

that the standard of orthodox belief is the faith as it is taught by the Roman See. Whatever conflicts with this is heresy, and the synod commands the full execution of the provisions of the Canon Law against heretics and their supporters, and against bishops neglectful of their duty of inquisition and suppression.

The main errors in England in recent years have centred around two points, the Primacy in the Church and the Sacraments. The synod does not construct any new formulary in which to set out the Catholic teaching, but is content to reproduce the century-old decree of the eighth general council at Florence, with its definition of the divine character of the Primacy of Rome which St. John Fisher had cited against Luther in the days before Henry VIII had ever dreamed of being a Supreme Head, ' Hoc unum concilium,' the saint's argument declared, ' sufficit pro omnibus.'

To another section of this canon we owe, seemingly, the modern form of tabernacle, for after recalling the existing legislation the canon proceeds, ' we add that this tabernacle shall be placed in the middle of the high altar, so prominently, that it can be seen by all, and so fixed that it cannot easily be moved away.' And it is ordered that, once again, ' to honour the Body of Our Lord Jesus Christ . . . a lamp or a wax candle shall continuously burn before It . . . a custom which, in almost all the churches of this realm, has in these late years been injuriously abolished.'

Few things in this life moved Pole to such indignation as the spectacle of absentee bishops. At every phase of the reform he did so much to promote, he had denounced it unsparingly, and when the question of his appointment to Canterbury was first stirred, he hesitated from the fear that he might end as one of these nominal bishops with which for a good century and a half the Church everywhere had been overstocked. The third decree of the synod treats of this matter, and outspokenly states that ' the great abuse flourishes that many bishops, not residing in the churches committed to them, abandon them to hirelings, which thing has been the cause of almost all the evils that afflict the Church.' In language removed very far from the stereotyped phrases of the usual constitutions de vita clericali, offenders of this sort are bidden to amendment, and ' since we often see it happen that the fear of penalties will move to fulfil their duty those on whom the fear of God has no effect ' the old penalties are renewed. Eight years later the council at Trent will find a still better remedy, in the provision of financial penalties that come into operation automatically.

The legate's rigorous conception of a bishop's duty shows no less evidently in the decree on preaching and catechising, for he insists that to preach is the personal duty of bishops, and that to delegate this duty to others is an abuse. The clergy are given a reminder of their special duty to those who have left the Church, and the synod stresses two kinds of sermon or instruction for which there is great need. The first is on penance, especially in view of the national sin of schism from which God has so lately freed the English people. The second subject suggested is that of the vices and abuses in doctrine and in morals that have so flourished in these last twenty-five years of schism, evils with which, says the decree, many yet remain infected.

It is admitted that there is a general lack of priests able to preach, and a book of homilies [1] is to be prepared which these unlearned priests shall read Sunday by Sunday in lieu of a sermon. The bishops are also to organise a body of itinerant preachers to tour their dioceses, and the faithful generally are urged to pray that God will send preachers.

There is in the earliest life of St. John Fisher a description of Wolsey, presiding as papal legate, with all possible pomp, at the National Synod of 1518—' called by my lord Cardinal rather to notify to the world his great authority and to be seen sitting in his pontifical seat, than for any great good that he meant to do ' [2]; and the life relates the saint's startling rebuke of his superior's worldliness. Pole, at that time, was an undergraduate at Magdalen. He had, since then, refused to be Wolsey's successor at York and now, the first papal legate England had seen since Wolsey, was, nearly forty years later, presiding over another National Synod. Its fifth decree condemns utterly all that state for which Wolsey stood—and the generality of bishops for many a

---

[1] ' These Homilies were never published. BURNET (II, p. 523) records that he saw a scheme of them among Parker's papers at Corpus Christi College Library, Cambridge. There were to be four books : (1) on disputed points, to guard the people from error ; (2) expositions of the *Pater Noster*, *Ave Maria*, *Creeds*, Ten Commandments and Sacraments ; (3) explaining the Epistles and Gospels for Saints' days and holy days; (4) on virtues, vices, and the rites and ceremonies of the Church.' (FRERE and KENNEDY, II, p. 40.)

[2] *St. John Fisher the Earliest English Life*, ed. Philip Hughes, London, 1935, p. 58.

year after Wolsey's fall. Pole's own simplicity in these matters is brought about by the inventory of his goods delivered to the crown on his death, a short list of personal belongings in which the word ' old ' recurs continuously. His decree enjoins moderation and forbids bishops and prelates to dress in robes of silk. Four courses at most does he allow them for meals, no matter what the rank of the guest they entertain, and the fourth course by indulgence only, and not as approving it. They must cut down the number of their suite to the minimum, and, not to fall under any suspicion of avarice, give the fruit of their economy to found burses for the education of poor scholars.

And the bishops must leave aside all secular business— following here again the example of Pole, though the cardinal does not say this. For although he did not live long enough to be himself the pastoral bishop he desired to see in Canterbury, he managed to steer clear of political life, despite King Philip's committing the realm to his care during his own long absence. One office alone would the cardinal archbishop undertake, to reconcile differences between the treacherous and unfriendly councillors. It was Nicholas Heath, the Archbishop of York, who became Lord Chancellor on Gardiner's death—though the office was Pole's for the taking, and the nobility would gladly have seen him accept it [1]—and Pole never took his share of political and administrative work as one of the Council.

The legislation which deals with benefices and ecclesiastical appointments is, as always, grimly sorrowful reading. The simple commonplace is repeated, as for centuries already and as it will be repeated for untold ages yet to come, that there is only one rule for authority to follow, namely to choose always the man most suitable for the place. Then, as the prohibitions grow detailed, there is revealed the whole familiar tableau of the miseries inseparable from the benefice system once ecclesiastical appointments had passed from the domain of the virtue of distributive justice to that of the Canon Law considered as a means to safeguard property and the right to property. There is the systematic promising of places not yet vacant, and there is also a connected abuse, the transfers of a patron's right to nominate —of which last the synod says roundly ' an abuse often met

---

[1] Pole to Morone, Feb. 5, 1556, quoted PASTOR, xiv, p. 388.

with in England.' Clerical patrons—even bishops—who so transfer (*lege* sell) such rights are to lose the particular right altogether for this present vacancy and for the next recurring. And whoever accepts the presentation after such a transfer is not only to lose the place, but to be for five years incapable of receiving any ecclesiastical office of any kind. Bishops are forbidden to institute such nominees. Inevitably, with such an abuse there is very often joined simony, and to quote the decree ' this pestiferous vice . . . in these last years has in England carried all before it.' All gifts of money, promises of revenues, pacts of any kind between the recipient of an office and the one with whom the appointment rests, no matter what the rank of either, are declared null and whosoever has received such gifts must restore them and, furthermore, is declared incapable, so long as he lives, of receiving any ecclesiastical promotion. If the guilty patron is an ecclesiastic he loses all rights of patronage over the benefice concerned and he becomes, *ipso facto*, infamous in law. Those who act as middlemen in these transactions lose all their rights in law, and, of course, must give up all they have received. Bishops must for the future be rigorous in administering to all those whom they institute to a benefice the sworn declaration that they are in no way guilty of simony.

The detail of this legislation and the severity of the penalties tell their own tale of the extent to which rank and office in the Church had become just so much merchandise in the years since the schism began. There had, of course, always been scandals of this sort, but never had traffic in spiritual matters been given so great an opportunity to develop and to become a national habit as in the country's first experience of the Royal Supremacy. The most notorious cases were, of course, the surrenders of ecclesiastical property, in return for personal pensions, made by different religious superiors, and the alienations of estates made by newly-appointed bishops as a condition of their nomination. In the tenth decree of the synod this last abuse is set out and provided for. For the future, all benefice holders are to compile an inventory of the goods of the benefice, movable property as well as lands, rights, and debts. This is to be witnessed in due legal form, and copies filed with the bishop. Once every three years, and whenever the benefice changes hands, this inventory is to be revised. Inventories of the possessions of the different sees are to be filed with the metropolitan, and that of the metropolitan see with the chapter of the archdiocese.

The most promising feature of the synod's work, however, is the provision it makes for the training of the future clergy, and here Pole anticipated the greatest of all Trent's reforms, which decreed that seminaries should be founded in every diocese. The sixth decree of the synod deals with the long-standing evil of episcopal carelessness in the matter of ordinations, which, says the synod, has resulted in the appearance of priests of such a type that there is a general contempt for the whole body of the clergy and for the whole system of worship. Bishops must not, for the future, leave to others the duty of seeing that the candidates they ordain are really fit subjects for the sacrament and the office. The procedure they should follow, as the synod gives it, affords a last glimpse of the medieval system, now about to disappear and give place to that carefully regulated seminary training which has made the parish clergy of these days almost a religious order in comparison with their medieval predecessors. In good time before the ordination is held, the synod decrees, those who wish to be ordained are to make known their wish to the bishop, that he may make all the necessary enquiries. On the Thursday before the appointed day—the Ember Saturday presumably—they are to appear and give in their names. That day and the Friday are given up to the examination as to their canonical fitness. The candidates are to bring with them certificates for all the details this includes namely, to prove that they are not heretics, nor of illegitimate birth, that they are of the required age, not under any censure, nor suffering any of the legal defects ; that they are of decent life, and sufficient learning ; and also the proofs of their title to some sufficient benefice, lest they be reduced, after ordination, to begging or to selling their Mass. They must also bring letters from their parish priest, from those who have taught them and from others who know them well, testifying to their good repute. They are to go to confession, and so to txpose their soul that the confessor will be able to advise them whether to proceed and receive the sacrament, and finally, at the ordination they are to receive Holy Communion. One who has been all through the carefully ordered system of these latter days may be forgiven if he opines, perhaps as one less wise, that it all sounds, by comparison, very happy-go-lucky.

But in the eleventh decree we come into another world, *That in cathedrals there be educated a certain number of beginners, from which, as from a seed bed, priests may be chosen who can worthily be placed in charge of the churches.*[1]

One of the crying needs of the time, the decree states, is the lack of ecclesiastics suited for important positions, and the most obvious way to provide for this seems to be the foundation in every cathedral of a *seminarium ministrorum.* Therefore, for the future, every cathedral church shall, according to its resources and the size of the diocese, provide for the education of a certain number of boys from the age of eleven or twelve. They must already be able to read and to write, and show signs that give a real hope of their one day being priests and devoting their lives to the ministry. Preference is to be given to the children of the poor, although boys of the richer class are not to be excluded, so long as they give real promise of a desire to serve the Church. These boys are to be taught grammar and the doctrine and the ecclesiastical discipline. All are to wear the tonsure and the clerical dress, to live a common life and to serve the cathedral offices. The seniors are to be ordained acolyte, and, together with the *toga liberalis*, they are to be paid a small annual allowance.

'As they come to the age fixed by law, if their character and proficiency in studies warrant it, the acolytes shall receive Holy Orders, and serve in the cathedral as the bishop and the chapter shall direct. This new school, as far as it is a school of grammar, is not to be exclusively clerical. Other boys of the town and diocese may be admitted. They shall, however, wear the same dress and follow the same way of life as the rest. If any of them show signs of a desire to serve God as a priest, they can later be found a place among the clerics when vacancies occur.

The decree ends with an elaborate direction as to how the bishop and chapter are to provide the funds for the new ' seminaries,' what benefices may be specially allotted, and what taxes laid on all benefices, for their support. In this decree the scheme is really only outlined, and more details are promised once the synod reassembles. As a matter of

[1] Ut in cathedralibus certus iniatorum numerus educetur, ex quo, tanquam ex seminario, eligi possint, qui digne Ecclesiis præficiantur.

history that reassembly never took place, and the scheme
remained no more than a scheme, so far as colleges in
England were concerned. But whoever knows anything
of the peculiarly English system of colleges where Church
boys and lay boys are educated together in the bishop's
school, and follow the same régime, and who knows anything
of the descent, direct or indirect, of all these schools from the
great college of Douay, will see how Pole's remarkable
scheme came to find its first executor in Cardinal Allen,
and what historical justification there is for the English
anomaly which, from time to time, still threatens to disturb
the peace of zealous Roman officials.[1]

The last decree of the synod deals with the subject of
episcopal visitations. Every three years the bishop is to
make the visitation of his diocese, and the decree prescribes in detail the order he is to follow. He is to preach,
to confirm, to absolve from reserved cases. He is to examine
into the whole state of every parish and ecclesiastical
institution, its temporal state as well as the spiritual. And
what seems to us stringent, and certainly calculated to make
the visitation a reality, the bishop in every parish is to
choose four or five parishioners of good life and take their
sworn testimony on all this detail, and among the matters
on which they are to be interrogated is the delicate business
of how their clergy conduct themselves.

If one may judge from the new spirit that inspires this
legislation, its simple acknowledgment that things have been
very wrong indeed, its severity towards future offenders,
and the importance of its constructive proposals—bearing
in mind always that the synod's plans are not yet complete [2]
—and if one may judge from the whole life of the man whose
character is reflected in every decree, and if one may judge
from the new kind of bishop that was now coming to be
appointed in England, the Catholic Church in England as
reformed by Reginald Pole would have had nothing to
fear in comparison with any of the churches of the Continent,
not even with Milan itself. Which brings us to say something
of Pole's hierarchy.

[1] The Council of Trent's legislation on Seminaries is in the 23rd session of
the council (July 15, 1563), chapter 18 of the series De Reformatione.

[2] The synod was adjourned at the beginning of Lent, 1556, until Nov. 10
following, and then further adjourned until May 10, 1557. In the event,
however, it never reassembled. By May, 1557, Pole had ceased to be legate,
and was under orders to return to Rome, vide infra, p. 111.

§ iii. The New Episcopate

When Queen Mary came to the throne, and to her chosen task of the Catholic restoration, three out of the twenty-six sees of the provinces of York and Canterbury were vacant —Rochester, Bangor, and Durham—and one prelate— Hooper—was bishop both of Worcester and of Gloucester.

There were, then, twenty-two bishops in possession of their sees. All of them were excommunicated, by reason of their adherence to Henry VIII in his schism and their own individual, explicit repudiation of the Pope's primacy. Only one of these bishops was a survivor from the hierarchy of Catholic times, that is to say owed his original appointment to the Pope. This was Thomas Cranmer, Archbishop of Canterbury. The rest had been made bishops solely by the king as Supreme Head after Christ of the Church of England, thirteen of them by Henry VIII in the years 1534–1545, and eight by Edward VI. A further complication was that the seven most recently appointed had been consecrated according to the rite provided in the new Book of Common Prayer. And twelve of the twenty-two were married ; six of these were bishops consecrated by the Catholic ritual. Four sees, in addition to the bishops in possession, had an ex-bishop also, the prelate whose deprivation had made room for the bishop actually in possession. The situation could hardly have been more complex for a queen anxious to restore the Catholic *status quo*.

The first action taken towards this curiously varied hierarchy was the legal dispossession of several of its members. The first to go were Ponet of Winchester and Ridley of London, the successors to two deprived prelates, Stephen Gardiner and Edmund Bonner, whose appeal against their deprivation as illegal was now heard—after a lapse of years —and upheld. Tunstal was at the same time restored to Durham, left vacant since his dispossession, and Veysey of Exeter replaced his own dispossessor, Miles Coverdale, while Day, in the same way, returned to Chichester in place of Scory.

In March, 1554, Catholic discipline, in so far as Parliament had again given it legal existence, came once more into play, and commissions were issued for an enquiry into the conduct or status of seven other bishops. The result was the deprivation of Holgate of York, Bush of Bristol, Bird of Chester, and Ferrar of St. David's on March 13 for marriage, and of Hooper of Gloucester,[1] Taylor of Lincoln, and Harley of Hereford, for heresy on March 15.[2] Barlow of Bath and Wells had already 'resigned,' and Cranmer had, in law, forfeited his see on his condemnation for High Treason in the previous December.

Mary had thus to find bishops for nine sees in addition to the two she found really vacant at her accession. But before coming to the men chosen for these sees something had better be said of the bishops who were retained, the motley episcopal relics of Henry VIII's activity as Supreme Head. There were fifteen of them in all.

Bishop	See	Appointed
John Veysey	Exeter	1519[3]
Cuthbert Tunstal	Durham	1530[3]
Stephen Gardiner	Winchester	1531[3]
Thomas Goodrich	Ely	1534
Robert Parfew	St. Asaph	1536
Robert Aldrich	Carlisle	1537
John Salcot	Salisbury	1539
Edmund Bonner	London	1540
Robert King	Oxford	1545
John Chambers	Peterborough	1541
George Day	Chichester	1543
Nicholas Heath	Worcester	1543
Robert Sampson	Coventry and Lichfield	1543
Antony Kitchin	Llandaff	1545
Thomas Thirlby	Norwich	1550

Five of these twelve 'Henrician' bishops were one-time abbots, who had peaceably surrendered their abbeys in return for comfortable pensions. King had been the head of Augustinian Oseney. The rest were Benedictines, Parfew, Abbot of Bermondsey ; Salcot, of the great abbey of Hyde ;

[1] And of Worcester also.
[2] The Commissions authorising these deprivations are printed in TIERNEY, II, App., p. clx ff.
[3] These three were survivors of the old, papally appointed hierarchy of Catholic times. The others were bishops of Henry VIII's own making.

Chambers of Peterborough—the last abbot and the first bishop—Kitchin, of Eynsham.[1]

Three of these fifteen bishops were not destined to play any great part in the Marian restoration, for they died in the summer of 1554 before the famous day of reconciliation came. These were Veysey, an old court prelate of Henry VIII's reign, and two of the typical Tudor diplomat bishops, Sampson and Goodrich. Sampson had been one of the select deputation sent to harry Mary into submission to her father, and Goodrich had been sufficiently sympathetic to heresy under the régime of Edward VI to be Lord High Chancellor, and to sign the proclamation of Lady Jane Grey's accession.

The five ex-monk bishops were none of them men of any great significance. King was a connection of Cromwell's, by the marriage of a brother, and this had helped him to become Abbot of Oseney in time to surrender the properties to the crown. It was his good fortune to be able to surrender, at the same time, the abbey of Thame of which also he was the head. King had been a bishop wellnigh thirty years in 1553, for it was in those last years of peace before 'the blessed divorce' rose above the horizon, that he had been consecrated, as auxiliary to John Longland, Bishop of Lincoln, King Henry's. confessor. Bishop King had made no opposition to the abolition of the Mass in Edward VI's reign, for all that the bodies of so many of his priests, in the time of the great religious rising of 1549, dangled from their belfries *in signum fidei*. The history of his religious opinions is such that the latest writer to touch on it has been able to suggest that, at the very end, he went over to plain heresy, after all his reconciliations.[2]

Salcot, the Bishop of Salisbury, if he graduated B.A. in 1488, must, by the time of Mary's accession sixty years later, have been a very old man indeed, and we do know that, for his age, he was dispensed from attendance at her coronation. He has the distinction that after his petitioning Clement VII to grant Henry his divorce that Pope refused to accept him as Bishop of Bangor, and so he was consecrated despite the Pope, the second English bishop to be consecrated on the royal authority. Of Salcot's share in the Catholic

---

[1] Six of the eleven bishops deprived in 1553–1554 were also ex-religious.
[2] A suggestion which, *pace* the author, seems to me extremely unlikely, but *cf.* GARRETT, *The Marian Exiles* (1938), sub voce *King*.

restoration we know nothing at all. And we must say the same of his fellow ex-Benedictine, Robert Parfew,[1] who, translated in 1554 from St. Asaph to Hereford, died just a fortnight before Salcot in September, 1557.

Chambers of Peterborough is described as ' a safe and conformable person,' and he owed his ecclesiastical success as much to his friendship with the rising house of Russell as to his timely surrender of his abbey to Henry VIII. Here again is a bishop of whose new zeal we know nothing, and about whom from all that is known of his career, we might not ungenerously prophesy that he would, on Elizabeth's accession, do just what his fellow, Antony Kitchin, actually did and ' turn once again.' Chambers was perhaps seventy when the legate reconciled him. Antony Kitchin was older still, if the generally accepted dates are true. He had been a monk of Westminster Abbey, and the head of the Benedictine College at Oxford. Henry VIII gave him a good pension when he surrendered his abbey, and promised him still better. The poor little Welsh see of Llandaff was all the ' still better ' that came, and this only when Kitchin was close on seventy.

This group of aged, ex-monastic nonentities among the reconciled bishops is balanced by an equal number of diplomats and legists. Tunstal, now in extreme old age, had been the intimate friend of Thomas More, and had enjoyed a really international fame as humanist, mathematician and legist. We have seen him as one of the heroes of the youthful Reginald Pole. Gardiner and Bonner were legists too and had laid the foundations of a prosperous episcopal career in whole-hearted efforts on the king's behalf at the time of the famous divorce suit. Both had been of Wolsey's household, and both had distinguished themselves by a personal violence of speech to the Pope. Clement VII had indeed been so far provoked, on one occasion, as to threaten Bonner with a hanging. All three of these bishops had managed to twist their consciences and to preach and write in defence of the Royal Supremacy. Pole had hardly been able to credit that Tunstal, whom he had admired for a lifetime, could have written what was published under his name. As to the past literary activities of Gardiner and Bonner, some heretic, now in Mary's reign—it was John Bale, ex-Carmelite friar and ex-(Edwardine) Bishop of Ossory—

[1] Or Warton.

had had the happy thought to embarrass these repentant champions of Henry VIII by translating into English Gardiner's book—*De Vera Obedientia*—and Bonner's anti-papal preface to it. Inevitably the matter was urged against the bishops as now, in the hey-day of the restoration, they presided over heresy trials, and with this advantage to us, that Bonner openly admitted that it was simple fear of the punishment for resistance that had won himself and Gardiner over to King Henry's way of thinking ; the pendant to which story is Gardiner's own exclamation as, while he lay dying, his chaplain read to him the Passion of Our Lord from the Gospel. The priest came to the story of St. Peter's fall and the bishop broke out : ' I denied like Peter, I went out like Peter, but as yet I have not wept like Peter.' And Tunstal in his will makes an unmistakably similar reference, when he uses the liturgical absolution of the dead with a special addition all his own : ' Enter not into judgement, I beseech Thee, with thy *runaway* servant, O just Judge.'

These three bishops were very prominent personages in the new reign, and not unnaturally, seeing they were three of the most experienced, the most capable and the most dis-interested of all the crown's servants. Tunstal remained at his post in the north, a kind of viceroy for the border counties. Gardiner, as Lord Chancellor, was the queen's principal adviser and executive officer. Bonner, as head of the diocese which, of all others, was the special seat of heresy, gained a new publicity from the innumerable trials and condemnations at which he had to preside.

Heath and Thirlby were diplomatists also ; Thirlby in constant employment as an ambassador, even in the first months of Elizabeth's reign. Both were Cambridge men, and while Thirlby had then been reputed a ' favourer of the gospel ' and had had Cranmer's friendship to thank for his rapid rise, Heath had been a fellow of one of the colleges—Christ's—in whose foundation St. John Fisher had had so great a share. But no more than Thirlby had he scrupled to follow the king when the testing time came.

All this group—save Tunstal—were much of an age, men in the middle fifties, with twenty-five years' experience of court and council and parliamentary life to guide their present action. To the protestantising of religion in the late reign they had all offered a satisfactory resistance. Heath had indeed been willing to use the new Ordinal though not

G 2

to put his name to it. But when the order went out to take
down the altars he refused, and was thereupon deprived of
his see and imprisoned, as had already happened to Gardiner and to Bonner. Tunstal, too, was imprisoned and
deprived, but Thirlby, although in the debates on the
Prayer Book he made a stand against the new heretical
doctrines, was left unmolested and the end of Edward's
reign found him still in confidential employment as ambassador to Charles V.

The two remaining bishops, of this group that was a
legacy to the restoration from the previous régime, were
Robert Aldrich of Carlisle and George Day of Chichester.
In both cases the early careers had been scholarly rather
than political. Aldrich had, in his Cambridge days, been
a pupil of Erasmus, and one of the great man's companions
in the celebrated pilgrimage he made to Walsingham.
From King's he had passed to be a master at Eton, and then,
after some years, to a prosperous university career. He did
useful service for the king in the divorce campaign, and a
Windsor canonry, with its *sequelæ* of the Provostship of Eton
and an appointment as almoner to Queen Jane Seymour,
were his reward. One of the bishop's memories of that
bygone time, which the news of Queen Mary's restoration
of the Sheen Charterhouse might now stir to life, was of his
visit to the London Carthusians in 1535 to persuade them
to accept the Royal Supremacy. As Bishop of Carlisle he
had, later, done his best to fight the liturgical changes of
Edward VI's reign, and he had distinguished himself as a
writer against the sacramental heresies.

George Day had been a still more active figure, for he
was a theologian by profession, as one might say. In his
early life he had been one of St. John Fisher's chaplains, and
Master of the saint's own foundation at Cambridge, St.
John's College. He had been public orator, and in that
office had, no doubt, laid the foundations of his later fame
as a preacher, ' the floridest preacher ' of his time, who in
the eventful year 1553 preached both at King Edward's
funeral and at Queen Mary's coronation. In all the
movement to rearrange creeds and services that filled the
last years of Henry VIII's reign and all the reign of his son,
Day had had an important share, even before his appointment to Chichester—at the early age of forty-two. He was a
member of most of the various commissions, and when the

sacramental heretics were able to show their hand openly, after the death of King Henry, Day stood firmly by the old beliefs. He voted against the Act of Uniformity and refused to put his name to the Prayer Book, and finally, for his active resistance to the protestantisers, his refusal, for example, to take down the altars in his diocese, he was deprived of his see and imprisoned.

Day did not live to see the end of the restoration. He died in 1556, in a fatal twelvemonth that saw the deaths of no fewer than six of these bishops. Aldrich, too, was among these, and the rest were four of the one-time abbots. Of the five pre-Marian Catholic bishops who survived to meet the changes of 1559 all were of the diplomatic group save one, and it was he, the sole remaining ex-abbot, who, this time, alone of the hierarchy failed. Tunstal, Bonner, Heath, and Thirlby in 1559 stood true. For these also the Marian restoration had not been in vain.

So much for the prelates whom the Marian restoration under the cardinal legate received as a legacy from the régime of the Royal Supremacy. What of the bishops who were the product of the restoration ? Between 1554 and 1558 eighteen [1] bishops were consecrated for the different English sees. Seven of these consecrations were of bishops to replace those deprived for heresy or for marriage. The other eleven were of bishops to fill vacancies caused by death or by translation of the previous bishop. As a body the new bishops offer many significant contrasts, by comparison with their colleagues of the earlier Catholic régime.

One of these new bishops, Holyman of Bristol, was a Benedictine, a one-time monk of the abbey of Reading in the time of the martyr abbot Blessed Hugh Faringdon. Hopton of Norwich was a Dominican,[2] and Goldwell of St. Asaph a Theatine. The rest were of the secular clergy.

They were most of them men in the very prime of life. Pole was fifty-six when he was consecrated Archbishop of Canterbury, in succession to Cranmer (March 22, 1556) and only five of the other eighteen new bishops were any older. Eight of them indeed were only in the early forties. And yet few of them were long-lived, for eight of the eighteen died before the year of crisis 1559, and another four in the twelvemonth following. Indeed, this curiously general inability of Pole's bishops to last, was to prove

---

[1] Including Cardinal Pole.   [2] Maurice Griffin, of Rochester, also.

one of the contributing causes to the ease of the Protestant victory in the parliamentary debates of 1559.

No single one of these eighteen new bishops had received his see as a reward for services to the crown in any secular capacity. There was not among them any who, like Tunstal, Gardiner, or Bonner, was primarily a lawyer and a diplomatist by profession. The breach here with a tradition more than a century old is very striking.

Four [1] of the new bishops had spent much of their life since the schism beyond the seas, exiles for the faith. Ralph Baynes, now appointed to Coventry and Lichfield, had made a name for himself at Cambridge as a vigorous opponent of Latimer. He had then gone abroad and won great distinction as a Hebrew scholar, and was indeed professor of Hebrew at the University of Paris. He has an honoured place in the history of scholarship as one of the pioneers of Hebrew learning in England. Christopherson, the youngest of the bishops, was also a humanist of repute, one of the leaders in the revival of Greek learning at Cambridge. He was of a later generation than Baynes, and apparently born too late to have known the church of pre-Henrician days. But when the general assault on the Catholic sacramental system began, at the accession of Edward VI, Christopherson made his way to Louvain. Like Baynes he was an author and he did useful service by extensive translations into Latin of the Greek Church historians. Pates of Worcester was the third of these returned exiles. He was of the generation of Gardiner and Bonner, and with them in Henry VIII's time he was employed in the royal service. It had been no small advantage to him that he was the nephew of John Longland, Bishop of Lincoln and confessor to the king. With such powerful patronage Pates had risen rapidly and ecclesiastical offices and revenues had showered upon him. He was, in fact, little more than thirty when, in 1533, he was sent as resident ambassador to the court of Charles V, and for the next three years he accompanied the emperor in his journeyings up and down Europe. It was while he held this post, in the critical years which saw Henry's repudiation of papal authority, and the first martyrdoms of the Catholics who remained loyal to the faith, that Pates changed sides. He refused to return to England when recalled and, a few years later, was attainted.

[1] Not including the cardinal legate.

Meanwhile, in 1541, he was named Bishop of Worcester by Paul III, and as Bishop of Worcester he attended the Council of Trent in its first series of sittings (1547) and again in 1551 when Julius III reassembled it.

The fourth of the returned exiles was Thomas Goldwell, Bishop of St. Asaph. He had gone abroad, apparently is, the very first months of Henry's anti-Catholic manœuvren and at Padua, in 1532, he met Pole. Thenceforward his life and Pole's never ceased to be closely connected. From 1538 to 1547 Goldwell administered the ancient Rome hospice for English pilgrims that was soon to become the English College and them in 1547, he joined the new religious order popularly called the Theatines. Here Goldwell made immediate contact with the very heart of the contemporary Catholic movement to reform the Church. This religious order was the creation of two remarkable personalities, the Count Gaetano da Tiene—St. Cajetan—and Gian Pietro Carafa, Bishop of Chieti. The purpose of the order was pastoral work among the poor—preaching, catechising, administration of the sacraments—and the Theatines were distinguished by an especially rigorous vow of poverty. Not only were the individual religious incapable of ownership, and the order also as an order, but the Theatines were not allowed in any way to beg. They lived in day-to-day dependence on what the Providence of God sent them. The order grew very slowly, but wherever it went, at Rome, at Naples, and at Venice, it gradually transformed the spiritual life of those cities which had been for so long the witness of clerical worldliness and indifference to spiritual duties. Carafa, by the time Goldwell became a Theatine, was a cardinal and one of the chief personages in the Curia. When Goldwell—now bishop-elect of St. Asaph—returned to Rome in 1555, as one of the English embassy of that year, Carafa was Pope, the *terribile* Paul IV. Goldwell's novitiate was interrupted in 1549 when he went to serve Pole as chaplain in the great conclave which so nearly elected a second English Pope. Then Goldwell returned to Naples, to be professed and to work for the next four years in the Theatine church there. The appointment of Pole as legate to England in 1553 drew Goldwell once more from his pastoral work. In the September of that year he rejoined the cardinal, and in November went to England as his confidential envoy to the queen.

Two of the new bishops—Morgan of St. David's and David Pole of Peterborough—were professional canonists, administrators of proved worth : Pole had been for nearly twenty-five years Dean of the Arches and Vicar-General to the Archbishop of Canterbury.

Six of the eight bishops who remain to be considered had spent the greater part of their lives in academic posts. Brookes, of Gloucester, was a one-time Master of Balliol ; Oglethorpe, of Carlisle, was the President of Magdalen ; Scott, of Chester, Master of Christ's ; Watson, of Lincoln, Master of St. John's College, Cambridge. White, Bishop first of Lincoln and then of Winchester, had been master and later warden of the famous Winchester school.

Gilbert Bourne, of Bath and Wells, had been for years in the service of Bonner. Brookes and Watson had been closely associated with Gardiner as his chaplains. Oglethorpe and Glyn were theologians of repute. Watson was perhaps the ablest man of all the new hierarchy. He was the friend of Ascham, and Cheke, and Sir Thomas Smith, and a force of the first importance in the Cambridge movement to revive and reform the teaching of Greek.

The eight bishops of this last group had all been close spectators, and even actors, in the religious revolution accomplished by Edward VI. How had they borne themselves in the hour of trial ? Of Turberville of Exeter almost nothing seems to be known. From the fact that Brookes of Gloucester was, during all this time, one of Gardiner's chaplains and that, in Mary's time—Gardiner being now all powerful—he was one of the first to be nominated to a see, we can safely deduce that, like his master, he did not conform to the new theology. And we can surely make the same guess about Bourne of Bath and Wells (consecrated along with Brookes), who had remained a faithful chaplain to another of the bishops imprisoned by Edward VI for resistance to doctrinal changes, Bonner of London. About the remaining bishops we know something more.

Watson was, apparently, deep in Gardiner's confidence throughout all his fight with the Council in the time of Edward VI, and twice—in 1547 and in 1551—like his master he found himself in prison, the first time for a sermon denouncing the heresies of the Protestant party.

Glyn, as Lady Margaret professor of divinity, could hardly escape the notice of the authorities if he remained true to

Catholic doctrine. He was, in fact, forbidden to lecture, and he played a great part, on the Catholic side, in the disputation about the Holy Eucharist which was one of the features of the visitation of the university by the commission of 1549. He was appointed to Bangor in 1555.

White also opposed the changes, and soon became known as a prominent cleric hostile to the new ways. He, too, was imprisoned, in the Tower, in 1551 charged with receiving books and letters from abroad and he remained in prison a whole year. And a year later he was excommunicated for his doctrinal insubordination.

The story of Owen Oglethorpe, Bishop of Carlisle from 1557, is less pleasing. He had a great repute as a theologian and had been a member of the commission which drew up in 1540 the statement of doctrine known as the King's Book. As President of Magdalen he had to rule a much-divided college. After the abolition of the Mass there were riots at Magdalen, for the Catholic majority ignored the law, and when they continued to celebrate the Mass the reformers protested. Oglethorpe never faltered in his beliefs, but now he yielded to force, and not only consented to celebrate the new service, but recorded in writing, for the Council, his repudiation of Transubstantiation and the practice of private Masses. Even so, he failed to convince the Government of his sincerity, and in 1552 they brought about his removal from the presidency. In this timorousness, and in the readiness to temporise with principle as a matter of expediency, we can perhaps see something of the spirit that guided Oglethorpe in the critical first few months of Elizabeth's reign. When the new queen asked him to omit the elevation, as he was vesting to sing Mass in her presence on Christmas Day, 1558, he refused. But, a month later, when all of his brethren had refused to crown her, realising by now that her oath to protect the Church would be perjury, Oglethorpe consented. And then, as the ensuing weeks made only too clear what Elizabeth's intentions were, he fell ill with anxiety and remorse. He lived long enough to refuse the Oath of Supremacy and to be deprived of his see, but died in the first days of 1560.[1]

[1] This § iii, *The New Episcopate*, is but a sketch of the section intended, which it has not been possible to complete. This sketch has already appeared in *The Clergy Review* and I have pleasure in acknowledging the willingness of those concerned that it should be reprinted here.

§ iv. The Repression of Heresy

Heresy is the sin committed by the Catholic who, on some point of the religion revealed by Jesus Christ, sets his own opinion in opposition to the Catholic Church's teaching. From the very beginning of Christianity such doctrinal rebellion has been held in horror, and the heretic—the Catholic, that is to say, who, instead of accepting *en bloc* the teaching handed down, picks and chooses his beliefs according to some norm other than that of the guarantee implicit in the fact that it is the Church which is teaching these things as true—has from apostolic times been the object of unqualified reprobation. It has always been for the Church a matter of the very gravest concern to bring about the repentance and conversion of heretics, and already for some centuries before the Reformation, Church and State habitually co-operated to punish the sin of heresy as an anti-social mischief of a very serious kind indeed. Long before Pole's time it had become a fixed universal belief in the Christian mind that heresy was a thing not to be tolerated, and this belief long survived the sixteenth-century breach of religious unity, all the great contending parties agreeing in this at least that whoever differed from the true belief was to be coerced into a better frame of mind or be punished for his obduracy. To take one instance only, where many might be quoted, and to cite it not in any indirect apologetic proof that there was something exceptionally humane about the burning of Protestants by Catholics, here is an extract from a letter written in 1548 by no less a personage than Calvin to the duke of Somerset, uncle of King Edward VI and at the time, as Protector, the ruler of England. ' As I understand, you have two kinds of mutineers against the King and the estates of the realm ; the one are a fantastical people who under colour of the gospels would set all to confusion ; the others are stubborn people in the superstition of the Antichrist of Rome. These altogether do deserve to be well punished by the sword, seeing they do conspire against the King and against God who has set him in the royal seat. Of all things let there be no moderation. It is the bane of genuine improvement.' [1]
Here is a position which all the Reform leaders accept,

---

[1] Calvin, *Opera* in *Corpus Reform. torum*, XLI, p. 68.

namely, that there is no place within the State for religious dissent.[1] And the Catholics cling to the traditional idea that to leave the revealed doctrine for any human wisdom is a crime that deserves death. Hence, that Pole's commission imposed on him the duty of repressing heresy and seeing to the punishment of heretics, was simply part of the common form of the universal public life of his century, and the revival of the English statutes [2] that regulated the process of the State execution of heretics, was a natural, if not inevitable, corollary to the legate's appearance in England.

But whatever the willingness of the newly reconciled State to play the traditional role of the loyal Catholic prince bearing the sword against the enemies of religion, the English situation was such that, while the State had its own good reasons for a policy of bloody repression, and showed a corresponding willingness to execute the law with a maximum of severity, the attempt to root out heresy was bound to fail unless it could be extended over a period of many years. Should the attempt fail, should the half-killed thing survive, and come back to a fullness of life, then its would-be executioners would necessarily have to bear an infinite burden of hatred. And this is, of course, what eventually happened.

It is a matter of historical fact that these heretics put to death in the Marian restoration of Catholicism were, very often, much more than just intellectually or emotionally enthusiastic about some special religious belief. They were a minority, a small minority indeed, of the general population, but in will and desire—and very often in act and deed—they were militantly anti-Catholic. For the religion they had abandoned—or from which they had been liberated—they had all the hatred which the Israelite of old bore to the

---

[1] Two other examples that illustrate contemporary feeling among the reformers on the question of religious dissent may be quoted. The first is a definition of heresy from the work which Theodore Beza wrote to justify Calvin's burning of Servetus, *That Heretics ought to be punished by the State*, published in 1554, the very year that saw the revival in England of the statute, *De Heretico Comburendo*. For Beza the heretic is one who ' breaks the peace and consent of the Church by holding a false doctrine and by persisting in spreading it ' (quoted GARRETT, p. 4, note 4, from *De Hæreticis a civili magistratu puniendis*). The second is Cecil's declared principle that ' No state could be in safety where there was toleration of two religions.' (PECK, *Desiderata Curiosa*, quoted POLLARD, p. 69.)

[2] 1 & 2 Philip and Mary, c. 6, reviving 5 Richard II, st. 2, c. 51, 2 Henry IV, c. 15 and 2 Henry V, st. 1, c. 7.

idolators among whom his lot was so often cast. Catholicism
was a thing to be destroyed. For the true follower of Christ
no truce with it was possible. No régime could be acceptable
in which there was room for the Catholic also. Mary,
the victim herself of persecution, began with ideas of
toleration, ' bloodshed was no part of her original design,' [1]
but she and her government were speedily made aware
that there was this strong and active minority among her
subjects with whom no truce was possible. Before any
persecution began, in the truce of the very first weeks of the
reign, it was made evident by a host of incidents, and the
flooding of London with pamphlets and broadsheets, that
heresy now, in London, in 1553, was challenging, not the
mistakes which as yet the régime had not had the time to
commit, but the régime itself. The government, ultimately,
after eighteen months of defiance and outrage, of religious
sedition and riot, and in the face of much parliamentary
opposition, acted like every contemporary government
faced with the like problem. The old heresy laws were
restored, and henceforth upon the bishop's certificate that
a man had been found to be a heretic and had remained
obstinate in his opinion, it was the duty of the sheriff to see
to his execution by burning him at the stake.

There were, however, special elements in the situation of
heresy in England, which perhaps are clearer to us who
write after the event than they were to contemporaries.
But before we pass to consider these—and they are the
elements which brought it about that the Marian repression
of heresy was a ghastly futility, the elements also which,
unfairly enough, bred the unhistorical legend so familiar
to us all—some contemporary witness may be cited as to
the fact that heretics were violent and that the source of the
violence was their heresy.

To the heretics the Edwardine settlement of religion
was divine. ' For truly,' say the petitioners of Norfolk and
Suffolk to the queen, ' the religion lately set forth by King
Edward is such in our conscience as every Christian man is
bound to confess to be the truth of God ; and every member
of Christ's Church in England must needs embrace the same
in heart and confess it with mouth. . . .' [2]

[1] POLLARD, p. 100.
[2] FOXE, *Acts and Monuments*, VIII, p. 121, quoted GAIRDNER, *Lollardy*,
IV, p. 272

The list of outrages and sacrileges perpetrated by these enthusiasts can be read in any text-book, dead cats vested to caricature the priest saying Mass, assaults on priests while celebrating, lampoons and satires, and violent resistance to the restoration of the old liturgy. And everywhere the situation was complicated by the association of heresy with sedition and treason. ' The Londoners do not desist from daily outrages against the Catholic religion,' a Venetian diplomatist writes to his government from England in March, 1555, ' having not only again mutilated the statue of St. Thomas of Canterbury, which had been restored and put back in its place, but even robbed several churches of the tabernacle of the Sacrament ; nor with this commencement does the Government deem fit to act with such rigour as is becoming, hoping by address and leniency, time, rather than severe punishment, may mitigate their rage and fury.' [1] The Venetian's astonishment at the leniency of the government, or rather at its slowness to act, was not shared by his colleague, the emperor's ambassador, Renard, who saw from the beginning how it might be even more dangerous to attack the evil than to leave it alone. ' It will be difficult to keep the heretics under without scandal,' he wrote to Charles V,[2] adding that Gardiner, Bishop of Winchester and Lord Chancellor, fully realised this.

The fact was, of course, that no matter how small the number of really conscientious and enthusiastic heretics was, in comparison with the mass of the nation, heresy had been free to air itself, to take root, and to spread, for almost a generation. The heretic had had time to become a familiar figure, and what is familiar is not easily recognised as a menace to the general well-being. Still more lastingly effective was the fact that recently, for the last six years and a half before Mary's accession, heresy had been in control of the State. For England, heresy had indeed, until yesterday, been orthodoxy, the official belief, and if it was now but a party in politics it was a party whose head, until yesterday, had been the king himself, a party that had counted the great chiefs of the aristocracy and the leading bishops of the Church, the Primate above all, among its members. Because heresy had aided Henry VIII in his own revenge against the papacy; had

[1] *Venetian Calendar*, VI, p. 32.
[2] Quoted, GAIRDNER, *Lollardy*, IV, p. 90.

partly inspired, partly supported, partly persuaded and in a manner coerced his successful defiance ; and because in his son's reign heresy had legally initiated and commanded the further advance ; there had been created, by the time of Mary's accession, a huge vested interest in heresy, and a penumbra of neutrals not actively hostile to heresy, which was of immensely greater extent than the heresy itself, and destined, ultimately, to decide the question of heresy's survival in England. In the fact of this far-spreading penumbra of neutrals is to be found one reason why the active repression of heresy in the years 1555–1558 lacked, what the like activity lacked nowhere else in Catholic Europe, the support of public opinion, the support that might have been expected from people who believed the government to be at odds with a serious menace to the national life.

A further reason for this lack of popular support was the deep-seated unpopularity of the régime by the time the heresy laws were revived. The two causes of this unpopularity were the queen's marriage to a foreigner and the parliament's act of submission to the Pope. ' The very name of Spaniard was odious,' Gardiner had truly said to Charles V's ambassador, ' and the English would never endure the Spaniards, who were so much hated in Flanders.' [1] And when the legate rode through the streets of London in the farewell procession of King Philip, in 1555, blessing the people as he passed, they openly laughed and jeered at him. The Spanish marriage was universally hated, and for the reconciliation with Rome none but a minority of sincerely pious Catholics was really enthusiastic. Elsewhere, in this matter, there was a rich variety of opposition, from simple inert indifference to active bitter hostility.

Not all the heretics taken up, condemned, and executed, were actively and sacrilegiously critical of Catholicism. And among them were not a few whom no heresy laws should ever have touched, since they were not heretics at all in the strict sense of being obstinately apostate Catholics. There had been a sufficient lapse of time, by the middle of the sixteenth century, for men to have been born in heresy and to have been bred in heresy, never knowing, personally, any other form of belief. To execute these as though they

[1] Renard to Charles V, Nov. 5, 1553, quoted in GAIRDNER, Lollardy, IV p. 116.

were apostate Catholics was to go in the face not merely of actual justice, but of the letter of the law. But no distinction was ever drawn in practice.

No one has made a detailed critical study of the Marian persecution. All the accounts of it we possess are heavy with the worst failings of the hagiographer and the apologist. And the distortions of the legend have done much to provoke exaggerated scepticism about the facts that are its foundation. There is, of course, no need to postulate any personal bloodthirstiness whether in the ecclesiastics who tried the accused or in the executive that initiated the policy and kept the ecclesiastics to their task. The terrible penalty of death was the usual penalty for serious offences of every kind, and as for death by burning, it was in England regularly inflicted on women, in lieu of a hanging, for two hundred years and more after Mary Tudor's reign, until wellnigh the close of the eighteenth century.[1]

By the standards of any country at any time before the French Revolution, there was nothing unusual in the severity of the punishment. Those who enacted such a penalty cannot, historically, be regarded as monstrous for that alone, nor can they be said to have been anything other than typical of their time because the offence for which they decreed the penalty was the offence of heresy. But ought they not to have known that, as conditions were in England, this particular method of repression was useless ?—that it did no more, could do no more, than terminate the lives of just so many individuals ?—and that along these lines nothing short of general massacre would really solve the problem of public order ?

No man in the Europe of that day had more experience of the varying chances of repressing heresy than Charles V. For thirty-six years he had fought a losing battle in Germany with Lutheranism, and, more recently, he had used methods every whit as bloody as those England was about to experience, to put down heresy in his own hereditary dominions, in the Netherlands and in Spain. The German policy of the emperor and his Spanish and Belgian policy were different, as the different circumstances seemed to demand. It is of the highest significance that such a supple politician did his best to dissuade the government of his

[1] The last burning is, I think, that of a woman condemned as a coiner in 1789.

English cousin from adopting in England the policy which he had sanctioned for Belgium and Holland and Spain.

When, at the outset of the reign, Mary's natural eagerness had seemed to the emperor to be full of danger for the prospective restoration of the Faith, and Charles had turned to Rome to check the speed of her advance, Rome had adopted his point of view, and, as we have seen, the Pope had bidden his own legate take his orders as to the appropriate moment, from this imperial Nestor. And, possibly, not impossibly at any rate, had the Pope whom Charles so won over, by his apparent grasp of the facts of the situation, been still among the living in the latter part of Mary's reign, something might have been done once more to temper English severity. But that Pope, Julius III,[1] died in the March of 1555, and after the short three weeks' reign of Marcellus II, it was to the Cardinal Gian Pietro Carafa that the papacy came, Pope Paul IV. Here was not only the lifelong bitter enemy of Charles and all his house, a Pope who was soon to engage in war with Philip, the emperor's son—now King of England as well as of Naples ; not only a Pope who made it a principle to disregard statesmanship ; but the creator of the Roman Inquisition, and the late Grand Inquisitor, a man who used to declare that had his own father been a heretic he would gladly have carried the wood to build his pyre, a man who, as his own treatment of Cardinal Morone showed, and indeed his later efforts to try Pole also for heresy, was hardly sane on this question of heretics. It was against the background of the least understanding of all the popes, and a Pope who was as despotic as he was rigid and short-sighted, that the desperate operation took place of saving the Catholic English State by the faggot and the stake.

It was Mary's third parliament which revived the laws *De Heretico Comburendo*, some two weeks after it had expressed the national repentance to the legate, in December, 1554. The act came into force on January 20 following, and in February the first heretic was burnt, John Rogers, at Smithfield in London. In March the first executions of laymen took place ; in August the first of the women were burnt. By the end of the year a total of seventy had been put to death.

---

[1] For Julius III, *cf.* PASTOR, Vol. 13, c. 8 ; for Paul IV, *ibid.* 14, c. 10.

The bishops concerned kept steadily to their task, speeded on, when they faltered, by letters from the Council. Bonner, of London, very soon fell under the suspicion of slackness and in 1555, when two months had gone by without any convictions, the Council took him to task. 'We . . . understanding now, to our no little marvel, that divers of the said disordered persons, being by the justices of peace for their contempt and obstinacy brought to the ordinaries . . . are either refused to be received at their hands, or if they be received, are neither so travailed with, as Christian charity requireth, nor yet proceeded withal, according to the order of justice, but are suffered to continue in their errors, to the dishonour of Almighty God, and dangerous examples of others. . . .'[1] And the bishop was warned to carry out the law.

There is some dispute as to the number of those who thus suffered death in the four years, nearly, for which the régime endured. But the total of those burnt can hardly be less than 300. It is not unimportant to notice that four-fifths of this total were burnt in London (where 112 suffered), East Anglia, Sussex, and Kent, that only one execution is recorded north of the Trent,[2] three only in Wales, and none west of Salisbury. Five of the heretic bishops were burnt and twenty-one of the lower clergy, but almost no gentry. Almost all the victims were poor people, working men, small traders, and their wives or widows, for no fewer than sixty women are included in the list.

It is true that many undoubted and known heretics went unmolested, Roger Ascham, for example, who had been Lady Jane Grey's tutor, Sir Thomas Smith, a former tutor of Edward VI, and one of the inner ring that planned the heretical triumphs of that reign, or again Matthew Parker, one day to be Pole's own successor at Canterbury. It may also be taken as true that among those put to death were many who were no better than criminal fanatics,[3] and many whom Cranmer, to say nothing of Calvin, would have condemned as readily as Gardiner or Bonner had the law directed his attention to their activities. There were already Protestants whom other Protestants regarded as hardly less

---

[1] May 24, 1555; Quoted, STONE, pp. 390–391, from FOXE, *op. cit.*, VIII, p. 86. The Act reviving heresy prosecutions is 1 & 2 Ph. and Mary, c. 6.
[2] At Chester.
[3] *Cf.* Pollard's statement about this, p. 138, *op. cit.*

noxious than papists and as, equally with the papists, to be rooted out of the land of the living.

But when all these allowances and deductions have been made, there remains the fact of a series of executions for heresy on an altogether unprecedented scale, and, by its very scale, a new phenomenon in English life, material for a saga-cycle, for a great folk-legend ready to the hand of any interested enthusiast with wit and imagination and some craftsmanship in letters. Such an enthusiast that very generation of the repression produced. He was John Foxe,[1] a one-time fellow of Magdalen College, Oxford, and, at this moment, an exile living in the colony of English exiles at Bale. Foxe devoted his leisure to the collection of whatever information was in circulation about the sufferings of his co-religionists in England, and presently, in 1559, there appeared the first edition of his great work,[2] but in Latin. That same year Foxe returned to England. He was ordained priest by the new Protestant Bishop of London, Edmund Grindal (who had been of considerable service to him in the compilation of the book), and in 1563 the first English edition appeared. It was, from the beginning, a huge success, and three more editions were called for in the author's lifetime.[3] The influence of his book was immediate and it was permanent. For generations the popular conception of Rome and of Catholicism was derived from its pages for, in 1570, Convocation ordered the revised edition of the book to be placed in all cathedral churches, and that all dignitaries should place copies of it, for the use of servants and visitors, in their homes, and on the quasi-public, quasi-official, reading of Foxe's *Book of Martyrs* which went on in many a parish church, no less than upon the reading of the new translation of the Bible, the spiritual life of the new Protestant Englishman was henceforth largely built up.

Foxe's Catholic contemporaries were not blind to the ruinous effect of his book. Fr. Robert Persons, who with great bitterness calls his veracity into question, declared that the book ' by the judgement of many men hath done more hurt alone to simple souls in our country by infecting and poisoning them unawares under the bait of pleasant histories, fair pictures, and painted pageants, than many the

---

[1] *Cf.* J. F. MOZLEY, *John Foxe and his book* (1940).
Acts and Monuments.   [3] Foxe died in 1587.

most pestilent books together . . . causing infinite spiritual hurt to many thousand souls of our country. . . . The minds of English Christians standing firm and fixed in one religion . . . now by reading this work they are all put out of joint.' [1] And such, in the opinion of Foxe's latest champion, was the precise intention of the martyrologist. ' If anything could make England protestant for ever, it would be the memory of the Marian terror ; and [Foxe] desired to burn his dreadful history into the minds of his countrymen, both high and low.' [2]

For the student of the Counter-Reformation in England, Foxe's undoubted effectiveness is of more importance than his much-discussed veracity. Dr. Maitland's severe criticism of this is well known,[3] and the later work of Dr. J. G. Gairdner [4] supports it. It is a fair and balanced statement which describes the book as ' a mass of unsorted fact and fiction, carelessly thrown together, often proved untrustworthy, rarely corrected, and at the best uncritical, one-sided, and violent.' [5] Mr. Mozley would probably demur to some of these qualifications. He finds Foxe a man more often abused than studied. Still he makes no bones about admitting that Foxe ' is not properly a historian at all, rather he is a compiler on a gigantic scale. His book is a colossal storehouse of material gathered from many quarters and of differing merit. This material he uses in a casual and unsystematic way.' [6] Also ' Foxe is temperamentally incapable of writing what is now called scientific history : he is no dry delver into documents, no dispassionate arranger of his discoveries, no follower of minute accuracy. He has too warm a heart for this and he lacks the patience.' [7]

This Foxian mass contains, however, all the elements of great popular literature, and it never lost its hold so long as that spiritual world which gave it birth survived. Here are horrors, here is pathos, human cruelty, human courage, daring men with bold tongues, extravagant pains and extravagant defiance, life not a little in the raw, and, as well as elemental vigour, skill and great gusto in the telling. Foxe's book ended all hope of popular support for the old

---

[1] *A Treatise of Three Conversions of England* (1603–1604), cited MOZLEY, *op. cit.*, pp. 177, 178.
[2] MOZLEY, p. 129.
[3] In *Essays on Subjects connected with the Reformation in England* (1849).
[4] *Lollardy and the Reformation*, Vol. IV.
[5] STONE, p. 370.   [6] MOZLEY, pp. 153–154.   [7] *Ibid.*, p. 155.

religion in England. It is not a book that Catholics know well, and I make no apology for a longish extract that will show something of its power. It is taken from the account of the death of the famous Dr. Rowland Taylor,[1] one of the first of the Protestants to suffer in Mary's reign.

Rowland Taylor was the parson of Hadleigh, in Suffolk, and it was apparently his vigorous opposition to an attempt of a neighbour, the parson of Aldham, to restore the Mass in Hadleigh church that led to his arrest. ' Thou devil,' said Dr. Taylor to the priest at the altar, ' who made thee so bold to enter into this church of Christ to profane and defile it with this abominable idolatry ? ' He was summoned to London and was examined by the Lord Chancellor, touching his marriage and his beliefs about the Holy Eucharist. Gardiner, we are told, greeted his prisoner with ' many villainous reproaches ' which Dr. Taylor repaid with interest, in the matter if not in the manner, when he recalled Gardiner's past subservience to Henry VIII. ' Art thou come, thou villain ? How darest thou look me in the face for shame ? Knowest thou not who I am ? ' so the chancellor had begun. And Taylor replied : ' How dare ye for shame look any christian man in the face, seeing ye have forsaken the truth, denied our Saviour Christ and His word, and done contrary to your own oath and writing ? With what countenance will ye appear before the judgment-seat of Christ, and answer to your oath made first unto that blessed king Henry the Eighth of famous memory, and afterwards unto the blessed king Edward the Sixth his son ? ' The end of the argument was that Taylor was committed to prison.

He was next deprived of his living as a married cleric and then, after a long interval, again appeared before the Lord Chancellor and other commissioners on January 22, 1555. This time he was condemned as a heretic and handed over to the civil authorities.

He was to die in his parish of Hadleigh, but his wife and children had, by this, come on to London. On February 5, at two in the morning, the sheriff came to the London prison to take him the first stage of his journey. ' Dr. Taylor's wife,' says Foxe, ' suspecting that her husband should that night be carried away, watching all night in St. Botolph's church-porch beside Aldgate, having with her

[1] FOXE, VI, 676-703.

two children, the one named Elizabeth, of thirteen years of
age (whom, being left without father or mother, Dr. Taylor
had brought up of alms from three years old), the other
named Mary, Dr. Taylor's own daughter. Now when the
sheriff his company came against St. Botolph's Church,
Elizabeth cried, saying, " O my dear father ! Mother !
mother ! here is my father led away ! " Then cried his
wife, " Rowland, Rowland, where art thou ? "—for it was
a very dark morning, that the one could not see the other.
Dr. Taylor answered, " I am here, dear wife," and stayed.
The sheriff's men would have led him forth, but the sheriff
said, " Stay a little, masters, I pray you, and let him speak
to his wife." Then came she to him, and he took his
daughter Mary in his arms, and he and his wife and
Elizabeth knelt down and said the Lord's prayer. At
which sight the sheriff wept apace, and so did divers others
of the company. After they had prayed he rose up and
kissed his wife and shook her by the hand, and said, " Farewell, my dear wife, be of good comfort, for I am quiet in my
conscience ! God shall stir up a father for my children."
. . . Then said his wife, " God be with thee dear Rowland !
I will, by God's grace, meet thee at Hadleigh ! " . . .
All the way Dr. Taylor was joyful and merry, as one that
accounted himself going to a most pleasant banquet or
bridal. . . . Coming within a two mile of Hadleigh he
desired for somewhat, to light off his horse, which done he
leaped, and set a frisk or twain as men commonly do in
dancing. " Why, master Doctor," quoth the sheriff, " how
do you now ? " He answered, " Well, God be praised,
good master sheriff, never better ; for now I know I am
almost at home. I lack not past two stiles to go over, and
I am even at my Father's house ! " . . . The streets of
Hadleigh were beset on both sides with men and women of
the town and country who waited to see him ; whom when
they beheld so led to death, with weeping eyes and lamentable voices, they cried, " Ah, good Lord, there goeth our
good shepherd from us, that so faithfully hath taught us,
so fatherly hath cared for us, and so godly hath governed
us " . . . with such other most lamentable and piteous
voices. . . .'
The journey was at last over, February 8, 1555. ' " What
place is this, he asked and what meaneth it that so much
people are gathered together ? " It was answered, " it is

Aldham common, the place where you must suffer, and the people are come to look upon you." Then said he, "Thanked be God, I am even at home!" and so alighted from his horse, and with both his hands rent the hood from his head. But when the people saw his reverend and ancient face, with a long white beard, they burst out with weeping tears and cried, saying, "God save thee, good Dr. Taylor; Jesus Christ strengthen thee and help thee; the Holy Ghost comfort thee!" with such other like godly wishes. Then would he have spoken to the people, but the yeoman of the guard . . . would in no wise permit him to speak. . . . When he had prayed, he went to the stake, and kissed it, and set himself into a pitch-barrel which they had set for him to stand in, and so stood with his back upright against the stake, with his hands folded together and his eyes towards heaven, and so he continually prayed.' One of the executioners, as the wood was heaped around the stake, ' cruelly cast a faggot at him, which hit upon his head, and brake his face that the blood ran down his visage. Then said Dr. Taylor, " O friend, I have harm enough— what needed that?" At the last they set to fire; and Dr. Taylor, holding up both his hands, called upon God, and said, "Merciful Father of heaven, for Jesus Christ my Saviour's sake, receive my soul into thy hands." So stood he still, without either crying or moving, with his hands folded together, till Soyce [1] with a halbert struck him on the head that the brains fell out, and the dead corpse fell down into the fire.'

[1] An executioner.

NOTE.—The phrase quoted, on p. 78 *supra*, as St. John Fisher's saying has really for its author Thomas de Vio, Cardinal Cajetan, arguing against the schismatic Council of Pisa in 1511.

CHAPTER V

THE LEGACY'S FATE AND FAILURE

IT has sometimes been argued as a serious blunder in Pole's administration that by his neglect to fill the sees as they became vacant, the cardinal weakened the Catholic forces in the coming parliamentary struggle over the Elizabethan Acts of Supremacy and Uniformity. The accusation goes back as far as the cardinal's Spanish opponents, and, notoriously, to the Count de Feria who was Philip II's ambassador in London at the end of Mary's reign. But the facts hardly bear out the accusation.

When Pole died, November 17, 1558, there were indeed five sees already vacant ; Salisbury since thirteen months before, Oxford since eleven months, Bangor since six months, Gloucester since nine weeks, and Hereford since seven weeks. But a bishop had been chosen for Salisbury— Francis Mallet, Dean of Lincoln, and Maurice Clenog was designated for Bangor, while it had been arranged that Goldwell was to go to Oxford.

Two other points must be mentioned. First, that the illness from which Pole died had had him in its grip for nearly twelve months. In March, 1558, the Spanish ambassador already described him to Philip II as a dead man. Secondly, for eighteen months before his death Pole had not only ceased to be Legate *a Latere* of the Pope, but had lost all his power and influence at Rome, and was actually under orders to return there to take his trial for heresy. And all five of these vacancies had occurred since Pole lost his legatine powers. On the other hand it must be acknowledged that the delays in nominating to the six sees that came vacant while he was legate and resident in England were, considering the critical need of bishops, somewhat extraordinary.[1] But where the fault lay, whether with the crown,

[1] These sees were Chester, vacant five months ; Winchester, vacant thirteen months ; Peterborough, vacant eighteen months ; Carlisle, vacant seventeen months ; Lincoln, vacant nine months ; Chichester, vacant fifteen months.

or with Pole, or with the Roman authorities, does not appear.

The removal of Pole from his office of legate was the crowning catastrophe of his chequered career, and, with a certain appropriateness, its cause lay very largely in the political preoccupations of the ruler of the papal states who was also, of course, the Pope.

Paul IV, the Neapolitan nobleman Gian Pietro Carafa, had all his life hated the family of Charles V and Philip II, the conquerors of his native country and the oppressors of his people. As an ecclesiastic he had an even more intense hatred for these princes as enemies of the Church's independence. For nearly fifty years, ever since the days when he served as nuncio in Spain, he had looked on with ill-concealed anger while a succession of popes temporised and placated and made concessions to the all-powerful Spanish state lest this, too, should abjure its spiritual allegiance. Now he was Pope it was for him a most urgent obligation in conscience to end what seemed to him the servitude of the Church to the Hapsburgs. And he proceeded to the work of emancipation in the spirit and with the weapons of Innocent III, unhappily not aware that the age in which alone these could be effective was long since passed. In all matters of politics and of warfare the Pope lived in a world of fantasy, where everything was in the greatest possible contrast with the reality of things.[1] And, for these matters he was unhappily in the hands of a man whom everyone except himself knew for a first-class scoundrel, his nephew Carlo Carafa, whom he had created cardinal and made his Secretary of State.

Given the superhuman strength of will which this aged Pope possessed, it needed only the slightest of accidents and there would be real danger of war between himself and Philip II, who, of course, as King of Naples, could be a most dangerous neighbour to the papal states. Within three months of Paul IV's election, a comparatively trivial act of insubordination on the part of a minor papal feudatory, done to the profit of Charles, set the whole scheme of their relations in jeopardy. Through the next year, 1556, the Pope's language grew more indignant, and against the imperialist design—for he was convinced it existed—to

[1] PASTOR, Vol. 14, p. 80.

make him a mere chaplain to the emperor, he began to
gather arms, to collect money. and to look for allies. And
then, September 1, 1556, the emperor's viceroy at Naples,
the duke of Alba, without the formality of a declaration of
war, moved his armies. Three days later they were across
the papal frontier and had taken the town of Pontecorvo.
In Rome the bulls were drafted for the excommunication and
deposition of King Philip.

The war dragged on for a full twelve months, a phase
of the general war between Charles and Philip on the one
hand, and Henry II of France. One of its incidents was
Philip II's instruction to all his subjects to leave Rome,
to which Paul replied by recalling his legates and nuncios
from all the dominions of Spain, April 9, 1557. This meant
the end of Pole's English career, and the news caused general
consternation at the English court and in the hierarchy.
Letters of protest came in from the queen and from the
bishops, and the English ambassador at Rome strove to have
Pole exempted from the decree. But the Pope was unmoved.
Mary, knowing Pole's delicate conscience, took the precau-
tion of holding up the Pope's messengers at Calais, and of
confiscating the official letters, so that the cardinal never
received them. But Pole, who, of course, knew all that had
happened, immediately ceased to act as legate, and put
aside his legatine insignia, and he wrote his own letter to the
Pope, in which he said nothing about his own case, but
merely pleaded that England should not be left without a
legate. If he was not himself to be legate any longer,
some other should be sent to replace him. The Pope replied
in the consistory of June 14, 1557, by creating cardinal and
naming legate William Peyto, an octogenarian Franciscan
of the friary at Greenwich. In a letter to the English bishops,
and in a brief to the king and queen, he explained that it
was not possible to restore Pole's dignity, for this would
involve a reversal of his decision. To Pole he wrote ordering
his immediate return to Rome. All these letters Mary
continued to intercept.

But Paul IV persisted, and he now made it evident
that something else, beside the fact that Pole's sovereign
and the Pope were at war, had moved him to recall the
English cardinal. Pole, he openly declared, was a dangerous
heretic, an even more dangerous heretic than his friend
Cardinal Morone, whom the Pope had had arrested some

two weeks earlier [1] and who was now lying a close prisoner
in the Castle of Sant' Angelo. Morone's trial had begun,
and it was the Pope's intention that Pole should share his
fate. That Pole was a heretic was, as has been stated, no
new idea with Paul IV. It had played a part in his opposition to Pole in the Conclave of 1549, and before Pole left
for England, four years later, he had gone to the trouble of
thrashing the whole matter out with Carafa, and had wrung
from the old man an admission that his suspicions were
unjust. Now, however, they had revived, and they were
given full play. Already in the previous November (1556),
so Morone then wrote to Pole, the Pope had thought of
recalling him, and now, in the heat of the war with Pole's
sovereign, he thought he saw his opportunity.

Morone was, of course, as innocent as Pole, and his
' trial ' showed this fully. He had no difficulty in clearing
himself, but the Pope refused to believe the evidence, and
for as long as he lived Morone remained in prison treated
like a convicted heretic and not even allowed to hear Mass.

Peace was made between the Pope and Philip II in
September, 1557, and the Pope, with great simplicity,
surely, now asked Philip to have Pole arrested and to send
him to Rome. Pole, he said, was the father—and Morone
merely a disciple—of ' this cursed sect . . . this house of
apostates.'

So long as Pole lived the suspicion endured and the
order for his return to Rome was never withdrawn. It was
his fate to die a heretic in the eyes of the Pope. But nine
months later, in August, 1559, Paul IV followed him to the
grave. On Christmas Day, 1559, a new Pope was elected,
the Cardinal Gian Angelo de' Medici, and it was he, Pope
Pius IV, who, in the first weeks of his reign, after an official
report by Morone's judges, the chief of whom was the future
Pope St. Pius V, vindicated Morone and, indirectly, Pole
also. In the consistory of March 13, 1560, the Pope declared
that the whole procedure was irregular in form and in
substance. There was not ever the slightest lawful reason
for suspecting Morone and the prosecution was declared
null, ill-advised, and unjust.

The most eloquent memorial of this calamitous incident
at the close of Pole's life is his own noble vindication of his
faith, made to Paul IV. And it is characteristic of Pole

[1] May 31, 1557, PASTOR, Vol. 14, p. 290.

that, having written it, he threw it in the fire with the scriptural phrase, ' Thou shalt not uncover the nakedness of thy father.'

It was on Thursday, November 17, 1558, that Queen Mary died, in the palace of Whitehall, and a few hours later, across the river at Lambeth, her kinsman, Reginald Pole, also passed away. The first phase of the Counter-Reformation in England was at an end. What had it achieved among the English people ?

Let us begin by setting out the judgement of an informed, but singularly unsympathetic modern scholar, Professor Pollard : [1] ' . . . the time for a real counter-reformation had not come in England and there were few signs of Catholic fervour in Mary's reign. The queen herself and Pole were the only religious enthusiasts ; there was little of the missionary spirit in Bonner, Gardiner, or even Tunstal. Neither the fathers of Trent nor the disciples of Loyola had yet done their work, and the Marian reaction was no part of the counter-reformation. Pole, indeed, endeavoured to effect some reforms ; but he appealed to deaf ears, and the bulk of Mary's clergy had not sufficient religious conviction to prevent them turning their coats again in 1559. . . . The reconciliation with Rome was the result not so much of popular impulse as of governmental pressure, and it stirred not a breath of spiritual fervour.' This writer is able to cite in support the testimony of important contemporary witnesses. 'With the exception of a few very pious Catholics,' the Venetian ambassador informed his government, in the last year of the reign, ' . . . with the exception of a few very pious Catholics, none of whom, however, are under thirty-five years of age, all the rest make this show of recantation, yet do not effectually resume the Catholic faith, and on the first opportunity would be more than ever ready and determined to return to the unrestrained life previously led by them. . . . They discharge their duty as subject to their prince by living as he lives, believing what he believes, and in short doing whatever he commands, making use of it for external show to avoid incurring his displeasure rather than from any internal zeal ; for they would do the like by the Mahometan or Jewish creed.' [2] Here we have a detailed comment on what the Spanish

[1] Op. cit., p. 173.
[2] Venetian Calendar, VI, pp. 1074-1075, cited in POLLARD, p. 131.

diplomat, Mendoza, had told Dandino in Brussels four years earlier, namely that the great truth to grasp about the England over which Mary had just begun to reign was that for a generation it had known all the luxury of living freely in heresy, in private judgement, in emancipation from the control either of ecclesiastical authority or of certitude in faith or morals.

The same Venetian, in the same report to the Senate, gives it as his opinion that the only reason why the Catholic religion and the authority of the Roman See prevail is that they are sustained by the power and presence of the Catholic queen. Her death will mean the utter failure of the restoration. Cecil is another witness to the truth of the same view. Discussing the prospects of Catholicism, and with Paget, framing his words to suit that piety which Paget had in common with him, he said : ' I fear rather an inundation of the contrary part, so universal a boiling and bubbling I see.' [1]   Renard too, an opponent of all those whom the French and Venetians patronised, was troubled with premonitions of coming catastrophe. If the queen did not bear a child, to be her Catholic successor, ' I foresee convulsions and disturbances such as no pen can describe.' [2]   And when Calais fell to the French, in 1558, Philip II's ambassador, Feria, reported a general falling off in assistance at Mass, ' not a third of those who used to attend go to church.' [3]

The first criticism one is moved to make—passing over several inexactitudes of detail—is that whatever the truth of these statements, they are based chiefly on observations of life in the capital, and although the dispositions of London might well be decisive in the success of any national policy, religious or otherwise, the fact that London was anti-Catholic need not mean any more than that the country was to be saddled with a policy congenial to those who dominated the capital. Nor is the ultimate success of such a policy any proof of the country's general sympathy with it. We need more than the success of a policy that came out of London as evidence that, throughout England generally, there was no attachment to the Mass at the end of Mary's reign, and a positive objection to the papacy.

Against the Spanish ambassador's view of the case we

<hr>

[1] Quoted in BIRT, p. 510.
[2] Cited in POLLARD (no date given), p. 142.   [3] *Ibid.*, p. 172.

may set the words of the envoy of the Duke of Mantua, writing in February, 1559 : 'The acts and decrees of Queen Mary and Cardinal Pole have vanished in smoke, but it is really surprising to witness the very great fortitude of many persons. . . . Mass is said in all the London churches before numerous congregations, who show much devotion. So it is evident that religion is not on such a sorry footing as was supposed ; for everybody is now at liberty to go or stay away.'[1]

One might also bear in mind Mr. Pollard's own remark,[2] to the effect that ' the " busy meddlers, in matters of religion, the preachers, printers, and players," against whom proclamations had been issued in August (1553) can only have represented a section of the people ; and the petitions in Kent and agitations in Essex for the retention of Protestant services were mainly local symptoms.' And long before the legal restoration of Catholicism had begun to take shape in any administrative action, one of Calvin's own correspondents bore striking testimony to the Catholicism of the countrysides. The country folk were so attached to the papacy, he wrote, that the ' Gospel ' could only be preached in the security of the nobleman's private chapels.[3]

We have evidence, too, from contemporary English reformers as to the serious conversions to Catholicism during the restoration. It was the opinion of Bishop Jewel, lately returned to England in 1559 after five years of exile, that many converts to Catholicism had been made in that interval,[4] and as for Oxford, he wrote to Vermigli that there were hardly two Protestants in all the university.[5] Edmund Grindal, bishop-to-be of London, wrote to much the same effect only two months later than John Jewel : ' We are labouring under a great dearth of godly ministers ; for many who have fallen off in this persecution, are now become Papists in heart ; and those who had been heretofore, so to speak, moderate Papists, are now of the most obdurate.'[6]

Yet a third returned exile and bishop-elect more than

---

[1] *Venetian Calendar*, Feb. 6, 1559, pp. 26–28.   [2] POLLARD, p. 103.
[3] Dodmer to Calvin, Dec. 17, 1553, quoted PASTOR, Vol. 13, p. 270, note 2, from Calvin's Works, *Corpus Reformatorum*, XLII, p. 706.
[4] PASTOR, XIV, p. 393.
[5] Jewel to Vermigli, Mar. 20, 1559, in *Zurich Letters*, 1st series, 10.
[6] Grindal to Conrad Hubert, May 23, 1559, in *Zurich Letters*, II, No. 8, cited SANDER, p. 258, note 1.

hints that, even in London, the mass of the people were far
from favouring the changes that were coming with Elizabeth. Edmund Allen describes to John Abell—still at
Strasburg—the great day when, in the cathedral of London,
it was announced that the Mass had been once more
abolished. 'The Lord Keeper, and the whole Council
being present the preacher proclaimed the restoring of the
book of King Edward, whereat the Lords and the people
made (or at least pretended) a wonderful rejoicing. Never
a Bishop or Canon of St. Paul's was present thereat.' [1]

The problem is, then, far less simple than the passage
quoted from Mr. Pollard might lead one to think. Neither
the Mass nor the Pope were, in the event, easily got rid of
by the anti-Catholic party in the hour when it came into
possession of the means of government.

What was generally and universally true, and what
needs to be recalled yet once again, is that Pole's twofold
task, of restoring Catholicism and of repressing heresy, lay
in a country where the factor chiefly active in the previous
phases of change was not doctrinal at all. It was not
enthusiasm for heresy that really mattered in Mary's reign
and in the first critical years of Elizabeth, but the reluctance
of a laity emancipated from the control of clerics, and, more
recently still, triumphant over the clerics, to submit to any
externally imposed reversal of this process : a laity, moreover, enriched with wealth taken from the clerics.

Down to the revolution of Henry VIII's reign the cleric
had ruled the layman, through the machinery of the Canon
Law, in a great variety of ways. It was not a question
merely of the regulation of the layman's behaviour when he
found himself between the four walls of his parish church.
Many things connected with marriage, its validity, legitimacy
of offspring ; wills, their validity and interpretation, supervision of executors, administration of intestates' property ;
sexual immorality, defamation of character, simony ; and
all that far-spreading business that related to the protection of the true belief, brought the layman within the
orbit of his bishop's jurisdiction and subjected him to
the activity of the bishop's officials. In a score of ways
he could fall foul of some excommunication and the

---

[1] Letter of May 28, 1559, quoted GARRETT, pp. 238–239, from *Foreign
Calendar*, 1558–1559, p. 287 ; Dr. Garrett ascribes the letter to the new dean
of St. Paul's, Alexander Nowell.

consequent writ *de excommunicato capiendo* which threw him into the king's prison until he sued out an absolution from the bishop. Also, a point of considerable importance, in all these matters of ecclesiastical jurisdiction the layman was not only very much the sheep in the hands of his shepherd, but, granted the gulf which, even then, separated the procedure and the spirit of the Common Law and the Canon Law, even somewhat the sheep before its shearer. Here was a world in which, because not a cleric, the layman was perpetually held *in statu pupillari*. It was the world of the spiritual and he was a patient in the hands of the practitioners of the canonical mysteries. These practitioners were indeed Englishmen, as English as the layman, but the law they administered had little resemblance in its doctrines or its procedure to the law which the laymen administered to one another. When the layman faced the Church as a great spiritual state, he faced a state whose organisation was absolutist, whose laws were the expression of a particular legal doctrine. It was a Christian doctrine and a Christian law, Christian because baptised, but before its baptism no other than the imperial law of ancient Rome.

Long before Martin Luther moved, or Henry VIII was born, there is evidence of a restlessness in English minds at this subjection to a spiritualty whose powers, rightful powers undeniably, are organised in such un-English fashion. The special contrast, peculiar to England—where alone the Roman Law had never taken root—between the Canon Law and the national law, added a special violence to the anticlerical spirit in which the Reformation in England began, and a special note of strength to the determination of the English layman never again to be the subject of clerical rule.

The Reformation began, in the parliament of 1529, as a strong protest against the abuses of clerical rule. With the rights and wrongs of the quarrel we are not here concerned, nor with the truth of the several accusations, the worth of the bishops' official reply, the sincerity of the king's intervention. But the movement set up by that protest did not end until the existing relation of cleric and layman was reversed, and a new religion set up in which the layman was supreme, and where everything religious, the very right of religion to exist as anything more than the private conviction in a man's soul, depended on the fiat of parliament.

The cleric was now the layman's servant, a functionary to minister to him spiritual goods. Henceforth the layman is wholly master of all his own life, answerable for his conduct to none but laymen, freed from all effective control save what the lay state imposes.

How much enthusiasm might reasonably be expected among the laity of 1554, not indeed for the restoration of the Mass, nor even for the abolition of the Royal Supremacy as an institution contrary to the divinely founded primacy of the Pope, but for the re-establishment of the rule of the cleric implied by the public recognition of the Church as a perfect society, with powers legislative, judicial, and coercive, independent of the lay state and yet reaching out to the lay state's members ?

The Church in 1532 had been induced to surrender its whole status and the jurisdiction deriving therefrom, and an act of parliament had noted that surrender, had accepted it and legally confirmed it, thus ending for ever, so far as the layman was concerned, the binding force of merely ecclesiastical legislation, or of sentences and penalties merely ecclesiastical. A later act of parliament had proceeded still further, and declared the omnicompetence of the royal jurisdiction where Englishmen are concerned, and indeed its sole competence. For Henry VIII's is an imperial realm, and if the Canon Law is the Roman Law domesticated by Christian baptism, here is the spirit of the Roman Law itself, called from a vasty deep indeed, to lay the heaviest stone of all upon the ecclesiastical jurisdiction's grave. Henry VIII is the heir, like Frederick II and Barbarossa before him, to Justinian, to Diocletian, to Augustus. What they were in their place and time, the King of England is in England. There is but one jurisdiction that binds his subjects, and henceforth, if they so choose, they may without molestation or any prejudice to property, liberty or life, ignore the opinions and dicta of the clergy. And the imperial power completes the revolution by forbidding the Canon Law to be any more taught in England. After twenty-five years of such emancipation, will the English layman in' 1554, whole-heartedly and enthusiastically, offer his neck to the yoke ? Or will he, broken-heartedly, lament the coming lay victory of 1559 ?

Nevertheless, even upon this very class, rich with gain from sacrilegious sources—the class whence came the statesmen and administrators, the members of the parliaments and the local justices—the prematurely blighted restoration of Mary's short. reign had one great effect. To those among them who had no inclination to the new beliefs, and who were not religiously indifferent, the reign of Edward VI had taught one important lesson, that the integrity of Catholicism was menaced once Catholics cut themselves off from the Roman jurisdiction, and to such Catholics as these the reign of Mary afforded just sufficient space for the necessary readjustment. When Fr. Persons made his famous venture into England, twenty-three years after Mary's death, he reported a new phenomenon to Rome : ' In Henry's days, the father of this Elizabeth, the whole kingdom, with all its bishops and learned men, abjured their faith at one word of the tyrant. But now, in his daughter's days, boys and women boldly profess their faith before the judge and refuse to make the slightest concession even at the threat of death.' [1] Here in the passive resistance of Catholics, in every class of society, to the re-establishment of heresy by Elizabeth, and in the firmness of their hold on the Roman primacy as the sole hope for orthodoxy, in this new very real grasp of the papacy's function in the Catholic Church and a new unshakeable devotion to it, is to be found the lasting effect of Pole's legacy. Neither the seminary priests nor the Jesuits of late Elizabethan times created that new spirit. It was their mission to foster it and to renew it, but they were themselves fruit of it, just as truly as the faithful people whose welcome made their ministry possible. The new spirit derives from the sincere appreciation, in some English minds at any rate, of the national repentance on St. Andrew's Day in 1554. It is fruit of the reconciliation there made. In what other school than that of Pole's restoration was Allen himself formed ?

[1] Persons to Agazzari, S.J. (Rector of the English College at Rome), July, 1581, quoted SIMPSON, p. 243.

BOOK II

CARDINAL ALLEN

CHAPTER I

THE RELIGIOUS REVOLUTION OF 1559

§ i. THE PROTESTANT PARTY, 1554–1559

As revolutions are the work of minorities, so usually it is no more than a minority that offers active opposition to their progress. The mass of the community, as it does not initiate, so it does not resist : 'the nation,' 'the people' acquiesces, and, whatever its sympathies, obeys the party which is *de facto* in possession of the means of government. The calculation as to what proportion of 'the nation' is, at heart, really sympathetic to the new régime or looks longingly back to the old and hopes for the day of its restoration, is too nice not to vary greatly according to the side from which it is made, and even 'the impartial observer' has generally to admit a lack of means effectively to check his estimate. Whatever Elizabethan England was, in religious sympathy, in 1603, it was not whole-heartedly Protestant in 1559 any more than Marian England was whole-heartedly Catholic in 1558.

The Marian restoration of Catholicism had been the realisation of the ideal of a party, or rather of two parties brought into unity by the events of the reign of Edward VI —the Catholics for whose position St. John Fisher and his fellow-martyrs of Henry VIII's reign might stand, and those whom it is becoming a fashion to call 'Henricians,' those who followed such leaders as Bishop Gardiner. What determined the accession of this alliance to power in the years following 1553, was the military failure of the Protestant party who had ruled in the previous six years. Now whatever its late fortunes, that Protestant party— whose supreme inspiration was Archbishop Cranmer—was, in 1553, it seems certain, a body with a very small following indeed. There is no evidence at all for any belief that there was anywhere among Englishmen generally, at that date,

123

such an enthusiasm for the new teaching about Grace or about the Holy Eucharist as there was for the anti-papal activity. Mary's immediate success seemed to mean the inevitable end of the party's hold on England and the likelihood of its extinction. Actually none of her measures to destroy the party succeeded. During her reign it merely went underground, and her death found it, still small indeed, but preserved, well-organised, with a definite aim—to ' de-Catholicise ' England—with a worked-out plan, with chosen men to play the leading parts and fill the key positions, and above all with a leader of genius, Sir William Cecil. And for the last years of Mary's reign the new queen, Elizabeth, had been hand in glove with the party. Cecil was with her when the commissioners came with the news of Mary's death, and it was Cecil whom she chose, in the first moments of the reign, to be her Secretary of State.

Mary died on November 17, 1558. Her sister succeeded without any sign of opposition from any quarter whatever. Two months later she was crowned and met her first parliament. Before recalling the way in which that parliament was brought to reconstruct the country's religion on the twofold basis, once more, of the Royal Supremacy and a new doctrine of the Holy Eucharist, the construction and personnel of the party deserve some attention, while something needs to be said about its history during Mary's reign and about the plan which guided its chiefs during the first critical months under Elizabeth.

The Protestant party, it has been said, went underground for the five years that Mary ruled—more accurately it went abroad, in a series of carefully planned, well-organised emigrations to selected towns [1] and, one is tempted to say, selected posts with special duties. For the party went abroad in order to prepare for the day of resurrection, and from its various strategically chosen hiding-places, Emden, Frankfort, Strasburg, and the rest, it waged a never-ceasing war on the régime in England which had taken its place. From the day of its self-chosen exile two purposes went hand in hand. The party would harass the English

---

[1] '. . . those and those only where the fugitives were preceded by one of the foreign congregations so lately their guests,' GARRETT, p. 46, who notes Zurich as the one exception to this, but there ' Englishmen needed no introduction.'

government, now restoring Catholicism, by a press propaganda of calumny and slander and lies, by the fomenting of an endless series of plots, risings, and assassination schemes, and it would train up a body of picked clergy, who when the time came would manage the Church for the party's leaders, the wealthy men who organised the emigration and financed it.

This is a very different picture of the religious exiles in Mary's reign from that usually given, from that which indeed we all of us believed until recently, from the story, that is to say, which the exiles themselves told of ' poor banished Englishmen,' driven from their own land by religious persecution. It is a different picture, but it is apparently the true picture.[1]

The earliest estimate of the number of the Marian exiles is that of John Foxe, the martyrologist, ' well near to the number of 800 persons, students and others together.' [2] Dr. Garrett's researches have confirmed Foxe as, here, accurate to the letter. We now know from the official lists kept in the several towns, the names and professions of all the exiles. In all 788 are thus accounted for. The first thing one notes about these exiles is that hardly any were of the working class. There is nothing, here, parallel to that exodus of poor weavers and labourers from the Continent which Edward VI's reign had seen harboured in London. Most of the English exiles were gentry and their households, or clergy. Of the rest the greater part were merchants. We have the names of 472 men ; their wives account for a further 100, and their children and young people for another 146. Women unaccompanied by men are given as twenty-five, and servants (names not given) total forty-five. The nobles and gentlemen account for the largest section of the 472, namely 148. The clergy are put at seventy-four, and there are ninety-nine named as students. Two-thirds of the men are thus accounted for by gentry or clerics or clerics to be. Forty of the rest are merchants, three lawyers, three physicians, and seven are printers. There are thirteen named as servants, three yeomen, and thirty-two artisans— forty-eight working men out of the total of 472.

---

[1] For its details the reader must be referred to the fascinating and scholarly volume, *The Marian Exiles*, Cambridge University Press (1938), p. 388, in which Dr. Garrett has set forth the result of her finds.

[2] GARRETT, p. 32.

Why did they leave England ? Fear of ' the wrath to come,' says Professor Pollard.[1] But there could not have been any such fear of persecution in the August of 1553, when the first plans were made, when Mary had been barely a month on the throne and when even her Catholic supporters seem to have been ready for any compromise, so slender were their hopes of her success proving lasting. No one could have said, either then or for a good twelve months afterwards, that there was any likelihood of Mary turning persecutor, or of her ever being in so strong a position as to be able to do this, supposing her character were now to change, and the queen become something she had never been hitherto.

There was, of course, the natural anxiety of a small group, whose chances of expansion would now be indefinitely lessened, not to be swallowed up in the nation at large, and there was the reluctance of such sturdy haters of everything Catholic to remain in a place where the idolatrous thing (for so undoubtedly they esteemed it) was allowed to breathe. ' The dominant note in all the letters and pamphlets of the period from August, 1553, onwards is " to flie the infection of the antechristian [sic] doctryne by departure oute of the realme " for fear of absorption.' [2]

The ' wrath ' which ultimately came for the Protestants in England, did not come until these exiles were comfortably established abroad, and it came, in no small measure, precisely because of the activities which occupied them abroad, and for the sake of which they had gone abroad. ' This we can assure you,' wrote David Whitehead, one of the pillars of the colony and church at Frankfort to Calvin, ' that that outrageous pamphlet of Knox's added much oil to the flame of persecution in England. For, before the publication of that book, not one of our brethren had suffered death : but as soon as it came forth, we doubt not but that you are well aware of the number of excellent men who have perished in the flame,' [3] The same might be said also of the literary labours of others too, notably of Thomas Becon and of Bishop John Ponet, an early English apologist of tyrannicide. The exodus was more truly described by

[1] POLLARD, p. 100.
[2] GARRETT, p. 40, quoting RIDLEY, *Piteous Lamentation*, Sig. C. 5vo.
[3] Letter of Sept. 20, 1555, quoted GARRETT, p. 15, from *Original Letters*, II, p. 761.

one among its members, Laurence Humphrey, who lived to write of it, in his life of Bishop Jewel, ' voluntarium in Germania exilium.' [1]

Study of the organisation of this exodus reveals in it the genius of William Cecil planning, very effectively, the first moves in the revolution from which has come the England of modern times. Cecil, at this time, was quite a young man, actually no more than thirty-three years of age, but already of rare and immense experience. He came of a family so obscure that even his great-grandfather's name is not recalled. He was born in the country where his family had begun to be prosperous, at Bourne, near to where Lincoln-shire touches Rutland and Northamptonshire. His grand-father had found some employ in the service of Henry VII and his father had been a page in the royal household. The grandfather was High Sheriff of Northamptonshire in 1529, and the father, Richard Cecil, High Sheriff of Rutland in 1539. Richard Cecil secured profitable grants of monastic property, and when he died, in 1552, William Cecil found himself, in the very opening of his public career, a really wealthy man. So it was that, later, he was to be one of the very few who were not beggared by a life given to the service of the mean and parsimonious Elizabeth. He was to find himself able to serve the State and to serve it honestly. Cecil's one great virtue was his inaccessibility to what is called ' graft.'

At fifteen he went to St. John's College, Cambridge; then ' the most famous place of education in England.' [2] It was the year in which the founder of the college, St. John Fisher, had given his life rather than accept that new doctrine of the Royal Supremacy which Wiliiam Cecil was, one day, to make the touchstone of English loyalty. Among the fellows of the college were Roger Ascham and John Cheke. Cecil, in 1541, married Cheke's sister, and on her death, in 1544, took for his second wife one Mildred Cooke. His erstwhile brother-in-law was now tutor to the heir to the throne, and his new father-in-law was the young prince's governor. *Funes ceciderunt in præclaris.* For a professional training Cecil had gone to the law, and when Henry VIII died, in 1547, he was able to share the new opportunities with Cheke and Cooke and the rest. Just a year later he

---

[1] *Vita Juelli*, cited GARRETT, p. 2.
[2] A. Jessop, in D.N.B., *Sir William Cecil*.

was made secretary to the Protector, Somerset, and though
he went to the Tower for a couple of months on Somerset's
fall, in 1549, he was politic enough—and already so well
understood as a knowledgeable man—to be able to cross
over to the side of Somerset's victorious rival, Warwick.

He now became Secretary of State (September, 1550) and
a Privy Councillor. With Cranmer, and others of the new
Protestant bishops, he was named a commissioner to try,
condemn, and burn the heretical Anabaptists, and when, in
October, 1551, Warwick had himself made duke of Northumberland and showered proportionate honours on all his
henchmen, Cecil was knighted. It was just seven months
later that his father died, leaving him wide estates in
Rutland, Lincolnshire, and Northamptonshire. The next
twelve months called out all Cecil's suppleness. Northumberland, his patron, was all-powerful, and Northumberland
was maturing his great conspiracy to maintain his hold on the
crown once the dying Edward VI passed from life. Cecil,
most reluctantly, did his patron's bidding, signed the act
devising the crown away from the lawful heirs—Mary and
Elizabeth—and also the oath to support the new succession.
When Edward died (July 6, 1553) and the reign of Queen
Jane began, Cecil's conduct was 'a miracle of evasion.'[1]
Never indeed were his great gifts of lying so marvellously
employed, nor more happily, if Cecil's own fortune is
considered. For Mary pardoned him, although she refused
to employ confidentially his singular abilities.

Sir William Cecil now became a most pious Catholic,
in his retirement at Wimbledon, begging the cardinal legate
for a dispensation to eat meat in Lent, for his stomach was
disordered, and, most vilely, making his Easter Communion
at the parish Mass in Wimbledon Church. Unmolested,
from behind this screen of sacrilege and hypocrisy he directed
the new venture that was to preserve Protestantism until
such a moment when it could once more be safely let loose
upon the English people. Sir William Cecil was now, in
fact, one of the four chiefs of the active Protestant party as
this continued after the executions of Northumberland and
Suffolk (1554). The other three were Suffolk's brother,
Lord John Grey ; William Parr, marquis of Northampton ;
and Francis Russell, afterwards earl of Bedford. Cecil was
the most powerful of the little group, the one man who

[1] POLLARD, p. 91.

GUL: CECILIUS Baro de Burghley Regni
Thesaur: Eques Periscelidis Obiit A.D.1598. Ætatis 77.

Sir William Cecil, K.G.

First Baron Burghley

(1520-1598)

'for years now had been familiar, intimately so, with the handling of executive machinery.' Here his gifts did not fall short of genius. Cecil is the experienced student of human nature in practice. He knows how the mass of mankind will act in any given situation, what motives will influence them, what arguments need to be proposed, and —which is perhaps of greatest importance—at what precise moment the argument must be proposed. And Cecil knew how committees work. Like every good secretary he knew how to work his committee. These four personages whom Dr. Garrett notes as a kind of executive for Protestant affairs in 1554, are later found to be a kind of executive for the alteration of religion in 1559.

By December, 1553, the body of twenty-six ' Sustainers ' had been organised, persons of wealth and influence who acted as a committee of ways and means. Five of the Sustainers 'were merchants who had already commercial affiliations with the cities of the Empire, especially with Strasburg,' [1] These five made themselves responsible for financing the scheme to train the students who should be, one day, the clergy of restored English Protestantism. Two months later, February 25, 1554, Peter Martyr, writing to Bullinger, records the arrival of the students at Strasburg. ' Each company travels . . . under a leader and is inevitably preceded by a courier sent ahead to make provision for it at its destination.' [2] The gentry, in similar fashion, travelled by households, and Mary's government, well aware of the migration, and seeing in it no more than the convenient departure out of the realm of troublesome extremists, put no obstacles in its way. [3]

Cecil's chief aids in the management of the party, once it was safely established abroad, were his father-in-law, Sir Antony Cooke, and a mysterious personage, who appears on every page of the record, but almost nowhere else in history, one Richard Chambers. Sir Antony Cooke was of the Strasburg colony, about which Dr. Garrett can note that the roll of its leaders is a ' catalogue of notabilities in Edward's reign, of conspirators in Mary's ' and that this colony was ' a centre for political propaganda . . . in constant touch with London, with Paris and with Rouen.' It was ' the foreign centre of Cecil's plans for the future.' Cooke's house was the ' headquarters of intrigue, from which

[1] GARRETT, p. 8.   [2] Ibid.   [3] Ibid., pp. 11–12.

emanated many of the mischievous pamphlets of Ponet
and Becon, which, by way of Emden, were carried into
England.' [1]

Strasburg was the headquarters of political activity.
The Emden colony was the centre of propaganda, where
were printed, and whence were put into circulation, the
pamphlets conveyed to London and the eastern counties
' by such agents of sedition as Trudgeover.' [2] The ' director
of propaganda ' was the scholar Sir John Cheke, tutor to
King Edward VI, and one-time secretary to ' Queen Jane '
tutor also once to Cecil and now brother-in-law.[3]

If Cooke's department was political organisation,
Chambers was in charge of the all-important matter of
finance. He is the agent continually *en route*, between
England and the Continent, and between the different
colonies, dispensing the alms, controlling the requests and
statements of cases. ' Œconomus et pater,' says Bullinger.
Frankfort was the headquarters of this ' centralised financial
control of the whole migration.' Frankfort was also the
scene of a most violent theological controversy which was
not without its effect on the later history of religion in
England. Here in fact there was produced, in 1555, a third
English liturgy largely—it would appear—the work of
Richard Cox, late Dean of Westminster, and an experienced
man in these matters, for he had been one of those who
compiled the Order of Communion in 1548, the First
Prayer Book of 1549, the English Ordinal of 1550, and the
Second Prayer Book of 1552. It was his leadership that
defeated John Knox's growing influence at Frankfort in
1555, and saved the colony (and perhaps the future of the
English State religion) from a total subjection to Calvin,
for whom Cox, thenceforward, stood for ' ostentation ; an
immoderate fervour in meddling ; and a proud and
confident manner in his carriage and language.' These are
curious characteristics for any friend of Knox to find
objectionable. They did not prevent Cox coming to the
logical—nay inevitable—finish, first as one of the private
committee which, in the interval between Elizabeth's
accession and the meeting of parliament, prepared the

[1] GARRETT, pp. 27–29.
[2] *Ibid.*, p. 116.
[3] ' This formidable alliance between the Protestant party and the Press is
one of the secrets of its rapid triumph over the Catholic majority.' GARRETT
p. 44.

Elizabethan edition of the Prayer Book imposed in 1559, and then as the first of the new line of bishops of Ely in 1560. An examination of the list of ' exiled ' gentry reveals the names of many of the best-known figures of Elizabethan history. There are the two Astleys, cousins of the queen, the famous duchess of Suffolk and her husband, Mr. Richard Bertie, over the concocted falsehood of whose piteous flight so many later generations were to shed tears, what time it fed their anti-Roman feeling. There are the chiefs of the great pirate families of Carew and Killigrew from Devon and Cornwall. The conspirator, Sir Henry Dudley, who came so near to accomplishing Mary's assassination, is on the list and several of his lieutenants. The Scarborough plotters of 1557—Cardinal Pole's nephew, their chief—are here, too, and with them some of those who were to be concerned in the treasons that preceded the French capture of Calais in 1558. There are various relations of Cecil—the close interrelation, by blood and marriage, of so many of this group is as interesting to notice as the like feature in the case of the Protestant plotters of 1688—and of the man who was to be almost as important as Cecil in the coming age, Sir Francis Walsingham, and there is finally Sir Francis Walsingham himself. Of these 148 nobles and gentlemen eighty-five only went to Germany. The rest went for the most part to France. In this French group were those for whom change of religion was chiefly important as a political opportunity and whose chief gravamen, after 1554, was the Spanish marriage. They were political conspirators pure and simple. It was in the German migration that the religious revolution was fostered through the Marian winter. Here were nurtured the seedlings that flourished in its second spring, and out of the eighty-five gentlemen gathered in Germany no fewer than forty-four are given as from the home counties and London. London and the home counties again supplied nearly a third of the ' students ' among the exiles, so far as the place of origin of these is known.[1] Nearly one-half of these students are university men (Oxford twenty, Cambridge twenty-nine), twenty of them fellows of their colleges.

The ordained clergy account for seventy-four names out of the 361 men settled in Germany. There are four bishops among them (Scory, once of Chichester; Ponet, once of

[1] Twenty-two out of seventy-four.

Winchester ; Bale, once of Ossory ; and Coverdale, once of Exeter). The deacons number twelve and those listed certainly as priests fifty also. Of these fifty all but nine had been ordained by the Catholic rite in the days previous to 1550, and nine were also ex-religious. The vast majority of the 110 clergy ordained under the new ritual of Cranmer's devising had, then, stayed in England, and for the most part there is no record of their molestation during Mary's reign—their deprivation for lack of orders excepted. It is also worth pointing out that only twenty-nine of these clergy who went into exile were married. Dr. Gairdner, for once, was very wide of the mark when he wrote that ' Hosts of married clergy also emigrated to the continent.' [1] We already knew that of the 360 priests deprived in the diocese of Norwich for marriage, only seven had crossed the seas, and that out of the sixty-nine similarly deprived in Bath and Wells all but one remained at home. Now we have the total list of married *emigré* clergy, and it is twenty-nine.[2] We do not know enough of the dioceses whence the fifty priests came to draw even tentative conclusions from the data, but we can note that nineteen of them came from the capital. Four only of these had been employed in purely parochial activities, and of the whole band of fifty, capitular dignitaries, university dons, chaplains, and tutors to various Protestant nobles account for more than a half. There were only fourteen parochial clergy out of the whole number of the exiles.

' There can be little doubt that the so-called " flight " of 1554 was not a flight but a migration, and as such, one of the most astute manœuvres that has ever carried a defeated political party to ultimate power.' [3] Nowhere is the importance of the personnel of the exile so strikingly shown as in the use made of it by Elizabeth in the first year of her reign. For from this tiny band are recruited almost all who will hold the key positions in the nascent Anglican establishment. Of the twenty-five sees vacant in 1559, by the deaths of ten Catholic bishops and Elizabeth's deprivation of fifteen more, fifteen sees [4] were immediately

---

[1] *English Church in the Sixteenth Century*, p. 391.
[2] FRERE, pp. 47–52, accounts for 1047 married clergy in seventeen out of the twenty-six dioceses.
[3] GARRETT, p. 1.
[4] Had Sampson not refused Norwich the number would have been sixteen.

filled from this group of exiled clergy while four others of the group became deans and seven archdeacons.

And the gentry came home too, some to sit in parliament and the Privy Council, and some, in these exalted places, to harass Cecil's plans in a manner quite unforeseen, for the years in which they had lain abroad had been years in which they had controlled their religious affairs with absolute freedom. They were the last of all mankind to rejoice in such an institution as the Royal Supremacy, and to the best of their ability they fought it off. In them and in their clerical allies lay the germ of the whole Puritan movement. But that is another story.

§ ii. THE PROTESTANT PLAN, 1558

Such was the Protestant Party at the moment when Elizabeth succeeded. We may now examine what they proposed to do, the dangers they anticipated and the means by which they hoped to escape them. All this we can find set out in the masterly exposition called the *Device for the Alteration of Religion*.[1] Cecil was probably, almost certainly, its author, for the paper reflects his policy and his ultimate action with such detailed fidelity that if it had not him as its first source we should have to posit as a power behind Cecil an unknown political genius superior even to him.

The *Device* is a short enough document, hardly too long to reproduce here in the text. The contents are arranged under seven questions : (1) When shall the alteration be first attempted ? (2) What dangers may ensue upon the alteration ? (3) What remedy for these matters ? (4) What shall be the manner of doing it ? (5) What may be done of her highness, for her own conscience, openly, before the whole alteration : or, if the alteration must tarry longer, what order be fit to be in the whole realm, as an interim ? (6) What noblemen be most fit to be made privy to these proceedings, before it be opened to the whole Council ? (7) What allowance those learned men shall have for the time they are about to review the book of Common Prayer and the order of ceremonies, and service in the Church, and where they shall meet ?

Religion, then, is going to be altered, and the first attempt

---

[1] Text in TIERNEY, II, App., p. ccxxx.

may not succeed. A selected body of divines meeting in
secret is to arrange the new Prayer Book. The arrangements
are to be first passed by a secret cabinet of four noblemen.
Among these arrangements some are temporary, to provide
a means for Elizabeth to halt between Catholicism and
Protestantism should the first attempt miss fire, and to provide that while Catholicism still remains a lawful and recognised religion the whole realm may yet be weaned away from
it. The *Device* is a singularly business-like piece of work.
It is ready with the names of the committee of 'learned
men as be meet to show their minds herein,' Dr. Bill, Dr.
Parker, Dr. May, Dr. Cox, Mr. Whitehead, Mr. Grindal,
Mr. Pilkington—the last four of whom recent exiles in
Germany. Sir Thomas Smith is to call them together and
it is in his house that they will meet with something more
than ' two mess of meat,' which ' is thought yet indifferent,
to suffice for them and their servants.' And let ' provision
be laid in of wood, of coals, and drink.' The inner cabinet
of nobles are the marquis of Northampton, the earl of
Bedford, the earl of Pembroke, and Lord John Grey.

The writer calls for the attempt to be made at the first
meeting of parliament : the sooner the trial of strength
comes the better. He reviews the reaction which may be
expected abroad. The Pope ' all that he may, will be
incensed,' but this will not go further than excommunications,
interdicts, and intrigues with foreign princes, although, ' by
reason of the clergy that is so addicted to Rome ' the papal
hostility will mean trouble in Ireland. Nowhere is there any
mention of Spain, the king of which country, Philip II, had
until within a few weeks been king of England too, and who
was still England's ally in the war with France. It is indeed
from France that the *Device* looks chiefly for trouble, and
from France's ally Scotland, whose young queen, Mary, was
lately married to the Dauphin. The English attack on
Catholicism, it is conceived, will encourage the French to
continue the war, as a struggle now against heretics also,
in which they may naturally expect aid from the English
faithful to Catholicism. This very serious danger the
author of the *Device* would counter by negotiating a peace
with France and by intriguing ' to help to kindle ' religious
controversy there. A like policy is urged for Scotland,
intrigues ' to help forward their divisions, and especially
to augment the hope of them who incline to good religion.'

The danger from the Pope is dismissed in a contemptuous couple of lines.

More important, however, than foreign reactions, is the question of domestic opposition. All the Council and office holders and supporters of the late Catholic queen will steadfastly refuse to assent. Every possible means is to be tried, therefore, to involve them legally in some offence, in order to destroy their credit and standing with the Catholic body. And they are only to be pardoned upon confessing their guilt. At the same time all who have, in the late reign, stood by Elizabeth must now, as a matter of elementary propaganda, ' be advanced with authority and credit.' Everywhere those professing Protestantism are to be put into office, for even ' if in the cause of religion, God's cause, they shall be slack, yet their own safety and state shall cause [them] to be vigilant, careful, and earnest. . . .'

The bishops and all the clergy ' in confession and preaching, and all other ways they can, . . . will persuade the people from it,' i.e. the alteration, and will shrink from no extreme. Wherefore, once again, every attempt must be made—' her majesty . . . must seek, as well by parliament, as by the just laws of England '—to involve them in an offence under the præmunire laws, and they must not be pardoned ' till they confess their fault, put themselves wholly to her highness' mercy,[1] abjure the Pope of Rome, and conform themselves to the new alteration.' ' By this means well handled,' the writer adds, ' her majesty's necessity of money may be somewhat relieved.'

Bishop Mathew has already vividly drawn the picture of Queen Mary's court, and shown the great officers, the ministers of state, and indeed the whole body of those personally devoted to her, as an elderly generation. And the Venetian ambassador's remark that no one under thirty-five has had any personal interest in the restoration of religion is testimony to the same effect. Now, in striking contrast, the *Device* urges that a bid be made to capture the youth, and those with fortunes to make. All the machinery of local government, the justices of the peace, for example, are to be put out and in their place ' men meaner in substance, and younger in years ' ; for lieutenants in every shire men

---

[1] This was, of course, the procedure adopted, successfully, by Henry VIII to bring the clergy to heel in 1531. He made an enormous sum of money out of it, £100,000, perhaps £2,000,000 of our purchasing power.

are to be chosen, known to be devoted to Elizabeth, and for captains ' young gentlemen which earnestly do favour her highness.' In these captains' hands are to be armed forces which will everywhere suppress ' murmurs ' and ' assemblies ' against the new arrangement. And, anticipating trouble from those Protestants for whom the new arrangement will not go far enough, the *Device* recommends ' strait laws ' and ' severe execution of the same at the first.'

The universities must not be neglected, nor Eton, nor Winchester, if only for the sake of the future.

What is to be done until the alteration is lawfully carried through and Catholicism has no longer any legal existence ? First of all a ' strait prohibition of all innovation, until such time as the book come forth.' This will secure that there is but one alteration for the country to witness. If change follows change the prestige of authority will suffer. Also such a prohibition will ' exercise the queen's majesty's subjects to obedience '—a further hint at the coming Puritan troubles. But while there is this ' strait prohibition,' the *Device* allows for the liturgical changes already made by the queen, and proposes these as the present limit of change, except communion under both kinds on the great feasts, and that all the priests assisting at Mass ' do always communicate in both kinds '—an ingenious addition of a rite that in no way contradicts Catholic doctrine, but at the same time insinuates a heresy and which is, in point of fact, a rite lately revived under heretical auspices and with a heretical intention. Finally, to ease the queen's conscience, until ' the book ' is lawfully commanded, ' some other devout set of prayers or memory said ; *and the seldomer mass.*' [1]

§ iii. THE PROTESTANT TRIUMPH, 1558–1559

Two days only after Elizabeth's accession, before she had even left her manor of Hatfield for the capital, the first step was taken, and a proclamation issued, that ' the Queen straitly charges and commands all manner our subjects of every degree not to attempt upon any pretence, the breach, alteration, or change of any order or usage, presently established within this our realm upon pain of our indignation, and the pains and penalties which thereunto may in

---

[1] Italics not in original.

any wise belong.'[1] This served at first to allay the fears of Catholics.

In the correspondence of the foreign ambassadors we can trace the way in which, during the next five or six weeks, opinions veered and speculation soared as to whether the new reign would mean the maintenance of Mary's restoration or the re-establishment of Protestantism in one form or another. Then, on Christmas Day, the queen began to show her hand. She sent a message, while the choir were singing the *Gloria in Excelsis,* to the bishop of Carlisle who was singing the Mass, bidding him not to elevate the Blessed Sacrament after the consecration. The bishop replied with a refusal and after the Gospel the queen and her attendants left the chapel. Here was change indeed. The queen had refused to make the most public of all acts of faith in the Real Presence, and she had also, deliberately, missed Mass, and she had chosen for her action the first great feast to happen in her reign. Two days later there came out the second proclamation,[2] cleverly worded to embrace a stern prohibition to enthusiasts who would anticipate the royal plans, but—more seriously for the Catholics—muzzling all comment from the pulpit on what was now about to be attempted in parliament. And the priest was allowed to read in English the Epistle and Gospel of the day, the Ten Commandments, the Lord's Prayer, the Creed, and—a hint here plain for all—'the common litany used at this present in her majesty's own chapel.'[3] This prohibition is to continue until parliament has come to a decision about the religious question. There is, then, change in prospect : this is a first official notification of it to the nation, and in it there is a threat of punishment for all who oppose ' the true advancement ' of religion, which ' her majesty most desireth and meaneth effectually by all manner of means possible, to procure and to restore to this her realm.'

The day fixed for the Coronation—January 15, 1559— was drawing near, and the bishops, certain of one thing, namely, that if the queen swore the accustomed oath to protect the Church she would be perjuring herself and,

---

[1] POLLEN, p. 18, quoting from STRYPE, *Annals,* i, ii, 389 ; this proclamation is not in GEE and HARDY.

[2] G. and H., No. LXXVII.

[3] A litany which still prayed for delivery from ' the tyranny of the Bishop of Rome and all his detestable enormities.'

fresh from her perjury, seal it with a sacrilegious communion, refused unanimously to crown her. Elizabeth had proposed not to take the oath, but Cecil, anxious that it should not be alleged against her that the rite of the crowning had been so seriously mutilated, persuaded her to the contrary. And, finally, one of the bishops, Oglethorpe of Carlisle, was induced to crown her. But the Mass was sung by a married priest, who omitted the elevation, and a sermon was preached by a notorious Protestant. All the bishops were present at the Coronation and testified to the oath, but when the Mass began they left the Church.

It was with the stage so set that parliament was opened ten days later, and on February 9 the government brought in their scheme for the alteration of religion. There is no need to repeat here, what has been told so often and so well already,[1] the story of the three months' struggle to pass the two laws which are the foundation on which is built modern England, the Elizabethan acts of Supremacy and Uniformity. It is a complicated story, where much still remains hidden. The first bill survived its introduction but a week—it was a measure which combined what both the acts afterwards effected. On February 22 a second attempt was made to do the trick with an omnibus bill. This got through the Commons in three days, but, after a first reading in the Lords on February 28, it was held up for a fortnight and then extensively altered in committee. The liturgical changes were cut out, and the Supremacy was left to the queen's choice. This Catholic rally may have been due to the strong unanimous protest of Convocation, occasioned by the news that traditional Catholic doctrine was once more in danger.[2] The Lords passed the bill as amended in

[1] *Cf.* Maitland's brilliant and masterly account—a *locus classicus* of English historical scholarship—in the *Cambridge Modern History*, Vol. II, ch. xvi : MAGEE does not accept it as proved that this was not a packed parliament ; he shows how the geographical distribution of the seats alr ady favoured Protestant districts ; he recalls what Maitland had already pointed out, the astonishing number of absentees from the debates in the Lords ; had all the Catholic lords appeared and voted, and had there been the full number of bishops, the Bills could not have passed : *op. cit.*, p. 15.

[2] This too little known document, a petition to the bishops from the Lower House of Convocation, deserves to be rescued from such limbos as Wilkins and Tierney, where it is only accessible to the specially interested student. It is not printed in Gee and Hardy's classic collection of documents which the general student is likely to want !

' Reverend Fathers in Christ, and most worthy lords.

' It has lately come to our notice, as a matter of general knowledge, that many dogmas of the Christian religion, received and approved up to this

committee on March 18—it was the eve of Palm Sunday. But meanwhile the Commons, on the 17th and 18th, had rushed through a new bill which revived and imposed the Prayer Book of 1552. When the amended bill came down to them from the Lords, they incorporated with it the new bill they had themselves just passed, and on Spy Wednesday —March 22—the Lords accepted this new arrangement and gave it its three readings in the one day. It only remained to give the bill the royal assent, and now hesitation on the part of the queen held it up.

What caused this hesitation is not known. The bishops had made a strenuous fight against every suggestion of change, and the speeches of two of them, Nicholas Heath,

by the public and universal agreement of Christian peoples, and handed down without discord from the Apostles even to ourselves, are being called in question, and notably the points written here below.

'Wherefore, We, the lower, secondary clergy of the province of Canterbury being gathered together (God so willing, and commanded by the orders of our most serene Lady the Queen, of the Dean and Chapter of Canterbury, by the writ of parliament and the wonted published ecclesiastical summons) have thought it to be among our present duties to make provision in every manner possible for the eternal salvation, as well of our own selves, so that of all those committed to us in cure.

'In which respect, moved by the example of our ancestors, whose lot fell often in times like our own, We have thought it well publicly to assert, for the praise and honour of God, for the fulfilment of our duty and that cure of souls which is laid upon us, the faith which we believe, and from our souls profess to be the true faith on the points here underwritten.

'We affirm and, so God help us in the day of judgment, we assert :

'1. That in the sacrament of the altar, by force of the word of Christ duly pronounced by the priest, there is present really, under the appearances of bread and wine, the natural body of Christ, conceived of the Virgin Mary ; and in the same way His natural blood.

'2. That, after the consecration, the substance of bread and wine does not remain, nor any other substance, except the substance of God and man.

'3. That in the mass the true body of Christ and His true blood is offered, a propitiatory sacrifice for the living and the dead.

'4. That, to the apostle Peter, and to his lawful successors in the apostolic see, there has been given, as the vicars of Christ, the supreme power of pasturing and ruling the church militant of Christ, and of strengthening their brethren.

'5. That the authority to treat of or to define whatever concerns the faith, the sacraments and ecclesiastical discipline has hitherto belonged, and ought to belong, to the pastors of the church alone, whom the Holy Ghost has placed in the Church of God for this purpose, and not to laymen.

'We, the aforesaid lower clergy, for the reasons we have mentioned, by the tenor of these presents, set forth to Your Paternities, this our assertion and our affirmation and our faith. We humbly petition that, since we have no means of making known otherwise, to those whom the matter concerns, this our opinion and our will, you, who are our fathers, will signify these things to the higher authorities. By doing which, You will—as we think— perform an office of charity and of affection, provide for the salvation of your flocks and set free your own souls.' (Latin text printed in TIERNEY, II, App., p. cclxi, from Wilkins' *Concilia*, Vol. IV, p. 179.)

the archbishop of York, and Cuthbert Scott, bishop of
Chester, still survive to testify to the identity of the faith of
the English Church at this moment with the faith of all the
thousand years that separated it from St. Augustine and
St. Gregory, as well as with the faith of all 'Roman
Catholics' of to-day. On the third reading of the bill as
the Lords had amended it—March 18—the bishops, by
no means satisfied, voted unanimously against it, and two
lay lords voted with them. They were, however, in a
minority of twenty (thirty-two—twelve). The bishops were
no less unanimous in the final division on Spy Wednesday.
How could a bill be said to be enacted 'by the Lords
spiritual and temporal' against which every spiritual peer
voting had voted at every stage ?

It has been suggested that it was with some hope of
breaking this episcopal *bloc* that the royal assent was delayed.
And it has also been suggested that the government hoped
to compromise some of the bishops in the coming public
disputations on religious doctrine. On the other hand Mr.
Magee argues [1] that the cause of the delay was that the Lords
did *not*, on March 22, accept the bill as the Commons had
sent it to them, and, in that one day, pass it through all its
stages. In support of this helpful thesis he quotes the
report of the Venetian ambassador (March 28), that parliament had adjourned for Easter with the two houses at a
deadlock. 'Although they (*i.e.* the Lords) had passed the
clause about the Supremacy of the Church,' the ambassador
writes, 'they did so under such restrictions that the Commons
would by no means consent to it. They are therefore in
greater discord than ever, and on Thursday, after the
Easter holidays, they will sit and reconsider the matter,
which is committed to four good and Catholic bishops, and
to four of their Protestants.'

Whatever the facts of this mysterious business, we know
that a royal proclamation was prepared, but not published,
announcing the restoration of the Prayer Book of 1552 as
accomplished, that as an incidental result of the disputation
of March 31 and April 3 two of the bishops were imprisoned
and the rest laid under bond to appear daily before the
Council, and that on April 10 an entirely new bill was laid
before the Commons. This was a bill to establish the
Royal Supremacy and this alone, and it passed without a

[1] MAGEE, p. 18.

division. It passed its second reading in the Lords on the 17th, and in Committee the penalties were considerably modified. Then, April 26, it passed its third reading, with eleven votes *contra*, namely all the bishops present and Viscount Montague.

The bill abolishing the Mass—the Act of Uniformity—was introduced in the Commons while the other bill was in Committee in the Lords, April 18. It passed the Commons without a division and it passed through the Lords without any Committee. But here it nearly met its fate, and the third reading passed by only three votes (twenty-one—eighteen), April 28. In the minority were the nine bishops at liberty and nine lay lords. Four spiritual peers (three bishops and one abbot) were hindered from attendance.[1]

Both acts received the royal assent, on May 8, when parliament was dissolved.

The Act of Supremacy set up, once again, the ecclesiastical creation of King Henry VIII. It revived the eight acts of parliament of his reign which had been repealed under Mary, and enacted that 'no foreign . . . prelate . . . shall exercise any . . . jurisdiction . . . spiritual or ecclesiastical within this realm . . . but the same shall be clearly abolished out of this realm . . . for ever.' Whatever 'jurisdiction . . . spiritual and ecclesiastical as by any spiritual or ecclesiastical power or authority hath hitherto been lawfully exercised . . . shall for ever . . . be united and annexed to the imperial crown of this realm.' As in King Henry's time, so now, there was provided an oath ; by this 'every ecclesiastical person,' judges, mayors, and lay officers shall declare their acceptance of the new doctrine : 'I, A— B—, do utterly testify and declare in my conscience that the Queen's Highness is the only supreme governor of this realm . . . as well in all spiritual or ecclesiastical things or causes as temporal, and that no foreign . . . prelate . . . hath or ought to have any jurisdiction . . . ecclesiastical or spiritual within this realm and therefore I do utterly renounce and forsake all foreign jurisdiction . . . and to my power shall assist and defend all jurisdiction . . . granted to the Queen's Highness . . . or annexed to the imperial crown of this realm.'

The penalty for refusing the oath was, for office holders,

[1] This account of the passage of the two acts follows that of Professor Pollard, *op. cit.*, pp. 200–208.

loss of office, and in the case of nominees to an office, avoidance of appointment. Four years later the penalties were increased.[1] A first refusal, after 1563, entailed the penalties of præmunire, *i.e.* loss of all goods and life imprisonment, while a second refusal was high treason and punishable with death. Those who in any way continued ' to affirm, hold . . . maintain or defend ' the papal jurisdiction now annexed to the crown, were liable [2] on a first conviction to a loss of all property (and if the property was below £20 value to a year's imprisonment also) : for a second offence the punishment was as in cases of præmunire, and for a third offence— adjudged high treason—death. The act of 1563 extended the obligation to take the oath to all members of the House of Commons, to all barristers and attorneys, to all officers of all courts, to schoolmasters also, and to public and private teachers of children.

The Act of Uniformity restores the Prayer Book of 1552 with certain alterations. From the feast of St. John the Baptist next (Saturday, June 24, 1559) it is this book alone which shall be used for all the services and administration of the sacraments in all the cathedrals and parish churches of the realm. Any ' parson, vicar, or other whatsoever minister ' [3] who (1) refuses to use the services as set forth in this book, or (2) uses any other rite ' openly or privily,' or (3) shall preach or speak in derogation of it is to be punished. For the first offence he will lose a year's income and be imprisoned for six months. For a second offence he loses his benefice and is sent to prison for a year. For a third offence he goes to prison for life. Lay critics of the book ' in any interludes, plays, songs, rhymes, or by other open words,' or who maintain priests to use other rites are, for the first offence, fined 100 marks and for the second 400 marks, while for a third offence they are to lose all their property and suffer life imprisonment. Finally, every inhabitant of the realm is, every Sunday and holy day, to attend service in his parish church, under penalty of a fine of 12d. for every time he is absent, the fine to be levied by the churchwardens and put to the use of the poor ; and the churchwardens are given power to distrain for the amount on the property of the offender.

[1] 5 Eliz. c. 1, PROTHERO, p. 39.
[2] By the act of 1559.
[3] It is of interest that the act does not say ' priest.'

This legislation came into force, the Act of Supremacy on May 8, the Act of Uniformity on June 24, 1559. Between that date and January 4, 1570, no Catholic was put to death in England for cause connected with his religion. As this decade is, for this reason, sometimes described as a period when Catholics were loyal to the queen and therefore undisturbed by persecution, and as it is from those who matured during these ten years that the more active Catholicism of the period 1570–1590 developed, it is as well to state exactly what freedom these acts [1] left the Catholic Englishman. He was indeed free, *i.e.* the law would not interfere with his property, his liberty, or his life, so long as he was content never to hear Mass again or to receive Holy Communion ; content that his children should be brought up without either ; willing to go Sunday by Sunday to his parish church to sit through a service he regarded as heretical and to listen to sermons which condemned his own beliefs as idolatry, superstition, and treason ; so long as he carefully refrained from any expression of opinion on these extensive changes ; so long as he had no ambition for a public career, no desire or need to be either lawyer or schoolmaster ; and so long as he did not have to sue a livery from the crown on coming into his property. Otherwise he was speedily enmeshed. From these very first months of the reign, before the Pope had even heard of England's apostasy, while Philip of Spain was still England's good ally, before any Catholic had so much as moved in thought against the victorious Protestants, in the very acts that refounded their religious establishment, means were ingeniously provided to make social life wellnigh impossible for all but the Protestant party and those who, by apostasy, would join them.

The Act of Uniformity gave the queen power to appoint commissioners to administer the Oath of Supremacy and to see to the execution of the liturgical revolution. They were nominated on the day the act came into force, fourteen of them in all, and all laymen but one, Edwin Sandys, a returned exile soon to be Bishop of Worcester. During the summer and autumn of 1559 the commissioners toured the country, everywhere offering the new oath to those bound to take it, and seeing to the destruction of altars, shrines, statues, stained glass, and all those hundreds of significant

[1] As completed by the act of 1563.

furnishings that accompany the cult of the Mass and of the
Holy Eucharist. At the turn of the year the first new
bishops were consecrated, and presently there began to
appear a new series of episcopal injunctions which, with
careful detail, restored the sacramental and ritual desolation
of the time of Edward VI.[1]

§ iv. The Outmanœuvred Catholics, 1559-1570

Everywhere the execution of the new laws met with opposition. Henry VIII had seen the whole body of the clergy
swear to his supremacy. Edward VI had seen a new
liturgy generally accepted. Few indeed were those who had
risked their heads or even lost their livings. But now, in
1559, every bishop, save one, stood firm and by the end of
the year all had been deprived of their sees and placed in
custody. Everywhere, too, the higher clergy stood firm,
the cathedral dignitaries, the heads of colleges, and the
professors in the universities. Nor were the religious
orders less loyal. Along with the bishops, seven deans of
cathedral chapters were deprived, ten archdeacons, seven
chancellors, twenty-five heads of colleges (nineteen at
Oxford, six at Cambridge) and, at Oxford, thirty-seven
fellows of colleges.

The parochial clergy were less resolute, or less attached to
the Catholic doctrines. We do not know the exact number
of priests in England in 1559, nor do we know the exact
number of those who took the new oath. There has,
inevitably, been much controversy about the proportion
that accepted the new arrangements. Gee—an Anglican
scholar—gives the total number of clergy in the four sees
of London, Norwich, Ely, and Coventry-Lichfield as 2200,
and of these he discovered that 1453 took the oath—roughly
two-thirds. Dom Norbert Birt, O.S.B., estimates the proportion, for the whole country, of those who remained loyal as
somewhat lower. He considers that the total number of
priests would be about 8000 and that 2000 refused the
oaths. This is the most generous estimate of any scholar
as to the proportion of priests who stood by the old ways.
Even if we accept it we must still be somewhat halted at

[1] The visitation articles and injunctions of the period 1560-1574 can be
read in Frere and Kennedy, *op. cit.*, Vol. III ; they reproduce, substantially, those summarised already, *cf.* pp. 16-17, 22-23.

surrender on such a scale, for the penalty (until 1563) went no further than deprivation.[1] How many of these men were Catholics at heart, and in their heart never denied the papal primacy, no man can say or even guess. Many of them we know, from various contemporary witnesses, continued to say Mass in secret while they celebrated the new liturgy in public. The state of mind and the theological knowledge which could allow such a sacrilegious incongruity as this, would be capable of anything. Certainly Habbakuk would hardly boggle at a mere oath of Supremacy. To understand the mind of such compromisers, of priests who could be Catholic in Mary's reign and Protestant in Elizabeth's, may not be easy, but the fact loses some of its first difficulty of acceptance when there is recalled the milieu which bred the most of those who were priests in 1559. For four years, it is true, there had been full opportunity and every inducement to be Catholic. But those four years were a very small proportion of the thirty years that had passed since England last knew the peace of normal undisturbed Catholicism. No priest under fifty, at the moment when the Elizabethan testing came, could recall any years of priesthood passed in that normal time. The majority of the clergy of 1559 had been formed in the years since Henry VIII broke with Rome, and they had learnt what theology they knew in the generation which saw, on the part of their seniors, a wholesale acceptance of the Royal Supremacy. What kind of doctrine *de Romano Pontifice* had been current in the Oxford and Cambridge schools after 1530 is too well known to need exemplifying. And for long years before Henry died there had been as much heresy about the Holy Eucharist—and heretical caricature of the Catholic doctrine—circulating in those learned places as there had been orthodox teaching. The marvel surely is not that so many of the clergy bred in that generation changed with every wind, but that so many were found, as the event proved, with sufficient grasp of principle to resist.

Of the many testimonies that remain to describe the confusion of the first months of the new régime we may cite John Jewell, returned exile and soon to be bishop of Salisbury, writing to Peter Martyr, August 1, 1559 [2] : ' Now that

---

[1] In Henry VIII's time it had always been death.
[2] Six weeks after the Prayer Book had been obligatory, three months after the passing of the acts.

religion is everywhere changed, the Mass priests absent
themselves altogether from public worship, as if it were the
greatest impiety to have anything in common with the
people of God.' Nearly a year later (July 10, 1560) another
very influential returned exile—Thomas Lever—writes to
Bullinger : ' Many of our parishes have no clergymen, and
some dioceses are without a bishop. And out of that very
small number who administer the sacraments throughout
the country, there is hardly one in a hundred who is both
able and willing to preach the Word of God.' Twenty years
and more after the settlement had been enacted, another
Lancashire man, a Catholic this time, Edward Rishton,
set himself to write—with Sander's notes to aid him—an
account of the religious history of the reign. He speaks of
the idea widely prevalent, in the early days of the new
establishment, that it was not wrong for Catholics to
conform with the queen's religion if they did so merely outwardly, from obedience to the queen. ' This opinion was
adopted also by the lower clergy, simple and parish priests,
not a few canons of cathedrals and collegiate churches,
who in their hearts hated the heresy, and for a time, listening
to the voice of conscience, refrained from the use of the new
service. So general was this, that after the day appointed
by the statute on which the true sacrifice was to cease and the
false rites were to begin, many churches throughout the
kingdom remained shut for some months ; for the old priests
would not willingly use the schismatical service, and the
new ministers were not yet numerous enough to serve so
many places.' [1]

For the first ten years of the reign we must see a considerable body of loyal Catholic priests, ' lurking ' is the
favourite adjective the new bishops use in their everlasting
complaints to Cecil about them, and a still greater number
of priests Catholic at heart but outwardly conforming to the
new discipline and doctrine—these last, by the law that
operates in such cases, year by year less Catholic and more
Protestant. And meanwhile there are beginning to be
ordained the first Protestant clergy, not at first, it must be
admitted, the most desirable of types, but, as the reign goes
on and the universities recover from the almost fatal blow
of 1559, approximating more and more to Calvin's ideal.
We know more of the harvesting of Allen's priests from the

[1] SANDER, p. 266.

college at Douay after 1574, and still more, perhaps, of the
epic year of Fr. Campion's great endeavour, than we know
of the work of the Marian priests in the years that went
before. Yet their sound, continuous and successful apostolate is implied in every recognition of the success of the later
generation, and the leading spirits of that later age plainly
acknowledge the debt. For these apostles, bred of Pole's
short-lived renaissance, that Mr. John Peel may stand as a
worthy instance, whom the *Douay Diary* commemorates : [1]
' a priest who for now sixteen years, at great danger to his
life, has laboured exceedingly, reconciling men to the
Catholic faith, and strengthening others lest they fail.'
Blessed Edmund Campion writes to his Father General,
and, describing the fervour with which the persecuted
Catholics approach the sacraments, says, ' for the ministra-
tion whereof we are ever well assisted by priests whom we
find in every place (quos reperimus ubique) whereby both
the people is well served, and we much eased, in our charge,' [2]
Another witness is Dr. Humphrey Ely,[3] once of St. John's
College, Oxford, then professor of Canon Law at Douay,
one of the company that came with Campion and Parsons
into England in 1580. He recalls the struggle in the first
years of Elizabeth's reign to keep the Catholics clear of
the Protestant services, and the great work of instruction
then done. 'The second praise of planting and teaching
this better opinion belongeth as well to many ancient
priests of Queen Marie's days that stood firm and stable in
their faith, and drew daily some out of the mire of schism
by preaching and teaching, whereof I myself am a witness,
having known many that were reconciled by them. . . .'
We have Allen's words also to the same effect,[4] and a report [5]
made to Rome, nearly forty years after the Protestant victory
of 1559, states that there are still between forty and fifty
Marian priests at work in different parts of the country.
As the pomp and circumstance of the ' Second Spring '
for long threw into the shade the solid work of the Vicars-
Apostolic from which so much of its achievement came, so,
it may be thought, devotion to the seminary priests and the

[1] KNOX, p. 104 ; Second Diary, May 12, 1576.
[2] November, 1580 ; translation in SIMPSON, p. 248, and POLLEN, p. 370.
[3] Quoted KNOX, LXII, from *Certain Brief notes, etc.*, p. 67.
[4] Letter to Vendeville, Sept. 18, 1578, or 1580, in KNOX, LXII.
[5] By Fr. William Holt, S.J., in 1596, printed KNOX, p. 378, from Archives
of the See of Westminster, IX, p. 443.

religious missionaries has somewhat unfairly obscured the important fact of the spiritual effect of the priests whom Pole and his bishops reconciled or ordained.

Violent hatred of the Pope, an almost insane hatred of the Mass, are the most obvious qualities of the early Elizabethan Protestantism, and after 1570 Foxe's *Book of Martyrs* and the new papal initiative against the Protestant government of England supply fresh occasion and further food for bitterness towards the Catholics themselves. But from the beginning the Protestants are well in the saddle: 'the new men held all the churches [*lege* pulpits, and understand the chief means of influencing public opinion], all public education, all offices, and the irresistible force of the Crown,' [1] And to this we must add the command of the press,[2] the most enduring means of forming and holding educated opinion, and add also the steady pressure driving the Catholic from all centres of political and social activity.

It is necessary thus to recall not only the thing done in 1559, but also what manner of men they were who did it, and by what manner of means the thing was done, for it is fundamental to any understanding of the Catholic reaction to realise that, to the Catholics, the religious revolution was simply the victory of a factious minority, of a clique which by skilful trickery had possessed itself of the confidence of the sovereign and the machinery of government. The nation, it was their constant contention, was still Catholic and a Catholic nation was, from 1559, in the grip of a small heretical minority.[3] What was the immediate effect of the change on the lay members of this Catholic majority ? The specialists begin by warning us they have not much to tell

[1] POLLEN, p. 44.
[2] *Cf.* GARRETT, p. 157 : ' To the close association between Foxe and John Day may in very large part be attributed the eventual triumph of the reformation in England,' and, *ibid.*, p. 104 : ' It was Day—the printer of much of the seditious literature of Mary's reign—who, to quote his epitaph, " first set a Foxe to wright how Martyrs runne." '
[3] *Cf.* Allen's *True, Sincere and Modest Defence of English Catholics*, 1584. ' We set forth the truth of all these actions for the honour of our nation, which otherwise, to her infinite shame and reproach, would be thought wholly generally to have revolted from the Catholic faith. . . .' The truth is that the disorder proceeds only from ' the partiality of a few powerful persons abusing Her Majesty's clemency and credulity . . .' and ' the whole state (excepting the authority of the Prince) may yet be rather counted Catholic than heretical,' *cf.* p. 5 of the 1913 reprint of this classic piece of English writing.

us. ' Particulars are, alas, hardly to be recovered now.' [1]
A few, very few, meagre statistics, and deductions from the
ever-recurring complaints of bishops to Council and Council
to bishops about the obstinacy of papists, occasional remarks,
obiter scripta, in the correspondence of the time, are all we
possess, outside the testimony of the Catholics themselves.
It seems fairly certain from the testimony of Catholics who
were witnesses of what they described, that at first the greater
part of the Catholics went to the new services, and the fight
against ' Church Going ' is the first sign of any real reaction
against the revolution of 1559. Simpson explains [2] that this
change of service ' was no great novelty to them. For thirty
years they had been used to these variations, some of which
had been made on illegitimate authority, some, as Mary's
restoration, rightfully ; but all had come proximately to
the people on the authority of the State, whether it was the
State acting schismatically or acting in obedience to Rome.'
Father Pollen [3] (who, however, thinks that ' the majority
simply kept away from Church ') speaks of the Catholics
as ' waiting for another change of the royal whim, of which
they had experienced so many. Three creed-compelling
sovereigns had died in eleven years and the reigning queen
was far from strong. Or again she might marry a Catholic,
for there was as yet no Protestant prince who was her peer.'
In any attempt to reconstruct the frame of mind of convinced
Catholics who could, at such a moment, give this apparent
approval of the change by assisting at the new services,
this also must be taken into account that the services were
for the most part simply the Morning and Evening Prayer
of the new rite, made up of psalms, readings from Holy
Scripture and prayers which were very largely translations
of prayers used in the Catholic services. For by a curious
paradox the Protestant heresy which had begun by taking
scandal that at the daily Mass so few communicated (and
at private Masses, not infrequently, no one at all), and which
to remedy this state of affairs taught that all the congregation must communicate whenever the Holy Eucharist was
celebrated, and which had so stressed the receiving of the
sacrament that the sacrificial nature of the Holy Eucharist
was all but denied entirely, the Protestant heresy, now
supreme, brought it about that the Communion Service
was one of the rare events in the Christian's life. Not even

[1] POLLEN, p. 94.   [2] SIMPSON, p. 201.   [3] POLLEN, p. 44.

once in the week was this substitute for the Mass made available. Whatever the cause for this comparative indifference, the injunctions of the first Protestant bishops testify that they were content if, in their very cathedrals, the Eucharistic liturgy was celebrated once a month, and in the parish churches it speedily became a quarterly service. The Catholic who went to the new heretical service did not often risk taking scandal from its major offence.

Professor Kennedy[1] quotes evidence from visitation reports and from the correspondence of the Protestant bishops, to show how, in the first years of the reign, there was strong opposition to the settlement and, with a widespread refusal to attend the new services, a general conspiracy to maintain the Mass in secret. And this was not confined to any one particular locality, for he has in mind, and quotes evidence concerning, the sees of York, Durham, Carlisle, Chester, Ely, Norwich, London, Chichester, Salisbury, St. Asaph, Hereford, and Bath and Wells. But ' by force or fraud it came to pass that the largest portion of the Catholics yielded by degrees to their enemies '—it is a Catholic contemporary who is speaking—' and did not refuse from time to time publicly to enter the schismatical church to hear sermons therein and to receive communion in these conventicles.' So Rishton,[2] writing in 1585, and he attributes the change to the whipping-up of the local Protestant officials by the bishops' visitations and to the consequent systematic fining of the absentees.

Cardinal Allen's recollections of these years, seem to bear out Rishton. In a long letter to his friend, the co-founder of Douay College, Dr. John Vendeville, he speaks [3] of his labour in England thirteen to sixteen years previously, and tells how his arguments and his instructions on the authority of the Church and the Apostolic See brought it about ' in a very short time that a vast number . . . abstained altogether from the communion, churches, sermons, books, and all spiritual communication with heretics.' Allen seems to suggest that it was all but inevitable that many should have fallen. Fidelity is ' a most difficult thing to obtain in that country, because of the iniquitous laws, and the punishment of imprisonment, as

---

[1] *Parish Life*, Ch. VII, ' Parochial Catholicism.'
[2] LEWIS, pp. 266–267.
[3] Sept. 16, 1578, translated in KNOX, p. xxiii.

well as other penalties, which it entails.' He always
preached that those who fell should be leniently dealt with
by their more fortunate brethren, and even forty years
later, by which time the position was clear beyond any
chance of doubt, his attitude won the approval of the Pope.
For Clement VIII, expressly reaffirming the unlawfulness
of assisting at Protestant services, ' added withal that such
as of fear and weakness or other temporal force or necessity
should do it, ought to be gentle dealt with and easily
absolved.' [1] One last example of how widespread was the
Catholic misunderstanding on this point, and of how long
it lasted, even after explicit declaration from Rome, may
be found in the petition of Mary Queen of Scots [2] to
Gregory XIII, in 1582, for a dispensation to allow her
Catholic servants to go to the Protestant services, and so
escape the penalties that otherwise must fall on them.

This great body of Catholics, whatever the degree of
their loyalty to the old faith, was, of course, entirely unorgan-
ized, and for this reason it has often been considered, by
Catholics of later times, fair criticism to speak of them as
though they were all feckless and incapable. That they were,
after 1559, for some years wholly at the mercy of their
victorious opponents was in the nature of things. The
very measures which secured the triumph of the highly
organized minority that now controlled the machinery of
government, had destroyed the organization of the Catholic
majority as a Catholic body. There happened what cannot
but happen when a revolution begins by making away with
all its chief opponents. No matter what the size of the
leaderless majority, for a time it is bound to be a mere
aggregate of individual opinions, schemes, and plans of
action. Like Gulliver on the shore at Lilliput the English
Catholics came from the Parliamentary struggle of 1559
to find their every energy minutely held. One first mood
was, seemingly, desperation. ' Nothing can be done,' the
Spanish Ambassador reports Archbishop Heath as saying,
' but we can suffer whatever God wills,' [3] And Simpson
has a passage which is a kind of taunting commentary on

---

[1] Allen to the Catholics of England, Dec. 12, 1592 ; *L.A.*, p. 345.
[2] The Queen to the Nuncio in France, printed KNOX, p. 335, from the
Roman Transcripts at the Public Record Office, London.
[3] *Catholic Record Society*, Vol. I, p. 15, quoted POLLEN, p. 37.

this text. ' They were all waiting,' he says, ' for something
to turn up ; waiting like the drunken man for the door to
come round to them, instead of shaking off their lethargy,
and walking out through the door. They were waiting for
Burghley to die, or for Elizabeth to die, or to marry a
Catholic husband, or for the King of Spain to come and
depose her ; waiting for fortune to change for them, instead
of trying to change their own fortune ; and forgetting that
fate unresisted overcomes us, but is conquered by resistance.
It was this English dilatoriness, this provisional acquiescence
in wrong, this stretching of the conscience in order that
men might keep what they had, which made it possible
that England should be lost to the Church, as it has since
lost many a man who was quite convinced that he ought to
be a Catholic, but waited till his conviction faded away.
The Catholics waited for the times to mend ; and they
waited till their children were brought up to curse the
religion of their fathers, till they had been robbed piecemeal
of their wealth and power, and found themselves a waning
sect in the land they had once occupied from sea to sea.'

We know, now that the archives of the great states have
given up their secrets, what Simpson could not know, not
so much that the sole hope of the Catholics lay in foreign
aid whereby to overthrow Cecil, but this most important
fact that the one monarch who could help them, Philip of
Spain, not only counselled a patient toleration of the
persecution but imposed this policy on the Pope and stood
between what appeals for violent action the Catholics made
to the Pope and any favourable hearing of those appeals.[1]
And, the impossible political action apart, the English
Catholics were far from being idle spectators of their own
tragic fate during these first ten years after the change.
There was, in every diocese, even in London and in Puritan
Norwich, the activity of the priests who remained true.
There were the efforts of such leaders as Nicholas Sander
and Maurice Clenog to persuade the Pope to excommunicate Elizabeth.[2] And there was the great literary venture
on the part of the Catholic scholars who had fled overseas,
to Antwerp and to Louvain. ' Books opened the way,'
said Allen, speaking, many years later,[3] of the militant

[1] MEYER is especially valuable for this matter.
[2] In 1563 ; cf. POLLEN, p. 76.
[3] Apologie of Two English Seminaries(1581), p. 26, quoted POLLEN, p. 111.

open defiance that characterised the middle period of the reign.

Fr. Pollen counts no fewer than eighteen Catholic writers who, between 1564 and 1567, published books of devotion, religious instruction and, most timely of all, religious controversy. Ten of these were Wykehamists, as was the priest whose book caused the greatest sensation of all, Thomas Harding, once chaplain to Stephen Gardiner and now the bold assailant of the hardiest of all the Elizabethan prelates, John Jewel, Bishop of Salisbury. In four years this active group produced some forty-one books, and then the outbreak of the great rising in Flanders against Philip II. brought all such scholarly activities to an abrupt end. But no less than 20,000 copies of these productions were smuggled into England and sold there despite the government's police measures, and Sander bears witness how much this vigorous counter-attack availed to raise the spirits of the Catholics at home. ' A new zeal for Catholic truth made the Catholics dare everything in order to learn about their Faith and to defend it.' [1]

For the story of these exiles in Flanders the reader must go to the work of Fr. Robert Lechat, S.J.[2] Here we may note that, like the foreign Protestants who sought shelter in England in Edward VI's reign, they were genuine religious refugees. A very high proportion were priests ; they had all made their way abroad with difficulty, and at their own expense ; and once arrived they lived for the rest of their lives in a destitution relieved only by the occasional alms of the Pope or the King of Spain.

It was from the practical genius of one of these exiled priests, William Allen, that the greatest achievement of this early Elizabethan Catholicism came, the founding of the college at Douay. For here, under God, was the principal means of preserving the Catholic Church in England for the next two hundred years. Superlatives come very easily, even to practised observers of human endeavour as history records it, but it is scarcely possible to exaggerate what the Catholic Church owes to the work of this Lancashire priest. The day of Douay's foundation, September 29, 1568, should be indelibly marked in the calendar of every English Catholic.

---

[1] *De Schismate Anglicano*, lib. III, MS. English College, Rome, cited POLLEN, p. 111.
[2] *Les Réfugiés Catholiques Anglais dans les Pays Bas Espagnoles.* Louvain, 1914.

§ v. The Reaction in Rome, 1559–1569

So far there had been singularly little movement from the Roman authorities towards the Catholics of England. Paul IV, when the news of Elizabeth's relapse reached him, was transported with the anger which characterised him all through life. But for the few months of life that remained to the aged Pope—he died in August, 1559—the King of Spain prevailed on him to wait a little longer and to watch. Then, for the rest of this critical year, the Holy See was vacant,[1] while in one of the longest conclaves ever known, contending policies strove for the mastery.

The Pope it elected, Pius IV, was the most conciliatory of men, a professional canonist and administrator, resolved before all else to reassemble the Council of Trent, and to bring its work to a conclusion, and, as an essential preliminary to this, to restore the good relations between the Holy See and all Christian princes, relations embittered almost everywhere during the reign that had lately ended. Philip II's pleas for patience towards Elizabeth were now welcomed and the Pope prepared to send an envoy to her The letter of Pius IV to Elizabeth is dated May 5, 1560, and it thus belongs to the first months of his reign. In it [2] the Pope gives expression to his good wishes for the queen's prosperity, promises his assistance, exhorts her to beware of evil counsellors, and finally invites her to take part in the coming general council. He chose as his envoy Vincenzo Parpaglia, the one-time associate of Reginald Pole, abbot now of San Solutore at Turin, whose journey to Rome in 1553 is one of the very first incidents in this story. The envoy left Rome on May 25 and by June 17 had got as far as Louvain. Here he was held up, and the story of the delay recalls, in many ways, that earlier adventure of the legate in 1553 already described.

The Pope, on the day he wrote the letter to the English queen, wrote also to Philip II and to his uncle, the Emperor Ferdinand, advising them of his move and asking their aid. By the time the news of what was toward had reached Elizabeth (the end of May, 1560), Philip II had acted. He wrote to Rome protesting strongly, and sent orders to his lieutenant in the Low Countries—his half-sister, Margaret

[1] Aug. 18 to Dec. 26.
[2] Text in Tierney, II, App., p. cccxxi.

Farnese, duchess of Parma—to hold up the papal envoy once he reached Brussels. Thus while Philip's ambassador in London, unaware of his sovereign's mind in the matter, was working Elizabeth into a position where she could not say she was unwilling to receive the nuncio, Philip himself was using all his power to prevent the nuncio's arrival.

The Spanish king, it was the old trouble of 1553 once again, was convinced that the French were behind the legate's mission. He suspected that Parpaglia was charged with some kind of ultimatum to Elizabeth, an ultimatum which she could not but defy, and defiance of which must involve her excommunication and deposition and a commission to himself to execute the sentence. While the ink was still scarcely dry on the treaty that had ended Spain's last exhausting war with France [1]—England being Spain's ally —and with the reorganisation of his government in the Low Countries just begun and already at a critical stage, Philip II saw the prospect before him of a papal mandate to make war on England, a war in which the French must ally themselves with Elizabeth and in which the Anglo-French alliance might lose him the very pivot of Spain's European hegemony, the states and cities of the Netherlands.

Moreover, Parpaglia was *persona non grata* with Philip II. Rome, dependent for the success of its plans on the king, to an indefinite degree, had chosen just the wrong man to be its agent. Parpaglia had been one of Cardinal Pole's circle—and while Pole had stood throughout his life for the dissociation of the Catholic cause in England from Spanish policies, he had been, on the other hand, an object of serious dislike to Elizabeth. The abbot's personal unsuitability for his mission was twofold. Worse still, he had himself already crossed Philip's path. Only eighteen months before this, the king had banished him from Flanders, under pain of death, as a French spy.

The King of Spain's protest was as effective at Rome as, eight years before, the protests of his father had been in the case of Pole. The new Secretary of State—that nephew of Pius IV who was one day to be St. Charles Borromeo—wrote, July 10, to Parpaglia, bidding him go no further than Brussels. Should he, however, already have reached London, he is, throughout, to follow the advice of Philip's ambassador there. Philip II's ambassador was to

[1] Signed at Cateau-Cambrésis, April, 1559 : it was now May, 1560.

control the legate to Elizabeth as Charles V's ambassador
had controlled the legate to Mary.

Parpaglia, however, was still at Brussels, and with the
Roman letter of July 10 the mission was at an end. It only
remained to get him back to Rome without advertising to
France that Philip II's influence at Rome was so strong that
he had forced the Pope to reverse an important public
decision. Pius IV, so the Spanish ambassador at Rome
declared, would even have been glad to have been able to
plead a refusal of his envoy by Elizabeth. Such an insult
would not have been easy to overlook, however, and it was
the ingenuity of Margaret of Parma that found the appropriate way out. She suggested that de Quadra, Philip's
ambassador in London, should now write to Parpaglia a
letter discouraging him from further action until the Council
met, and explaining that there were really great difficulties
in the matter of getting passports for him. Which letter de
Quadra did indeed write, July 25, 1560. With it he sent a
letter for Margaret also, which told her that Elizabeth, before
issuing the passports, would ask to see the despatches Parpaglia
carried. She would also insist that she was addressed with
her full style and all her titles ; the Pope must still acknowledge her as Defender of the Faith ! And she had told the
ambassador that she would rather die than change her faith.

Parpaglia waited a little longer and then, in October,
1560, he returned to Rome. It is, I think, impossible to say
what Elizabeth wanted—if we are to base an opinion on her
own declarations. It is true that she told de Quadra, when
the news of the proposed mission first came, that she wished
to receive the nuncio. Undoubtedly the Pope's letter was a
recognition that ended all doubts whether Pius IV would
regard her as a usurper because of the sentence of
Clement VII upholding the marriage between her father
and Katharine of Aragon. If the Pope could somehow
have become an additional instrument of English diplomacy,
undoubtedly he would have been welcomed. But Elizabeth's conversations with the Spanish ambassador—who
was himself a bishop—can hardly have inspired in him any
belief that she ever intended to give him any real guidance
thereby as to her intentions. Did she not one day tell him
that she longed to be a nun, in some quiet convent cell ?—and
again, apropos of Leicester, that she would be so glad to
tell him all about it, under the seal of confession, ' For I am

no angel ? '—and yet again assure him ' that she could not disregard the grace which Our Lord had given her, and that it would be her delight to live and die a pure virgin ? '

Pope Pius IV, who had not the advantage of that detailed knowledge of the queen which it is now so easy to gather from the printed despatches of half the embassies of Europe, continued to hope. A chance remark of Elizabeth's ambassador in France in December, 1560, passed on to Rome by the Duke of Savoy, set him to cast round for a more suitable envoy, and in February, 1561, he persuaded a noble Venetian, the abbot Girolamo Martinengo, to undertake the difficult, if not hopeless, commission. The history of 1560 was repeated, with some significant variations.

Martinengo was instructed (March 9, 1561) to consult the Spanish authorities in Flanders, but, in London, he was to lodge in his own quarters and to see that the Spanish ambassador was not present when he had his audience of Elizabeth. His business with the queen was to invite her to the Council, and only after this was he to raise the further question of the release from prison of the Catholic bishops.

Already, before this, Philip II had heard of the new project and he had again strongly protested, and even after it had been explained to him that nothing more was intended than this invitation to the Council, he persisted in his opposition and, in April, wrote to Flanders that Martinengo was to be prevented from going to England. But by the time these instructions arrived, negotiations had already been begun between Martinengo and Elizabeth through Margaret of Parma and the Spanish ambassador in London.

Elizabeth, once again, told de Quadra how pleased she was, and revealed her embarrassment by her immediate recital of all the difficulties which must first be overcome. The greatest of these was the sacrosanct law of the realm which forbade her to acknowledge Pius IV as anything more than the Bishop of Rome. Cecil also was deputed to raise difficulties and to devise delays, yet without any mere undisguised refusal, such as might inevitably draw the papacy to reprisals and endanger the tacit understanding with Spain. But de Quadra played his part, too, and had pushed Cecil as far as naming the palace at Greenwich for the nuncio's reception, before Cecil was ready with his final check. This was the Secretary of State's discovery—announced on April 28 —of a ' plot ' between leading English Catholics (a number

of whom had recently been thrown into prison for hearing
Mass) in which de Quadra was, of course, involved. This
and the fact that there was already a nuncio at work in
Ireland—Fr. David Wolfe, S.J.—stirring up the Catholics
against the queen, made it, of course, impossible to grant
Martinengo his passports.

A way had been found to delay the nuncio indefinitely
without a point-blank refusal, and so without embarrassment to Philip II. And now the question was allowed to
be discussed by the Council.

A report of this meeting—May 1, 1561—survives among
the State papers of the reign,[1] and also an enlightening
letter, giving the news of the Council, from Cecil to the
English ambassador at Paris, Sir Nicholas Throckmorton.
The English Secretary of State admits the difficulty he was
at to overcome the impression made on the Council by de
Quadra's diplomacy. ' He had taken faster hold to plant
his purpose than was my ease shortly to root up.' He admits
also that, until just before this meeting of the Council, the
tendency had been to receive the nuncio, ' I have imparted
this answer for the nuncio to sundry places, lest our former
inclination had been too hastily spread by the adversaries.'
And he tells us what he had found of great assistance in
moving away from ' our former inclination,' thus : ' When
I saw the Romish influence toward, about a month past,[2]
I thought it necessary to dull the Papists' expectation by
discovering of certain Mass-mongers and punishing them,
as I doubt not you have heard of them.' Here surely speaks
Thomas Cromwell's successor, and the smooth note ends, ' I
take God to record I mean no evil to any of them,[3] but only
for the rebating of the Papists' humours, which by the Queen's
lenity grow too rank. I find it hath done much good.'

' So much was the contrary labour by prevention,' says
Cecil, that ' yet was I forced to seek byways.' Even
Elizabeth had had to be dealt with, for ' God, whose cause
it is, and the Queen, whose only surety therein resteth . . .

---

[1] Printed in TIERNEY, II, App., p. cccxxii.

[2] The letter is dated May 8, 1561 ; it is printed (in part) in POLLEN,
pp. 70–71, from Record Office, *Foreign Elizabeth*, XVIII, p. 103.

[3] Fr. Pollen, *op. cit.*, p. 71, comments : ' Such, however, was the man's
hypocrisy, that while calling God to record that he meant no harm to any of
them, he was keeping scores in prison, some to remain there for months,
some for years, some for life. Those capable of paying were not freed
without the fine of 100 marks, a large sum for those times [*i.e.* £33 3s. 4d.,
say £5/600 of our purchasing power] ; nor even then could any go free
without taking the Oath of Supremacy.'

have ended the matter well,' God ' by directing,' the queen
' by yielding.' The Secretary sighs his grateful relief,
' Howsoever the end is, the way was full of crooks,' and his
gratitude goes out *nominatim* to Sir Nicholas Bacon, the earl
of Pembroke and the marquis of Winchester.

The report of the Council meeting—' A note of the consultation had at Greenwich, May 1, 1561, by the Queen's
majesty's commandment . . .'—is in quite another tone.
It speaks of a unanimity of feeling on the matter ' without
any manner of contradiction or doubt moved by any,' and
professes to give only ' the chiefest ' of the reasons which
they all urged. The really determining argument was,
presumably, that which recalled ' the laws lately made,'
the Act of Supremacy with its rejection of the spiritual
jurisdiction of the Pope ' and therefore it is not only against
the laws of this realm, that any such nuncio shall come
hither, but also that any person should, by word or deed,
allow of his coming.' Councillors who voted for Martinengo's passports would by the fact, it is suggested, be involved
in an offence that might even be treason.

The diplomacy of Pius IV was then unsuccessful, as
regards its main object, but it was far from being wholly
barren. Twice within twelve months a papal envoy had
made a contact with the English Catholics exiled in Flanders.
He had been a channel through which much information
had passed to Rome, and Rome, because of the envoys, was
now aware of the exiles as a possible means of future action.
The exiles had, through the envoys, received their first alms
from the Pope, and they had seen the envoys plead their
cause with the Spanish authorities in the Low Countries.
Here were the beginnings of a new relation between the
papacy and the English Catholics, a relation in which the
Pope began to be in very deed their father, and, in a most
intimate sense, their leader and their only hope. It was not,
indeed, until the coming of Gregory XIII, ten years later,
that these relations matured, and became very evident
features in the scheme of European politics, but the beginnings of those relations were undoubtedly the contacts made
in 1560–1561 between the exiles and the two envoys Parpaglia
and Martinengo. And if Parpaglia was unwelcome to
Philip II because of his association with Pole, this very link
made him all the more welcome to the exiles, and all the
more useful as a liaison between them and the distant papacy.

CHAPTER II

THE COUNTER-ACTION THROUGH SPIRITUALS

§ i. ALLEN'S PRIESTS

BY the time of Gregory XIII's election [1] the exiles had, of their own initiative, taken the most important decision of all and established the seminary at Douay. The foundation was the outcome of a conversation between William Allen, of Rossall in Lancashire, and John Vendeville, professor of Civil Law at the new University of Douay. The two were returning from a visit to Rome in the spring of 1568, Allen a pilgrim, his companion a somewhat disappointed suitor. Vendeville in fact had in his mind a great plan to further the missions to the Indies, and he had gone to Rome to lay his schemes before the Pope, Pius V. To his great sorrow the whole winter went by without any chance of a hearing, and when it was made clear that the papal attention was crowded with nearer problems, the pioneer made his way home. One day as he spoke of his schemes and lamented that they would, now, hardly ever be realised, Allen spoke of the needs of England. In the course of time death would carry off the existing clergy, and what would be the plight of the faith if, when the expected restoration came, there were no English priests ? Even though Elizabeth died and a Catholic succeeded, heresy would triumph if there were not Catholic preachers, writers, and priests to seize the opportunity. It would be an excellent thing to have always ready men of learning outside the realm, to restore religion when the proper moment should have arrived.[2] A college would serve to gather all that Catholic talent which, homeless, and without means of living, for now eight years and more, was slowly decaying in half a dozen cities of the Low

---

[1] May 13, 1572
[2] Allen to Vendeville, Sept. 16, 1578, in KNOX, xxvi ; the text of the letter is in *L.A.*, 52–68.

Countries. The students could finish their education; the priests could perfect their studies. Priests could be formed; books could be written. The English Church would possess once more an essential instrument of its continuance, a shelter for its intelligence, a hearth whence its faith might continue to be fed.

Allen could not have urged his cause to a man more qualified to help, for it was to the initiative of Vendeville that the erection of the University of Douay itself was due.[1] Vendeville, at the time of his well-deserved success with Philip II in this matter, was a very young man. In 1568 he was only forty-one, five years older than Allen, and as might be guessed an enthusiast for educational improvement as the best of arms against the menacing heresies of the time. He was himself one of the most celebrated teachers of law his generation knew, and at the same time a practising lawyer of such ability that at twenty-nine, already professor of Civil Law at Louvain, he had been recommended for a place on the Council that governed the Low Countries for Charles V. He was not appointed, seemingly because he trusted to his abilities and his recommendations and neglected the innumerable little intrigues and sycophancies which are so often essential to success in such ventures.

From this moment his life changed. He took one of his colleagues in the faculty of Theology into his confidence, and under this expert direction re-modelled his whole life. One ideal alone now possessed him, to work for the extension of the Kingdom of God on earth. He exchanged his chair of Civil Law for that of Canon Law, and directed all his studies to the problem how best to deliver Europe from heresy. One of the best means, so history, he considered, taught him, was the well-organised, well-educated religious order. The new foundation of St. Ignatius Loyola was later, very naturally, to find in him a strong champion, and it is not idle to see something of this side of Vendeville's mind in the early organisation and life of Douay College, whence came students as rigorously formed and as well trained as any Jesuit. Later in life Vendeville became Bishop of Tournai, and, like many another bishop of the Counter-Reformation, he turned to the great Society, and did not turn in vain, for trained auxiliaries to institute the necessary working reconstruction of Catholic life. Was it from

[1] CARDON, p. 62 seq.

Vendeville that Allen took, what was to distinguish his
apostolate too, that great esteem for the Jesuits and that
gift of working harmoniously with these capable men whom,
yet, so many of the prominent Catholics of the time
suspected and disliked ?

Already, nine years before this memorable discussion
with Allen, Vendeville had urged upon the Council of the
emperor that colleges and seminaries were the best weapons
with which to fight heresy, and it was from this standpoint
that he had pressed upon his new sovereign, Philip II, the
foundation within his dominions of a university which would
be for the French-speaking provinces what Louvain was
for the Flemings and the Dutch.

The new university was solemnly inaugurated October 5,
1562, and among its first professors, very naturally, was
Vendeville, once more in the chair of Civil Law. The highest
chair of all, that of Theology, went to an Englishman,
Richard Smith, late of the University of Oxford and now the
only man at Louvain to come up to the requirements of the
exigent town council of Douay, determined that the first
generation of the professors of the new foundation should be
men of mark. They were resolved ' emploier et mectre en
œuvre gens forts excellens ' in this matter of theology, for
was it not precisely and principally to produce good theological thinking that the new university had been founded ?

We shall never see Allen's great venture for the thing it
was, unless we see it as one of the most important elements
of this brilliant, newly founded University of Douay. And
if we wish to form any idea of the kind of men England lost
in 1559, we can do it, once more, by studying the contribution they made to the several faculties again of that same
university. Nor is it without profit to compare this flourishing renaissance across the seas in the Flemish dominions of
King Philip II with the desolation, almost academic
destruction, which at Oxford and Cambridge followed upon
Elizabeth's legislation.

To the new University of Douay, Catholic Oxford, as it
disappeared, gave five of its first professors, men, all of them,
proved in the event to be of uncommon distinction. Richard
Smith has been mentioned already. The chair of Canon Law
went to Owen Lewis ; Allen was given the practical post
of the chair of Catechetics and next of Controverted Doctrine,
while Thomas Stapleton, following Allen in both these posts,

lived to be the most celebrated doctor of them all. Lewis was rector of the university in 1568 and Stapleton in 1573. All these men, save Lewis, found time to write voluminously, in English for the benefit of the Church at home, in Latin for the still wider audience of learned Europe. And in the town library of Douay there still lies the unpublished manuscript of Allen's lectures on Peter Lombard. Lewis, like Vendeville and many another, combined with his scholarship a talent for the practice of the law and in 1574 he surrendered his chair for the service of the diocese of Cambrai as *officialis*, and was given the dignity of Archdeacon of Hainaut. It was through his management of the affairs of this diocese in important suits that he first came to be known at Rome, and so passed from Flanders to a wider sphere of influence, as the Vicar-General of St. Charles Borromeo at Milan and then as Bishop of Cassano. After Allen he was the most distinguished, and perhaps the ablest, of all the exiles, and his relations with Allen remained close and cordial to the very end. Allen lived long enough to see the national antagonism between English and Welsh breed a real feud, and to know that the contending parties swore each by the names of himself and Lewis. But nothing could make a breach in that remarkable charity, and the remark with which he ended a long conference with Lewis, in the very last months of his life, is characteristic : ' Well, Abraham and Lot were both good men, but their shepherds could not agree.'[1]

The presence of so many Englishmen in the professorial corps, and the fact of there being in the town an English college, attracted many English to the university, apart altogether from those who, in the college, were preparing for the priesthood. There were, for example, in 1576, eighty students at the college and in the university no fewer than 120 English. Douay was steadily becoming another Oxford overseas when, in 1578, came the calamity of civil war once more and, as a result of the temporary Calvinist domination of the Catholic provinces, the English seminary left the town for more friendly Rheims. With the return of the college to Douay, in 1593, the old relations with the university were resumed, and although the *seniores* of the college never again played in the university such a part as

---

[1] Quoted KNOX, p. ciii, note 3, from WATSON, *Decachordon of ten quodlibetical questions*, p. 98.

in the first ten years, the college continued to live very largely by the life of the university, and to matriculate a large proportion of its students and present them for the various degrees.[1] The doctorate was then a rare distinction. In the faculty of Theology only twenty-three doctors were created between 1562 and 1600 : of these, four were English exiles and connected with the English College, namely Allen and Stapleton, doctors in 1571, Richard Bristow in 1575 and Richard Hall in 1577. The doctorate in law was rarer still. In the same period of thirty-eight years it was conferred only fifteen times, and in the promotions of 1568 Owen Lewis's name finds a place *utriusque iuris doctor*.

The possibilities of developing, under the ægis of this new royal university, a really formidable counter-attack to the victorious, but scarcely triumphant, Elizabethan Protestantism, were, then, very great. Allen set himself to make the most of them. Vendeville seems to have been the means of finding the scheme's first patrons in a material sense, patrons whose generosity would provide the money to buy a house and keep the community in food for the first few years. He did much out of his own fortune, and he enlisted the sympathy of three Benedictine prelates, the abbots of St. Vaast in Arras, of Anchin and Marchiennes. All three abbeys were on that list of fourteen from which both the king and the Pope hoped to draw a considerable annual sum towards the upkeep of the new university. All three contributed to the best of their ability and, considering the incessant wars of which their country had for fifty years been the theatre, contributed generously. The abbots of Anchin, and Marchiennes, Jean Lentailleur, and Arnould Ganthois, were typical of the new renaissance, ' L'humanisme dévot,' at its best. They were products of the new spirit moving strongly for now a generation in the University of Paris, savants, reformers of the monastic life, good administrators, enthusiasts for the better education of the clergy and men of saintly life. When Vendeville approached them for aid towards the new venture they were, both of them, already involved in all the anxiety and expense of founding colleges themselves in the university, the Collège d'Anchin and the Collège de Marchiennes, colleges where the humanities and philosophy should be taught and where the

---

[1] CARDON (p. 353) gives the following statistics of students of the English College entered also in the university : 1575-1576, 153 ; 1592-1605, 286.

teachers were to be Jesuits. But these abbots were also men
of the type to whom no cause that is Catholic appeals in vain.
And they generously gave to Allen's college also.[1] He
bought two large houses and the gardens attached and on
Michaelmas Day, 1568, the English College opened, Collège
des Prêtres Anglais, to Douay, or again Collège du Pape.

The new college opened with four English students.
Their names deserve a record for that fact alone ; they
were Richard Bristow, late fellow of Exeter, Edward Risden,
of the same Oxford college, John Marshall, late fellow of
New College, and John White. Four years later the first
priests were ordained. Six were ordained in 1574 ten in
1575, eleven in 1576, and by the end of 1578—after ten years
of work—the college had produced seventy-seven new
priests, and not only priests, but priests who were returning
to England to work there. For, in 1574, the idea had come
to one of the recently ordained not to await in Flanders the
hour of the Catholic restoration, but to cross over to England
and, while awaiting it, help on the good work done in such
secrecy for now fifteen years by the priests who had refused
to bend to 1559. This first of the ' missionary priests ' of
Douay was Lewis Barlow, and with him, that same year,
there went Henry Shaw and Martin Nelson. Six years
after this new venture—henceforth the main purpose of the
college—there were a hundred Douay priests at work in
England (1580). By the end of Elizabeth's reign (1603)
450 had been sent from Douay to the English mission.
The Catholicism of the English was not to die a painful,
if natural, death of starvation, and Allen swiftly became a
person of the first importance to the English government.

The college grew rapidly. In 1578, the year it was
transferred to Rheims, there were fifty-five students in
residence. In 1580, 112, and in 1582, 120. The next year,
1583, brought eighty new students in six months, and from
this time to the end of the century there were always about
200 studying in the college, while others are mentioned
as attending schools in the town, younger students these
last, still working through their humanities.

Douay College was not, however, any garden enclosed
where, in seclusion from actuality, the future English

---

[1] In the next generation the Abbot of St. Vaast was to found a college in
the university, the Collége St. Vaast, and also a Benedictine house,
dedicated to St. Gregory, for the English Benedictines ; this last is now the
great Abbey of Downside.

clergy were trained. It was set in the heart of a busy university city, and its superiors were also important personages in the university world, as many of its students were pupils of the Alma Mater. The college speedily became the chief centre of English Catholic life, and its secondary activities were little less important than the main purpose of training priests. There was, for example, the care of the laymen who came to Douay to study the humanities and philosophy and to take their degrees in arts, the Catholics who desired not only education but a Catholic education, and of those ' best wits ' who despaired of finding education at all in the Oxford and Cambridge of that time, ' where no art, holy or profane, was thoroughly studied and some not touched at all.' Protestants doubtful of the new faith came also, and Catholics who had apostatised at least in outward act. Such were ' duly catechised and reconciled to the Church by penance for their previous life and schism.' More than 500 had been so instructed, Allen could report in 1578. Other visitors came out of mere travellers' curiosity, interested to see what had happened to these men who had left England years ago now, and of whom England was beginning once more to hear. Some of these visitors were ministers of the new religion. Not a few were converted, stayed, and, becoming priests, passed on to the English mission and even to martyrdom. There was also, to occupy the leisure of every member of the community, a devoted apostolic correspondence with old friends and associates still in England. Simpson describes this as one of Allen's greatest discoveries, and (with the *Rambler* recently suppressed and Newman before his eyes shelved in semi-disgrace at Edgbaston) comments feelingly: 'Allen was not the man to let the force that was in an educated convert run to seed or to allow him to stand all day idle in the market-place for want of employment.'

Finally the college served a most practical purpose in providing a temporary home for the priests who, without leaders, without help or encouragement of any kind, from any source save their personal friends, had fought the battle in England since their deprivation now so many years ago. These came to Douay too ; they found there, wearing their native dress, that peace of normal Catholic life which they had thought to have lost for ever, and they also found there a means to refurbish their theological armament.

It cannot be too often stated, it is the highest proof of the
man's greatness and of his magnanimity and of his incredible
large-heartedness, that the secret of it all was Allen himself.
' All that came to Douay or Rheims were received and
welcomed ; none were rejected, had they money or had
they none, brought they recommendations or brought they
none.' So one who knew well the time of which he wrote.[1]
' The name of Douay is now famous throughout England,'
the future martyr, Blessed John Payne, could write in 1576,
and indeed the appearance of these new priests, trained
specially for the new work, trained ascetics, trained cate-
chists, trained controversialists, the first evidences English
Catholicism had known of the Catholic renaissance active
elsewhere in Europe for a good forty years now, all this
cannot but have told surprisingly. Allen tells us of one alone
of these new priests who, in one day, reconciled eighty of
the lapsed flock. ' And this in the meantime is my joy and
comfort in Christ that whatsoever the fearful or unskilful
think of this practice, by their travails as also by others of
the like calling and endeavour, God is daily glorified and
served in our country with great increase of the Catholic
faith, and more and more be daily won all sorts of men, and
that innumerable now confess their faith and abhor all
communion and participation with the sectaries in their
service and sacraments that before, being Catholics in heart,
for worldly fear durst not so do, and that there is daily such
joyful resort of many to this side the seas to learn their
belief and to take experience of the Church's discipline by
our said priests' special exhortation, that it is wonderful to
strangers and comfortable to us to behold. For my part
I should think all my poor pains and desires well rewarded
in God, if every one that laboureth there could but recover
one soul from schism and perdition, as I have assured
intelligence every one gaineth full many.' [2]

All his contemporaries were left with one abiding
memory of Allen, that he was a born ruler of men. He lived
through storms, and passionate controversies in which he
had friends on all sides. He kept his own views, never con-
cealed them—nor ever ceased to express them—and he never
lost a friend. He is literally the one man of all that time,

[1] Humphrey Ely.
[2] Allen to Chauncy, Aug. 10, 1577, *L.A.*, pp. 34–35.

actively engaged in the public life of the time, of whom all
are agreed he never made an enemy. Douay College
flourished and all it had for rule was the will of its president,
his conviction that none was less earnest than himself for
the common aim, and the great dread of all to cause him
any pain or add to his anxieties. The intimate history of the
college in those years is truly idyllic, and its secret is the
character of Allen and the love and veneration he inspired
in all. ' A little government there is and order,' he wrote
himself, ' but no bondage nor straitness in the world. There is
neither oath nor statute nor other bridle nor chastisement ;
but reason and every man's conscience towards other.' [1]

Our best source of information about the details of the
system which, in Allen's day, trained the Douay missionaries is Allen himself. In the long letter to Vendeville [2]
he tells us a great deal of his ideal and the means by which
he hoped to reach it. In a spirited defence of his priests
against English clerical critics of an older generation he
tells us still more, [3] while a letter written by Vendeville to the
president of the privy council at Brussels, Viglius, completes
this very full first-hand witness. [4]

To begin with, we might recall how all this work of restoration was clerical and scholarly. All these pioneers were
clerics and learned men, scholars, ' dons ' if you will, of the
English universities, and the two university cities of Louvain
and Douay were the centres whence it all came. It is not
surprising to find, in the new missionary seminary, a strong
adherence to university ideals, to note there a real reverence
for learning as such, and much of the etiquette preserved
which testified to this. Some twenty-two of the students proceeded to degrees in theology in the university, between
1568 and the removal to Rheims ten years later, and it was
only the lack of money to pay the fees which stood in the way
of still other promotions. [5]

The doctors had their special place in hall, receiving an
extra allowance of food and also wine, and the visitation of
the college in 1612 is testimony that the tradition still sur-

[1] Allen to Hopkins, April 5, 1579, *L.A.*, p. 176 ; the whole letter should
be read.
[2] Sept. 16, 1578, text in *L.A.*, pp. 52–67 ; translated, in great part, in
KNOX, pp. xxxviii–xliii.
[3] Letter to Dom Maurice Chauncy, Aug. 10, 1577, text in *L.A.*, pp. 31–37;
translated, in great part, in KNOX, pp. xlv–xlix.
[4] Nov. or Dec., 1568, in *L.A.*, p. 22.
[5] KNOX, App., p. 304.

Photo by Emery Walker

William Allen
(1532–1594)
Cardinal of S. Martin ai Monti

vived of Allen's care that special honours should be paid
to the learned men of his community, ' doctores, assistentes,
et lectores, quorum semper particularis ratio habita fuit
a Cardinale Alano et aliis.' ' When D. Bagshawe and D.
Stafferton came to Rheims and had signified to him [Allen]
that they were doctors . . . the next day at dinner he
brought them into the hall and placed them himself in their
due places next to the other doctors in divinity, the one
above M. Licentiate Parkinson and the other above me
being but doctor of laws. And this place they kept so long
as they remained to all men's liking and contentment.' [1]

Allen was above all things practical. He had no desire,
of course, to produce clerical archæologists. The need he
strove to supply was for a competent working clergy, and
so he could write : ' Our students, intended for the English
harvest, are not required to excel or be great proficients in
theological science . . . but they must abound in zeal for
God's house, charity and thirst for souls.' [2] Yet Allen is not
of those who so readily cry ' scientia inflat.' He goes on to
explain what the knowledge is that his priests must possess,
and, very pointedly, to tell of the restricted sphere to which
he destined the less educated of his clergy. Deep knowledge
is not any hindrance, in his opinion, to a priest's usefulness :
' . . . the more knowledge they possess concerning the
Scriptures and controversial divinity, and the greater the
prudence and discretion they couple with this knowledge,
so much the more abundant will be their success.' If only
the missionaries ' have burning zeal, even though deep
science be wanting, provided always that they know the
necessary heads of religious doctrine and the power and
nature of the sacraments, such men, among the more skilled
labourers whom we have in nearly all the provinces of the
kingdom, also do good work in hearing confessions and
offering sacrifice.'

To hear confessions and to say Mass—it was to these
points that the training was especially directed, and the
first and most fundamental part of the training. ' Our
first and foremost study,' was to brace the aspirant ' to a
zealous and just indignation against the heretics ' by placing
all his college life in the setting of the liturgical offices of the

---

[1] ELY, op. cit., p. 92, cited KNOX, p. xxxii, note 4.
[2] KNOX, p. xxxviii, Allen to Vendeville, Sept. 16, 1578 or 1580 ; text of
the Latin letter in L.A., p. 62.

Church, carried out in the best manner possible, as the best of all means to awake their minds to the ruin and desolation of their native land. And while encouraged to this hatred of the forces which had wrought so much ill, the student was reminded that the source of all ills is man's sin, and that all men are sinners, and he was bidden dedicate himself to the work before him in a spirit of contrition and reparation for all his own sins. To make amends for the routine confessions of past years, ' when for custom's sake we confessed once a year,' there is now a special devotion to the sacrament of Penance and, a most important detail of the spiritual formation of the missionaries, they make ' the spiritual exercises under the fathers of the Society.' The student must never lose sight of the land he has left, of the evils there wrought, of the sufferings of his kinsfolk and friends at the hands of ' the impious persecutors.' This will brace him to sacrifice himself utterly for his calling, 'they are happy to whom it is given to suffer something for their country, kinsfolk, religion, and Christ. . . . There is nothing, then, which we ought not readily to suffer rather than see the evils of our nation.'

As to the actual course of studies, Allen first speaks of Sacred Scripture. It is of the utmost importance that the missionary priest shall be thoroughly familiar with the whole of it and ' have at his fingers' ends ' the passages in dispute between Catholics and the Reformers. Hence there is (1) a daily lecture in the New Testament ; (2) a running explanation daily of a chapter of the Old Testament in the refectory after dinner, and of the New Testament after supper ; and (3) a dictation of all the controverted passages with notes of the arguments for the Catholic interpretation and answers to the Protestant case. Finally, every week there is a disputation, students being trained not only to put the Catholic case but to understand the Protestant side by themselves defending it, as well as by putting the Protestant objections, and twice a week a student makes a kind of scriptural sermon on one or other of the controverted points. ' The holy bible is always read at dinner and supper, while all listen attentively . . . four or at least three chapters at a time,' and every one reads over daily, in his room, the passages read in the refectory and those expounded. ' Those who are able to do so read them in the original. In this way the old Testament is gone through 12 times every three years or thereabouts . . . the new Testament is read through sixteen times in the same period ; and this is a great help towards acquiring a more than common familiarity with the text.' [1]

'Those who are able to do so,' says Allen in the passage just quoted. The rest of these students who, it will be recalled, ' are not required to excel or to be great proficients,' are ' successively taught Greek and Hebrew, so far as is required to read and understand the Scriptures of both Testaments in the original, and to save them from being entangled in the sophisms which heretics extract from the properties and meanings of words.'

To what great achievement this Douay devotion to Holy Scripture led is known to all, the translation of the whole Bible into English, accomplished during these very years by Gregory Martin. Allen, in explaining the care taken to train the students in preaching, has much to say, that is of great historical interest, about the often disputed point whether there was, in pre-Reformation times, a Catholic Bible in the English tongue. He notes it as one of the great handicaps to Catholics in dealing with the heretics, that these have a Bible in the vernacular, while the Catholic preacher does not ' commonly have at hand or quote the text of Scripture save in Latin.' Unless there is some ' English version of the words,' and he remembers it, the preacher must, there and then, translate ' on the spur of the moment,' and this, unfortunately, ' they often do inaccurately and with unpleasant hesitation.' 'This evil might be remedied,' Allen continues, ' if we too had some Catholic version of the bible, for all the English versions are most corrupt.' Then comes the momentous phrase : ' we, on our part, if his Holiness shall think proper, will undertake to produce a faithful, pure, and genuine version of the bible, in accordance with the edition approved by the Church. . . . Perhaps indeed it would have been more desirable that the Scriptures had never been translated into barbarous tongues ; nevertheless at the present day . . . it is better that there should be a faithful and catholic translation than that men should use a corrupt version to their peril and destruction.'

The students are taught to preach by weekly exercises on the Sunday epistles and gospels, and: 'We preach in English in order to acquire greater power and grace in the use of the

---

[1] Letter to Vendeville as translated, KNOX, p. xli.

vulgar tongue, a thing on which the heretics plume themselves exceedingly, and by which they do great injury to the
simple folk. In this respect the heretics, however ignorant
they may be in other points, have the advantage over many
of the more learned Catholics. . . .' Allen was well aware
of the weaknesses in the Catholic Action of his time, and willing enough to learn where the enemy's superiority could
teach him.

The theological teaching given in the seminary is set out
in less detail. There were two lectures daily on ' the Summa
of St. Thomas. For we teach scholastic theology (without
which no one can be solidly learned or an acute disputant)
chiefly from St. Thomas, though sometimes also from the
Master of the Sentences. Once a week there is a disputation
on five specially chosen articles of the Summa.'

There are two classes weekly in moral theology, the manual
of Azpilcueta, called Navarrus, serving as a text. Cases
of conscience had a place of their own in the time-table,
and those sent in from England and those of more frequent
occurrence were written up in a book and the student took
a copy for future guidance. As a preliminary to these
studies, and as a kind of preparation, the students ' were
most carefully instructed in the whole catechism.' Particularly did the course lay stress, in dealing with the matter of
ecclesiastical censures, on ' the marvellous power and
authority of the Sovereign Pontiff.' It was ' the exceeding
neglect and contempt with which this was treated by pastors
and people alike,' says Allen of the time preceding the great
change of Henry VIII's time, ' that God has punished with
the present miserable desolation.'

The letter from which this is all resumed, ends the account
of the studies with a list of the books recommended for private
reading, ' as most needful to men of our profession.' These
are the dogmatic decrees of the recent Council of Trent ;
the decrees of the English provincial synods, that is Lynd-
wood's *Provinciale* ; ' the whole of church history, especially
that of Venerable Bede, in order that they may be able to
show our countrymen from it that our nation did not receive
in the beginning any other than the Catholic faith which we
profess, and was converted to no other form of Christianity
except that we preach to them, and that their forefathers
bore the name of Christians and were such only as members
of this Catholic Christendom '—a truth still urgently

necessary for England and never more forcibly put ; St. Augustine against the heretics of his time, especially ' on the unity of the church, his letters to certain Donatists,' the *De Utilitate Credendi*, and the *De Cathechizandis Rudibus* ; St. Cyprian, *De Unitate Ecclesiæ* ; Vincent of Lérins ; St. Jerome against Vigilantius and Jovinian ; Thomas of Walden for his refutation of Wickliff, ' the father of all modern heretics.'

The spiritual life of the college is simply provided for. All say the Divine Office and all use ' the Blessed Virgin's rosary with the meditations attached.' They hear Mass together each morning at five, and before Mass they say the Litany of the Saints, for the Church, and for the conversion of England. Every Sunday and on the greater feasts they receive Holy Communion. Those who are priests say Mass every day. The feasts of St. Gregory the Great, St. Augustine the apostle of England, and St. Thomas of Canterbury, were kept with special solemnity, days of solemn intercession ' for the conversion of our country,' and for this same intention the college fasted twice each week.[1]

Allen ceased to be the active centre of all this life when, in 1585, the Pope claimed him for work in Rome. It was then twelve years since the first Douay priests had been ordained. Three of that group of four were dead, Bristow and Gregory Martin worn out prematurely by overwork, Ford a martyr in 1582. But the English Catholics now had their English Bible, and the college which produced this had in the twelve years sent 256 [2] trained missionary priests to their assistance, of whom twenty-five had valiantly given their lives in testimony of the faith.

There was criticism, of course, and this (as represented by Dom Maurice Chauncey, one of the London Carthusians of St. Thomas More's time, now in exile and prior of his monastery) may be best considered for the light it throws on something much nobler and more generous, the character of Allen. In his reply to Chauncey the founder paints the portrait of the missionaries of the first generation, gives, yet again, a valuable hint about the condition of things on the eve of the Reformation, and reveals very strikingly his

---

[1] The basis of this account of the college life and studies is Allen's letter of Sept. 16, 1578, to Vendeville.

[2] Knox, *Diarium Primum* (of the college), pp. 24–38.

own practical prudence in the general direction of the new
work. Chauncey had taken scandal that the priests did
not go about England in their cassocks but wearing lay
dress. He objected to their youth, their lack of professional
knowledge, and their indiscretion. Allen replies that none
were under twenty-five when despatched to the mission,
and indeed, all of them, rather more. The most of them were
not only skilled in Latin and the other learned tongues but
also 'brought up to degree in art or divinity.' Even so
'I neither sent [to England] all that would and perchance
could do good there, neither bestowed like faculty and
authority to all that went thither.' Only to those over
thirty, in fact, did he give faculties to reconcile Protestants,
or apostate Catholics. As for the less skilled : 'To some
that be of no great study, judgment or capacity I grant no
further authority but only in uplandish places, where
there is no other better learned than themselves, to hear
the common [1] Catholic people's confessions, or of that house
only where for the time they dwell.' Whatever the shortcomings of any, in this respect of ecclesiastical learning,
'none be so unfit but that they have had much more convenient institution in all kinds of pastoral doctrine than the
common sort of curates had in old time, as you may better
than I remember their want then in manner even of necessary
knowledge. . . . Many of the elder sort of priests long since
made in England, coming hither to see our trade and tarrying
with us some good time, will bear us witness in that
point. . . .'

There have not been, so far, he thanks God to be able to
say it, any worse things to report than that some 'have
unadvisedly uttered in their sudden fear some places and
persons of their resort and catholic exercise.' And then the
president flares in defence of his pupils. They are not so
learned as they might be ? 'It is not requisite, as you full
well know, that every one should be so profound to resolve
all cases that may fall, specially in man's life and conscience ;
and if any of our order in England should be so presumptious
or his master before him, to challenge so much cunning,
he were too proud [2] to be a priest or ghostly father ; as he
also is over simple or rigorous that would have none admitted
to hear confession that be not resolute in every point that

[1] *I.e.* ordinary, the word has not the modern disparaging sense.
[2] *I.e.* in the real sense of the word ; *cf.* St. Thomas Aquinas' definition of
pride as an inordinate desire for excellence.

may be propounded, or of so perfect life that no man may possibly reprehend them. Would God all could be so, for then should we poor sinners be so also ; but that golden world is past, if ever any such were.' They are not, in age, sufficiently mature ? ' Alas ! I have no old expert men to teach, nor am not able to teach such : such use not much to come to the school. And though they were never so old, would there be no faults spied among them think you ? Would all such live and teach and deal in those matters without all offence trow you ? It were to be wished, but it is not to be hoped.' Surely these men deserve a more patient judgement ' whose faults many a man spieth that prayeth not for them, as most men mark their misses and few consider in what fears and dangers they be in, and what unspeakable pains they take to serve good men's turns to their least peril. . . .' Already in this letter we can see the trenchant style that will one day mark Allen's pamphlets.

William Allen was himself no more than a mortal man. He, too, had his weaknesses, and the most serious of all, in its ultimate consequences, was a failure to realise that, as the years go by, a country and its people may so change as to become wellnigh wholly different. Simpson describes this weakness with something of his wonted acridity, ' the usual penalty of exiles—entire ignorance of the movements and feelings of his country, and the crystallisation of his brain in those feelings with which he first left England.' It was in 1565, as a man of thirty-three, that Allen saw England for the last time. Already by the date of his letter to Maurice Chauncey, twelve years later, the state of parties had greatly changed. Twelve more years of Protestantism in possession, in possession of the State, of the law, of the univer-sities, of the churches, of the pulpits, of the press ; twelve years of steady growth of the Protestant prestige ; twelve years during which Catholicism disappeared ever more deeply underground, in which the fines continued to be exacted and the ostracism from any career became ever more rigorous ; twelve years in which the Protestants became more and more venturesome, and more numerous, and in which the Catholics had grown more and more discouraged ; years in which a Catholic rising had failed, miserably, disastrously ; years that had seen, what we must next discuss, the Pope's deposition of the queen and a new trial for Catholics thereby ; years in which serious additions

had been made to the penal code ; years in which the
English people's dislike of Spaniards was rapidly becoming
a hatred of Spain ; these twelve years had passed, and of
their great effect on England Allen had but a notional
apprehension, for he could not, living in Flanders, make
any contact with the reality itself. Had he been able, in
1577, to spend six months wandering about England, what
a different thing English history might have been ! As it
was, he never seems to have seen the problem before him
except in terms of that Catholic restoration on which he
had gazed as a young man. The revolution of 1559 had
been due to trickery, and it was a minority that had
triumphed. Such a triumph could not endure. One day
the heretical success would collapse, and the great scene of
St. Andrew's Day, 1554, be renewed. Meanwhile, patience,
prayer, the work of the colleges and the aid of the Catholic
princes. Two years before his death, four years after what
we regard as the final blow to such hopes, the defeat of the
Spanish Armada, Allen, now an old man, wrote his spiritual
testament to the English Catholics,[1] and the letter shows him
still the same. ' Doubt ye not, my most sweet and faithful
coadjutors and true confessors, that our adversaries iniquities
are now in God's sight near accomplished and at the height :
on the contrary side the numbers of our brethren that are
to suffer for his truth are near made up and shortly to receive,
not only in the next, but in this world, the worthy fruits
of their happy labours. God Almighty and all merciful
will not suffer long the rod of the wicked to lay so heavy
upon the lot of the just, neither let us be tempted more
than by his grace we shall be able to bear, but will shorten
these days of affliction for the elect's sake. Comfort
yourselves herein, my loving fellows, and in the most
Christian and glorious cause that ever God's priests or
people suffered in.'

Douay did not for long remain the sole seminary for the
mission to England. In 1579 Gregory XIII transformed the
ancient Roman hospice for English pilgrims into the still
existing English College, and Douay sent a group of students
to colonise it. Ten years later the energy of Fr. Persons
brought about the foundation of Valladolid. Presently, to
anticipate the chronological sequence of this story, the

---

[1] Letter of Dec. 12, 1592, printed in *L.A.*, p. 343 *seq.*   the quotation is
rom p. 344.

ancient religious orders began to revive. There were once more English Benedictines, Franciscans, Dominicans, and these presently began to appear in England as missionaries, working side by side with the seminary priests, sharing their prisons and the sled that drew them to the gallows for the dreadful end which ever hung over every man of them. In all the chief towns of the Low Countries, in many other places, in France and Spain and Portugal, there were soon patent evidences, in the shape of English seminaries, monasteries, convents, and schools, not only of the persecution of the Catholic faith in England, but of the virility of English Catholicism.

Douay, with its great college of the secular clergy, its Benedictine monastery of St. Gregory's, its Franciscan monastery, too, and its several convents, must have worn a rarely English look for centuries to the passing English traveller.[1]

The resources of Douay College were always scanty. In the first years it was the general charity of the faithful and the alms of the neighbouring Benedictine abbeys that provided for the little community. Then, in 1570, Allen was named one of the regius professors in the university, and he made over, immediately, the whole of his salary, 200 gold crowns a year, to the common fund. He did the same when Gregory XIII, some years later, conferred on him a canonry in the wealthy cathedral of Cambrai. But the first signs of financial security only came when, in 1575, Gregory XIII assigned the college an annual pension of 1000 gold crowns.[2] Three years later Philip II made a grant of 1600 florins a year, in 1580 the papal pension was increased by a half and in 1582, thanks very largely to Fr. Persons, the King of Spain raised his contribution to 2000 florins. Nevertheless the college finances continued to be a chronic source of anxiety, for the papal pension was not sufficient for the keep of more than forty students. The students who had means paid for their keep, and there were certain amounts paid for tuition by laymen, and occasional legacies. The first of these was from Allen's old Oxford tutor, Morgan Phillips, who went with him to Douay, and, dying there in 1570, left all his property

[1] *Cf.* GUILDAY, *The English Catholic Refugees on the Continent*, London, 1914.
[2] This Pope also granted 1500 gold crowns towards the cost of printing the Rheims translation of the New Testament.

to the new foundation. But Allen, seemingly, never refused any whose talent and character gave promise of a useful missionary and so, for himself, this first period of rapid expansion and successful work remained 'these five most laborious and painful years.' [1]

§ ii. THE ENGLISH JESUITS

To complete this picture of the English mission as Allen organised it in the years that followed the foundation of the college, something must be said of a very momentous step he took in 1579, namely his request for the aid of some of the English members of the Society of Jesus.

The Society was, at this time, still something of a novelty. It was barely forty years since Paul III's bull had given it authorisation, and only twenty-three since the death of its founder, who, as yet, was not even beatified. The astonishing successes of the fathers of the first generation, the revival of religion in the great cities of Italy and Spain of which they were a leading cause, the work of Lainez and Salmeron at Trent, of St. Francis Xavier in the Indies, of St. Peter Canisius in Germany, the work now being done by Maldonatus at Paris—everywhere, in every department of the Catholic revival Jesuits were to be found in key positions —all this had produced a pro-Jesuit enthusiasm which is easy to understand if only because it must still seize hold on any reader of imagination who will study the surviving records of those times.

The very novelty of the new order, religious without a habit, without enclosure, without the choral office as the centre of their life, had, from the beginning, raised up hostile critics on all sides. The successes of the Jesuits, too, made them as many enemies, one feels, as friends. Already by 1580, the superiors of the Society needed all their prudence if, from the hostility of other Catholics, the work they were commissioned to do was not to fail. Nowhere did the antagonism show itself more keen than in the university towns, and Paris and Louvain were soon to be the scene of great conflicts.

Not every Jesuit, even then, was a saint. New orders, especially when to their novelty rapid success is added, and the apparent favour of the highest authorities, have no difficulty in recruiting new members. Not all those who

[1] Letter to the Cardinal Secretary of State, Jan. 16, 1585, KNOX, p. lxxvi.

apply, nor indeed all those accepted, are by any means what the founders envisaged. The letters of St. Peter Canisius testify to the speed with which this most delicate, if most efficient, instrument of the Counter-Reformation, began to break down once the human element declined from that heroic standard which the spirit of the Society demanded on all hands.

The Jesuit was, however, by the last quarter of the sixteenth century, justly reputed everywhere the trained man *par excellence*, the man with the new technique, the very type of the Renaissance caught and spiritualised. And, were he but true to his origins, his influence on the men of his generation was a thing to wonder at. By this time many Englishmen had joined the Society, and it was no doubt very largely the desire of enlisting auxiliaries of such worth that moved Allen to approach the Jesuit General. An additional reason, it may well be, arose from the turbulent events—' stirrs,' our forefathers would say, in whose history, for the next sixty years, the word is to recur wearyingly— in the newly founded English College at Rome. The fact of national antagonism between English and Welsh lay at the origin of these first disputes. A Welsh administration in a college where the majority were English had given the ancient feud its chance, and in the end the Holy See had surrendered to the wishes of the students and, for their Welsh superiors, substituted Jesuits. If Jesuits were to train the future missionaries for England, would it not be better that Jesuits themselves should share in the work of the mission, as Jesuits had, for years now, been sharing the work of the mission in Germany ?

Allen had known and esteemed the Society for years already. His first contacts with it were, apparently, through his friend Vendeville. He used the Jesuits for the spiritual direction of his college and he was personally known to the General, Everard Mercurian. It was in fact this priest, then superior of the province in which Douay lay, who had been commissioned to deal with Vendeville and the abbot of Anchin in the negotiations which followed the abbot's invitation to the Society to staff the new college he was founding at Douay. Allen was, at that very moment, engaged, again with Vendeville, in the first anxieties about his own college. It is hard not to believe that Mercurian and he came together. Then, in 1574, in one of the first contentions between the Society and the University of Douay regarding the status of the students of the Collège d'Anchin, Allen was one of the arbitrators appointed to decide the matter. When, two years later, Allen was seeking aid for his college from the Pope, the Douay Jesuits wrote to Rome for him, and Mercurian, now the General of the Society, backed up his appeal.

When Allen, in 1577, wrote the letter to Chauncey in which he defends so sturdily the good name of his students he described the Jesuits as ' men called of God to raise the necessary discipline of the Church and the best ghostly fathers that the Church hath.' [1] That his admiration moved as closely as might be to its logical end, namely imitation of the methods of the great Society, we can be assured from a striking passage in a letter written, one year later still, this time to the General, Fr. Everard Mercurian : [2] ' I have also taken great care that our students should be chiefly formed in the same zealous aims, studies, and discipline as your own, than which there is to-day nothing more productive of learning and a sincere piety, nor anything better adapted to a zealous gaining of souls.'

Then had come the commission to the Jesuits to administer the new English College at Rome. By the time Allen suggested that English Jesuits might be sent into England, he was already on as intimate terms with the Society as any man could be who was not himself one of its members.

Oceans of ink—seas at any rate—once flowed around this great question of the effect of the Jesuit co-operation in the mission to England. Much might have been spared the patient reader if the writers had had before them—what we can now read—the first reply of the Jesuits to Allen's suggestion. The reply shows that the Society was most unwilling to accept that suggestion, and it sets out in detail, in prophetic detail indeed, the probable consequences. It would be hard to find a document in which the practical prudence, the ability ' to deliberate well about what is good or expedient,' [3] which is the proverbial gift of the Society, is more clearly stamped on every word.

The Jesuits first of all pointed out that the English government would assuredly denounce them as political agents, and would, in advance, poison opinion against them,

[1] *L.A.*, p. 33.   [2] Letter of Oct. 26, 1578, *L.A.*, p. 69.
[3] ARISTOTLE, *Ethics*, VI, 5.

denature their actions and make any apostolic work among
the Protestants impossible. For to unravel this web and
detect the fallacy would require more wisdom than can be
expected in the mass of men. Next they objected the
spiritual perils to which the missionaries themselves would
be exposed ' obliged to go about in disguise and hide their
priesthood and their religious profession under the garb
and swagger of soldiers ; they must live apart from one
another and consort with men of doubtful character ;
they would be sent back to that world to escape which they
had sacrificed themselves. They would be overwhelmed
with business, and there would be no facilities . . . for
renewing their relaxing fervour by frequent retreats.' Finally
—and in the light of what was to happen these next prescient
sentences deserve to stand out in capitals—' on occasion of
disputes with the other priests, there were no bishops in
England to exercise ecclesiastical jurisdiction ; and it seemed
difficult to believe that so many priests and religious could
live together in one realm without jars and discords.' [1]

However, the discussion ended with a consent from the
General and he selected two of his English subjects, Fr.
Robert Persons and Fr. Edmund Campion. The miscalcu-
lations of the one were to be the foundation of the English
anti-Jesuit legend—his virtues ignored, while the radiance
of the other's spiritual genius, the richness which in him
grace perfected, was such that later generations of Catholics
have hardly seen any other figure in the Elizabethan Church.
It may safely be said that Fr. Mercurian, in the spirit of
the founder, gave of his best to the desperate venture.

' The army of missionaries was led by Dr. Goldwell, the
Bishop of St. Asaph ; with him were Dr. Morton,
the Penitentiary of St. Peter's, and four old priests of the
English hospital, Dr. Brumberg, William Giblet, Thomas
Crane, and William Kemp ; Laurence Vaux, the old
[Warden] [2] of Manchester was drawn from his cell at Louvain,
and several young priests . . . joined in the company.' [3]
These others were Ralph Sherwin, Luke Kirby, Edward
Rishton, priests, the Jesuit lay-brother Ralph Emerson, and
two young students, laymen, Thomas Bruscoe and John
Pascal. With Persons and Campion there were fifteen in all.

[1] This account is taken from Simpson's summary and not from the
original document.
[2] *I.e.* of the collegiate church there.   [3] SIMPSON, p. 142.

The movement of this caravan towards England in the early summer of 1580 is the event still described by otherwise serious historians as ' the Jesuit invasion,' and for the misleading adjective Catholics, too, must bear some responsibility who, only too often, have spoken and have written as though in the remaining twenty-three years of Elizabeth's reign, Jesuits hid behind the wainscot of every popish manor house. The anti-Catholic legend of Jesuit omnicompetence in crime is helped by the legend of more friendly creation—the no less clamorous ' rooting ' of the Jesuit ' fans ' who see the action of the Society in every Catholic success, as a certain type of Catholic critic sees it in every catastrophe. The facts are more simple. There were priests who played a leading part in the Elizabethan life of plot and counter-plot, but they were the exception. Jesuits in England there were constantly to be, henceforward from 1580, but it was not until the seventeenth century that they were at all numerous. In Elizabeth's reign there were rarely as many as a dozen of them at work in England at any one time.[1] Of the beatified martyrs of the reign eleven are classed as Jesuits, but all but four of these were wholly trained outside the Society and entered it while they were actually prisoners for the faith in England. On the other hand three of the fully trained Jesuits who suffered under Elizabeth were, in natural gifts and natural attractiveness, the finest flower of all their generation. That the memory of what they were, Edmund Campion, Henry Walpole, and Robert Southwell, and of what they did, has survived so vigorously as to shape our whole idea of the Elizabethan persecution is the tribute of time to a rare combination of natural genius and great holiness of life. And, to mention only three of the rest of the little band, Robert Persons, Henry Garnet, and John Gerard were personalities who must have stood out well above their fellows whatever the age in which they lived. But although this tiny band of Elizabethan Jesuits was so rich in personalities it remained, also, a tiny band until the end, and *pace* all writers, Catholic and Protestant, pro-Jesuit and anti-Jesuit, there was no Jesuit invasion of England in Elizabeth's reign.

Meanwhile, of course, the expedition had made its way

---

[1] In 1593, seven out of a total of thirty English Jesuit priests ; in 1598, sixteen (two in prison) ; 1610, fifty-two ; 1625, 133 ; 1632, 164 ; *cf.* FOLEY, VII, pp. lxvi–vii, lxix, lxxiii–lxxv.

into England, and its chief, Fr. Persons, was soon writing
to his Roman superiors : ' There is immense want of a
Bishop to consecrate for us the holy oils for baptism and
extreme unction and for want of which we are brought to
the greatest straits ; and unless his Holiness makes haste to
help us in this matter, we shall be soon at our wit's end.' [1]

§ iii. THE EXCOMMUNICATION OF THE QUEEN

The fortunes of that party which set out from Rome in
1580 have been told often. Its fate interests us here because,
telling the story of a missionary enterprise, we now make a
first contact with another side of the Roman action against
the Reformation in England. We enter the world where
ecclesiastics seek to attain their ends through political and
military means. What members of the party of 1580 met
their death beneath English gallows in 1581 and 1582,
did so after condemnation as traitors, convicted of plotting
the death of the sovereign, upon indictment under the Statute
of Treasons[2] of King Edward III. The story of the years
1564–1580 has been surveyed from the point of view of
religious propaganda. It must now be looked at from the
point of view of diplomacy and arms.

Let us begin with Rome. Paul IV, it has been noted,
was moved to hot anger at the news of Elizabeth's reversion,
in 1559, to the reformed religion. There was already some
talk of excommunication in French quarters, prompted by
the claim of the young dauphiness—who in this same year
became Queen of France—to the English throne. But when
Pius IV succeeded Paul IV (December 25, 1559) the King
of Spain had no difficulty in winning him round to a policy
of conciliation. The proposal to excommunicate Elizabeth
was frowned on, and as well as the Emperor,[3] the legates at
Trent urged patience and still more patience. The pressure
which had now (in 1563) occasioned these last declarations
was English and its chief agent was Dr. Nicholas Sander.

Three years passed and then, in 1566, came the election
of another new Pope, the Dominican cardinal Michele
Ghislieri, known to later history as St. Pius V. It was
perhaps this Pope's greatest service to the Church that he

---

[1] SIMPSON, p. 245.   [2] 25 Edward III, c. 1.
[3] ' Never have I seen him more moved,' the nuncio, Delfino, wrote to
Rome, June 17, 1563, describing Ferdinand's reception of the idea ; quoted
in POLLEN, p. 63.

R.C.R.

personally saw to the execution of the new laws of the recent
Council of Trent, and this in his own see first of all. Rome
had for long been a byword among Catholics as the place
where always the excellent Roman decrees were first
ignored and violated. This reproach St. Pius V removed,
it might be said, overnight, and by nothing so much as by
the force of his own constant example. He was not a
canonist, like Pius IV who preceded him and Gregory XIII
who was his successor, but a theologian ; and for some years
before his election he had been the Grand Inquisitor, an
appointment that only crowned a lifetime's work in the
struggle against heresy in Italy. Upon all who came in
contact with him St. Pius V left the ineffaceable impression
of one who never ceases to see God, and for whom nought
else exists but God's will and God's service. Never was
there a Pope, it has been said, in whom the priest so strikingly dominated all else. The witness of contemporaries
to this is unanimous. From the hardened ambassadors
of worldly Venice to our own Francis Bacon, all recognised
in him the holy one of God and bent in reverence before this
triumph of Grace.

To such a Pope what mattered first, and most, and all the
time, was the moral quality of those he was asked to help,
and the moral quality of the means proposed to him. The
politic toleration of wrongdoing in order to gain an easy
passage for Catholic schemes, he must abhor and turn away
from utterly. Such a Pope would hardly resign himself to
be a passive spectator of the slow strangulation of Catholicism
in England, and his correspondence shows that, from the very
first months of his reign, St. Pius V was far from regarding
Elizabeth as the legitimate queen.[1]

The history of the bull *Regnans in Excelsis* of February 25,
1570, by which the Pope ultimately excommunicated the
queen has never been completely reconstructed.[2] When
Mary Queen of Scots, eighteen months earlier, met her
final defeat at the battle of Langside and fled to Elizabeth's
protection, the Pope had already come to regard her as a
woman more sinned against than sinning, and as a reliable
Catholic. The Scottish queen's plight offered justification

---

[1] Elizabeth ' quæ se pro regina Angliæ gerit ' ; brief of May 2, 1566,
to Philip II, cited PASTOR, Vol. 18, p. 196, note 3.
[2] *Cf.* POLLEN, p. 143 ; history of the bull ' about which we unfortunately
still know very little.'

and opportunity for a dynastic revolution in England, and
the means of a Catholic restoration. The Pope's own story
about the origin of the excommunication scheme gave as its
one real motive the desire to quieten the consciences of the
English Catholics, who scrupled to free themselves by arms
from the tyranny that oppressed them, so long as they had
not some official declaration that Elizabeth was a heretic,
and that their oaths of allegiance no longer bound them.[1]
It was because the Pope's intention was primarily to relieve
the minds of the English Catholics that the bull was only
published in England. No Catholic prince was deputed to
carry out the sentence it contained, nor, even, was official
communication of it made to any Catholic prince. Copies
were indeed sent to Flanders and to France, but to both
places in view of the number of English exiles there to be
found. It was never displayed, as all bulls were then
displayed, in the Campo de' Fiori at Rome—whence a
certain amount of controversy as to the bull's validity—and
four months after it was published the papal nuncio at
Madrid had still only heard rumours about it. As far as
such a matter could be kept secret, while yet preserving its
essentially public character, the excommunication of
Elizabeth was muffled in secrecy.[2]

Already in March, 1569, St. Pius V was sounding the
duke of Alba, Philip II's governor in the Low Countries
and the greatest soldier of his age, as to the chances of an
invasion of England. Alba was, what he remained to the
end, discouraging in the extreme. Later on in that same year
the Pope made use of Dr. Nicholas Morton, a one-time
prebendary of Canterbury and now a penitentiary of
St. Peter's, to sound the leaders of the English Catholics
and discover how the project seemed from their point of
view. Dr. Morton was of the school of Sander, and as early
as 1564 he had been pressing the Holy See to attempt something for the ' reduction ' of England.[3] In the spring and
early summer of 1569 he went about England from one place
to another, interviewing notables and also working as a
priest with extensive powers to reconcile lapsed Catholics.
The great anti-Cecil conspiracy, in which the most varied
elements of the nobility had combined, was coming to
maturity during these months, and when Morton returned

[1] *Cf.* PASTOR, Vol. 18, p. 213 and fol.
[2] PASTOR, *ibid.*, pp. 215–218.   [3] POLLEN, p. 143.

N 2

to Rome, in September, 1569, he reported that England was ready to rise.

Morton—so Fr. Pollen [1]—was one of the chief causes of the Roman activity that produced the excommunication. However, the English situation was, as always, much more complex than any visitor could gather. The Leicester-Norfolk-Northumberland conspiracy failed entirely and then, just as Cecil was secure, the northern earls fell into the trap and, November 14, 1569, rose in hopeless rebellion. That very week new reports were coming in to Rome that all England was about to move.[2]

The Rising of the North does not concern this story, for it was not engineered from Rome nor was it, in actual fact, a Catholic rising, although the restoration of Catholicism would have followed on its success, and wherever it was successful Catholicism once more came into the light. The Rising of the North was a feudal rising, of Catholic lords and their Catholic tenantry. But there were Catholic lords on the other side too, and probably the army which put down the rising was as Catholic as the forces it opposed.[3] And once the royal army had the upper hand, the rebels were punished with even greater severity than Henry VIII had punished the Pilgrimage of Grace. At least one man was hanged in every village from Leeds to Newcastle.

One of the first acts of the two nobles who led the rising—the earls of Northumberland and Westmorland—was to write to the Pope begging his aid. This letter, written on November 7, 1569, did not, however, reach Rome until February 16, 1570. St. Pius V had not waited for such official news that the rising had begun. On February 5, at his command, the process, or trial, of the queen had begun in the Roman courts.[4] For a week various English exiles in Rome were heard, in testimony of the charges made, e.g. the imposition of the oath of supremacy, the deprivation of the bishops, the intrusion of heretics into the different sees, the imprisonment of Catholics for hearing Mass, the introduction of heretical services and sermons. Thirteen witnesses in all were heard, ten of them priests. Their

[1] *Op. cit.*, p. 143.
[2] Pastor, *ibid.*, p. 199.
[3] It was also, of course, with an army—a mercenary army—in large part Catholic, that William of Orange forced out James II in 1688.
[4] For a detailed account of the process, *cf.* Pollen, pp. 142–159, and the sources there cited.

names, and their status in the time before 1559, are of interest : Thomas Goldwell, Bishop of St. Asaph ; Maurice Clenog, bishop-elect of Bangor ; Nicholas Morton ; Henry Henshaw, rector of Lincoln College, Oxford ; Edmund Daniel, dean of Hereford ; Edward Bromburgh, fellow of New College, Oxford ; William Gyblet, priest ; William Allot, priest ; Dr. Richard Hall, of Pembroke College, Cambridge, later professor of Canon Law at Douay University, and, if not the author, then the translator into Latin of the earliest life of St. John Fisher ; Thomas Kyrton, priest. The laymen were Sir Richard Shelley, Grand Prior of the English Tongue of the Knights of St. John, a veteran from the days of Henry VIII, whom he had served for long as an ambassador, Richard Shelley the younger, and Henry Kyrton, LL.B.

These gave their testimony, the cardinals gave their counsel, and on February 12 the Pope pronounced his sentence. Four days later came the news from the northern earls that they were ' up.' The Pope sent them an encouraging letter on the 20th—the rising was, of course, all over and finished already eight weeks ago—and on February 25 the bull was published.[1] From the long elaborate sentence the defining words should be studied.

' We declare the said Elizabeth to be a heretic and an abettor of heretics, and that those who adhere to her have incurred the sentence also and are cut off from the unity of Christ's body.

' And moreover we declare that she is deprived of her pretended right to the said kingdom ; and that all her nobles, subjects, and peoples of the said kingdom, and all others who have in any way sworn allegiance to her, are absolved for ever from such oath, and from any obligation of lordship, fidelity, and homage, as now by the authority of this bull we have absolved them.

' We deprive the said Elizabeth of her alleged right to the kingdom and of all the rest aforesaid ;

' We command and we forbid all and singular her nobles, subjects, peoples, and whomsoever else we have already named, to dare to give any obedience to her counsels, her commands or to her laws.

[1] The Latin text is in TIERNEY, III, App., p. ii, an English translation in SANDER, pp. 301-304, and a resumé in POLLEN with an interesting photograph of the actual document—never, of course, sent to Elizabeth. Who would have offered to deliver it ? It is now in the Vatican Archives.

'Whoever shall act otherwise we bind with the sentence of like anathema.'

For the English Catholic who was anxious to know how the Pope felt about Elizabeth—and Sander tells us of many who put this question to him—or who was tormented by the problem of reconciling his duty to defend the faith with his allegiance to the queen, all this was excellent. Nothing could now be clearer to any Catholic who wished to rise in arms against the queen than that he was free in conscience to do so. But by the time this soothing declaration came to his knowledge, Catholics, as the whole country was well aware, had already risen, had been defeated and had been terribly punished. For an immense number of Catholics, we may be very sure, interest in this particular case of conscience would be henceforth largely academic. Yet the solution of their problem had been published, and, officially or unofficially, all the world knew it, knew that the Pope had declared that Elizabeth was not Queen of England, had declared that her subjects owed her no allegiance and, more, knew that the Pope had forbidden the queen's subjects to obey her under penalty of sharing the same excommunication. Amongst those who knew all this were, of course, the queen herself and her ministers, and lest there should be any doubt about it two Catholics, greatly daring, pasted a copy of the bull on the door of the Bishop of London's town house near St. Paul's. One of these, John Felton, was taken, admitted what he had done, and being condemned as a traitor was put to death with the usual fearsome barbarities.

The bull of St. Pius V was to be a leading element in the government's action towards Catholics for the rest of the reign. Before we come to that, it may help if some opinions of contemporary Catholics are now set down.

No copy of the bull had been sent to the King of Spain. But when the news of it reached him, he expressed himself angrily to the nuncio, wrote to his ambassador at Paris that the bull 'will embitter feelings in England and drive the queen and her friends to oppress and persecute the few good Catholics who still remain in England,'[1] and to Elizabeth herself the king wrote that no act of the Pope had caused him such displeasure.[2] Alva, to whom a bundle

[1] *Cf.* POLLEN, p. 152, with references there printed.
[2] *Cf.* PASTOR, Vol. 18, p. 218, quoting MEYER.

of copies had been sent for distribution, was no less angry. He refused to have anything to do with the matter and wrote to the Spanish ambassador in Rome that it was morally impossible for the English Catholics to obey the Pope, and that the conflict in conscience which must now ensue could not but be greatly harmful to religion. To London Alva wrote still more peremptorily, telling the ambassador there not to let anyone guess he had so much as heard of the bull.

Even the Pope seems to have wondered, later, whether he had done the best thing. In the consistory of August 3, 1570, he spoke with much lamentation of the bad situation in England, and, very pointedly, said that the issue of the bull had had the strong support of Cardinals Buoncompagni [1] and Santa Croce.[2]

The most embarrassed of all were, of course, the Catholics who had to live in England. It was just about this time, within the twelve months which followed the bull's arrival in England, that Edmund Campion left England. When, two years later, he went to Rome one of the cardinals, Gesualdi, asked his opinion about the bull. 'I said it procured much severity in England, and the heavy hand of her majesty against the Catholics.' Sander indeed wrote a defence of it, but his friends persuaded him to suppress it, and when Allen touches on the matter he immediately reverts to apologetics.

Never since 1570 has any Pope excommunicated any sovereign in such a way as to declare the subjects free from their allegiance and bound to rebel, and the history of the next century gives us an actual papal reference to the excommunication of Elizabeth which is worth recording once again. In 1641 or 1642 Urban VIII was urged to excommunicate Louis XIII of France, because he had allied himself with the King of Sweden against the Catholic champions, Philip IV of Spain and the emperor Ferdinand III, in the Thirty Years' War. The Pope replied : 'We know we may declare him excommunicate, as Pius V declared Queen Elizabeth of England, and before him Clement VII, the King of England, Henry VIII, and all at the instance of the House of Austria and the Spaniards. But with what success ? The whole world can tell. We yet bewail it with tears of

---

[1] Later pope as Gregory XIII.
[2] POLLEN, p. 155, citing MAZIERE BRADY, *Episcopal Succession in England*, II, p. 337.

blood. Wisdom does not teach us to imitate Pius V or Clement VII, but Paul V, who in the beginning, being many times urged by the Spaniards to excommunicate James, King of England, never would consent to it. . . . . '[1]

Parliament met in 1571 and the reply of the government to the excommunication can be read in two new penal statutes, which, because they were the occasion of more than one Catholic's losing his life, call for notice. The first was *An act whereby certain offences be made treason.*[2] To say that Elizabeth is not, or ought not to be queen, to say that any other person should be king or queen, to say that Elizabeth is a heretic, schismatic, tyrant, infidel, or usurper—all these offences are henceforth high treason. The second measure is *An act against the bringing in and putting in execution of Bulls and other instruments from the see of Rome.*[3] Anyone is a traitor who, after July 1, 1571, makes use of any bull, writing or instrument of absolution or reconciliation with the Roman see, who absolves or reconciles another, who receives such absolution or reconciliation or who obtains from the Pope ' any manner of bull or instrument . . . or shall publish or by any ways or means put in use any such bull.' Aiders and abettors of such traitors are liable to the præmunire penalties. Failure to denounce one who offers such absolution or reconciliation is misprison of treason. Anyone who brings into England the ' thing called by the name Agnus Dei or any crosses, pictures, beads, or such-like vain and superstitious things ' from the Pope, ' and divers pardons, immunities, and exceptions granted by the authority of the said see,' and anyone who receives such, are liable to the præmunire penalties. Three years before the first of Allen's missionaries had appeared in England, and indeed before the idea had even been mooted that the Douay priests should proceed to England, Cecil's government had riveted still more narrowly the life of the Catholic English. And by the time those first missionaries did arrive something else was also happening.

[1] SIMPSON, p. 519, quoting S.P.O., Italy, 1641–1665 ; a reference I have not been able to verify.
[2] 13 Elizabeth, c. 1 ; for the text *cf.* PROTHERO, p. 57. The act also makes it a serious offence to write or print in support of any person's right to be Elizabeth's heir ' except the same be the natural issue of the queen.'
[3] 13 Elizabeth, c. 2 ; *ibid.,* p. 60.

CHAPTER III

THE REPLY THROUGH THE TEMPORAL ARM

§ i. ROME AND THE SPANISH CHAMPION, 1559–1588

ST. PIUS V had died in May, 1572. His successor was that Cardinal Buoncompagni who had so strongly supported him in the business of the excommunication. The new Pope took the name of Gregory XIII. He has his place in history as the real founder of the system of permanent nunciatures, and also as the founder and generous supporter of a host of colleges and seminaries for the propagation of the faith in countries menaced by heresy or infidelity. Gregory XIII was already an old man of seventy at the time of his election, but he was a man of extraordinary energy, and of long administrative experience. From the first days of the reign the pace of the papal action began to increase, and in nothing more rapidly than in what related to England. It is this Pope who comes so effectively to the rescue of Allen's foundation at Douay. St. Pius V had approved and blessed the work. It was his successor who provided for it financially. And it was this same successor who set himself to a systematic effort—that only ended with his life—to dethrone Elizabeth by force of arms.

Already St. Pius V had, in 1569, sounded Alva on the chances of an invasion of England. He had written—too late, of course—an encouraging letter to the leaders of the Rising of the North, and in 1571 he had given ear to the wild schemes of that vague intriguer Ridolfi, a Florentine banker resident in London and agent there for the business of the Holy See. Ridolfi's mind constructed a great plan for England's deliverance. The Pope and the Spanish king would supply money and troops, Alva should be generalissimo, and a rising in England headed by the duke of Norfolk (not a Catholic) would seize Elizabeth, and liberate the Queen of Scots. Norfolk would declare himself a Catholic and, marrying Mary, reign with her over the England of the new restoration. How far this scheme really existed outside Ridolfi's fertile brain it is hard to say. It certainly took in the Roman authorities, and it was Ridolfi's dealing with Norfolk that brought that unfortunate young nobleman to the block in 1572. Ridolfi had, by that time, long left England behind him. While, as he thought, all was yet hidden from the English government he had crossed the seas to beseech the co-operation of Rome and Spain. Alva received him coolly, and the opinion of the soldier on this incompetent intriguer, written in a warning letter to Philip II,[1] might well be written at the head of every page of this part of the story, for it explains very much more than the particular failure of Ridolfi.

' I have seen,' writes the duke, ' the discourse which Ridolfi has given on what may be done in England. When the man that makes the discourse has no one to criticise the suppositions on which he argues, he will draw his conclusions most happily. It is like a judge passing sentence after hearing one side only. And a man like this, who is no soldier, and has never seen war in his life, thinks one can pour armies out of the air, or keep them up one's sleeve, and effect with them what his fancy depicts. For to talk as though one might have one army to take the Queen of England, another to free the Queen of Scots, and at the same time to seize the Tower of London and capture the ships in the river—really I think that even, if your Majesty had agreed with the Queen of England to do these things, you would not have enough to do it in an instant, as he proposes that it should be done. Wherefore, Sir, in the case of men of such little comprehension of what is practicable, nothing at all should be risked upon their words ; but only on their deeds, when their part is actually executed.'

Ridolfi passed from Brussels to Rome, and from Rome, with letters of recommendation, to Madrid. Here he met with a cooler reception, but the Council meeting at which his plans were debated [2] has another importance for us. Now, for the first time, the question arises of murdering Elizabeth. No one, be it noted, is recommending this. No plans are made for it. It is merely mentioned as a possibility that may

---

[1] POLLEN, p. 163, quoting GONZALEZ, *Apuntamientos MS.*, pp. 198–209, the letter is dated Aug. 29, 1571.

[2] July 7, 1571, POLLEN, p. 179.

happen during the campaign. No one is horrified, there is no
record of shudders. Elizabeth's disappearance from this
life would be a good thing all round, and she might disappear this way in a general revolutionary movement. The
possibility is mentioned, is noted, and the Council proceeds
to the next point in its agenda. We are in the sixteenth
century, not half-way through the twentieth.

Pope Gregory XIII did not, then, initiate the new papal
policy that strove to liberate the English church by force of
arms, but he took it up with an enthusiasm that never
flagged, showing ' extraordinary pertinacity ' [1] in urging
Philip II to this holy duty. And the point is of the utmost
importance, for this papal founder of seminaries was to
choose as his chief English agent in these political activities
the president of the college at Douay, Dr. William Allen
no less. We are now approaching the real crux, not of
Allen's personal history only, nor of any study of the evolu-
tion of the theory that popes may rightly depose Christian
princes, but of the history of the Catholic Church in England.
Allen's career as a politician began when, in December,
1575, Gregory XIII summoned him to Rome to give his
opinion on the proposed joint expedition—the Pope and
Spain—to free Mary Queen of Scots. Allen was in favour
of the idea.[2] From now on he plays a dual role in the great
drama, and, not through his own fault, a singularly sterile
role, for all these schemes and projects were vowed to futility
from their first inception. But the Counter-Reformation in
England henceforth proceeds by a double method, and, in
the opinion of some of its chiefs, it does so necessarily.
Twenty years after Allen's début as a political leader, when
Gregory XIII was dead and Allen too, and when a new
spirit was beginning to inspire the Roman Curia, Sir Francis
Englefield, one of Allen's old and closest companions-at-
arms, wrote his last letter to Philip II, and in it he set out the
purpose which had inspired Pope Gregory and his collaborators. ' Without the support and the troops of Spain,' he
declared, ' it is scarcely probable that England will ever be
overcome and solidly established in the Catholic religion :
and although the seminaries are the most powerful means
and the most certain, to prepare men's minds, they must fail
to achieve the desired end, if temporal forces do not assist

[1] POLLEN, p. 200.   [2] *Ibid.*, p. 220.

at the appropriate moment.' [1] The missionary movement
could not survive unless Cecil and all that he stood for were
driven from power, and only Spanish armies could do this.
On the other hand, the seminaries would serve to prepare
men's minds—according to the King of Spain's view of the
matter ; the best policy for the present being, he wrote in
1582, ' to gain souls by way of teaching, and thus to fortify
the Catholic party for its time and occasion, without
precipitating matters through impatience.' [2]

The drama of the next twenty years must, of course, be
seen historically. It must not, under pain of falsifying the
truth and leaving the story a mass of incomprehensible
contradictions, be envisaged as a conflict between the
Catholicism of this mid-twentieth century and modern
Anglicanism. The personalities of the opposing leaders do
not resemble less those of their present-day successors than
do the problems of the sixteenth century those we now have
to face. The moral law, of course, never changes. What is
in itself wrong in one age is wrong in all ages. Treason
never ceases to be treason. Murder is always murder. Yet
we (who have never been faced with the terrible question
who is our lawful ruler ? to which of rival claimants—one
certainly king *de facto* and the other just as certainly not—
do we, as to the *de jure* sovereign, owe in conscience aid and
allegiance ?) may spare a little patience to the casuistry of
generations to whom this was desperately practical. I write
this not with reference to the men whom in our own time
the Holy See has set up for our veneration as martyrs and
who were, many of them, executed as convicted traitors,
but with reference to such Catholics as Allen and Englefield
and Persons, who undoubtedly schemed to levy war on the
de facto sovereign and to deprive her through foreign arms.

We must make the effort to see the events as they happened.
It is all very unlike the home life of sovereigns (and popes)
of later beloved memory, but what 1575 ought to have been
cannot be judged by what 1940 is. And the first thing to
grasp is the menace which Calvinism, in this generation,
presented to all that the greater part of Europe knew as
civilisation. In one country after another, wherever the
Calvinist doctrine and organisation had penetrated, there

---

[1] Sept. 8, 1596 ; text in TIERNEY, III, App., p. xlviii *seq.*
[2] Philip II to his ambassador at Paris, quoted SIMPSON, p. 279, but
without any reference.

had been a general wreckage of the old order. Everywhere
the reform of religion had been the means of a minority,
a minority well endowed with wealth, seizing the instruments of government. It was not merely a question of
the simple artisan who, through his vernacular Bible and the
competent sermons of his trained Calvinist pastor, through
the systematic instruction and the modern devotions, found
himself spiritually and his kinship with God. This was
maybe the final and the lasting effect of Calvinism at its
rare best. But it was as the powerful organisation of wealthy
minority groups, mastering first of all separate states and
then threatening to master in similar fashion the commonwealth of Christendom, and wherever it was master destroying ruthlessly the old religion it held for idolatry and all that
society whose basis was the Catholic Church, it was as the
universal menace that the popes of the period 1559–1592
saw and fought in every part of Europe *la religion prétendue
reformée*, and never ceased their endeavours to league the
Catholic princes in the battle against it. Whether this view
was correct, this was their view, and, in a time which has
seen political minorities dominate and exploit, to the
imminent danger of all we hold dear, two of the greatest
states of the world, we can shed the nineteenth-century
prejudgement that the sixteenth-century Catholics cannot
have been sincere in their passionate anti-Calvinism
because such things just cannot happen in that way.

Related to this dread of Calvinism as the universal menace,
is the second permanent feature of the later sixteenth-
century popes' view of their office, namely, their duty to
liberate the Catholic peoples from this tyranny that oppressed
them. These popes saw England, rightly or wrongly, as
a country where a leaderless Catholic majority was dominated by a clique of heretics, possessed of the sovereign's
ear and of all the means of government. And ceaselessly,
from 1570, the popes strove to enlist the one Catholic prince
whose hands were free of rebellion at home, and who was
possessed of armies and captains, in the liberating crusade
which they planned. The Spanish king's problems were, we
can see it now from the most cursory study, very much more
complex than the Roman diplomacy realised. It is one of
the basic causes of the failure of so much activity that, from
the beginning, the popes tended to over-simplify the English
situation, the European situation and the infinity of cross-

purposes of which the lonely man in the Escorial was the centre. They were sometimes theologians, and sometimes canonists, diplomatists or administrators, but over and over again their action suggests that, in political and military matters, they are but ecclesiastics and hopelessly out of their depth. On the unfortunate Gregory XIII—who, however, went serenely to his end without guessing the tragic failures that centred round his reign—the historians, the Catholic historians, have of late been very severe. Pastor speaks of his efforts as ' unfortunate in their results and lamentably misinformed.' [1] Fr. Pollen roundly declares that his zeal was not according to knowledge, that it was not practical, that it was lacking in simplicity. He taxes the Pope—and we must bear in mind that it is a man in his seventies of whom he writes—with habitual refusal to look squarely at the objections to his plans. He finds ' a want of straightforwardness ' and notes how the nuncio in Spain was snubbed so badly when he sent information which did not tend to confirm the papal view of things, that he practically ceased, thenceforward, to send any real information at all. It was ' impious to entertain doubts.' In Rome there was ' a determination to see things in their own way,' and, most disastrously of all, there is the ' support of an obviously risky measure on the fatalistic assumption that God must bless and prosper what was undertaken for a good purpose.' We shall now pass to the summary of the political activities of the reign (1572–1585) and keep in mind the last writer's pertinent comment, that ' in reality [Gregory XIII and his advisers and helpers] were provoking instant destruction for the men they were trusting and a fearful retaliation on their own friends.' [2] He also says, and, in fairness to Fr. Pollen, this should not be omitted : ' If they had appreciated the risks to which they were exposing the English Catholics we may be sure that they would never have acted as they did.' [3]

What exactly were these political schemes against Elizabeth in which, for twenty years (1569–1588) successive popes were so busily engaged ? The full tale is too long to tell here, but some kind of chronological catalogue is essential to any understanding of the subsequent history of the English who remained Catholic. The first project was

[1] Vol. 19, p. 404.   [2] POLLEN, p. 200.   [3] Ibid., p. 199.

that Ridolfi's plot already mentioned. Here the originating mind was not Roman, but the Pope gave the scheme every encouragement once it was brought to his notice. By the time this plan had broken down, the autumn of 1571, there had reappeared in Rome a dissolute swashbuckling scoundrel from Devonshire, one Thomas Stukely by name. This impudent adventurer had already striven hard to win a living by his wits out of Catholicism, but, so far as St. Pius V was concerned, without success. Now, with the merit of a brave share in the great fight of Lepanto, he returned, and this time the Pope listened to his plans for a war on Elizabeth, was even impressed, and wrote to Philip II suggesting Stukely as a likely generalissimo and offering to launch the expedition under the flag of the Holy See, if Philip would help with arms and men and money. Philip, however, declined, January 11, 1572, and then, in May of that same year, the Pope died.

His successor owed his speedy election, a matter of half a day's conclave, with as many as fifty-one cardinals taking part, almost entirely to Philip II's influence. The king's agent was his minister at Naples, that Cardinal Granvelle whom already we have seen active with considerable effect on English affairs at Brussels in 1554. Granvelle arrived in Rome as the conclave was about to begin, May 12, 1572, and it was an alliance of his contriving—he came as the Spanish king's accredited voice—with Farnese, personally the most influential of all the cardinals and the 'favourite' for the election, and with Bonelli, the late Pope's nephew and the chief of the *bloc* of cardinals created by him, that decided the matter. The three agreed on Ugo Buoncompagni, a man sympathetic to Philip II ever since he went as legate to Spain for Pius IV in 1565, and the election was settled. There would be no more of the friction between Rome and its principal champion now that, to a theologian whose attachment to principle seemed fanatical to politicians, there succeeded this practical administrator, with his more supple jurist's mind. Buoncompagni showed his understanding of the power that had made him Pope by giving his own vote, in the purely formal ballot that gave official value to the decision, to Cardinal Granvelle.

Philip II had now a friend in the supreme place, but Gregory XIII, if he did not continue along the lines of Pius V in his dealings with Spain, did not betray his predecessor by any surrenders, and in regard to Spain's co-operation against England he showed himself still more interested and indeed, in his demands, importunate.

Before a year had elapsed he had sent on to Philip, the agent of the exiles in Flanders, Nicholas Sander. Philip, by no means so eager as the Pope, contrived to stall this fiery theologian, and while he champed impotently, Gregory, in February, 1574, made a new assault on the king through the nuncio. Seven months later his importunity won him a kind of answer. Stukely had now produced a scheme for a raid which would free the Queen of Scots. The King of Spain was, at any rate, ' not averse ' ; the papal secretary, Galli, Cardinal of Como, was keen, and the Pope, curiously, somewhat hesitant. But only at the beginning. Gradually, as quickly as the slowness of a post would allow that took weeks to pass between Rome and Madrid, and Rome and Flanders, and Flanders again and Madrid, during the year 1575, the project took shape. It was finally decided that February, 1577, would be a suitable time. The expedition should go under the papal colours. Don John of Austria should command it. The excommunication should be renewed and Mary, once liberated, should be put in place of the dethroned Elizabeth—or if not Mary, then the next surviving heir of the Yorkist line. Don John of Austria was, however, to be employed on other business in the months when he should have been fitting out the English expedition. The whole of 1576 was taken up with a most serious crisis in the affairs of the Low Countries, and all the energies of Spain went to preserve the hold of Philip II on his most valuable provinces. By the end of the year the king brought the English scheme to an end.

But in 1577 it was revived, by Don John himself, fired with a romantic devotion to the imprisoned queen and an ambition to use his great powers free from the cramping paralysis of King Philip's habitual delays. He found a most enthusiastic ally in the Pope, who sent him a special nuncio, and also an immense subsidy. Yet once again a renewal of the crisis in Flanders was an obstacle, and the way in which the affair had been negotiated with Rome threatened a diplomatic breach between Philip and the Pope. Then, October 1, 1577, Don John's sudden and untimely death brought this particular scheme to an end.

The Rome of Gregory XIII did not, however, suffer

any lack of willing champions and adventurers for anything anti-Elizabethan, and while the last scenes of the enterprise just mentioned were being played in the camp before Namur, Stukely had persuaded the Roman authorities to give him men, arms, ships, and money. By this time Stukely's real character had become apparent to the Cardinal Secretary at any rate, though it still took in the learned Owen Lewis and his compatriot, Maurice Clenog. But the Cardinal of Como behaved with almost incredible ' levity.' [1] If the expedition did no good, it could do no harm, he declared, and at any rate Stukely might serve as a thorn in Elizabeth's side, much as Orange was a thorn in the side of Philip II. Como had been warned from Spain that Stukely was ' a braggart and a bankrupt,' [2] and all he can say is that if he is no worse than that, good service may yet be expected of him. So the Pope made the adventurer marquess of Leinster, and in January, 1578, he set out. At Cascares in Portugal he fell in with the last of the crusaders, King Sebastian, then about to lead an army against the Moors. Stukely joined forces with him—Como consenting ! —and at the disastrous defeat of Alcazar, August, 1578, with King Sebastian, Stukely, too, was killed.

Another iron, papally placed, had gone cold. There were yet others warming. The year which had seen the first moves in the scheme that ended at Alcazar had brought also to Rome in search of aid a man of far different type from Stukely. This was James Fitzmaurice, a kinsman of the earl of Desmond. Gregory welcomed him also, and gave his proposed expedition the spiritual status of a crusade. All who joined his army or aided him in any way were granted the indulgences granted to those going to war against the Turks. [3] The Pope also gave him monies and Como gave him letters to the papal representative at Lisbon, to aid him in finding a ship. Once Fitzmaurice had raised the revolt reinforcements would be sent. The Irishman left Rome with this encouragement, and then there followed a series of heart-breaking experiences, waiting on the King of Spain's irresolution, at Madrid, until finally in November, 1577, Fitzmaurice set sail for Ireland from Lisbon, with the

---

[1] Fr. Pollen's word for it, *op. cit.*, p. 225.
[2] *Ibid.*, p. 225.
[3] *Cf.* Brief of Feb. 25, 1577, in M. V. RONAN, *The Reformation in Ireland under Elizabeth* (1930), p. 560.

Franciscan Bishop of Mayo, Patrick O'Hely, and perhaps eighty soldiers. In January, 1578, they lost their ship, by a mutiny, and then came a further year and a half's wait in Portugal and Spain, what time the concrete papal favour went to Stukely. After the Stukely debacle, the scheme to assist Fitzmaurice was taken up once again. Once more there were conferences, councils of war, projects, memoranda, correspondence between Rome and Madrid, and then, after nine weary months, the expedition set sail from Ferrol, June 17, 1579. In view of the menace it was made to sound, when, later on, Dr. Sander and his warlike ventures were quoted as justification for the next step in the persecution of the English Catholics, it may here be noted that the total force was one small ship, which carried a dozen ecclesiastics and perhaps fifty soldiers. 'Their strength,' wrote the nuncio at Madrid, Filippo Sega,[2] 'lay in Fitzmaurice's name . . . in their being representatives of the Pope, and in the precious banner blessed by His Holiness' hands—on which was emblazoned a Christ upon the Cross.'

The crusade was soon ended. Fitzmaurice landed at Dingle Bay just one month after he had sailed from Ferrol. On August 18 he was slain in a skirmish at a place not satisfactorily identified, somewhere to the east of Limerick. About the same time, and perhaps on that very day, Bishop O'Hely was hanged at Kilmallock, after torture, by the Lord President of Munster, Sir William Drury. The tiny garrison which Fitzmaurice had left at Smerwick held out for some months yet, and finally in August, 1580, the promised reinforcements left Spain, six hundred men with arms for another two thousand. The new force was soon surrounded, and after three days it surrendered, only to be butchered with unusual savagery (November 10, 1580).

While these things were happening on the remote borderland of Kerry and West Cork, Philip II was chiefly occupied with the affairs of Portugal. The death of King Sebastian at Alcazar (August 4, 1578) had brought to the throne his aged great-uncle, the Cardinal Infante Henry. When he came to die who would rule in Portugal ? Philip II had a claim, for he was the eldest son of the cardinal-king's eldest sister. The cardinal-king died in 1580, and the year of crisis found Philip concerned solely for the conquest of

[1] Quoted RONAN, p. 610, from *Relazione Compendiosa* (*Vat. Arch.*).

Portugal, despite the unceasing pleas of the Pope that he would turn his armies rather against England, and despite the Pope's offer of generous subsidies.

By the time the Fitzmaurice expedition came to its bloody end, the Holy See had been for six years, without intermission, seeking to effect a change of government in England by force of arms. Gregory XIII had yet another four and a half years to reign, and as undismayed by the failures in Ireland as by Stukely's treachery, he continued to bend himself to the task.

The scenes of the chief activity in the next phase of this movement are Paris and Scotland, and as well as to Philip II the Pope now looks for help to the great French family of Guise, the nephews of Mary Queen of Scots, the leaders, more and more, of the militant Catholic party in France, and the allies in spirit, as the determined enemies of the Huguenots, of Philip II. What turned the mind of the Roman politicians to these new allies and changed a little the direction of their attack, was a revolution that occurred in Scotland in this year 1580. The young king James VI, the son of Mary Queen of Scots, was but a boy of fourteen, and since his mother's captivity Scotland had really been ruled by two men of iron, first by his half-uncle the earl of Moray, and then, after Moray's murder in 1570, by the earl of Morton. These men were, both of them, typical politicians of their time, and, not being Catholic, were fanatically anti-Catholic. The disappearance of Morton—at the hands of the public executioner—was already something of a gain for Catholicism, but the advent to power, a month later, of the king's kinsman, Esmé Stuart d'Aubigny, soon to be duke of Lennox, sent Catholic hopes soaring. For Lennox was a Catholic and he had, apparently, all the precocious boy-king's confidence. In the centres abroad where politically-minded Catholics gathered, plans and combinations leapt, almost unbidden, to the minds of all. And here it is that Fr. Robert Persons, S.J., makes his first steps, not indeed as a plotter or a politician, but as a spiritual adventurer in the high field of royal consciences. The news of the happenings in Scotland in the summer of 1580 prompted him, in 1581, to send to Scotland an English secular priest, one William Watts, to study the chances of James VI's conversion to the faith of his mother. Presently a great scheme took shape. James would become a Catholic, Mary would be set free, Cecil would be driven out and Elizabeth given the choice between acceptance of Catholicism and deposition. The means were simple. The converted James would cross the border with an army, and the English Catholic nobles would rise in arms. By December, 1581, the Pope was interested in the scheme, and in January, 1582, he sent [1] Fr. William Crichton, a Scottish Jesuit, to Paris to take part in a great council of ways and means. The nuncio at Paris, the ambassador of Mary Queen of Scots, the duke of Guise, and Fr. Persons, these were the other counsellors, and from their deliberations Fr. Crichton went on to Lennox in Scotland. Allen, too, was in the secret. May found Crichton back in Paris with Lennox's agreement and some details, and while Crichton went on to Rome to report, Persons was given a like commission to the King of Spain. The Pope, however, had grown more cautious now. He would pay out no money until the troops had moved. Philip II was no readier. He did his best to prevent Persons coming to him, but vainly, for the Jesuit had left Paris before Philip's letter reached the Spanish ambassador there. And Philip left the exhortation of Pope Gregory, this time, without an answer. Here, if ever, Pope and king must share the honours. It was truly the case of Lord Chatham and Sir Richard Strachan, and while each awaited the other, the golden hour had slipped by. On August 23, 1582, a counter-revolution in Scotland—the Raid of Ruthven— drove Lennox from power and put James VI once more under the control of the Calvinists.

Nine months later the indefatigable crusaders produced a new scheme. The Spaniards should land an army, either in Scotland or in the north of England—Allen drafted a strong memorandum pleading it should not be in Scotland —while an army raised by Guise would descend on Sussex. The Pope would contribute 13,000 ducats. It was in May, 1583, that this scheme was prepared. In June the King of Scotland escaped from the nobles who had held him captive since the previous August, and now both Guise and the Pope managed to get into communication with him and in his letters he showed himself willing to co-operate. Once more Crichton took the road from Paris to Rome,

[1] This should be noted, *i.e.* that it was at the Pope's bidding that the Jesuit took part in this political action. Is it too much to guess that it was this same high authority which threw Persons also into activities of this sort ?

while Persons again journeyed south to Madrid. He urged
that the Pope should renew the excommunication of Elizabeth, and Gregory consented, and a draft of the proposed
new bull survives to this day, it appears, in that Archivio
Vaticano that holds so many memorials of schemes that
missed fire. Allen, it was arranged, should go as papal legate
with the army that would invade the north, and to give
him a good local standing he was to be consecrated Bishop
of Durham. The Pope was now showing himself as keen as
seven years before, and lavish in his offers of money towards
the King of Spain's expenses. But, as seven years before,
a crisis in the wars in the Low Countries, with repercussions
in France that involved the Guises in a conflict with the
crown, halted the whole business. By the new year, 1584,
James VI was anxiously ' cooling off.' If the Pope's help
were not prompt and really powerful, he was writing to
Guise, he must necessarily go over to the Protestants and
throw himself into the arms of Elizabeth (February 19,
1584). He could not resist any longer. And while this was
being written from Scotland, the rank and file among the
exiles, English and Scots alike, were rapidly losing hope.
In August the careful Philip II had come to the conclusion
that the affair would cost at least two million crowns, and it
must therefore wait. All was now over, and it only needed
James' ambassador to the Paris conference to betray the
whole thing to Elizabeth, which he did, *en route* from
France to report to his master. As for the French king,
Henry III, Mary Stuart's brother-in-law, he declared to
her, in May, 1584, that he would see Elizabeth queen even of
Scotland rather than ally himself with the Guises and Spain,
even for Mary's liberation, a queen-dowager of France.

In June, 1584, Henry III's sole remaining brother died,
that Duc d'Anjou who had courted Elizabeth, and around
whose courtship the hopes of some of the English Catholics
had for a time centred. From this moment the political
situation on the continent was bound to change, and
rapidly. The chief reason for this was that, by this prince's
death, the Huguenot leader, Henry of Navarre, became
heir to the crown of France. The militant Catholics,
banded now in the Holy League, would never be brought
to allow a heretic to rule over them. Guise was their leader,
and the King of Spain would be their strong ally. France
was drifting to what promised to be the most dangerous of

all civil wars, and before Philip II lay the chance of a
new route to European hegemony, and, incidentally, a
new opportunity of settling the problem of England. He
could now afford to notice openly the long English aggression, the immense damage done to his commerce and to
his prestige by a country which stood out to contemporaries
not only as a centre of heresy, but as a great pirate state.[1]
For the first time the Spanish king could think of a war with
England in which France would not be able to stab him
in the back through Flanders.

Curiously enough, this moment at which Philip II was
preparing to take the lead in ' the enterprise of England '
found Allen and Persons in what looked like final despair of
all political schemes. ' Dr. Allen and I . . . had resolved
to leave cogitation of such matters,' wrote Persons, ' and to
follow only our spiritual course, whereupon all dependeth
though in longer time.' And then in the autumn of 1584
Fr. Crichton was captured at sea, and with him all the
undestroyed papers relating to the scheme of 1583.   Elizabeth's government now had all the proof they wanted that
Rome and Spain were really leagued against them.

Gregory XIII did not survive the failure of 1584 long
enough to make another move in the war against Elizabeth.
He was now well past his eightieth year, and on April 10,
1585, he died, somewhat suddenly. Just a fortnight later
the cardinals elected, most unexpectedly,[2] and before the
King of Spain's instructions could arrive, one whom Gregory
had for thirteen years kept out of all public employment,
the Franciscan Felice Perretti, known as the Cardinal of
Montalto.   He took the name of Sixtus V.

The new Pope was one of those titanic personages, more
common in the century of the Renaissance than in this
later age of the Counter-Reformation. He had all the
driving force of Julius II and the violent hatred of clerical
slackness and crime which marked Paul IV. St. Pius V
had been his great patron and was now to be his exemplar.
And with all this immense power of action there was joined
in Sixtus V an extremely acute sense of what was practically

---

[1] *Cf.* Dasent in his Introduction to *Registers of the Privy Council*, VII,
1558–1570. ' It is scarcely an exaggeration to say that the keynote of the
present volume is piracy.'

[2] By ' an ecclesiastical and religious election.' PASTOR, Vol. 20, p. 9.

possible. In the time of Pius V the first initiatives in ' the enterprise of England ' had come from English exiles like Morton and Sander. In the next reign the initiative had lain with the Pope himself, while the King of Spain was dragged into the successive schemes more or less reluctantly. Now, at the moment when Philip II was making the settlement of Elizabeth his primary concern, there had been elected a Pope with a mind of his own—as to ends and means—about England and about every other Catholic and European problem, a Pope, moreover, whose ideal of the relations that should exist between the Pope and the Catholic champion was medieval. Philip II, if he expected the blessing of God on his arms, should place himself at the service of the Pope, and purify himself for the holy assault by penance for past sins ; and for no sin so much as for his ceaseless encroachment on ecclesiastical jurisdiction.

Sixtus V, indeed, suspected to the end the purity of Philip's motives in this role of champion of the Faith. He made no secret of his suspicions and no political considerations ever held him back from his duty of resisting the King of Spain's usurpations in spiritual matters. With the tacit consent of earlier popes Philip had become, in some ways, as supreme over religion in Spain as Elizabeth was over religion in England. More seriously still, he seemed to be on the point of controlling the very papacy. The day might come when he would simply nominate the Pope, and in that day the Church would fall more catastrophically than even before Luther or Calvin or Elizabeth. From the point of view of this menace presented by the Catholic champion to the liberty of the Church, the reign of Sixtus V is all-important. For he so wrenched the papacy away from the tutelage of Spain that, although he did not himself live to see it, the century ended with the papal action more independent than at any time since the election of Charles V.[1] Never since the reign of Sixtus V has there been any real danger of a papacy surrendered to the will of the Catholic prince. To have brought this about is perhaps the greatest achievement of this Franciscan Pope, greater even than his great construction of the *Curia Romana*, as all later centuries have known it, or than any of the other mighty works that filled the short five years of his reign and which the two well-packed volumes of Pastor can do little more than list.

[1] 1519.

The collaboration of such a spirit with Philip II in ' the enterprise of England ' has an interest all its own. It is Philip who now takes the lead, and the Pope who, more or less grudgingly, enters into the political scheme and always with great care that guarantees are given which will leave the papal supremacy intact, and that no monies will be paid until the fruits of victory are, at any rate, grasped.

The year 1585, memorable for the change of policy on Philip's part and for the appearance of the dynamic Sixtus V, saw, as the first result of this new combination, Allen's departure from Douay, and the end of his actual direction of the college. In September of that year the new Pope summoned him to Rome, and at Rome he remained for the rest of his life. Once in Rome Allen worked hand in hand with Philip's ambassador there, the Count of Olivares, to engage the interest of the suspicious Pope and enlist his sympathy. It was Allen's single-minded enthusiasm, his genuine devotion to the cause of restoring the faith, which finally broke through the Pope's reserve, and by February, 1586, Olivares could report to Spain that Allen had ' inspired the Pope with a great desire for the enterprise of England.' [1] And during these same months Philip II began a siege of the Pope to obtain the red hat for the Englishman.

The suspicions of Sixtus V were not the sole obstacle which had to be overcome. There was also, for instance, the rival scheme to annihilate Protestantism by the conquest of Geneva, and there was the notion, which never left the Pope, that Elizabeth, properly handled, might be converted. One of his agents, so he believed, actually penetrated to the court and made to her the offer of the Pope's friendship. But though the Pope never altogether abandoned the hope of ' Jezabel's ' conversion, from 1586 onwards he took his share in the political activities as constantly as Gregory XIII.

The great affair now was, of course, the preparation and despatch of the Armada. Mary Queen of Scots was put to death in February, 1587. At the end of July in that same year the Pope and the King of Spain came to terms. Sixtus promised a million scudi and Philip pledged himself that the fleet would sail this same year, that he would name as King of England some Catholic accepted by the Pope (who would receive his kingdom as from the Pope), and

---

[1] Text in *L.A.*, p. 51 ; translated in *L.A.* Introduction, p. lxxiii.

that all church lands and properties held in England by laymen would revert to the Holy See. This was to be kept a profound secret, as also was the fact that Allen, created cardinal August 7, 1587, only a week later than this pact, was to go with the expedition as legate and play the same role in the restoration of 1587 that Pole had played in 1554.

There is no need to tell yet again the story of the Spanish Armada, how Drake's daring destroyed the fleet as it was being prepared in 1587, how the superior seamanship of the English harried and broke the great fleet when, in July, 1588, it finally neared the shores of England. With the resounding defeat of Philip's first great offensive against Elizabeth, the mainspring broke of all that Papal-Spanish political alliance which had been active for now twenty years, and it broke beyond repair.

In its last stage Allen had been at the very heart of the manœuvres. ' Parma by order, as I take it, of the King of Spain,' he wrote to Mary Stuart, ' acquainteth none particularly and fully with these things but myself, [Parsons] and Owen.' [1] Now he was to suffer the full force of the reaction in Rome, a reaction all the more evident after Spain was defeated in the conclave that elected Clement VIII, in January, 1592. This was the fourth conclave in eighteen months, and the defeat followed on three Spanish victories, the election of the short-lived chaplain-Popes of Philip II, Urban VII, Gregory XIV, and Innocent IX. These transient pontiffs gave place in 1592 to Clement VIII, a Pope who combined the determination of Sixtus V with the tact of Pius IV, and the policy of Gregory XIII, with regard to England, was laid aside, once and for all. Clement VIII had never known the pre-Reformation Church—he was no more than fifty-five at his election in 1592 ; he had none of that sense of the Spanish champions as simple gifts of God to the heresy-endangered Church which had been almost inevitable in so many of his predecessors. And in another respect also his election was the sign that a new age had come, for Clement VIII's memory did not go back so far as the foundation of the Jesuits. He was the first of the Popes not to have known the Society as an astonishing novelty of spiritual efficiency, a very revolution in spiritual technique, an apostolate that

[1] Feb. 5, 1585 ; *L.A.*, p. 247.

put the Church, so to speak, very heavily indeed in the debt of the fathers. The new Pope, like all mankind since, had always known the Jesuits. Their great achievement was, by his time, part of the accepted order. The time was already taking it for granted, and, detached from wonder and from awe, showing itself as critical of the Society as of any other Catholic institution.

Allen survived the dawn of this new age, in which, at Rome, Spain and the Society were counting so less considerably, for nearly three years. It was as the future legate of the English reconciliation that Sixtus V had given him his hat, rather than as the preserver of Catholicism in England, which is surely his title to glory. Otherwise this Pope had little use for the great scholar and administrator that Allen had proved himself. Pastor speaks of him as esteemed indeed, in a Rome that did not guess at a tithe of his great capabilities, and Olivares has left us a picture of Sixtus V treating him 'like a nigger.' The English cardinal was, it is true, employed on the commission for the revision of the Vulgate text, both by Sixtus V and Clement VIII. He had his place as the Cardinal of England, and the titular head of his nation, and as such he remained the single force, which, after thirty years of dissolution, still bound together the heterogeneous and conflicting remnants of English Catholicism. Otherwise few troubled about his needs or his wants. Philip II, in 1589, nominated him to the archiepiscopal see of Mechlin, but the see was bankrupt and Allen far too poor to be able to accept it. Olivares describes that poverty for us : 'No one has given him anything, since he does not fill any of the offices which others turn to their account, nor does he seek after those means of which men who have not his regard for propriety avail themselves. Thus he could not go forward nor backward, and that he might not drop from hunger I am forced to help him with Your Majesty's money.' Three years later things are no better : 'Though his style of living is narrow and pinched [it] has not been enough to allow of his buying cloth to hang his rooms, nor a bed to sleep on, for the one he uses is mine, and with all this he owes some money, as I can also in part testify.' So the great leader who had never spared his own fortune, nor his very life so far as he could give it, who for all his great abilities was so singularly free from ambition or any thought of self, slowly came to his end, crowned with empty honours that only set off the dereliction in which he was left, a dereliction that was a fitting symbol of the fate of his own people. But even that dereliction was not to be final, though it was to go as far almost as utter ruin.

Allen, in the founding of Douay, had ensured that the light of faith in England should never lack those who alone can tend it, and he had had the grace to be the schoolmaster of martyrs. 'The instruments [for the conversion of England] are his disciples,' Olivares declared to Sixtus V in 1587, pleading for Allen's elevation, ' of whom so many have suffered martyrdom that the scarlet of his hat may be said to have been dyed in the blood of the martyrs whom he has formed.' Indeed the thought of the martyrs never left him. He had formed them, he had defended them against the slanders of Burghley, he had been the first insistent advocate of their cause at Rome, and when he came to die it was in their company and in their spirit. The hideously painful strangury which had nearly killed him in 1585, took hold of him once more in 1594, and almost his last words to Philip II's ambassador, faithfully attendant to the end on this last and greatest of Philip's one-time English subjects, words carefully recorded and sent on to the king, were these : ' That the greatest pain he suffered was to see that after God had given him the grace that by his persuasion so many had borne imprisonments, persecutions and martyrdom in England, he had deserved by his sins to end his life on that bed.' He died on October 13, 1594, sixty-two years old, and was buried in the English College church.

The defeat of the Armada marks the end of the alliance between the papacy and Spain for the forcible reduction of England to the Roman obedience. Of all the schemes proposed and decided on during something like twenty years, two only matured, the Irish expedition of Fitzmaurice in 1579 and the Armada itself. There were, however, other schemes, which we may more exactly style plots— since they were the work not of sovereign princes, but of discontented individual subjects—during this same period, and the story of them can be read in all the text-books which treat of Elizabeth's reign. There are, for example, the plots of Francis Throckmorton in 1583, of Somerville and Arden in that same year, of Antony Babington in 1586.

In all these plots to try to bring about a change of government, Catholics were, it is true, participators. But none of these plots had their origin in Rome, nor did the popes in any way direct them or have a share in them. It is indeed an ironic circumstance that while the popes were planning —and always vainly—to bring about a rising in England, Englishmen should actually be setting themselves to the good work and the Pope be ignorant of their endeavours until all was over and the plots discovered. These several plots apart, there remain for our consideration yet a third variety of schemes. Here the plotters are again private individuals among Elizabeth's subjects. Their aim is to murder the queen, and the charge has been brought that the popes were cognisant of these plots and encouraged the plotters. The charge is too serious to be neglected.

The first time we hear any talk of Elizabeth being murdered, is at the Spanish Council, when Ridolfi's scheme is under discussion, in July, 1571.[1] One important detail of this project was the capture of Elizabeth : ' to seize the person of the Queen of England in order to secure for myself that of the Queen of Scotland,' Norfolk says in the *Instructions* for Ridolfi which he signed. Alva, writing to Philip II about this part of the scheme, moves a step farther in this meditation on Elizabeth as a possible security for Mary, and he says : ' In case the Queen of England were dead, whether by a natural death or not, or if they seized upon her person, without our having anything to do with it— then all would change.' By the time the matter is discussed at Madrid it is no longer merely the chance that Elizabeth may be killed that appears in the papers, but the alternative ' killing or capturing.' But in Alva's final letter on the subject, ' killing ' drops out altogether. It is a question merely of ' capturing.' Can Ridolfi be said to have plotted to murder Elizabeth ? or indeed, can anyone, in 1571 ? In any case all this belongs to Spain, and in no way does it involve the Pope. The Pope at this particular time was Pius V, the last of the popes to be canonised, and it would be something calling violently for explanation that such a pope was involved in an assassination. Yet this is precisely the charge made against him by no less a person than the great Catholic historian of the last century, Lord Acton.

[1] For Ridolfi, *cf.* POLLEN, pp. 160–184.

Because of the religion and the scholarly standing of the accuser the charge is still current, and from time to time it is revived, and therefore it is well worth reprinting the learned note in which Fr. Pollen disproves it and, most usefully, shows how Lord Acton was misled into making it.

' " Pius V, who had been the only Pope proclaimed a Saint for centuries, commissioned an assassin [i.e. Ridolfi] to murder Elizabeth, and the confirmation is found in the official life of Pius in the *Acta Sanctorum*." [1]

The reference here is to *AA.SS.*, May 1, § 173 (ed., 1866, p. 661) : " Pius cogitabat . . . illam malorum omnium sentinam, seu (ut appellabat ipse) flagitiorum servam, de medio tollere." These words, if they had stood quite by themselves, might no doubt have been interpreted as meaning assassination, *e.g.* " Pius thought of *making away with her, who was the cesspool of all evils*, or, as he called her, the slave of crime." and therefore he sent Ridolfi. If we look into the context, however, we soon find reason to pause, and all doubt is at an end if we consult the original Italian, from which the Latin is translated. The Italian sentence is very long and laboriously balanced ; the essential clauses are these : " Pensando Pio, da una parte di soccorer la Reina di Scotia . . . dall'altra . . . *di levare a un tempo la sentina di tanti mali* (nodrendo Elizabetta dissentioni . . .) deputo alcuni homino . . . de'gli cattolici gliene dessero contezza." " Pius, thinking on the one hand, of helping the Queen of Scotland, and on the other of *clearing the cesspool of so many evils* (for Elizabeth nourishing dissensions, etc. etc.) deputed certain persons among the Catholics to give him information " (Girolamo Catena, *Vita del Glorioso Papa Pio V*, Mantua, 1587).

The clause, which might, apart from its context, bear a sinister meaning, is perfectly innocuous in the original language. The passages are quoted in full in C.R.S., xxi, 335.' [2]

Sixtus V—as violent in his language against Elizabeth as was ever Pius V—and the co-partner of Philip II in the business of the Armada, is himself a witness that proposals were made to him to have Elizabeth murdered and that he invariably refused to listen. But with regard to Gregory

---

[1] This first sentence is *The Times* summary of Acton's charge. Fr. Pollen accepts it as a faithful account.

[2] POLLEN, p. 215, note 2 ; C.R.S. is Catholic Record Society publications.

XIII, who comes between these two popes, the case is by no means so simple.

Somewhere about the year 1580 an unnamed English nobleman had spoken about murdering Elizabeth to Dr. Owen Lewis, as we know from the archdeacon's letter of March 1, 1582, to the Cardinal Secretary of State.[1] The would-be assassin asked a reward of 10,000 gold crowns. To this noble it was apparently all one, from the point of view of morals, whether the queen were ' removed ' by an armed expedition or a personal attack ; a confusion of thought not uncommon, even nowadays, with untrained minds, in the case of war against a desperate and invincible enemy. We can understand the nobleman, though we deplore that he would only kill for pay. But what about the priest—pious, a celebrated canon-lawyer—to whom he went with the project ? Fr. William Crichton, S.J., faced four years later with a similar proposal put forward by William Parry, answered as, to-day, all of us would answer, and unanimously, ' omnino non licere,' ' it is altogether unlawful.' Dr. Owen Lewis did not indeed approve the project. ' But I am by no means inclined to any such scheme,' he told the cardinal, ' it does not beseem me as a priest to have anything to do with deeds of blood, so I gave him no reply.' It is the last phrase that one would like to emphasise. On the lips of a good and holy man, as was assuredly this Vicar-General of St. Charles, it has to us a curious and unhappy insufficiency. Things seemingly clear to us as crystal were somewhat less clear, apparently, three hundred and sixty years ago.

The incident of Dr. Lewis prepares us a little for the next incident, a plan to slay Elizabeth in which the Secretariate of State was certainly concerned, though not as originating it. This is the subject of the famous Sega letters, found in the Vatican Archives fifty years ago by an English scholar, and first printed in full (from the transcripts in the Public Record Office in London) by the German scholar, Arnold Oscar Meyer. They appear also in the appendix to the English translation of this work made by Fr. J. R. McKee of the London Oratory.[2] The simplest way to tell the story is to print a translation of the two letters :

[1] PASTOR, Vol. 19, p. 444 *seq.*
[2] *Ibid.* ; MEYER, pp. 269–272, and, for the Italian text, pp. 489–491.

1. The nuncio in Spain (Mgr Philip Sega, Bishop of Piacenza) to the Cardinal Secretary of State, November 14, 1580.

' Among the other things about which this Dr. Humphrey Ely spoke to me, he told me one with great secrecy in the name of certain nobles of the Island where the said Jesuit fathers are.[1] It is this. The aforesaid nobles would resolve to try and kill the queen with their own hands, provided that they were assured, at any rate verbally (and he says that they would put faith in this if he wrote it to them, or he would take the reply to them personally) that His Holiness would give them assurance that in so doing they would not fall into sin—for there is the danger that a matter so serious and perilous would cost them their own lives. I have given him this reply, that by the words of the sentence of Pius V of holy memory it appears that these gentlemen can reassure themselves, since the sentence expressly gives all vassals leave to take up arms against the wicked [2] queen, with this in addition that I shall not fail to send on their proposal, that I may know more specifically what are His Holiness' commands ; having further declared to him that should the Pope not go so far as to wish to make any declaration before the event, he could at least be certain that His Holiness would give, to all who should survive this deed, whatever absolutions and declarations might be necessary, or abundant safeguards for the persons of the aforesaid survivors. I further remarked to him " nocuit quandoque differre paratis " [3] since if this scheme has come to the knowledge of more than one or two, it is inadvisable to keep it in suspense, because of the inherent danger of its being discovered. Moreover they ought to know how to make use of their opportunity. I am now engaged in persuading him to return to England, not even trusting to writing as he had agreed with his friends, pointing out to him that if by chance the letters were to be intercepted, their not being in cipher but in veiled terms would be

<hr>

[1] ' In nome di alcuni nobili de la isola [e] de li medesimi padri giesuiti ' ; so MEYER (p. 490) prints the passage. The word he thus brackets is not in the original transcript.

[2] MEYER prints : ' La regina impune,' but the transcript reads very clearly ' impure.'

[3] ' Delay is sometimes dangerous when all the preparations are made,' a reminiscence of a verse in Lucan's *Pharsalia*, as MEYER notes.

the occasion of long imprisonment and torture to any of the nobles who happened to fall into the hands of the queen. I do not know what he will decide, but I shall write it with my next. Meanwhile we shall be together to-morrow, he and I, with the words of the sentence before us, to consider them a little more particularly. If, notwithstanding his knowledge of the danger he runs in returning to England, he yet resolves to go back rather than to write, when he has come to some decision I shall let you know the result as soon as I can. I further notify your lordship that these gentlemen do not ask of His Holiness either brief or bull but just a mere statement. It will be enough if you will send it to me in cipher, and I shall arrange a cipher with him and a way to receive my letters safely. In case I have gone forward a little too speedily in this affair, so that some absolution from His Holiness is needed, I beg of Your Lordship to ask it for me, for certainly in this matter " the zeal of the Lord's house hath eaten me up." '

2. The Cardinal Secretary of State to the nuncio, December 12, 1580.

' There can be no doubt that while that guilty woman of England holds the two noble Christian kingdoms she has usurped, and while she is the cause of such great harm to the Catholic faith and of the loss of so many millions of souls, whoever moves her from this life with the due end of God's service, not only would not sin, but would even be doing a meritorious deed, especially as the sentence still stands which Pius V of holy memory pronounced against her. However, should these English gentlemen decide they ought to undertake so fine a business Your Lordship can assure them that they will not incur any sin, and it is to be hoped in the blessed God that they also escape all the dangers. As to Your Lordship, in case you have in any way incurred any irregularity, His Holiness sends you his holy blessing.' [1]

[1] The last sentence is the absolution for himself which Sega asked in the last sentence of his own letter, e.g. not the sacramental absolution for sin, but the removal of the ' irregularity ' called Lenitas (supposing he had incurred it), to wit a forfeit incurred, under the Canon Law, by a cleric who participates—even lawfully—in a deed that involves the killing of another. The effect of this impediment is to prevent the reception of further degrees in the sacrament of Holy Order, or the lawful accomplishment of the functions of one's present status.

The nuncio, then, hears from Humphrey Ely, doctor of laws, that in the island where the same Jesuit fathers are —we are not given the whole of the letter : evidently there has been other news of the island and of the Jesuits— certain noblemen have a plan for Elizabeth's assassination. How far is this true ? We have no means of knowing. Who were these noblemen ? What credentials had Ely to ask this astonishing question in their name ? We know nothing. We have no means of knowing, and the interest of the correspondence lies elsewhere. It lies in its revelation of what the bull of excommunication authorised, according to this seasoned papal diplomat ten years later, and according to the Cardinal Secretary of State. The bull authorises all Englishmen ' to take up arms ' against Elizabeth, therefore these nobles may with a safe conscience attempt her assassination ' with their own hands.' Evidently these two highly placed ecclesiastics hold the same view of the business as that expressed by the nobleman who consulted Owen Lewis in this very same year. It is not only not sinful (cf. the bull of Pius V which still stands), but, says the cardinal, if we consider the immensity of spiritual evil of which ' that guilty woman of England ' is the source, the act would be meritorious. Without wishing to enter into anything like moral comparisons, one may surely say, immediately, that this is not—we flatter ourselves perhaps—how we should to-day regard such a matter. We should all say with Fr. Crichton, S.J., *omnino non licere.* How are we to explain the mentality of these papal diplomats and legists ? Meyer, it seems to me, misses the point altogether and, for once, writes unscientifically when he says : ' Gregory XIII adopted without hesitation all the political methods of his time. He alone among the popes of the Counter-Reformation regarded assassination, when employed in the church's service, as a work well-pleasing to God.' This suggestion of a man indifferent to the commission of crime where crime is profitable, is altogether at odds with the meticulous legalism which was the essence of Ugo Buoncompagni's character and the habit of all his long life. Given all our knowledge of that character and life, the first doubt to leap to the mind is whether Gregory XIII would regard the killing of Elizabeth as assassination. And if he did not, how did he come by his opinion ? And how is it that his opinion was not universally accepted, even among the plotters, *e.g.*

Fr. William Crichton, S.J. ? We do not actually know the workings of the Pope's mind. But we do know something of the general teaching of moralists about the killing of tyrants, and we have a most valuable clue to the Pope's line of thought in the phrase of his secretary's reply to Sega, ' especially as the sentence of Pius V still stands against her.' For that sentence, depriving Elizabeth of her right to rule, made her no more than a usurper. We know enough to be able to draw a very real distinction between what the Pope conceived himself to be blessing and that political assassination which was so common a feature of the time. Elizabeth, for example, more than once strove to have Mary Stuart murdered. She planned the assassination of Gregory XIII and of Philip II about this very time that the Sega letters were written,[1] as she planned the murder of Don John of Austria somewhat earlier.[2] Philip II set a price on the head of his tenacious opponent William the Silent, and Henry III had murdered, by his forty-five guardsmen, his own two great opponents, the duke of Guise and his brother the cardinal. But we have no warrant for saying that Gregory XIII and his advisers were indifferent to murder, or that they blessed those about to commit murder in their interests. What they had in mind, what they intended, was something very different indeed. It is never lawful for a private individual, acting on his own judgement that a ruler is a tyrant (or acting on the like judgement of other private individuals), to kill that ruler—and this is true whether the ruler is judged to be, and is in fact, a usurper of lawful power or, on the other hand, is a lawful ruler judged to be ruling tyrannously. The private individual who so acts is a criminal.

On the other hand—supposing the tyrant to be, not the lawful ruler ruling tyrannously, but a usurper of lawful power, a ruler, that is to say, with no right to rule, whose authority rests solely on what force he can command—if there is any higher public authority to decide and declare this, and that authority does so decide and declare, then, since the ruler is now, by public sentence of authority, the declared enemy of the State, and since the individual pro-

[1] So PASTOR, Vol. 19, p. 448, quoting PLATZHOFF, *Die Theorie von der Mordbefugnis der Obrigkeit im 16 Jahrhundert*: *Historische Studien* 54 ; Berlin, 1906, a reference I have not been able to control.
[2] Spanish ambassador in London to Philip II, May 8, 1578, *Corresp. de Felipe II*, V, p. 227, quoted PASTOR, Vol. 19, p. 448.

posing to kill the ruler is no longer acting on his own private judgement, that individual, if he kills the ruler in order to save the State, commits no crime and his act is a good act.[1]

This is a very different state of things from the anarchy that would allow every citizen to be the judge and the executioner of his ruler.[2] It is a very real system of justice ; but in order that the system may really work justice, and not lead men back to the jungle, it is necessary first that there be in existence this higher public authority that can judge sovereign princes, judge whether they are indeed princes *de facto* or *de iure*, and next it is necessary that this higher authority be recognised to be such by all concerned.

That higher public authority empowered to judge the sins and status of princes, any citizen of Western Europe in the time of St. Thomas Aquinas would have readily recognised in the Catholic Church.[3] In that age, if ever, the

---

[1] *Cf.* the commentary in BILLUART, *De Iure et Iustitia Diss.* X, Art. II. on St. Thomas Aquinas' discussion of the question, *Whether to Kill a Malefactor is lawful for a private individual ?* (*Summa Theologica*, 2a–2ae, Q. 64, a. 3.) St. Thomas teaches very directly and simply that to put malefactors to death is the business of public authority alone. Against this conclusion three objections are commonly urged, says Billuart. Is it not lawful for anyone to kill an outlaw ? Is it not lawful for a man to kill his wife taken *flagrante delicto* in adultery ? Is it not lawful for anyone to kill a tyrant ? In replying to the third objection he draws the distinction between the tyrant who is the lawful ruler, and the tyrant who is an usurper—following here St. Thomas in the saint's Commentary on Peter Lombard. Billuart states it as the common teaching that it is lawful to kill a tyrant who is a notorious usurper, ' given certain conditions.' These conditions are (1) it must be certain that the tyrant has no right to the kingdom ; (2) that there is no higher authority to whom recourse may be had ; (3) that the commonwealth is not opposed to the killing of the tyrant ; (4) that from the killing there is to be hoped the tranquillity of the state, and not rather still greater evils than the present.' And he ends with the reminder that the second alternative in (4) is the more usual, and that the particular remedy is rarely to be advised. A more modern summary of this once very famous question, by Pére Spicq, O.P., is to be found in the edition of the *Summa Theologica*, published by Desclée et Cie, *La Justice*, Vol. II, pp. 221–227. In conclusion we may note that the indiscriminate slaughter of tyrants by all and sundry was condemned by the Church long before the troubles of the Reformation, when at the 15th session of the General Council of Constance the following proposition was condemned : ' Any tyrant can be slain, and can be slain lawfully and meritoriously by any of his vassals or subjects.' (DENZINGER, *Enchiridion*, n. 690.) There is nothing to lead us to think that so competent a jurist as Gregory XIII was ignorant of the elements of this classic discussion. Nor is there any reason either to deal gently with his alleged indifference to murder, the Pope being the child of his age (which is Meyer's judgement), or to shudder in embarrassed retrospect (which is Fr. Pollen's attitude). The fault to be found with this Pope is that, through lack of information he so misjudged the circumstances that what he sanctioned as the lawful execution of a tyrant was actually, and in fact, murder.

[2] The state of things condemned by the Council of Constance in 1418.

[3] So it is generally stated.

system was a practical reality. But, although the Catholic Church still subsists, and all its intangible jurisdiction, the general recognition of such jurisdiction has long since disappeared. A condition vital for the working of the system has gone, and all men—not least the supreme authority in the Catholic Church—are aware that because a *sine qua non* for this particular exercise of jurisdiction is gone, the power is in practice obsolete. That world in which alone it could produce its effect is no more—nor can it return. The citizen of to-day, if he be oppressed by tyrants, whether this be the ruler he himself so cheerfully elected some years ago, in happy unconsciousness of latent treachery and viciousness, or whether it be a ruler brutally thrust on him against his will and the will of all the nation, can look for no remedy deriving from any belief common to the whole world in which he lives. The higher authority is still here, but the general acceptance of it, the habit of deference to its word, has ceased to be even a memory. ' The case is wholly altered.'

That higher jurisdiction, then, no longer functions, and, as it cannot help the Catholic of to-day in his difficulty, so also it cannot embarrass him in his relations with his fellows. It did not embarrass the Catholic of the thirteenth century, although then it functioned very fully ; and it helped the Catholic of the thirteenth century considerably. That the exercise of this jurisdiction both embarrassed the standing, as a citizen, of the Counter-Reformation Catholic and at the same time failed to help him, was inevitable, for the lot of the Counter-Reformation Catholic was cast where the tides swirled and eddied with bewildering violence while the old Europe gradually gave place to the new. Such turning-points of history try with impossible severity those whose duty it is to administer systems of law and those whose extremity drives them to seek the remedy law affords. One age is slowly giving place to another, century-old allegiances to systems of belief and to codes of morals are yielding, universal general consents about the fundamentals of common life, of politics, of ethics are, not indeed in process of transformation, but about to sink for ever and leave no trace. Such moments are critical because, though the victim of extremity knows only too well that something incalculable is holding him, a situation without precedent indeed, it is in the nature of things that the administrator begins by applying the traditional remedy whose worth time has proved. Already in England, in 1570—and in Europe too—that world in which popes were Commanders of the Faithful had so far ceased to be, that the papal writs no longer ran save where princely interest and the opportune moment coincided with their issue. Although no man knew it until the experiment was seen to fail—and indeed no man could know it until then—the papal sentence against the Catholic prince fallen into heresy but not from power, was, and henceforth was always to be, sterile from its very declaration. And if this were so, what of the Catholic unable to know (what his grandchildren might guess) that the hour in which he lived was this precise hour of terrific transition, when jurisdiction fell into the nominal, and sanctions thereby lost their justification, what of the good Catholic with his good plan to shoot or poison the queen in execution of the just sentence ? To the new world which refused all recognition to any higher court than those of the realm, which denied indeed that there could be such higher jurisdiction, just as the excommunication was a mortal insult and the deposition so much vain brag, so the Catholic with his dag was but a murderous traitor. And such he has remained in the estimation of later generations of his people, who are as ignorant of the reality of the tyranny that drove him to seek from the higher jurisdiction the sole lawful remedy, as they are ignorant of the real meaning of the system of law that supplied the remedy. To the new world—and it is in this world that we still live—it appeared all one with political murder. To the older world which, to its cost in many, many particulars, did not as yet so much as know that there was any other world, a people was to be delivered from a tyrannous usurper, declared to be such by competent authority's public sentence, and the hand which struck the blow would no more be the hand of a criminal than was the hand which held the axe that felled Mary Stewart, or that other which fired the pile wherein burnt Mary Tudor's (or Elizabeth's) Anabaptists. It is only at the cost of some study, and at the price of a strong purging of pre-judgements, that we can get back to that older world where all men saw things in this light. But at whatever cost, return to it we must, if we are to understand the sixteenth century, for the riddle of this century is very largely the effect of an old world's survival long after the new has come into being.

The point where the Roman action stands in need of light and study—I will not say defence—lies elsewhere than in any association of the popes with the heinous crime of murder. It lies rather in their chronic lack of anything like adequate information about conditions in England, of information, that is to say, adequate for any prudent judgement whether or no the general body of the nation accepted the queen as its ruler. For on the truth of that judgement the whole morality turned. Moralists, when discussing in the abstract the morality of killing an usurping tyrant, are careful to point out that once the nation consents to accept the usurper as its ruler, such killing by a private individual is simply murder. What was the feeling of the English nation towards Elizabeth by the time that Humphrey Ely came to put his questions to Monsignor Philip Sega in November, 1580 ? It was now ten years and some months since St. Pius V had excommunicated the queen and declared her to be stripped of all right to rule. How far had the body of English opinion rallied to the papal sentence in those ten years ? How far would her death at the hands of a Catholic enthusiast be welcome to the greater and saner part of her people ? No one, I suppose, will deny that the nation as a whole still continued, after 1570, to take her for its ruler. What disaffection particular laws or policies had produced in the next ten years was by no means so strong as to justify the conclusion that only by *force majeure* did the queen succeed in maintaining her hold. Unless by some species of legal casuistry—that heresy, by the fact, proves a man not be of the *sanior pars*, or that support of the queen, again by the fact, proves as much—it is hard to see how the common opinion of England can have been understood, even by contemporaries, as anything but willingly loyal to Elizabeth. Such consent of the majority to the fact of her government did not, indeed, destroy the force of the papal sentence against the queen ; it could not restore what that had taken away, her right to rule ; but it did very definitely so alter the case that for any private individual to slay her was murder.

Were, then, the high ecclesiastics who encouraged and blessed the projects of private individuals to kill Elizabeth, patrons of murder ? I should say No. They did not admit —the Pope, that is to say, the papal Secretary of State, the nuncios in Spain and in France—that the mass of the nation accepted Elizabeth as queen. We may ask how came these high ecclesiastics to be so ill-informed—as undoubtedly they were. Had they never any suspicion that what information they possessed was incomplete, was, as we say, one-sided ? And that it could hardly have been otherwise, given the moral distance and the moral obstacles that lay between Elizabeth's London and the Counter-Reformation capital? Was it even possible for the procedure which issued in the sentence of 1570 to be according to the strict demands of prudence ? These questions must sometime be answered : but only with more information than this writer possesses, who if he does more here than ask the questions will, from his own lack of information, fail disastrously too. Let it suffice to say that it was for lack of information that Rome came to bless what to England, then and since, could only look like murder, and what, objectively, was murder.

In 1583 there is once again a plot to murder Elizabeth. This time it was the duke of Guise and his brother, the duke of Mayenne, who proposed it. They had a plan, and had found an agent. He wanted, however, 100,000 francs for reward. The duke would not approach the Holy See for this money or for any part of it. But as for the money that would be required for the further project of invading England and liberating the Queen of Scots, he thought the Pope might be willing to assist. Hence his communication of the matter to the nuncio at Paris and the nuncio's letter to the Cardinal of Como (May 2, 1583). We have the Cardinal Secretary's reply of May 23. It does not refer to the assassination at all. It is in very general language and taken up with but one point, the delivery of England from Elizabeth. Philip II also was told of it, by his ambassador in Paris, but at first in very general terms indeed. It was mentioned as a ' project which on account of its risk I dare not set down here, but which will make a noise if it succeeds.' [1] Six weeks later,[2] when the affair had fallen through, the ambassador was able to be more explicit. ' The project,' he explained, ' *was a deed of violence* against this lady. . . .' It is pertinent to our attempt to understand something of the general morals of politicians at this time (and this is the only justification for the digression) to know

[1] May 4, 1583, *L.A.*, xlviii, p. 412.
[2] June 23, 1583, Teulet, V, p. 281.

that this despatch has come down to us with the Spanish king's own annotations. The underlining above is Philip's and in the margin he has noted : ' It was thus, I believe, that we understood it here ; and if they had done it, it would have been no harm ; though they should have made provision of certain things beforehand.

Nowhere is there a hint of uneasiness as to the morality of the deed proposed, nowhere a hint that it was necessary to justify or excuse it as something unusual, an exception to the ordinary laws of behaviour. The nuncio knew of it and the Cardinal Secretary also. The Spanish ambassador vaguely referred to it and Philip II guessed, immediately, exactly what was afoot. The extraordinary unanimity in this absence of reprobation is a problem of much more complexity than an agreement of thugs about a new victim.

The last count in the series which would indict Pope Gregory XIII with scheming to murder Elizabeth is the complicated adventure of Dr. William Parry [1] whose life ended at Tyburn, March 2, 1585. This story has the further interest for the evidence it affords of the bad faith of the English government in its statement of the position, now always asserted, that Catholics are, by the fact, traitors really and not only traitors in any merely legal sense. We see here the kind of man Cecil used as an agent. We see the elaborate device to procure from Catholics, and from high Catholic authority, explicit sanction of a murder plot. We see also the incredible, cocksure levity of the Cardinal Secretary of State lending himself to the device. We see the agent entangled in his own web and his employers, at the chosen moment, punishing his pretended complicity as though it were real, thereby ending all chance that the spy would ever prove the case against them, and thereby, also, affording all London and England ocular evidence, in Parry's trial and execution, that Catholics aimed at Elizabeth's murder and that, when they were butchered, they were but receiving just and necessary punishment : *ex uno disce omnes.*

Like a far greater proportion of Tudor notabilities than is always realised, Parry was a Welshman. Cecil had employed him as a secret service man for some time in the 1570's. He married a wealthy widow, spent her fortune, got deeply into debt, and then bungled the murder of his principal creditor. Cecil saved him from the gallows and set him once

[1] *Cf.* PASTOR, Vol. 19, pp. 449 *seq.*

more to his old job on the continent. For a time he failed
to suit his master. He never had anything of importance
to relate. Also he complained that Cecil paid him all too
little. Parry now turned to exploit the chances of promotion
through spying on the Catholic exiles. He found a Jesuit
to receive him into the Church at Lyons, and began to talk
to as many of his co-religionists as would listen, about a plan
to murder Elizabeth and so end the persecution. It was now
that Crichton uttered the *omnino non licere* which has already
been quoted, and went to the pains of explaining carefully
to Parry that no goodness in the end can ever justify the
use of means that are bad. Parry met with no better success
with another Jesuit he approached—one Palmio. Fr.
Persons refused even to see him, and Allen's reception of
him was such that he did not even dare to introduce the
subject.

From Venice, in 1583, he made an approach to the Holy
See itself. He wrote to the Cardinal of Como for a passport
to go to Rome, where he had an important plan to lay before
the Pope. Then he changed his mind, and went instead to
Paris, still doing his best to get approval of the murder plan
from some English priest or other. In this he still failed, but
on December 10, 1583, he wrote once again, a letter
which has survived and which was the beginning of the end
of Parry. In this he said : 'I informed Crichton, before
I came to Paris, of my state and intention (*stato e intentione*),
and I write to beg you to obtain a Plenary Indulgence for
me from the Pope. I have always lived a Catholic and I
hope to die one notwithstanding that in matters of State I
have wavered to some extent, which much grieves me.
Pray do not attend to what is said of me by envious people,
but refer to the Archbishop of Glasgow, the Bishop of Ross,
Father Crichton, Charles Paget, Thomas Morgan. I shall
do nothing without their direction.'

This is a simple request for a Plenary Indulgence—a
favour not so easily come by three hundred years ago as in
later times—from one who claims to be a Catholic and ready
to do the Holy See a service. The letter was forwarded
by the nuncio. He knew well what reputation Parry had,
and he warned Como explicitly of the kind of man with
whom he was dealing. 'I send the letter of William Parry,
of whom I have received a bad account, and I am warned
that he is not to be trusted. . . . The Pope must be cautious

how he trusts those who say that they are English Exiles for Religion. Very many of them are spies.'

On the first day of the new year, 1584, Parry wrote again to Como. He repeats his request for an Indulgence, encloses a certificate to show he has already been to confession and, in the most guarded way in the world, refers to a scheme he has in mind to put into execution for the good of religion, a scheme which—his way of writing implies—is known to the cardinal also. Here is Parry's letter : ' Most Holy Father, If the enterprise (impresa) which with the grace of God, I intend to undertake ere long (and I undertake it for the public good and the peace of the whole of Christendom, for the restitution of the Kingdom of England to the ancient obedience to the Apostolic See, and for the liberation of the Queen of Scotland the only true and undoubted Catholic heiress of the Crown of England from her long and weary sufferings), produce that good effect which I hope for and greatly desire ; then I beg your Holiness, with all submission and humility that, as I am resolved to take upon myself this enterprise so full of danger without looking further, without any promise of hope, so it may please you out of the plenitude of your power grant me (being to-day confessed and communicated as I am) a Plenary and Absolute Indulgence and remission of all my sins, and to repute me the obedient and devout son of the Holy Catholic and Apostolic Roman Church, in the bosom of which and in the favour of your Holiness, I am most desirous to live and to die.'

In sending on this request with its vague allusions— dangerously vague since they came from one known to be almost certainly a spy in Cecil's pay, and since they were designed to draw an answer in writing—the nuncio again warned the Cardinal Secretary of State : ' The writer is all too well known. Here his reputation is certainly bad.' [1] Parry in his first letter had hinted that attempts would be made to paint him unfavourably. The Cardinal Secretary took Parry's anticipatory disclaimer in preference to the warning from his own official in Paris. He laughed at the fuss made about Parry's bad reputation, as he had made light of the earlier anxieties about Stukeley, and wrote to the nuncio [2] : ' Parry's two letters deal with a matter in which we cannot lose anything by giving him confidence,

[1] Jan. 8, 1584.   [2] Jan. 30, 1584.

so long as he does not go on to anything further.' The man
merely wanted, at the moment, his Plenary Indulgence and
a blessing on his good intention of doing something for
Holy Church. Had there never been, in all this time,
any hint of political action by Catholics, or had there never
been any vaguely described, verbally veiled but definitely
intended acts of violence, of insurrection and, also, of murder,
Como's attitude would not be unnatural ; although for a
man in such a position to disregard so flatly warnings
definitely given by his own observers is no less than criminally
foolish. But there had been all manner of plots, and all
manner of ways of insinuating knowledge of them, and it is
not to be wondered at that Como's reply to Parry should,
in this atmosphere where nods and winks and shrugs were
so often quasi-official means of communication, have told
in the end so damagingly against the credit of the Holy
See, and especially against the good name of Catholicism
in England. For when Parry was arrested and tried for
plotting the queen's murder, all this correspondence was
produced and read in court. Parry pleaded that the plot
was fictional, so far as he was concerned. There had been
a real intention on the part of the Cardinal Secretary and
the Pope. Like a good spy he had wormed this out of them.
Like a loyal citizen he had passed on the information to the
State. But the State preferred to believe that Parry was
the English accomplice of the cardinal and the Pope, and
as their accomplice he was condemned and hanged, drawn,
and quartered.

What did more than anything else to hang him was the
Cardinal of Como's letter of January 30, 1584. Here it is :
' His Holiness hath seen your letter of the first, with the
certificate included, and cannot but commend the good
disposition and resolution which you write to hold towards
the service and benefit public ; wherein His Holiness doth
exhort you to persevere and to bring into effect that which
you have promised, and to the end you may be holpen
by that good spirit which hath moved you thereunto he
granteth unto you his blessing, Plenary Indulgence and
remission of all your sins, according to your request, assuring
you that besides the merit you shall receive therefore in
Heaven, His Holiness will further, make himself your
debtor to acknowledge your deservings in the best manner
that he can, and so much the more so in that you use the

greater modesty in not pretending anything. Put therefore
your holy and honourable purposes into effect and attend
your health, and to conclude, I offer myself heartily unto
you, and do desire all good and happy success.'

What did Parry intend the word ' enterprise,' in his letter
of January 1, 1584, to mean ? What did Como understand
by it ? Fr. Pollen takes the view that Como must have
understood that some kind of assassination was in project,
and that his reply cannot escape the charge that it is a kind of
toleration of what was intended. The Como letters ' remain
simply detestable,' he says, ' and no one will blush more for
them than those who admire Pope Gregory most.' Fr.
Pollen speaks with a knowledge of this period to which very
few historians can lay claim, and it may be blatantly rash,
publicly to dissent from his verdict. But, for myself, I am
not convinced that it is not a sufficient explanation that
Como acted here as he acted time and again—and as
others in that same place acted, and were to act, throughout
all these disastrous years where English affairs were concerned—with a cocksure superficiality bred of poor information and of an utter failure to understand the English
character. The root of the trouble is an over-simplification
of the English problem, and productive of what Fr. Pollen
has rightly called ' levity.' This, if a true judgement, is
serious enough in all conscience. That popes could break
the fifth commandment is no more impossible than that
they could break any of the others, but something much more
definite than the history of Dr. William Parry will be needed
before we can demand of Gregory XIII and his Secretary
of State that they rise to reply to a charge of wilful murder.

§ ii. The Catholics in England, 1570–1588

We are now at the end of this somewhat lengthy survey of
the Roman intervention in the affairs of the English Catholics
during the first thirty years of Elizabeth's reign (1558–1588).
What of its effect in England ?—upon the Catholics, and
upon the government's action in their regard ? The first
directly spiritual activities of the popes, the decision that
Catholics must not assist at the services of the new religion,
and the new faculties to priests to reconcile those who had
lapsed, undoubtedly halted any general drift towards
Anglicanism. And of this something has already been said.

Engraved by H.Robinson

Pope Gregory XIII
(1572–1585)
(*Ugo Buoncompagni, born* 1502)

But what of the later politico-religious activities of the popes and their English clerical agents ? Here we are, apparently, faced with a most dramatic contrast. When we leave the high political circles in which Ptolemeo Galli, the nuncios, Allen too and Persons, have been seen so continuously active, and return to the Catholics in England itself, whether in London or in the shires, we seem to pass into another world. It is safe to say that while all the Catholic body knew about (and were indeed deeply harassed by) the papal sentence of 1570, the innumerable papal attempts to bring about its execution were utterly unknown to them. How they would have acted had a wholly papal army landed on the English shore is problematic, but there is little doubt that they were, and remained throughout the reign, as sturdily anti-Spanish as their Protestant neighbours, or their own Catholic fathers of Queen Mary's time. And the impression which the Spaniards themselves had of these same Catholics in England was that, as a body, they were too cowed and terrorised by the persecution to dare anything at all.

Let us begin by tabulating the new anti-Catholic laws that were a reply to the new Catholic activity of the Douay mission and, ostensibly, to the papal-Spanish political activities.

There is first of all the act passed in the early months of 1581,[1] *An Act to retain the Queen's Majesty's subjects in their due obedience.* By this statute six new treasonable offences are created. The acts henceforth treasonable are, in themselves, purely religious acts, matters of conscience, and routine activities in the practice of the Catholic faith. All six of these new treasons centre round the fact that conversions to the Catholic faith from Protestantism are taking place, and that repentant apostates from Catholicism are being reconciled to the Catholic Church. The act of 1571, so the statute opens, has proved insufficient to halt the conversions and recon- ciliations. Wherefore, from now on (*a*) all who absolve, persuade or withdraw any subject ' from the religion now by Her Highness authority established . . . to the Romish religion,' or who move him to promise any obedience to Rome, or make any attempt to do any of these things ; and (*b*) all who are so absolved, persuaded, or reconciled,

---

[1] 23 Elizabeth, c. 1 ; third session (Jan. 16–Mar. 18, 1581) of the Fourth Parliament ; *cf.* PROTHERO, pp. 74–76 for text.

are traitors. All who aid and abet them are guilty of mis-prision of treason, and likewise all who fail to denounce them within twenty days. The fine of 12 pence for each absence from the church service on Sundays and holydays inflicted by the Act of Uniformity is now increased one hundred fold. For his absence from such service the Catholic over sixteen years of age must now pay £20 a month—an amount greatly in excess of a year's income in the great majority of cases, and doubtless designed to be effective from the mere terror its announcement would cause. If any Catholic is so hardy as to resist for so long as a year, he shall, beside paying the £240 to which the fine amounts, find two sureties of £200 each at the least, for his good behaviour until such time as he conforms. The saying of Mass had already been forbidden. Now a fine of 200 marks (£66 6s. 8d.) and a year's imprisonment were enacted as penalties for the priest each time he said Mass, and half that sum and the same imprisonment for all who heard Mass, those convicted to remain in prison so long as the fine was not paid. Catholics were made responsible that the schoolmaster they employed assisted at the Church service. If they employed one who neglected to do so, or one not licensed by the Protestant bishop, they were liable to a fine of £10 a month, and the schoolmaster to a year's imprisonment. The device of keeping a priest disguised as the children's tutor would no longer work, and a further tightening up of the administration is provided by the clause that makes offences against all acts ' touching acknowledging of her Majesty's supreme government in causes ecclesiastical ' triable by justices of the peace for the twelve months that follow the offence. The fruits of the fines are to go, one-third to the queen for her own use, one-third to the poor of the parish, and one-third to the informer who brings about the conviction.

Four years later comes the better-known *Act against Jesuits, seminary priests and such like other disobedient persons*,[1] Since the act of 1581 just described, the first Jesuit had been captured and, with a number of Douay priests, had been tried for plotting to murder the queen. The accused had, of course, been condemned, but the trial had been so much more evidently than most State trials the mummery pre-cedent to murder, that the government never again

---

[1] 1585 ; 27 Elizabeth, c. 2. PROTHERO, pp. 83–86.

attempted to despatch priests in precisely this way. All
laws enacted so far had called for proof by the Crown of
some act on the part of the priest, his refusing an oath, for
example, or reconciling, or putting into use a papal bull.
The statute of 1585 did away with this necessity. All that
need now be proved was that the accused was a seminary
priest or Jesuit. This status and his not having sworn the
Oath [1] made him a traitor. For the act provided that all
priests, secular and regular, ordained beyond the seas
since the day on which the Act of Uniformity came into
force [2] (i.e. since the day when it had last been legal to ordain
a priest in England), must depart the realm within forty days.
Any such who remained, or any who after that time came
into England, and did not within three days take the Oath
of Supremacy were, by the fact, traitors. Any who aided
them in any way, gave them shelter or maintenance, were
guilty of a felony. Students in seminaries and colleges are
given six months in which to return, and two days more
in which to take the oath. Should they fail to do this, they,
too, are, by the fact traitors.

This act of 1585 is, of course, no more than a last, sup-
plementary development of the Act of Supremacy, in so
far as it touches the priest. First of all the priest is to swear
to the new dogma under pain of losing his benefice (1559).
Next (1563) he is to swear to it under pain of life imprisonment and, on a second offence, of death. So far he only
offends if he refuses the oath when it is officially tendered
to him. Now, from 1585, it is his business to come forward
and take the oath, and it is with his failure to do this that he
becomes liable to a sentence of death. From now on any
priest, except the Marian priest, is by his mere presence in
England liable to arrest as one hostile to the supremacy,
and therefore guilty of treason. There is no longer any
need to prove conspiracy, overt acts, or indeed any knowledge of any hint about conspiracies or plots. The government has reverted for proof of loyalty to the simple test of
the Oath of Supremacy. If the returned priest will take
this oath, the new act will not touch him. The reason given
in the act itself is that the new priests have come into the
realm 'to stir up and move sedition, rebellion, and open

[1] I.e. not, any longer, his refusal to swear the oath when it was officially
tendered to him.
[2] June 24, 1559.

hostility.' But the test whether a man is seditious and a rebel
is his willingness to accept the queen as supreme governor
in all causes spiritual and to abjure the spiritual authority
of Rome. Such an instrument can destroy many more than
rebels or traitors in the real meaning of the words ; it can
destroy every Catholic who receives Holy Orders and
returns to England for as long as four days. It can with
speed, and without any legal clumsiness, destroy the nascent
English Catholicism. The government can slay as a traitor
whatever priest they choose, without any need on their part to
prove his plotting, and yet, by styling the offence treason, they
can hope to escape the odium of persecuting for religion.

The act goes on to visit with the heavy penalties of
præmunire all who send abroad money or other relief to
any of these ecclesiastics or to the colleges, and it forbids the
sending of any minor overseas without the special licence of
the Crown, under penalty of forfeiting £100. There is the
inevitable spy clause that makes it an offence, punishable
with fine and imprisonment *at the queen's pleasure*, to fail to
denounce priests who are in the realm contrary to the act.
Finally, those who submit are not, for ten years, to come
within ten miles of where the queen shall be, under pain of
losing all the benefit of their submission.

Legal ingenuity, anxious to simplify the task of ridding
England of its new Catholic clergy, could add nothing to
this statute of 1585. The two acts of the reign which remain
to be noticed deal chiefly with the Catholic layman. The
first,[1] 'to avoid fraud and delays' in the collection of
recusancy fines, orders that once a Catholic has been convicted for not going to church over a certain period and has
paid his £20 for every month mentioned in the indictment,
there is no need of any second indictment should he continue
to offend : he is simply, for the future, to pay in twice yearly
to the Exchequer the amount due from him. Should he
default 'in any part of any payment aforesaid,' the Crown
can, by suit in the Exchequer, take all his goods and two
thirds of his landed property, 'leaving the third part only
of the same lands, tenements (etc.) for the maintenance of
the same offender, his wife, children, and family.'

The last act of all is that of 1593.[2] The object now, so it

[1] 28 & 29 Elizabeth, c. 6, in the Sixth Parliament, Oct. 29, 1586–Mar. 23,
1587. PROTHERO, p. 88.
[2] 35 Elizabeth, c. 2. *An Act against Popish Recusants.* PROTHERO, p. 92.

is stated, is ' the better discovery and avoiding ' of traitorous conspiracies against the queen. ' Sundry wicked and seditious persons,' Catholics by profession and spies in reality, are secretly wandering and shifting from place to place, corrupting and seducing the queen's loyal subjects. So the new statute enacts that no Catholic over sixteen who has been convicted for the offence of being absent from divine service is, for the future, to move more than five miles from his home, under pain of forfeiting all his goods and his life interest in his lands. Then there is a last stone on the cairn below which lies the right of the priest to live. Suspected priests who refuse to answer directly whether they be priests, Jesuits or no, are to be kept in prison until they do so.

One of the earliest witnesses that the English Catholics had as little love for the foreigner as the rest of their fellow-countrymen is the duke of Alva, who, so early in the history of the political action as 1571, warned Philip II that the national pride of the English would not easily put up with aid that came from abroad.[1] And from that time on, the testimony is constant to the same effect. Niccoló Ormaneto, who had been for so long Pole's intimate friend and secretary, and who was by 1573 nuncio at the Spanish court, is just as emphatic.[2] Twenty years later, after the long persistent endeavour of Allen and Persons, with the long papal encouragement of rebellion a still present memory, and the Elizabethan persecution a still bloodier reality, the very students of the college in Rome, it is reported by their rector, ' rejoice at the Spanish disasters, e.g. the late affair at Cadiz. They are depressed at the news of Spanish success as, a little before this, at Calais.' [3] It was about this time, too, that Philip II, meditating his last assault on England, the despatch of a second armada in 1597, had enquiries made on the chances of support from the Catholics actually in England. In one report that has been published,[4] and which is described as typical of the rest, the Spanish king is plainly told that ' as for the Catholics, he hath only those who depend upon the direction of the Jesuits, who are few,' and

[1] Aug. 27, 1571, quoted PASTOR, 18, p. 235.
[2] Ibid., 19, p. 406.
[3] A. Agazzari, S.J. (rector of the college), to Persons, S.J., Aug. 27, 1596 ; in TIERNEY, III, App., p. lxxv.
[4] Ibid., p. lxvii.

R.C.R.   Q

that, for reasons given, ' it will be more hard to hold England than to enter it.'

Allen was to the end of his days whole-heartedly pro-Spanish. The occupation of England by Spanish forces, the future of England as a part of Philip II's empire, seems not only to have no terrors for him, but to have seemed an ideal to be realised. And this motion so possessed him that he thought all other good men must share it. So, in a letter to Philip II of March 19, 1587,[1] he can speak of the country, now for so long ruined by the rule of the feeble, incestuous Elizabeth, as awaiting Philip's coming, longing, in fact, to receive him for the recollection of his former rule, his known zeal in the restoration of the faith and his descent from all the ancient kings. This, it might be urged, is simply a stylistic compliment with which a humble priest begins a letter to the lord of half the world, but Allen goes on to say explicitly : ' I think there can be very few indeed who love their country and religion who do not from their hearts desire to be once more subject to your most clement rule.' And to all his letters he signs himself, invariably the king's faithful subject.

But this attitude of mind is by no means typical. Allen is, in this respect, almost in a class by himself. Even Fr. Persons, so often held to be, as Simpson describes him, ' wholly Espaniolated,' never goes this length. In more than one place, in private letters to his own brethren, Persons says explicitly he has only one care, that England shall have a Catholic sovereign. Spaniard or Scot or Englishman is all one to him as ruler, if only the faith be safe, and his one reason for so persistently supporting the Spaniard is that, to him, Philip II offers the surest prospect of all. But for Spaniards as such, the Jesuit has little more affection than had the worthies who fought them in the ships of Drake and Hawkins. There is, notably, one letter from him in which we can see very clearly the torment in his English heart at the treatment their English allies receive from the dominant Spaniards. This one letter,[2] too long to quote in full, lights up the whole situation.

Persons had found, in the winter of 1590-1591, no fewer

---

[1] *L.A.*, p. 272.

[2] Text, from a MS. in the archives at Stonyhurst College, in *L.A.*, pp. 329-332 : the translation here printed is from Fr. Knox's remarkable introduction to that volume, pp. cxiii-cxv.

than ninety-three of his fellow-countrymen slaving in the King of Spain's galleys at Seville. He had visited them, aided them, and converted them. Now he was anxious about their future. Are they to go back to England ? This would be better for them, from a worldly point of view. But is the king indifferent to the service these men could do him if they remained in his dominions ? Upon this the Jesuit proceeds gradually to open his heart to his correspondent, Don Juan de Ydiaquez, one of the Secretaries of State. ' I have nothing to add but to tell you plainly . . . that I have been amazed at the lukewarmness with which the willing submission of the English . . . has been received. . . . Certainly I for my part feel sure that if our enemies had a like opportunity of doing honour to themselves and damaging us by means of our own people, they would not let it slip in this way. . . . Most certain it is that to think it possible to get the upper hand in England without having a party within the realm is a great illusion, and to think to have this party without forming it and keeping it together is no less an illusion ; nor is there anything so opposed to the accomplishment of this as the distrust with which up to the present time the English, even those who are Catholic, have been treated on all occasions : and I could relate these to your Lordship one by one, if what took place at the time of the Armada, when it was manifested before the whole world, did not suffice for all ; since on that occasion, though his Majesty had more need than ever to avail himself of his party, no account was made of it, nor was any confidence placed in any living person of the nation either within or without the realm, though there were many who could have given assistance, and who had before then offered their lives to serve his Majesty.

' This was deeply felt . . . it also gave much pain to hear some of his Majesty's principal ministers were in the habit of saying that they did not understand there were any Catholics in England. . . .

' From this your Lordship sees what would have happened to the poor Catholics, if the victory had been on our side ; . . . and since God, as I take it, would not let His servants be thus outraged by our own people after they had suffered what they have suffered from the heretics, He let the expedition meet with the fate which we have seen. . . .

' Where there is suspicion and distrust there is neither

love nor fidelity, nor is there anything in the world so
calculated to make men desperate as to be treated with
distrust in return for good will. . . .'

The Jesuit gives as one great example the Spanish treatment of the exiles in the Low Countries, ' men of quality
who lost what they possessed as a consequence of joining this
side and others remained in England on the watch to follow
them if it should turn out well with them : but they have
never met with confidence in any thing of importance, and
so they have all in fact come to nothing . . .' ; then there
is Colonel Stanley, ' to keep him here doing nothing is to
put him to a thousand deaths.'

Again, at the very time when the Pope and the Spaniards
are first coming together in a combination seriously dangerous to Elizabeth, in that very year when Allen and
Persons, the nuncio at Paris, the duke of Guise, and the
Spanish ambassador are holding their momentous conclaves,
two most trustworthy authorities, one from each side of the
conflict, are agreed that there is no danger threatening the
queen from inside England. The exiles may compile their
lists of likely chiefs, and plan where to land the invading
armies, but Walsingham's spies report that there is no sign
of movement among the English Catholics and Mendoza,
Philip's ambassador, describes them as paralysed with fear.[1]

Gregory XIII found the King of Spain slower than slow
to take up the schemes he prepared, and Sixtus V made no
secret that he suspected Philip's motives to be in large part
mere imperialism. The fact was, and Philip II knew it
well, that the popes did not by any means intend that his
victory over Elizabeth should add yet another great province
to his empire. That victory gained, another titanic struggle
would follow with the Pope, and in the course of it who
was to say whether Philip would not come as near a sentence
of excommunication as Elizabeth, or as he himself in the
war of 1557.[2] ' The Pope, in talking of the affairs of
England,' the Spanish ambassador at Rome informed Don
John in 1575, ' never failed to say that no Spanish or French
claimant of the crown must be put forward, but that they
must support the claims of some native-born Catholic.'[3]

[1] PASTOR, 19, p. 465.
[2] Cf. supra, p. 111.
[3] June 24, 1575, quotedi n POLLEN, p. 197, from STIRLING-MAXWELL,
Don John of Austria, II, p. 106–107.

Sixtus V was equally careful, in the pact made with Philip preparatory to the Armada, to insist that the independence of England was not to be endangered. The new king was to be chosen by the Pope. Only a year earlier Sixtus had definitely refused to grant Philip the English crown.[1] There can be no doubt that, for all these men, the English clerical politicians and the popes whom they served, whatever the political nature of their activities, religion and religion alone was the end of all their endeavour. In France a detached and cynical observer of the scene looked on, unable to interfere, whatever his wishes, the last of the Valois kings, Henry III. His comment, if blistering where the naïveté of the clerics is concerned, yet witnesses to the sincerity of their intentions, no less than to the realism of the Spanish king. 'The Spaniards,' he said, 'are not friars, and they will not give up the fruits of their victories in obedience to a command from the Pope.'[2]

The English government knew well, by the time that Philip II began to lead this movement in 1585, that Catholicism was steadily reviving in England ; it knew that Spain and the Pope had long been planning a military offensive in support of it ; it knew that many of the queen's subjects were among their agents. The government knew well, that is to say, the dual character of the Counter-Reformation. Upon the fact of the dual character of the Roman effort much of later English history has turned.

Cecil's primary aim in 1558 was the destruction of Catholicism in England. It was a fundamental theme of his politics that there must not be more than one religion in the one state.[3] His party, the religious party which had made him and which he had already served so well, was still a minority party. An offensive against the religion which, until the very last days of the old régime, had persecuted his party was not so much natural as inevitable. The destruction of Catholicism was an essential condition of the survival of Protestantism as anything more than the private, very private, religious opinion of individual souls. And so the policy of the Device was carried out to the letter, and most successfully. Catholicism was attacked at home, through Catholics, and anti-Catholicism was helped in

[1] PASTOR, Vol. 22, p. 50, quoting POLLEN in The Month, Vol. cl, p. 561 (1903).
[2] Quoted PASTOR, ibid., p. 49.   [3] Cf. supra, p. 97.

every neighbouring state whence help might have come to Catholicism in England. The Pope, as the Device anticipated, did no more, for some years, than growl spiritually. Spain, of which the Device says not a word in anticipation of any hostility, acted with a benevolent neutrality.

The Cecilian policy towards Catholics at home was one of slow strangulation. The execution was so carefully done that later historians have sometimes failed to see the marks, and have been inclined to support a verdict of death by natural causes. There was, it has often been said, no persecution of Catholics in England until the Pope's sentence of excommunication, or until the ' Jesuit invasion ' and the plots, some ten years later still. All that this means is that a Catholic, after 1559, was free to remain a Catholic, could be a Catholic without suffering any penalties, so long as he pretended to be a Protestant, went, for example, regularly to the new religious services which the chiefs of his own religion condemned, and so long as he was willing to give up all attempt to practise his religion, to hear Mass for example, to go to confession, to have any commerce of whatever kind with a Catholic priest, or with his spiritual chief, the Pope. The first result of the revolution of 1559 was not a truce between the two religions, but a Protestant offensive. The Catholic reply to this was immediate. The Catholics refused to be quietly strangled by the acts of 1559 and 1563. They combined to resist, whence the new books and the literary movement from Louvain, the petitions to Rome for a definite ruling about church-going, and the active apostolate of men like Sander and Allen and Morton, who toured England in these years, encouraging the Catholics to stand firm. It was at the culmination of this first phase of the resistance that the two new features made their appearance in the second decade of the reign, the missionary movement of which Allen's college at Douay was the chief centre and the political movement which had the Pope at its head.

From now on, that is to say from about 1574—the year when it was first decided to send the Douay priests into England as missionaries, and the year in which the Pope began the long effort to rouse Philip II to his role of Catholic champion—the dual character of the Counter-Reformation in England is very evident. There is the purely spiritual movement, that trains preachers, religious controversialists and theologians, whose aim is to provide the English

Catholics with Mass and the sacraments. There is also the resort of the papacy to the temporal arm, first to secure the future of the harvest the missionaries are sowing, and then for the punishment of the heretics.

Here, then, are two distinct movements, distinct because the actors in each are wholly separate groups of men. But the chief of both movements is the same. Both movements have one single ultimate source, the Pope. And not only are they thus co-ordinated in the Pope, but, for as long as the duality continues, the Pope has, for both movements, one single chief English agent, William Allen. This personal union of movements so distinct in character in the person of the ecclesiastic who was, for practical purposes, the primate of English Catholicism, was the source of innumerable problems to the English Catholics, and it was the source of as many opportunities to the English government.

Of the two movements, the spiritual movement was the more dangerous to Cecil's aims, and the more purely spiritual it was, the greater the danger it presented. To introduce into every town and county of England men of utterly selfless lives, dedicated wholly to the service of God trained in charity, instructed in faith, and to maintain a constant supply of such unworldly apostles might easily, even after twenty years of Protestant ascendancy, turn the scales against 1559, for Anglicanism was by no means, as yet, out of the critical stage and certain to survive. Cecil will not attack the spiritual movement as a spiritual movement. Nowhere is it ever said that the specific Catholic doctrine on the controverted points is itself something noxious to the public well-being. Whatever the Protestant theologians may say, no Elizabethan Act of Parliament declares the Mass to be idolatry, not even when the act is drawn to make it impossible to say or to hear Mass. The queen will not quarrel with theological ideas or theories. It is obedience to law she exacts, and disobedience to these particular laws about religion which she is increasingly ready to brand as treason and to punish as treason. The spiritual opposition is not attacked except as a treasonable opposition, and it is, of course, branded as a treasonable opposition by anticipation, in the very laws that are the occasion of the opposition forming.

The actual formulation of an anti-Elizabethan movement

in temporalibus is of course an immense opportunity for
Cecil. He now violently attacks the spiritual opposition—
the missionary movement is but its new phase—alleging
that this is really a treasonable conspiracy, the domestic
branch of the continental conspiracy, and he protests, ever
more strongly, that with purely spiritual matters he has no
quarrel at all.

The success of the political movement, for which Gregory
XIII may stand as chief patron and promoter, is, in actual
fact, the only hope for those who wish to make the England
of Cecil safe for Catholicism. Allowing even the hypothesis
that the majority of the English are Catholic in sympathy at
this time (1574–1592), the only way to restore their hold on
the government of England is a political and military victory
from outside England. Without such a victory the Church
in England can never be delivered from what must end in
her destruction.

The popes, then, shoulder the task—and responsibility—
of calling in the temporal arm. In doing so they risk a great
deal. They risk playing into Cecil's hands, supplying him
with abundance of matter that can be worked up to prove
his charge that Catholicism in England is simply a treasonable conspiracy, or, more subtly, that the spiritual activity
of the missionaries is but the means to a political end.[1] If
the popes ultimately won in the political struggle, Cecil's
misrepresentation would cease to matter, his pamphlets and
his propaganda be soon forgotten. But the popes lost, lost
heavily and completely. Their failure was, for Cecil's policy,
its great opportunity, and thence onward Catholics are
easily branded as only half-English, as anti-national, half-
foreign, and as, indeed, necessarily traitors. Cecil has
henceforward a free hand to use much more violent means
to destroy Catholicism, means much more rapidly effective
than strangulation, and to use them against the men and
the movement he knows to be purely spiritual.

The popes failed in their political endeavours, failed
to bring about the Catholic conquest of Elizabethan
England, and with the election of Clement VIII in 1592
these schemes were laid aside for ever. But a fatal influence
descended from these days of the dual endeavour into still
later generations. There continued to be in Rome, in the

---

[1] Which is what Philip II, too, can be held to have thought ; *cf. supra*,
p. 194.

very heart of the Counter-Reformation, a strong body of
opinion which, for the restoration of the faith in England,
looked primarily to the conversion of the reigning sovereign.
This school of thought was for years in conflict with that
other which based all on the extension of the colleges, the
improvement of the instruction given to the priests, and the
restoration of ecclesiastical government. Nor did this
second school of thought really come into its own until all
the hope of the other school was patently dead, even to the
most naïvely optimistic, and by that time it was too late
to look for more than the preservation of the faith in the
small groups of Catholics who still survived. But here we
anticipate the events of the next century. Long before that
tragedy had opened, there were victims enough, confessors
and martyrs, of whose trials Cecil's ill-will to the faith was
the sole cause, whatever the occasion supplied by the political
manœuvres of the contemporary popes.

CHAPTER IV

THE ELIZABETHAN MARTYRS

THE story of the Elizabethan martyrs has been pronounced by a leading authority to be the brightest page of all the Counter-Reformation epic. This is a much nobler place than their countrymen usually allot them, even their fellow-countrymen who also share their faith. Professor Meyer more than justifies his great claim by the whole of his book, and particularly by his chapter ' The Heroic Period of the Mission,' [1] which must for long remain the last word on its subject. These martyrs only come within the scope of the present book in so far as they were Rome's agents in the Counter-Reformation in England, and the particular way in which they appear is the old debate, were they really martyrs, or were they men justly put to death for treason ?

The Elizabethan martyrs are the 189 priests and layfolk, men and women put to death [2] in England between January 4, 1570, and February 17, 1603, under various acts of parliament, and who were either beatified by the Holy See in 1886 and 1929, or whose process of beatification has so far proceeded that they are styled ' venerable.' They formed the greater part of the total of the 316 English martyrs. Of the 189 there are 110 beatified and styled therefore ' Blessed,' and seventy-nine styled ' Venerable.' One hundred and twenty-seven of these martyrs were ecclesiastics —126 of them priests, and of these 126, there are one Benedictine, one Dominican, two Franciscans, and eleven Jesuits. [3] The remaining 111 are secular clergy.

[1] Pp. 189–214.
[2] Actually 188, for Bl. Philip Howard, earl of Arundel, died from the rigours of his imprisonment while in the Tower under sentence of death.
[3] Of the eleven Jesuit martyrs of this reign only four had been actually trained in the Society. The others are Jesuits by virtue of vows made (sometimes in prison) which martyrdom and not any more regular process perfected. The same is true of the one Benedictine martyr. All these martyrs of the regular clergy had been trained at Douay, in whole or in part, except Bl. Henry Walpole, S.J., and he was an alumnus of the English College at

Four out of this total of 126 priests were Marian clergy——*i.e.* already priests at the religious revolution of 1559. The remaining 122 had been trained since 1559 in religious orders and in the new colleges founded beyond the seas, no less than 113 of them at Douay. Fifty-five of these priests were university men, ten from Cambridge and forty-five from Oxford ; forty-nine of the total were converts, nine indeed of them converted ministers.

If we turn to examine the milieu whence came the sixty-two lay martyrs, we find every condition of life represented. The earl of Arundel was a kinsman of the queen; Bl. John Roche was an Irishman who earned his living as a Thames waterman. Here is the full analysis as far as the rank and occupations of the martyrs are known to us : nobles two, gentry twenty-six, the Bar three, schoolmasters two, student one, farmers and yeoman four, serving men four, and one each of the following : merchant, printer, bookseller, tailor, joiner, ostler, glover, waterman, and a dyer's apprentice. Of the three women martyrs, Margaret Clitherow was the wife of a prosperous York tradesman, Margaret Ward and Anne Line are given as gentlewomen.

Rome. Bl. Mark Barkworth, O.S.B., was, in part, an alumnus of the English College at Valladolid, and it was there that he was ordained. This preponderance of the martyrs of the secular clergy over the regulars in Elizabeth's reign did not continue, during the next century, in the same degree. During Elizabeth's reign there were practically none but secular clergy at work in England, which was one reason for the bitterness of the opposition to what was considered a Jesuit scheme to manage the Church in England. But, as the seventeenth century advanced the revived Benedictines and Franciscans, and especially the Jesuits, increased very rapidly in number, and this is reflected in the statistics of the martyrs. With the figures I also set down, for the interest of the comparison, an analysis of the martyrs in the time of Henry VIII.

	Total	Laymen	Clergy	Secular Priests	Regulars i.e.	O.S.B.	O.F.M.	O.P.	S.J.
Elizabeth	189	62	127	111	16	1	2	1	11
James I									
Charles I	}52	8	44	23	21	7	4	–	10
Commonwealth									
Popish Plot	25	4	21	6	15	1	3	–	11
Henry VIII	50	5	45	12	33	5	5	–	—
Total Eng.	—	—	—	—	—	—	—	—	—
Martyrs	316	79	237	152	85	14	14	1	32

The sixteen Regulars of Elizabeth's martyrs include one Friar Minim not yet ordained.

The ten Jesuits of the next period include two lay brothers.

The Benedictine of the third period is a lay brother.

The thirty-three Regulars of Henry VIII's time include eighteen Carthusians (six of them lay brothers), three Knights of St. John, one Augustinian friar, and one Bridgettine.

Of the total of eighty-five regulars seventy-two are priests.

The greater part of the priest martyrs were very young men indeed when they came to their high fate. Two-thirds of them—eighty-five out of the 126—had not been ordained more than five years when they were martyred and—the Marian priests apart—only eight of the whole 126 had been ordained above ten years. Nine indeed had only been priests for a matter of months, nineteen for just a year, another twenty for only two years.

These 189 martyrs were not the product of any one particular district. An immense proportion—fifty-three—were Yorkshiremen, fifteen were from Lancashire, and a dozen were Londoners. Five were Irishmen, one a Scot, eight were Welshmen. For the rest the Englishmen came from almost every county in England, those districts excepted which provided so many of the first Protestants, for there are no martyrs in this reign from natives of the counties of Suffolk, Cambridge, Huntingdon, Bedford, or Hertford. Nor are there among them any natives of Warwickshire, Surrey, Wiltshire, or Berkshire. The West of England (Cornwall, Devon, Somerset, Dorset, Gloucester, and Oxfordshire) contributed twenty-three, the Midlands twenty (the counties of Lincoln, Nottingham, Derby, Stafford, Leicester, Rutland, and Northampton). It is not without some significance that almost half the martyrs are from the north, ninety-three out of the 189.

The list of places where the martyrs suffered is worth some study. The largest number were put to death in London (seventy-eight), and at York (forty-one). The cathedral towns of Carlisle (one), Durham (ten), Lincoln (two), Gloucester (three), Oxford (four), Rochester (two), Canterbury (four), Chichester (two), Salisbury (one), Winchester (five), and Exeter (one), were scenes of the executions of others. There were also martyrdoms in the north, at Newcastle-on-Tyne (two), Gateshead, and Darlington. At Lancaster there were six, at Derby three, at Dorchester six, at Isleworth two, in the Isle of Wight two, and an execution, with one martyr, at each of the following places : Launceston, Andover, Kingston-on-Thames, in the southern half of the country ; at Warwick and Stafford and Oakham in the Midlands ; at Chelmsford and Ipswich in the east ; and at Wrexham and Beaumaris in Wales. By the end of Elizabeth's reign no district where there was anything of a Catholic revival to be feared was without its memories of the terrible fate in store whether for the Catholic priest or the faithful Catholic layman.

Once the statutes of 1581 had provided more easily provable charges on which Catholics might be sentenced to death, the executions never slackened so long as Elizabeth lived. From 1581 to 1603 every year had its victims. The total for the twenty-two years is 180. The worst five years were 1586–1590, when seventy-one were put to death. In the last three years of the reign twenty-three suffered. In the four summer months of the Armada year [1] no fewer than thirty were martyred, ten of them laymen. Twenty-one of these martyrs were put to death in London, fourteen of them in the two days, August 28 and 30.

Of the heroic quality of the lives of all these nearly two hundred martyrs no one can say anything that has not been excellently said many times already. It is our greatest glory that we can call these men and women ' our ' martyrs. And if ever a sense of the true scale of values returns to our country they will be the great boast of every truly national historian. Beside the splendour of their simple achievement, the dubious glory of Elizabeth and Cecil, of the semi-pirate, semi-slaver sea-kings, of the semi-atheist, wholly lascivious court, and the hardly more reputable world whence came Marlowe and Shakespeare himself, all these shall be seen for a fitful tawdry pageantry indeed.

Nor can the Catholic kings, nor even ' the glorious popes of the Counter-Reformation,' stand the ordeal of comparison with this fierce whiteness of Christian heroism, of unsullied, entire devotion. The story of the Elizabethan martyrs is indeed ' the brightest page in the whole Counter-Reformation epic,' the one page that no human imperfection, no grievous lapse, has spotted. Here, at any rate, can the Catholic reader breathe freely, and look on without even a half-fear that somewhere there lurk unpleasant skeletons.

But were not these Elizabethan martyrs really traitors ? The accusation continues to be made, and in many popular historical works it is taken as proved. Held back by some last hold of this tradition, hardly anywhere does a non-Catholic historian give to this epic of heroic endurance that fullness of admiration, that supreme admiration, which is its due.

---

[1] *I.e.* after the defeat of the Armada, after the display of Catholic loyalty, in a kind of triumphant holocaust with Cecil and Walsingham jointly officiating. *Cf.* BURTON and POLLEN, Introduction, pp. xxiv–xxix.

If the question, Did these martyrs really commit treason ? is to be fully answered, the first point to clear up is the meaning we attach to the term ' treason.' A standard dictionary defines it as ' overthrowing the government, betraying the state,' and treason in this sense of the liege man acting against the lord to whom he is bound by allegiance, is a crime against the natural law, like theft or murder ; a crime that exists independently of and antecedent to any legislation. Let us call this, treason in the real or natural sense, natural treason.

At a certain defined date legislation steps in and, providing penalties against those guilty of treason—against traitors—distinguishes various ways in which treason may be committed and lays down the amount of evidence required in proof of the crime. This the law did in England through the Statute of Treasons, enacted in the twenty-fifth year of King Edward III (1352), establishing thereby in England a legal doctrine of treason, and this we may call legal treason, treason in the eyes of the law. What is legal treason according to the act of 1352 ? The question is most relevant to the position of the Elizabethan martyrs, for it was under this act that some of them were put to death. And, of course, this old act of 1352 is still the law of England, and little more than twenty years ago a man was tried under it and put to death by virtue of it.

There are seven main points in which treason may be committed, says this act. Three only concern us here. They are :

1. ' When a man doth compass or imagine the death of our lord the king, of our lady his queen, or of their eldest son and heir.'
2. ' If a man do levy war against our lord the king in his realm.'
3. ' If a man be adherent to the king's enemies in his realm, giving to them aid and comfort in the realm, or elsewhere.'

The statute provides that the accused must be shown to have committed some overt act and that this is to be proved by the testimony of two witnesses. In respect of the three acts enumerated, legal treason is identical with natural treason.

The penalty for the crime of treason is death, and until

a century ago, not only death but death in this particular
way that the criminal is dismembered and disentrailed while
still alive—a medieval endeavour, it is said, to secure that
all traitors die as Judas, the greatest of them all, died.

The English law had not, however, yet finished with
treason. As the years went by, it suited the various kings
to bring under the scope of the Treason Act, and to render
liable to its horrible penalty, other offences which had no
connection with treason at all, either in the natural sense
of the term or in any sense used by the Statute of Treasons.
And presently treasons were so multiplied, the Statute of
Treasons was applied and made to serve as a kind of represser
for so many crimes, that a day came when the crown had to
revoke these more recent legal fictions of treasons, and an
act was passed restoring the purity of the old legal doctrine
of treason. In other words, since Edward III there had
been constituted by law what we may call fictitious treasons,
and now these were all abolished.

Parliament we know is sovereign. It can make it an
offence to smoke after a certain time—it has not yet done
this, though it has allowed it to be made an offence to smoke
in certain places. And, were parliament mad enough, were
the day to come when it should suit some powerful vested
interest to see a close connection between smoking and some
rival interest, why we might see parliament declare smoking
to be a treasonable act, and if it did so we should be helpless
before the court were we taken *flagrante delicto*.

This practice of attaching the name and penalties of
treason to acts not of their own nature treasonable, began
to revive in the reign of Henry VIII, despite the act which
forbade such extension, and that king brought it about
that for a Welshman to steal cattle was treason, and centuries
later than this, in the reign of Queen Anne, it was made
treasonable to affirm in writing that the king and parliament cannot limit the power of the crown—which at first
sight seems a very curious kind of treason indeed.

The simplest way to clear up this question whether the
Elizabethan martyrs were traitors is to find out under what
statute they were indicted and tried, and to discover
whether it was a statute dealing with real or fictitious
treasons, whether it was a statute that merely gave the
natural idea of treason legal expression and definition or
whether, to quote the actual title of an Elizabethan statute

we shall have to consider, it was a statute ' whereby certain offences be made treason.'

If it is under a statute of this second kind that the martyr is convicted, and if the trial has been fair, then though legally a traitor, he is morally only guilty of the particular offence which the law has, for the time being, made treason. I say ' for the time being ' because, all these acts ' whereby certain offences be made treason ' have long ago been repealed, while the Statute of Treasons is as good law to-day as ever it was. Treason, real treason, natural treason, is always a crime and the law cannot ever be so altered that it ceases to be a crime.

But if it was under the statute of real treason—the act of Edward III—that the martyr was indicted, then we need to examine whether the trial was fair, whether the evidence was true and whether the charge was proved.

Of the 189 Elizabethan martyrs some twenty were tried and found guilty of treason in the natural sense of the word, under the act of 1352. That is to say they were accused of rebellion or plotting to murder the queen, or of plotting a foreign invasion. The rest—and this is the great majority, 169 out of 189—were tried under acts passed in Elizabeth's reign, acts whereby certain offences are made treason, tried for treasons, that is to say, which were only treasons by a legal fiction.

The number of the martyrs condemned under the several acts is as follows :

Act of	1352 (25 Edw. III. c. 1)	1559 (1 Eliz., c. 1)[1]	1571 (13 Eliz., c. 1)[2]	(13 Eliz., c. 2)[3]	1581 (23 Eliz., c. 1)[4]	(23 Eliz., c. 2)[5]	1585 (27 Eliz., c. 2)[6]
Martyrs [7]	20	11	3	2	18	4	123

Most of the martyrs were put to death in the eighteen years that followed the act of 1585, i.e. 146 out of these 182, and of these 146, as many as 123 were indicted under the act

[1] Cf. p. 141, sup.   [2] Cf. p. 190, sup.   [3] Cf. p. 190, sup.
[4] Cf. p. 227, sup.   [5] Cf. p. 255, inf.   [6] Cf. pp. 228–30, sup.
[7] The total of martyrs considered is thus 182 : the seven martyrs not included in these analyses are Bl. Margaret Clitherow, indicted under the act of 1585, but not condemned, for she refused to plead and was therefore pressed to death as the law then provided ; Bl. Philip Howard, earl of Arundel, who died under sentence of death, condemned under the act of 1585 ; BB. John Roche and Margaret Ward, condemned for rescuing a priest from prison ; VV. Nicholas Tichborne and Thomas Hackshott, for the same : V. Robert Bickerdyke, condemned for ' traitorous ' speech under what act I do not know, cf. the record of his several trials in BURTON and POLLEN, I, pp. 251–259.

of 1585, which is admirable testimony to the practical usefulness of this statute. Its passing was the equivalent of the introduction of the guillotine into France two hundred years later. Particularly was it an efficacious instrument for the despatch of the priests, for of the ninety-nine priests executed between its passing and the end of the reign, ninety-six were victims to it. The other three were, two of them, priests ordained before 1559 and one was condemned for circulating Allen's reply to Lord Burghley's pamphlet defending the condemnation of Edmund Campion and his fellow-martyrs.

In this later stage of the persecution (1585–1603) the proportion of lay martyrs rises. In the earlier stage (the fifteen years between the death of the proto-martyr Bl. Thomas Plumtree, January 4, 1570, and the coming into force of the act of 1585, May 10, 1585) a total of thirty-six suffered death of whom only nine were laymen. In the next eighteen years (1585–1603) 146 died, and of these forty-six were laymen, and more than half of these forty-six (twenty-seven) were martyrs to the act of 1585.

The method by which this question, Martyrs or Traitors, can best be decided is to ask in each case two questions : What was the martyr accused of ? Was he really guilty of it ? And according to their indictments the martyrs, as persons accused of crime, fall into three great groups : I. those accused of overt acts of high treason, in the ancient and the current sense, under the statute of 1352 ; II. those accused that having a certain status (namely being priests ordained abroad subsequent to June 24, 1559) they have returned into England and not taken the Oath of Supremacy; also those who harbour them ; III. an intermediate group accused indeed of acts, acts newly made treasonable by certain statutes. To the first class belong twenty of the martyrs, to the second 123, to the third thirty-nine.

I. The twenty indicted under the Statute of Treasons of 1352 include two groups (ten tried together in 1581 and five in 1584), and the following five who were tried and condemned individually : BB. Thomas Plumtree (1570), John Felton (1570), John Storey (1571), Thomas Percy, earl of Northumberland (1572), and John Payne (1582). The case of the martyrs who make up the two groups and of Bl. John Payne presents no difficulty. The trials were very evident shams, as the records that remain show to whoever

will read them.[1] The charge in all these cases, involving
all told, sixteen priests, was the very definite accusation of
plotting together, in places named and at times specified,
to murder the queen. In no case was there any evidence
offered which proved this, and in so far as they were allowed
to question the witnesses the accused had no difficulty in
breaking down their testimony. The crown lawyers—the
accused were not, of course, allowed counsel [2]—chiefly
addressed themselves to violent attacks on the bull of excommunication, and the judges were openly active in the pressure
they brought to bear on the jury. In the trials of 1584, for
example, Bl. James Fenn objected that he had never been at
Rome in his life (one of the places where the accused were
alleged to have plotted together), that at the time he was
alleged to have been at Rome he was actually in the Marchal-
sea prison in London, and that he had never so much as
seen his alleged fellow-plotter, V. George Haydock, until
they met in the dock. To which the judge merely answered
that these were but details. Neither witness nor any
evidence soever were produced, the judge simply directing
the jury to bring in a verdict of guilty.[3] 'The affair of
James Fenn,' said Lord Burghley, ' was very ill-managed.' [4]
The trial of Bl. John Payne (at Chelmsford, March 30, 1582)
was really void in law because only one witness was brought
to prove the charge, the crown counsel relying on ' pre-
sumptions from Mr. Paine's having gone beyond the seas, and
having been made priest by the Bishop of Cambray ' to bring
home to the jury that he had plotted Elizabeth's murder.[5]

The trial of Edmund Campion and his fellow-martyrs
was a legal scandal that sounded all over Europe, and Cecil
was driven to defend it in a once celebrated pamphlet.

The first intention was to try Campion under 13 Eliz.,
c. 1, ' for absolving and reconciling ' . . . ; a man is caught
in a dangerous treasonable conspiracy and the government
propose to try him for unlawfully administering a sacrament ! This would too obviously seem like making away
with one of the most famous men of the day, for religion

---

[1] Cf. 1581, SIMPSON, pp. 393–442; 1582, CAMM, pp. 82, 436–39; 1584,
BURTON and POLLEN, pp. 46, 66–67, 73, 100–101.

[2] A feature of English criminal law proceedings that endured until well
into the nineteenth century.

[3] Account in CHALLONER, *Memoirs of Missionary Priests* (edition 1924),
p. 92.

[4] Quoted, without any authority given, in BURTON and POLLEN, I, p. 67

[5] CHALLONER, p. 40.

pure and simple. Whence a second thought and a second indictment, this time a bogus plot and Campion's share in it ; a plot in which there were three other conspirators, Allen, Persons, and Dr. Morton ; a trial in which Campion alone would be in the dock.

Then the government changed its plan once more, and lumped together all the other priests recently arrested, eleven in all and two laymen with them ; there was now a total of seventeen conspirators, and the indictment could only cover them all by imagining a new plot of more generous dimensions.

To the eloquence of the prosecuting counsel, Serjeant Anderson, denouncing, in general terms, the papal malevolence towards England as the cause of ' all the treasons and rebellions that have been conspired since the first hour of the queen's coronation,' instancing Storey, Felton, and the Rising of the North, and presenting the accused as the successors to these earlier traitors, Campion made the all-sufficient reply : ' The wisdom and providence of the laws of England, as I take it, is such as proceedeth not to the trial of any man for his life and death by shifts of probabilities and conjectural surmises, without proof of the crime by sufficient evidence and substantial witness . . . probabilities, aggravations, invectives, are not the balance wherein justice must be weighed. but witnesses, oaths, and apparent guiltiness. . . . These matters ought to be proved and not urged, declared by evidence and not surmised by fancy. . . .' This great trial of November 16, 1581, resolved itself principally into the trial of Edmund Campion, and, indeed, into a debate between himself and the prosecution that ranged over a world of issues, the background of presumption against which it was desired to set the alleged, but never proved and never provable, treasonable conspiracy. The only direct testimony—direct by comparison with the rest—was that Campion, in a sermon, on the text of Our Lord weeping over Jerusalem, had spoken of a coming day of Catholic triumph.

Against Sherwin all that could be urged was his refusal to give a plain answer to the thorny question of the Pope's power to excommunicate the queen, and an alleged statement that ' by the fireside in the English seminary beyond the seas ' he had spoken of what might be done in the west of England, and how the best place for a landing would be

R 2

St. Michael's Mount. To Cottam, who also, before the trial, had refused to answer about the deposing power, it was said very simply by the queen's counsel : ' You came into England at or near the time that the rest came ; so that it must needs be intended a match made between you, for the furtherance of those affairs which were then a brewing ; and how answer you thereunto ? ' Actually Cottam was meant for the mission to the Indies, and he was in England merely to recruit his health before leaving for the East.

In Johnson's case it was Eliot—the betrayer of Campion and the solitary witness in the coming year, 1582, against Bl. John Payne—who gave the sole testimony. This was to the effect that about the time, at Christmas, 1579, that Payne had tried to seduce Eliot from his allegiance, Johnson had come in search of Payne—who by this ' had conveyed himself away and was no more to be heard of '—and not finding him had remarked, ' he is gone beyond the seas, fearing lest you would discover his secrets,' and had warned Eliot not to disclose any of them.

Luke Kirby's share in this conspiracy to murder the queen was proved by the evidence of an apostate seminarist, one Sledd. Kirby had spoken to him, abroad, of the coming of a great day, when the Pope and Spain should make another alteration in England. He had been present at a sermon in which Allen exhorted the seminarists to work upon the fidelity of the English to Elizabeth, and, moreover, one of Kirby's familiar friends, Tudor by name, had violently repudiated the suggestion that he was of the queen's kin, calling her ' that whore of Babylon, that Jezebel of England.'

Campion's speech to the jury followed, and after an hour, the jury brought them in guilty.

Never in the whole trial is there any attempt made to prove any of the treasonable activities of which the prisoners stand indicted. Never are the required two witnesses produced to prove whatever is actually alleged. State trials, in the days of the Tudors and Stuarts so Lord Macaulay has somewhere said, were simply murder preceded by mummery. The description fits the trials of all these sixteen men. So far as the trials go they must be declared innocent of any of the offences which the act under which they were charged professed to punish and of which they stood indicted, the treason of plotting to murder the sovereign or to levy war against her.

The case of the other four martyrs in this first group is not so simple. The earl of Northumberland was, of course, one of the two chiefs who had led the Rising of the North, and it was for this that he was condemned. He figures as a martyr because he was offered his life if he took the Oath of Supremacy. It is for the like reason that Bl. Thomas Plumtree, one of the chaplains to the rebel army, has his place in the list. Bl. John Felton's offence was his making known the bull that deposed Elizabeth by posting it at the gates of the Bishop of London's palace near to St. Paul's. This, it seems to me, is the one case in the whole list where a Catholic, for the sake of Catholicism and moved by the action of a Pope commits an arguably treasonable act. It is true that the bull was, in substance, a spiritual sentence ; that it had in view primarily the consciences of a group of English Catholics ; that the Pope did not, in the bull, call on any prince to put into execution its consequences, namely the queen's deposition. It is true that only in England was it ever promulgated in a legal sense, and that outside England no one had legal congnisance of it. Yet the bull did declare Elizabeth to be no queen, and it not only freed her subjects from allegiance to her, but forbade them to continue loyal, forbade them to obey her laws. Felton's conscience bade him not only obey the Pope, but do his best to make the Pope's will known more generally.

Here was a case where English law and that more general reality, the law of Christendom, were in conflict. England, so the traditional conception held, was but a part of Christendom, living, like any other part, by the life of the whole. No man could be really harming England who called in the chief of the Christian commonwealth to heal England's troubles. But this conception of national law as subordinate to a higher reality, the welfare of Christendom, and of national welfare as deriving from the general welfare of Christendom, to which St. Thomas More had appealed at his trial forty years nearly before Felton, was no longer a thing of universal acceptance. This conception was indeed already rapidly falling into the eclipse which has since so generally covered it. The English answer to any such conception was stated with the maximum of brevity in Henry VIII's Statute of Appeals, to wit that England is a realm that is imperial. It is a closed commonwealth, self-sufficing, and politically and spiritually autonomous. All

jurisdictions, other than the king's are, in England, foreign
jurisdictions ; whoever introduces them to the prejudice
of the king's jurisdiction cannot but be a traitor.

Dr. John Storey was one of the most distinguished legists
of his time, an expert in both the Canon Law and the
Civil Law, and Regius Professor of Civil Law at Oxford. He
had inevitably played a notable part in the heresy commissions during Mary's reign, and in the first parliament of
Elizabeth's reign he had courageously opposed the bills for
the alteration of religion. Most of the next four years he
spent in prison, but in 1563 he managed to escape, became
a naturalised Spaniard and received employment in the
Low Countries from King Philip. In 1570 he was kidnapped at Antwerp by Cecil's agent and brought home to
England, to be tried for his life on the double charge of
plotting the queen's death and succouring the rebel leaders
who had escaped to Flanders after the Rising of the North.
We know nothing of his trial except what hostile sources
report. But these tell us that the martyr refused to plead,
claiming to be no longer an English subject. He was,
however, condemned and sentenced. His appeal to his
own sovereign went all but unnoticed, and the sentence was
carried out ' with horrible cruelty,' Cecil and others of the
Council attending personally in order ' to gloat over the
dying moments of the man they both hated and feared in
Queen Mary's days and detested still.' [1]

II. It is the second group of the martyrs which is the largest
group of the three, 123 martyrs in all, ninety-six priests and
twenty-seven laymen. The priests were all executed simply for
being Englishmen who had returned to England as priests and
had not taken the Oath of Supremacy, the laymen for assisting
the priests in various ways. Of this statute under which so
many suffered, the late Fr. Harrington has very justly said :
' This Act is not merely a retort to the Bull [i.e. of excom-
munication], it is the logical sequel to the opening acts of
the reign. The Elizabethan settlement is a uniform system,
little affected by the Bull *which merely provided an additional
incentive.*' [2] Those who devised the statute, however, professed to relate it to the statute of 1352 and to the political
activities which followed the bull of Pius V rather than to

---

[1] R. Simpson in *The Rambler*, New Series, Vol. VII (1857).
[2] *English Martyrs*, p. 208 ; italics not in original.

the settlement of 1559. There has come down to us the detailed report of one trial under the 27 Eliz., c. 2, in which the argument for the prosecution is set out at some length. The jury are told that it is not for any new offence that the prisoners are to be tried. The treasons of which they are accused are treasons by the common law and mentioned in the act of 1352. For the accused have been 'adhering to her majesty's enemies, compounding and originating the deprivation of the queen from her regal authority and life.' This, says the crown, was undoubtedly their intent, and their intent only needs to be proved for them to be convicted. But here the common law demands that some overt fact be adduced in proof of intent. By overt fact alone can the intent be proved, to satisfy the common law. Which is where the new statute of 27 Eliz., c. 2 begins to function. The sole purpose of this act is to make it easier for the jury to discern the treason in the activities of the accused, 'the statute did no more but to make certain the overt fact, for the ease of the jury that should try the treason by their overt fact.' The statute of King Edward III says all who adhere to the king's enemies are traitors. It is a kind of major proposition in the argument. The statute of 1585—the crown suggests—says that all who take orders beyond the seas are 'adherers' to that mortal enemy the Pope. Here is the minor. *Ergo.*

In other words ordination beyond the seas by the Pope's authority is the overt fact which proves the treasonable intent. 'No man will doubt that the Pope is the queen's capital enemy, as one that hath gone about by his sentence to deprive the queen of her estate, and to absolve her subjects of their fidelity and allegiance . . . and therefore each of them being natural born subjects to her majesty, and going out of the realm, and there adhering to the Pope, and by or under his authority taking an order of the priesthood, and returning to win the queen's subjects to their faction, were without any question even by the common law to be adjudged traitors.'

In this argument, which convicted the two accused to the satisfaction of a Sussex jury, there are two vital points which are not proved but assumed. The weakness which underlies the whole attempt to justify the martyrdoms as lawful executions of traitors shows here also. The accused are proved to have gone overseas, and to have been by the

Pope's authority ordained to the priesthood, but the charge stated between these two charges, and stated as a separate charge, ' and there adhering to the Pope,' is not proved. It is taken as proved, assumed as an activity inseparable from the other two charges. Next it is said not only that they returned, but that they returned ' to win the queen's subjects to their faction,' a phrase which is dangerously equivocal. The martyrs' reply to this was that they returned ' to win people to the Catholic faith ' and the argument returns to the question, is the Catholic religion a political faction ? Did the accused, having gone abroad, ' adhere to the Pope ? ' Is the Catholic religion a political faction ? These are the charges in which real treason lies, and they are charges nowhere proved. They are stated, because vital to the argument, and their truth is taken for granted.[1]

The laymen condemned and executed under this act of 1585, suffered for ' harbouring ' priests, that is for assisting them in various ways. The harbourer of a priest might be the host to whom he acted as a kind of chaplain, he might be the guide who took him from one Catholic household to another, he might be a serving man in the family that lodged a priest, he might merely be a Catholic found in the priest's company when the priest was arrested. He might be the tailor who made him a suit, the ostler who did him service in an inn, and in one case he was no more than the charitable Catholic bystander who clapped his hat on the priest's bare head as he was led away to gaol. Two of these harbourers were women, Margaret Clitherow of York, who scrupled to torment the jury's conscience with a conflict between their own safety and the sin of an unjust verdict, and so was pressed to death, and Anne Lyne, an aged woman who had to be carried in a chair to her trial.

III. The third group of the martyrs—those executed for religious activities made treasonable by the new Elizabethan statutes passed between 1559 and 1581—offers the great interest that the most of these were laymen, twenty five of the total thirty-nine. Twelve of these martyrs—five priests and seven laymen—were put to death by virtue of the Act of Supremacy of 1559, i.e. for denying the queen to be the

---

[1] For an account of this trial, of BB. Ralph Crockett and Edward James, at Chichester, Sept. 30, 1588, cf. their lives by FRANCIS P. HOGAN, B.A., in BURTON and POLLEN, pp. 473–498 ; the report, by the crown prosecutor, is in R.O., Dom. Eliz., i, 1588, Sept. 30, and was published by Simpson as long ago as 1857 (April) in The Rambler (N.S., vii, pp. 279–283).

supreme governor of the Church of Christ in England and maintaining the papal primacy.

There were three executions under the first statute of 1571, one priest (in 1578) and two laymen (1591 and 1598) for styling the queen a heretic ; there were two executions under the second act of the same year, the priest Cuthbert Mayne in 1577 for bringing into the country the expired papal bull announcing the Jubilee indulgence of 1575, and a layman, Roger Ashton, for obtaining a papal dispensation to enable him to marry his cousin. The second of the statutes of 1581 made it a felony, and punishable with death, to write, print, or circulate books which slandered or defamed the queen, supposing such actions could not be brought under one or other of the different treason statutes. This law brought four martyrs to their death, the priest, Thomas Alfield, and a dyer's apprentice, Thomas Webley for circulating Allen's reply to Lord Burghley ; William Carter for printing a tract by Dr. Richard Bristow, the Douay professor ; and James Duckett, a bookseller, for having in stock Bl. Robert Southwell's *Supplication to the Queen*. But of this second group of thirty-nine martyrs, nearly one-half suffered under the act of 1581 which made it treason to persuade any one to become a Catholic, to reconcile any one to the Church or to be so reconciled. Under this act five priests suffered, one for persuading, two for reconciling, and two—old Marian priests who had conformed after 1559—for being reconciled. Among the reconciled there were also the son of John Felton, a religious (but not a priest : he was only twenty) of the order of Minim Friars. The twelve laymen were, seven of them, condemned for being reconciled to the Church, and the other five for persuading others to become Catholics.

If we pierce the legal terminology and look to the actual cause of the deaths of the sixty-two layfolk who suffered death in Elizabeth's reign we find, then :

Treason	1
Denial of Supremacy	9
Making use of a Roman marriage Dispensation	1
'Treasonable words'	2
Printing or Circulating Catholic Books . .	3
Persuading to Popery	5
Being reconciled	7
Harbouring Priests	27

To these add Philip Howard, who died in prison under sentence, Margaret Clitherow, Robert Bickerdyke, and the four who died for helping priests to escape.

Now though parliament called it treason to deny the king to be the head of the Church of Christ in England, parliament cannot make that denial treason.[1] Nor can it make really criminal a man's association with traitors of this sort.

It has, of course, often been suggested that such statutes as that of 1585 were a natural rejoinder to the political schemes of Gregory XIII. We can allow, with Fr. Pontifex,[2] that ' politics and religion were inextricably interwoven at this time. Their inter-relations and mutual reactions are so close and multifarious that the two are almost one for historical purposes.' And this was as true for Gregory XIII and Sixtus V as for Cecil, but how far was it true of the offences for which these 189 suffered ? Our case for them is that there was the clearest of distinctions between their mission to England, or the way they conducted it, and the political activities which occupied their religious superiors. There was so great a distinction that the missionaries were not only innocent of this political scheming, but in large part wholly ignorant of it. And it is the traditional Catholic case against Cecil and the Elizabethan statesmen, that they knew of this innocence, were aware of this ignorance, were fully conscious of the loyalty of the mass of the Catholics,[3] and that, while they fought the political schemes of the papacy through the execution of these innocent men, they so arranged the procedure as to misrepresent the innocents and make the Catholic faith seem identical with treason to the mass of the English people of that time.

---

[1] To this very evident distinction more than one of the martyrs drew attention, e.g. Bl. John Body, to the sheriff at the place of execution, Andover, Nov. 2, 1583 : ' You may make what you will treason ; but I have committed no treason, although indeed I suffer the punishment due to treason.' Cf. BURTON and POLLEN, I, p. 19 ; Bl. Everard Hanse (at Tyburn, July 31, 1581), asked if he acknowledged Elizabeth as his sovereign, answered : ' That he did take her for his Queen, and that he never offended her Majesty otherwise than in matters of his conscience, which their new-made statutes had drawn to matters of treason. And whereas,' said he, ' I understand it has been given out that I should say " Treason was no offence to God," I protest I neither meant nor said any more, but that these new-made treasons, which are nothing else indeed but the confession of the Catholic points of religion, were no offences to God.' (CHALLONER, p. 16.)

[2] FR. DUNSTAN PONTIFEX, O.S.B., in E.M., p. 145.

[3] Cf. BURTON and POLLEN, Introduction, p. xxv.

It was Cecil's good fortune that the papal policy placed
the Catholic body in a position that could be easily exploited
to its permanent disadvantage, and he took full advantage
of his opportunity. But the Catholics—their priests at any
rate—were just as aware of the false position in which,
through no fault of their own, they were placed. Fr.
Persons, for example, in his life of Bl. Edmund Campion,
describes how, as they were about to leave Rheims on the
eve of sailing for England, Allen told them of the papal
expedition to Ireland of 1580. ' We were heartily sorry,' is
his comment, ' . . . because we plainly foresaw that this
would be laid against us and other priests, if we should be
taken in England, as though we had been privy to or partakers thereof, as in truth we were not, nor ever heard or
suspected the same until this day.' What then ? And here
we see for a moment the great soul of this Jesuit pioneer.
' As we could not remedy the matter, and as our consciences
were clear, we resolved, through evil report or good report,
to go on with the purely spiritual action we had in hand ;
and if God destined any of us to suffer under a wrong title
[*i.e.* as traitors] it was only what He had done and would be
no loss to us, but rather gain, in God's eyes who knew the
truth, and for whose sake alone we had undertaken this
enterprise.' [1]

The secular clergy were no less keenly conscious of the
hideous ambiguity. Their innocence is as evident as their
uneasiness, in their demand of Campion and Persons that
they make clear the totality of their commission. They
feared, said the London priests, that ' all their spiritual and
ecclesiastical functions might be brought into obloquy and
hatred with the people, and much cruelty inflicted both on
the said clergymen when they should be taken, and on all
other Catholics for their sake.' [2] And this, of course, is
precisely what came to pass. The story of the next twenty
years is the story of little else, and it is now that there are
laid the deep foundations of that barrier which even yet,
for very many Englishmen, shuts out Catholicism as even a
possibility in the national life.

Nor did the mitigation of the sentence of 1570 which
Gregory XIII granted in 1580—and which the two Jesuits
now made known to the priests who were consulting them—
really lessen the Elizabethan Catholics' difficulty.

[1] SIMPSON, p. 146.   [2] *Ibid.*, p. 183.

It was, apparently, the practical sense of the Jesuit superiors that won this concession from the Pope in 1580. From the very first news of the excommunication there had been a movement to bring about, if not its revocation (from the nature of the thing this was not possible), at least its practical reduction to nothing, by some mitigatory pronouncement. The Spanish ambassador in Rome was busy to this end in 1570. He reported that the Pope was willing to cancel, at any rate, the clauses that punished with excommunication all Elizabeth's subjects who obeyed her. In that same year St. Pius V, replying to Alva's protests, gave him leave to make it known that Catholics in England would not incur excommunication by reason of their failure to rise against the queen.[1] The matter went no further than this in the time of St. Pius V, and his successor, as we have seen, was from the first years of his reign far too inclined to a policy of aggression to make any changes that would allow Catholics to defend their country against a Catholic invasion with a clear conscience. Then, as the party of Campion and Persons were preparing to leave Rome, in reply to a petition from the Jesuits, Gregory XIII made this concession, namely, that the sentence of 1570 ' in no way bound the Catholics, things being as they are (rebus sic stantibus), but then only when the public execution of the said bull can be carried out.'[2]

This was on April 14, 1580, and to anyone conversant with recent happenings at the papal court, it must have seemed an astonishing volte-face if intended as a nullification of the bull, for only eight weeks earlier the bull had been reprinted and distributed to the various ambassadors by Cardinal Bonelli.[3] At this very moment, moreover, the nuncio at Lisbon was doing his best to whip up reinforcements to go to the aid of the tiny papal army, fifty soldiers strong, which, the previous year, had sailed with Fitzmaurice and Sander to Ireland. And—a fact luckily hidden from the eyes of all until the year of grace 1886—only six months after this concession to Campion and Persons, and while they in all good faith were using it to quieten the harassed consciences of Catholics up and down England, and all no doubt were breathing more easily at the thought that there could be no more severities from the government

[1] Cf. PASTOR, Vol. 18, p. 219.   [2] Text in MEYER, p. 487, §11.
[3] PASTOR, Vol. 19, p. 389.

on account of the *Regnans in Excelsis*, at this very time the Cardinal Secretary of State was writing from Rome to the nuncio at Madrid, that, given the *Regnans in Excelsis*, it should be self-evident that whoever killed Elizabeth, from proper motives, would be doing something meritorious in God's sight. Luckily for the Catholics of the next two centuries this letter never fell into Walsingham's hands. But the mitigation did, only a short time before Campion's death,[1] come into the government's possession, and Cecil made great play with the *rebus sic stantibus* clause in his pamphlet defending the execution of Campion and his companions. The English Catholics were now, it appeared, to remain loyal to Elizabeth, by the Pope's permission, until such time as the papal policy changed. And, what the missionaries of 1580 could not know, the papal policy was to change in 1583 when Gregory XIII prepared to renew the excommunication, and it was to change in 1588 when his successor, Sixtus V, also planned a new promulgation of it. And while Pope Gregory's intentions were soon known, through the capture of Fr. Crichton and his papers, the plans of Pope Sixtus were broadcast in the famous declaration to the English people which Cardinal Allen wrote, for distribution once the Catholic armies had landed.

The mitigation of 1580 was a concession made to Catholics living in England. It was in no way a mitigation of the sentence on the queen. Rome, in 1580 as in 1570, had intervened and spoken in order to relieve the scrupulous consciences of Catholics in England. In 1570 the dilemma of the pious Catholic was whether to rise in arms for the defence of Catholicism would not be a violation of his oath of allegiance ; in 1580 the dilemma was how not to disregard the papal sentence of 1570 in a situation where obedience to the queen and her government was unavoidable. In 1570 Pope Pius V abolished the tie of allegiance ; but in 1580 Pope Gregory XIII did no more than suspend the Catholic's obligation to rise in arms, and although to rise in arms was not, for the time being, a matter of obligation, it still remained lawful and, in fact, a blessed deed.

That the English government refused to be impressed by the famous mitigation is not surprising, little as they knew of these other proofs that the papal will remained immovable.

[1] PASTOR, Vol. 19, p. 453.

But it is a far cry from any papal stimulus of rebellion to the actual movement of individual Catholic citizens. In all the years of this endless mining and counter-mining, these never moved, and Cecil and Walsingham knew, better than any man, that they had never moved and that they were not likely to move, and why. That a private direction meant to ease a man's innermost conscience could, once it was published, so easily seem nothing else but a skilful move in a political game, is true. The mitigation played into Cecil's hands as all the political schemes had done, and ultimately it was the innocent who, once again, paid for the Roman mistake and misfortune.

Persons, writing reminiscently in 1594, laments the coincidence in time of Sander's expedition and the mission of 1580. ' Though it belonged not to us to mislike this journey of Dr. Sander, because it was by order of his superiors,' he says, ' yet were we heartily sorry . . . partly because we plainly foresaw that this would be laid against us, and other priests, if we should be taken in England, as though we had been privy or partakers thereof, as in very truth we were not, nor ever heard or suspected the same until this day.' [1]

It was then with this unwelcome knowledge in their minds that the two Jesuits had met the London priests, and had given them, when asked for advice, the only counsel possible, namely to go on with the work in hand, the only work for which they were accredited, and to leave it to God to defend their sincerity and to preserve the good work through the inevitable suspicion. Persons and Campion show a simplicity quite out of keeping with what—using the small letter—it used to be fashionable to call jesuitry, when they say confidently that if any priest is taken he has only to stand to the truth and challenge his adversaries to prove the charge of political conspiracy. ' They fondly hoped,' says Simpson, ' that a condemnation would be almost impossible, since they knew that no fact, attempt, or intention, however slight, could ever be proved.' [2] And they showed a real understanding of the futility of human striving against malice when they ended : ' This is all the satisfaction we can give. And if this will not serve, we can only seal it with our blood, and if it comes to this, it will not signify whether we are believed, or whether, like Our

[1] SIMPSON, p. 146.   [2] *Ibid.*, p. 184.

Lord and His apostles, we are reckoned among the wicked and put to death as the enemies of Cæsar.' [1]

Well, indeed, may Meyer, for whom ' it was not a fight in open day, but in the twilight and the dark,' write that ' the true heroes of this warfare were those who entered the forbidden land in spite of all dangers, and risked their lives for no other object than the spread of the Catholic faith.' [2] It is truly ' a calculating and pitiless spirit of statecraft ' that ' pervades the Elizabethan persecution of Catholics,' [3] and, as always in such a case, ' it was the exiles and the oppressed who were purified ; it was the oppressors who were brutalised.' [4] And the conclusion to which this patient and dispassionate scholar is drawn is that ' the mission was strictly confined to its own particular field of operation— the cure of souls. . . . It was neither meant to be a means of spying out the land preparatory to invasion, nor as an instrument of stirring up rebellion against the queen. . . .' [5]

It was always an important part of Allen's strategy that his priests should have no chance but to be innocent of all political action. In the college English political affairs were never mentioned. They were banished from conversation as from the lecture-room. For, a curious testimony to the stage of transition through which these matters were passing, the then very actual and very thorny and very hotly debated questions as to the nature of the papal power in temporal matters were never even touched on by the Douay lecturers. Allen is quite clear about this, and even had he not told it to us we might have guessed as much from the stumbling amateur way in which those of the martyrs who were plied with interrogatories in these matters answered their tempters and tormentors. For although a priest was arrested as a priest, and was to be condemned to die and to be executed simply as a priest who refused to take the Oath of Supremacy, it was rarely that his captors did not try to cast about the event something to show the world that it was a politician and a plotter, in intention if not in act, that was going to his doom. Hence what came to be so well known to the terrified Catholics as the ' Bloody Question.'

The priests were asked—often under torture—what opinion they held of the Pope's authority to depose the

[1] SIMPSON, p. 188.   [2] MEYER, p. 92.   [3] Ibid., p. 175.
[4] Ibid., p. 177.   [5] Ibid., p. 143.

queen ; what they thought of the opinions of such Catholic publicists as Sander and Bristowe who had dealt with this thorny (and involved) question ; also, what action they would take if a papal army should land in England.[1]

Such procedure was, of course, a thing foreign to the whole nature of English law, as Cecil was quick to point out when Archbishop Whitgift devised a like system to convict Puritans. The statesman now gravely objected that it ' is conceived after the Roman fashion ' and that it ' smacks too much of the Roman Inquisition.' [2]

Another procedure used in the elimination of Catholics, in which also the Roman Inquisition had no monopoly, was the torture. At no period in English history was this abominable business so habitual, and its processes brought to such a shameful refinement, as in the last twenty years of Elizabeth's reign when it was employed to induce the missionaries to declare themselves conspirators, to reveal the names of those to whom they had spiritually ministered, and occasionally for the mere satisfaction of the torturers. Cecil and Walsingham had sunk very low when they came to provide the human material which Topcliffe's sadistic habits increasingly called for.

The innocence of the missionary priests and of all these Elizabethan martyrs is after all best attested by the records of their trials, and here the challenge thrown down by Allen himself, in the very height of the persecution, still stands.

The last word of all we may best give to one of the martyrs. Bl. John Boste spoke for all his fellows and the whole missionary movement when, rebuking one of the rare political priests of the day, the unhappy John Ballard, who later went to the scaffold with Antony Babington, he said : ' Thou and I are priests : it is our function to invade souls, and not to meddle with these temporal invasions ; they belong not to us.' [3]

[1] *Cf.* TIERNEY, III, App., pp. iv–xviii, who prints (from Allen's *Brief History of the Martyrdom of XII reverend Priests*) the question put to Bl. Edmund Campion and his fellows, and also the tract published by Elizabeth's government giving the detail of their answers.

[2] PASTOR, Vol. 19, p. 477, quoting FRERE, *History of the English Church*, 1558–1625, pp. 229 *seq.*

[3] TIERNEY, III, p. 141, quoting from Fr. Holtby's report to Fr. Henry Garnet, 1594, in Stonyhurst MSS. Anglia, A, ii, 12. That there should be such unfortunates as Ballard was an almost inevitable consequence of this long politico-religious warfare. The wonder is that they were so rare, and the

Long as is the time given to this one special question, of the loyalty of the martyrs, much more would be needed to describe, even summarily, the whole extent to which the persecution was pushed in the forty years which followed the passing of the acts of 1581 and 1585. It is a tale of tens of thousands of imprisonments ; [1] of thousands of families ruined through the fines and confiscations ; of raids by pursuivants, of spies and *agents provocateurs* ; all the horrors and all the miseries—and with the heroism all the defects and tragic falls—inseparable from a system of government more familiar to us who have lived to see the Ogpu and the Gestapo than it was to such judicious chroniclers as Charles Butler and Mark Aloysius Tierney. As we call to mind the immense wreckage, spiritual no less than temporal, wrought by the Cecilian system, we should recall, too, the reason that underlay it. These Englishmen were ruined, imprisoned, slain, they saw friends and families broken and tormented, they were made to be outlaws and foreigners in their own land solely because they refused to change a habit and way of life traditional in England for a thousand years. If only they will accept and swear to the new doctrine, not yet fifty years old, that the queen is the supreme ruler of Christ's Church in England, deny that the Pope has any spiritual jurisdiction in this country, all will change for the better for them, and it will change immediately. The fines will cease, the prisons will be opened, the very noose will be taken from round their necks as they stand in the cart beneath the gallows. They are not being punished because they have brought in something new, some novelty of doctrine that will disturb a social order centuries old. They are not even accused of that kind of change which, everywhere, for a thousand years, has been looked upon as heinously criminal, the change called heresy. Those who

rarity is a great testimony to the seminary training. Of this clerical underworld, so carefully fostered by Walsingham, Meyer (p. 154) says : ' The few priests who thus gravely injured the dignity of their mission were all men far removed from the typical character of the Catholic missionary in England ' : *e.g.* Ballard ' lived as a man of the world and did not exercise his priestly functions ' ; Antony Tyrrell was ' a character that was the complete opposite of the missionary trained to inflexible fortitude ' ; as for Gilbert Gifford he was nothing but a spy, and his only motive in procuring ordination was the better opportunities this would give him to watch his co-religionists.

[1] When, in 1621, James I, as part of the preparations for the expected marriage of the heir to the throne with the daughter of Philip III of Spain, released the imprisoned Catholics, some four thousand returned to their homes.

inflict these penalties dare not say : ' Your religion is
treason and rebellion against God's truth, something evil
and bound to breed further evil, therefore you must die.'
Nevertheless they hate all Catholics as though Catholicism
were itself an evil thing—as, of course, they verily believe—
and the sole justification they put forward for this hate-
inspired persecution is that some Catholics are traitors.
Some Catholics have committed treason, all Catholics shall
be punished as traitors.

The persecuting government ' carefully avoided the open
and avowed persecution for religion which had made
Mary's reign so odious, and had rendered the Protestant
reaction possible, they were determined to make a distinction
without a difference, and under the name of treason to
repress Catholicism as effectually as Mary's government had
repressed Protestantism under the name of heresy.' [1] It is
surely in the light of all this that we should review, not merely
the failure and the mistakes, but the hopes and the aims of
Cardinal Allen and Fr. Persons. There is no need to
apologise for what they hoped to do. Had they succeeded
they would, in popular esteem, be among the greatest heroes
of our history, men thanks to whose efforts England would
have been delivered, not from a possible menace to its peace
—such as the successful plotters of 1688 are supposed to have
averted—but from an actual reign of terror, which for the
combination it presents of cruelty, rapine, and hypocrisy in
the ruling clique has never in English history been surpassed.

But what about the means by which Allen and Persons
endeavoured to effect the deliverance ? We do not need to
waste time about the old myth of ' the people's will ' being
the justification of the Elizabethan religious tyranny. The
age when the will of the people mattered had not only not
yet dawned, but no man, so far, had thought of such a thing
as even desirable. ' God save us from such a visitation as
Knox has attempted in Scotland ; the people to be orderers
of things ! ' is Archbishop Parker's comment on the ' demo-
cratic ' reformation north of the Tweed.[2]

As Allen, Persons, and those who thought with them,
saw the position of affairs after 1559, an interested and power-
fully placed minority was destroying the national tradition
and plundering the national heritage. Allen and Persons
represented another group, the opposition, whom, in

[1] SIMPSON.   [2] Quoted POLLARD, p. 198.

historical fact, a series of accidents had deprived of power, and placed in very jeopardy of life. This opposition now gave itself to organise resistance against the minority in power, and to the task of capturing the government from them. Theirs was not any Catholic endeavour to destroy a Protestant England. There was not, in the first twenty years of Elizabeth's reign, any Protestant England to destroy. There was an England in course of being ' protestantised '— which is a very different thing—and the agents through whom the change was being realised were the minority who were in possession of the instruments of government. It was this ' protestantisation ' that was Allen's real foe, and it was the agents of this movement who were the source and cause of the deaths of the martyrs. The England of those years was ' protestant-ridden,' and Allen and Persons, believing that the mass of Englishmen, once the gang that ruled was dispossessed, would gladly rally to the old ways, set themselves to displace the gang. The mass of the people at home, leaderless, helpless, cowed by the severity of the laws and held at every turn by the cruel ingenuity of the system, would drift inevitably from passive acquiescence in one generation to active co-operation in the next, unless signs were given them that the Protestant régime was not to be eternal.

The means which this active Catholic group employed were those always and everywhere employed under similar circumstances. They were the means that have been employed at every turn of English history, by real rebels and by lawful claimants alike ; the only means indeed that could be employed before the system developed of government by a cabinet, dependent on parliamentary majorities and with general elections to procure these last. Those means were the raising of armies abroad with the sympathy and aid of foreign princes ; the intervention of foreign princes who were in some way related in blood to the line of English kings, and, at the appropriate moment, insurrection at home. These devices have been tried over and over again in the course of our national history, in the interest first of one dynasty, then of another, and, finally, in 1688, in the interest not of any dynasty but of a small group of extremely wealthy men. Sometimes the devices have succeeded, sometimes they have failed. Some of the successful ' rebels ' have been favourably judged by the popular opinion of later times, some unfavourably. And so, too, has it been with the rebels who failed. But never, save in one instance, is there any expression of horror, scorn, and indignation at the means used, at this device of foreign armies, a foreign prince and insurrection at home—save in one case. And that is the case of that group of English Catholics, who used the device not to serve any dynastic interest, nor to secure the hold of any wealthy clique upon the national life and resources, but in order to preserve an England they loved from becoming a different kind of England, an England corrupted by what all decent men for a thousand years had held in detestation—heresy.

Nowhere, be it noted, is there any suggestion that Allen or Persons schemed to bring about the reduction of the country to the state of a foreign dependency. Nowhere is it suggested that the English should be transformed into Spaniards. Never, indeed, did there live Englishmen more ruggedly, awkwardly, undiplomatically English than these exiles, and anyone at all familiar with the story of their relations with Spain must bear witness to this. And, of course, though to us this may seem but heraldry, Philip II of Spain had been for four years Philip I of England, and acts of parliament still, to this day, run in his name. He had not been any mere prince-consort, and the reign in which all these men had passed part of their youth was that of Philip and Mary. Philip II was not so inevitably the impossible foreigner to them as he is to us, who see him first of all as the defeated enemy of the long naval war.

As to the other royal personage to whom the thoughts of the Catholic politicians turned—Mary, Queen of Scots— she had, of course, a very much closer claim to the throne. True a statute of Henry VIII made no account of her family's rights and after the end of Henry's own descendants, gave the crown to the family of his younger sister Mary. But statutes are not eternal, and men will not cease to be moved by the realities which statutes ignore or contradict. The fact was that the Queen of Scots was the heir to Henry's eldest sister. It was also a fact, that many people continued to believe that Elizabeth's mother was never Elizabeth's father's wife. These again may seem to-day legal and moral pedantries. But when both these women were alive and in conflict they were singularly live issues. And upon Elizabeth's death there was no question who should succeed her

—the son of Mary of Scotland, and this in virtue of his mother's right.

It remains, of course, that there were murder plots. But there is no evidence that either Allen or Persons had any hand or part in these. Even the mysterious reference in the Sega letter, if it means anything, means, it seems to me, that Persons refused to sanction such a scheme.

St. Thomas More, at his trial, appealed from the new English laws and the court that administered them, to the common judgement of Christendom. For a man to speak like this to-day would only be to brand himself as possessed of a strong personal eccentricity. There are, of course, still people who judge in this manner of contemporary events. But such people, however numerous they may be, are no more now than so many individuals. This has come to be an individual opinion merely. But St. Thomas More, making such an appeal, spoke a language that was still universal. He appealed not to a mere mental creation, but to an objective reality. There was a really existent, common judgement of Christendom, held everywhere to be the court of final appeal. This had been the greatest factor in European civilisation for a thousand years and it still remained a thing which could actively influence the course of events. And fifty years after the martyrdom of St. Thomas, it was still a thing sufficiently evident and active, a thing of real enough concern to the innovators as to Catholics, for Allen and Persons likewise, confidently to appeal to it for justification. It is by this that we must judge the morality of their aim, whatever be our judgement on the suitability of the means which they adopted to achieve their aim.

BOOK III
RICHARD SMITH, BISHOP OF CHALCEDON

CHAPTER I

THE BREAK-UP OF THE COUNTER-REFORMATION UNITY, 1594–1608

§ i. The New Age and the New Policy

CARDINAL ALLEN'S death [1] was a turning-point in the history
of the Catholic Church in England. He had been a man of
note since even so far back as thirty years before, when,
in his early thirties, he had played his great part in the
campaign against ' Church-going ' and had made one of the
little band of scholarly controversialists writing at Louvain.
With the foundation of Douay and the appearance of the
first Douay priests, Allen's prominence had grown into
recognised leadership, and for the last twenty years of his
life the whole Catholic world knew him as the untitled
primate of his people. The great learning of the Cardinal
of England, his immense charity, his unwearying patience,
the common-sense realism with which he viewed the needs
of the English mission, his long personal acquaintance with
all the chiefs of the Counter-Reformation, the high place
he held in their esteem—the gifts and experience thus
uniquely combined in Allen had given him unique power.
And now, inevitably, their disappearance meant that Allen
would be uniquely missed. He was indeed one of those
rare men of whom it can literally be said that they are
irreplaceable. For the best part of a generation the memory
of Allen had been supremely powerful to keep faithful to
his task many an isolated and abandoned missionary. It had
been no less potent to check rising divisions. Such divisions
had shown themselves, in the colleges, from time to time,
and nowhere more than in the college at Rome. But Allen
was the least factious of men, and the least self-interested of
leaders. Before such real humility and self-denial, in matters
of policy and prestige, as he habitually showed, the bitterest
partisans yielded, and with the recollection of his kindly

[1] Oct. 16, 1594.

strength the fiercest tempered of these Elizabethan clerics
bit hard and kept silence. That furnaces burned beneath
the deceiving ash none knew better than Allen himself,
and as he once wrote, in a revealing moment, it would be
easier to govern a thousand at home than a hundred in
exile.[1] Within twelve months of his death the flames had
begun to leap, and controversies to crackle whose smoky
trace is even yet not wholly effaced. *Incedo super ignes*, the
very chronicler three hundred years and more after the
event cannot but realise its truth as he begins to set down
the story.

In the half-century that separates Allen's death from the
outbreak of that civil war in which the absolutist English
monarchy met its fate, that Roman activity we call the
Counter-Reformation continued its uneasy and uneven
course among our people. Its aim, as the age of Elizabeth
passed into that of James I, changed, however, considerably.
The defeat of the Armada in 1588, the conversion of Henry
of Navarre in 1593, the destruction of the second Armada in
Cadiz harbour in 1597, and the peace of Vervins between
Spain and France in 1598, the death of Philip II in that
same year, after forty years' occupation of the central place
in European affairs, all these events announced very clearly
to the calm, level-headed Clement VIII [2] that the sun of
Spain's primacy had touched its meridian. And in those
same years, while this Pope was shaking off the last traces
of the Holy See's dependence on the Spanish champion,
it was borne in on the Roman authorities that not only
would Spain never be able to conquer England and make
safe the work of the missionaries there, but also that England
was no longer a country where a Catholic majority was
oppressed by a government in heretic hands.

The Counter-Reformation does not indeed cease to use
political means in England, but its political object is henceforward different. The Pope's anxieties centre, first of all,
around the question of Elizabeth's successor. Is it possible,

---

[1] *Cf.* also, in this same letter of May 28, 1582, to Fr. Agazzari, S.J. (rector
of the English College, Rome) '. . . this exile, which of itself breeds murmur-
ings, complainings, contradictions, and discontent. When Moses leads the
people through the desert he suffers much. . . . This is the peculiarity of
exiles ; but we must not faint ' ; text in *L.A.*, p. 136.

[2] Elected Jan. 30, 1592 ; yet another canonist Pope, whose life had been
almost wholly spent in the tribunals of the Apostolic See and in administration.

in these last years of her reign, to ensure that a Catholic shall follow her on the English throne ? Who is it that is most likely to succeed her, and what can be done, in these last few years before the great moment comes, to bind that successor to Catholicism ? And this question of the succession proves a new source of controversy among those English Catholics who are politicians. Some of them are still for Spain, and for the daughter of Philip II as the nearest Catholic descendant of Edward III, to the raging dismay of other Catholics who favour the Protestant son of Mary Stuart.

It is this James VI of Scotland who, in the event, becomes king, on March 24, 1603, easily, without any hint anywhere of opposition, thanks in no small part to the management of yet another Cecil, Sir Robert, younger son of Sir William who, Lord Burleigh since 1571, had died in the same year as King Philip. Whatever promises James had made for Catholic support while yet the great prize remained to be won, it was not any Catholic's activity that won it for him. The new régime was Protestant, and as the reign advanced, whatever the Catholicism of the new queen, Anne of Denmark, it became ever more clear that the Protestant hold on the government of England had not been shaken in the least by the change.

And now there begins to be perceptible a change in the goal towards which the leaders of the English Catholics bend their endeavour. The dream of another St. Andrew's Day, 1554, disappears for ever. It is not any restoration of Catholicism that occupies them, but a toleration of Catholics, and it is for this that they look to the goodwill (as yet to be captured) of the new sovereign.

For a good fifteen years they looked in vain, while the king shamelessly repudiated his promises.[1] But when James I—who had multiplied and increased the fines and confiscations, and who had sent priests to the gallows as readily (if not so frequently) as Elizabeth—sought to marry the Prince of Wales to a Catholic princess, their hopes once again rose high. The first marriage scheme indeed fell through, but a second succeeded, and James' heir, as King Charles I, actually married a Catholic, and for sixty years

---

[1] ' Na, na, we'll nae need the Papists now ' ; thus James to William Watson, the secular priest who had been the most active of all his partisans among the English Catholics.

from 1625, the royal family was semi-Catholic. Of the children of this marriage all who survived an early death came in the end to the Catholic Church. Both the sons who succeeded to the throne married Catholics, and both embraced the religion of their mother and wives. This most unlikely sequel to the Cecilian régime proved a distraction impossible to resist for the Roman diplomacy of the last stages of the Counter-Reformation, and indeed of several generations later still. What wonder if, so long as there were Catholic Stuarts, there were also during all the 160 years between the coming of James I and the death of James III, influential personages in the Curia too dazzled by the chronic Catholicism of the house not to base all on its aid ? Popes, let us hasten to say, were not prominent in this set, but among those who were prominent not a few were able to influence policy profoundly.

This book has not anywhere offered itself as a general history of the Counter-Reformation in England, and, to my regret, in this last part it is going to fail even to attempt what it promised to be, namely a history of the Roman effort in that great affair. For the last twelve months the important archives of the Archbishop of Westminster have been buried behind protective sand-bags, and the writer of these pages has been living seventy miles away from libraries as well as from these all but essential archives. For which really excellent reasons it might seem that he should not risk botching a good subject by the inevitably inadequate treatment which is all that, in such circumstances, can be given it. If, however, with the book two-thirds written, he proceeds to do what he can to fulfil his engagement, it is very largely because he has something to relate which has not hitherto been told, or at any rate papers to make known so far unpublished and undiscovered, and because what is put forth fragmentarily and, admittedly, from one point of view only, may be of service in a day yet to come to some scholar better placed, writing in more favourable surroundings. Sir Charles Oman, in one of the most delightful books of historical method that can ever have been put together, has recently warned all practitioners of this craft, that a false ambition to write the perfect book has hindered the production of untold useful books. With this very much indeed in the forefront of my mind, and recalling that St. Thomas somewhere defines pride as 'an inordinate appetite for excellence,' I proceed to set out some of the fruits of researches made many years ago now in various Roman archives. The picture is one of the *Ecclesia Anglicana* in its supreme hour of desolation. I shall try to say how this came about and why it was allowed to continue, and incidentally throw some light, it may be, on the reasons for the astonishingly rapid decline of Catholicism in England in the all but last hour, the fifty years that lie between the Revolution of 1688 and the consecration of Richard Challoner in 1741.

In the background of all the Catholic activity of seventeenth-century England there is one permanent feature, one endless, and it may be thought somewhat monotonous, overshadowing element, and this is the feud between the secular clergy and the Society of Jesus. At every turn we meet signs of it. Whatever the subject of correspondence between public authorities, sooner or later this feud is mentioned. No Catholic of any prominence can escape its influence. At times one feels that it dogged those generations much as the Liberal-Conservative dichotomy used to dog all little boys and girls who managed to be born alive. And to what bitter extremes it could drive men, let the story of John Sergeant, as Major Hay tells it, bear witness.[1] Two things need to be borne in mind, from the very outset of any attempt to write about this feud. First, that no side is ever entirely in the right, and, secondly, that while it is no more possible to convict a community than to indict a nation, individuals are, in the long run, only too often taken as representative of the official attitude of the body to which they belong. These are extremely commonplace truths and they have usually been entirely forgotten by those who have told this story. The misdeeds—whatever they were—of Fr. Robert Persons, for example, have been often gleefully seized on as evidence that the spirit of the Society is essentially mischievous. The offences of his opponents have been taken to justify whatever design the Jesuits had to capture the machinery of the Catholic Church in England, to 'jesuitise' English Catholicism. And, of course, nowhere, once these dreadful feuds begin, is it allowed that a man may honestly forget this year what he said or wrote last year. Only too often every discrepancy has

[1] *The Jesuits and the Popish Plot*, London, 1934.

been seized on as proof of deliberate bad faith, and if a man is caught out in an apparent untruth it has been cried to the heavens as final damning proof that, with him and his, morality is but a name. In a word the atmosphere of these long-dead controversies has also, only too often, been the atmosphere in which the record of them has been set down in later times. The fortune of the Catholic Church in seventeenth-century England still awaits its historian largely, one suspects, because those who know most about the matter know also the fate that has so often overtaken writers who have already essayed the task, the fresh controversies in which these were themselves speedily involved, the bitterness and acrimony which sooner or later crept into their own writing. It is indeed a story as full of shadows as of light, scandals of all kinds are frequent, the greatest of them all the chronic dereliction of the *Ecclesia Anglicana,* and even if we accepted, uncritically, all the allegations made against the Jesuits, the ultimate responsibility here, as in the age of Allen, lies elsewhere, in a higher region altogether.

The main battle of the feud centres round the episcopate of Richard Smith, consecrated Bishop of Chalcedon in 1625 and sent to England with the powers of a diocesan bishop for England and for Scotland. But that battle would never have been so sharp, would probably never have been fought, had not the England to which the bishop came, been for thirty years already, the scene of lesser fights between the two groups. The trouble went back indeed so far as the death of Allen, and in its real cause—the human nature of the contendants—further even than that. It has been related what admiration Allen had for the Society, its spirit and its methods, and how he strove to approximate the training of his students to that of the young Jesuits. Bl. Edmund Campion is witness how much the Society owed to the secular clergy, the warm welcome given in England to its first missionaries sent there : ' The priests of our country themselves being most excellent for virtue and learning yet have raised so great an opinion of our Society, that I dare scarcely touch the exceeding reverence all Catholics do unto us.' [1]

None the less, in this connection, we must recall the prophetic foreboding of the Jesuit General, Fr. Mercurian, when, in 1580, he was first asked to send Jesuits into England.

---

[1] Letter of Nov., 1580, in SIMPSON, p. 248.

How could it be expected, said this long-headed Fleming, that, in a land where there were no bishops, priests could live long together without friction and worse ?

These earlier troubles can be grouped round four events. These are the ' stirs ' at Wisbeach Castle in 1595, in which the animosities first showed above the surface ; then the battle about the succession to Elizabeth between Jesuit-led [1] Catholics, who favoured a Spaniard, and others who hoped for the King of Scots ; next there is the controversy about the appointment of an official head for the secular clergy, the archpriest ; and, finally, there are the fights about the new oath of allegiance. The roots of the opposition to the Society on the part of good men, the charges which they allege to justify their opposition and suspicions, are apparently two. They dislike Jesuits for an alleged superiority complex, and they accuse them both of having no interest in works that originate outside the Society and of ceasing to be interested in anything the Society cannot control. The opponents of the Society, in the England of three hundred years ago who were good men—I say nothing of those jealously driven by the spectacle of Jesuit successes—thought they saw in the contemporary action of the fathers all the proof they needed of these two charges. Whence, gradually, it became a matter of principle to oppose the Jesuit advance universally, and when, generations later, the first churches began to be built and the first ' parishes ' established, it was by no means infrequent to insert in the deeds a clause providing that no Jesuit should ever be placed in charge. No story is so depressing as the story of good men, whose aim is one, quarrelling desperately about the better means. It is a story that no humorous

---

[1] There was undoubtedly in the sixty years and more that followed Allen's death (1594) a feud between Jesuits and Seculars. But not every Jesuit, nor every secular priest, was an active participant. And although the leaders in the dispute were, on both sides, the ecclesiastical superiors of these various bodies, it would be going too far to deduce from this that each superior had his men so organised for the fray, that Jesuits and Seculars (and later Benedictines) with their lay clientele faced each other like rival armies in formation. When one speaks of ' the Jesuits ' or ' the Seculars ' or ' the Regulars ' what is to be understood is the element in these various bodies that was active, with what spontaneous support and encouragement from the rank and file it is not always easy to discover. In this controversy about the succession, for example, although Fr. Persons strained every nerve to aid the Spaniards, his fellow-Jesuit, Fr. Crichton, was no less active on behalf of the King of Scots, and as critical of Fr. Persons as any secular priest.

touch can lighten. It is tragedy itself, and in a case such as this where what is at stake is the preservation of a people's faith, none but minds diseased could find amusement in the spectacle.

§ ii. THE FIRST DIVISIONS—WISBEACH

The half-ruined castle of Wisbeach served for many years in Elizabeth's reign as a kind of depot [1] for the imprisonment of Catholic notables. Here died, in 1584, Thomas Watson, the last Catholic bishop of Lincoln, and, in 1585, John Feckenham, the last resident abbot of Westminster, and with them slowly rotted and died many another. For Wisbeach, to-day the centre of miles and miles of smiling fruit orchards, was, three hundred years ago, isolated from the rest of England by noxious and impassable fens and marshes. Among the prisoners in this dismal jail was the Jesuit father, William Weston. The troubles originated in a very human way. The prisoners of Wisbeach, after years of the stiff régime of solitary confinement, were from about 1593 allowed to live a kind of life in common. Soon the tedium of this enforced companionship without employment had its natural results. All the symptoms of what we should call ' liver ' and ' nerves ' began to be pretty general. Sooner or later, it may be presumed, there would have been quarrels whether Fr. Weston had been there or not. To live the hard life of strict enclosure, but without vocation, or religious duties, and without any natural liking for such a life; to endure through years with the fullness of Christian charity or even common courtesy, the personal peculiarities of such near neighbours, the enforced close companionship of all and sundry ; to come safely through such an ordeal calls for something more than what ordinary humanity can accomplish. Fr. Edmund—as the Jesuit was generally called—had a great name as a missionary. He

---

[1] Could we not say ' concentration camp ' ? There were several of these :
' Banbury was apportioned for the recusants of Warwick, Oxford, and Northampton ; Tremingham for those of Norfolk and Suffolk ; Kimbolton for those of Huntingdon, Buckingham, and Bedford ; Portchester for those of Surrey, Hants, and Sussex ; Devizes for those of Dorset, Wilts, and Somerset ; Melbourne for Stafford, Derby, Leicester, Lincoln, and Nottingham ; Halton, in Cheshire, for Lancashire, Cheshire, and North Wales ; Wigmore, in Montgomeryshire, for Hereford, Monmouth, Worcester, and South Wales. Those proposed for the north were Middleham, Knaresborough, Durham, and Barnard Castle.' Cf. SIMPSON, p. 234.

was able and he was austere, something, alas, of a *censor morum* by nature, and admittedly he believed in severity for others too.

According to the account sent to the Jesuit General [1] by the head of the Jesuits in England, Fr. Henry Garnet, Weston was perturbed by the general disorder of the life. There were endless quarrels and disputes, too much drinking, some shiftiness in the distribution of alms and at least a suspicion of immorality, in the narrowest sense of the term. Weston had been a member of this community for some years. He had already made one effort to better its ways, and now in January, 1595, thinking that things were steadily growing worse, he struck, and disappeared from the common table, announcing that unless the rest were willing to promise to live by some kind of a rule he proposed to have nothing further to do with them. He was not alone in his views, and of the thirty-three prisoners, nineteen joined themselves to him, and chose him for their superior.

Were things quite so black as they are here painted ? Was Weston's move due to such spontaneous disgust ? The points have been hotly debated. At one stage in the interminable series of negotiations to bring the parties together, the chosen arbitrators got so far as to ask about the misdeeds which had brought about the formation of the associates. The Jesuit and his companions, says Fr. Garnet, were partly unwilling to speak about the matter, for it filled them with shame to be accusers of other men, and were partly unable by reason of the conditions in which the inquiry was set. These were that the inquiry should be according to canon law procedure, that the accuser who failed to prove his charge should submit to the penalties which the accused would have suffered had he been proved guilty, and that the accused should be secured against further proceedings in any ecclesiastical court. Certainly Fr. Garnet's long letter to Dr. Christopher Bagshaw,[2] the leader of the minority at Wisbeach, is far from conveying the impression that he is dealing either with a priest whom he believes to be living an evil, or careless life, or with a leader of such. Why do you quarrel, he says in effect, with your companions who have chosen to live under a rule ?

---

[1] Letter of July 12, 1595, printed in TIERNEY, III, App., p. cv, from Stonyhurst MSS. Anglia, A, ii, 4.

[2] October 8, 1595, in TIERNEY, III, App., p. cix–cxiv.

Are they not free to do so ? What injury does this do you ?
'You others, meanwhile, live as it pleases you ; that is as
learned and pious priests, which up to now you have
done.'

We need no testimony of eye-witnesses to guess how those
who refused to join the association would regard the elect,
nor of how—almost inevitably—they would from now on
construe their every gesture, and see in the very formation
of the little group, a damning criticism of their own way of
life.[1] As the months slipped by, the news of the dissensions
at Wisbeach leaked out, and soon the discussions had spread
through the whole body of the missionaries and had become
known even to their flocks. What finally brought the
divisions to an end—after much abortive negotiation—was
the action of two of the best-known of the secular clergy,
John Mush and Richard Dudley, acting together with Fr.
Garnet. New rules were drawn up, which all accepted, and
on November 8, 1595, after nine months of conflict, the
common table and common life were resumed. A letter
from the two arbitrators survives that describes the scene
of reconciliation and, incidentally, bears witness to the tense
emotional atmosphere in which all these contending clerics
had been living. 'You would have wondered to have seen
the vehemency of God's spirit, in one moment to make all
hard hearts to relent ; and where there was most froward
aversions immediately before, there was suddenly seen to
be most intense affections and tenderness. Such humiliation
one at another's feet ; such wringing, clipping, and
embracing ; such sobs, tears, and joyful mourning—that
for joy also our hearts were like to burst among them.
And verily, father, neither among themselves, nor to our
sight, they appeared, after, the same men they were before.
We thought it one of the joyfullest days that ever we had
seen.'[2]

The ' stirs ' at Wisbeach were ended, but how far the
reconciliation was radical with some of the principles may
be fairly doubted. There are evident and serious contra-

---

[1] According to TIERNEY, III, p. cx, note 1, Fr. Weston himself declared
(in a letter to the Jesuit provincial of Germany, Fr. Oliver Manare) that the
object of the separation was to shame the other party. Tierney does not
print this letter, but gives the reference Stonyhurst MSS. Anglia, A, ii, 34.
[2] Dudley and Mush to Fr. Garnet, Nov. 8, 1595, in TIERNEY, III, App.,
p. cxv.

dictions in Fr. Garnet's letters,[1] both about Bagshawe
himself, the leader of the anti-Weston party, and about the
charges laid against his associates, and when the Jesuit
came to file the correspondence he endorsed the last letter
from the Weston party : ' A general letter of the good at
Wisbeach, of their union.' Such controversies indeed rarely
end with a real restoration.

§ iii. Division on the Question of Elizabeth's Successor

The involved story of the divisions among the more active
of the English Catholics caused by the question of the
succession to Queen Elizabeth has, for this book, no more
importance than what the controversy contributed to the
growing mutual mistrust of Jesuits and Seculars.

Elizabeth's heir, at the time when Fr. Persons came to
England as a missionary (1580), was, in the eyes of Catholics
and by whatever rights primogeniture conferred, the captive
Queen of Scotland, the grandchild of Henry VIII's eldest
sister. But by English law the succession went to the heirs
of Henry VIII's younger sister Mary, queen-dowager of
France and duchess of Suffolk. The position of these heirs
was, however, complicated by the fact that the marriage,
between the eldest grandchild of this princess and Lord
Hertford, whence sprang the older line of her descendants,
had been declared to be no marriage by Elizabeth's first
Archbishop of Canterbury. And while the claim of the
senior line was thus rendered doubtful, the representative
of the line descended from a younger daughter of the duchess
of Suffolk—the earl of Derby—had thought it prudent to
renounce any claims he might have. The problem who was
to succeed Elizabeth was, then, not a problem for Catholics
only. In law none of Henry VII's descendants had, by 1587,
any longer a claim. Then in 1587 the axe of the executioner
removed the only one of these descendants who was a
Catholic, and the Catholic leaders, Allen and Persons, set
themselves to search for the nearest heir who remained loyal
to the old faith.

The Queen of Scots had bequeathed all her rights to the

---

[1] As there are in the letters of Dr. Christopher Bagshawe. ' It is
melancholy to contemplate these contradictions,' Tierney said, contemplat-
ing them just a hundred years ago.

King of Spain. This was already a pointer as to the direction in which orthodox Catholic political thought ought to travel. Mary's son, James VI, was now a man of twenty, and his late manœuvres while his mother's life lay in the balance showed him concerned only to win Elizabeth's favour and her goodwill as the future King of England. Albeit his Calvinism went no further than appearances, zeal for Catholicism would never consume this sorry son who—we know it now—had assisted his mother to her death on a foreign scaffold. Allen and Persons were, for once, not wrongly inspired when, in their search for a future Catholic king, they wasted no time in contemplation of the unfortunate denatured changeling at Edinburgh. But where their inspiration led them, and by what paths, needs to be read in more detail than there is here space for, if it is to be believed. For, with what insufficiency of genealogical information they themselves are witness, they now set themselves to plot the claim of Philip II himself. Mary had been the lawful heir, they held. She had transferred her claim to the King of Spain. The theologians, turned heralds, would prove him also to be the rightful king by descent, for Philip II had the best claim among the Catholic descendants of the old Plantagenet line. To prove this the investigators had to go back a long way indeed, and, in the first scheme they drafted, they went as far as the younger son of King Henry III, Edmund Crouchback, earl of Lancaster, who had died three hundred years before.

There is no need to describe the elaborate genealogical discussions by which the claims of other Catholic princes of the continent were ruled out—Alessandro Farnese, Prince of Parma, among others who, had the Armada been successful, might not impossibly have urged his right as a right by conquest. The claims of the House of York were easily dealt with, for by this time not one of its chiefs was Catholic, and heretics, of course, lost all their rights of succession. So, to those who reasoned in this way, and who had the necessary historical information, Philip II was now, in 1587, the only rightful King of England, and since he knew that to assert the claim for himself would only add to the difficulties of the situation the king named in his stead his daughter Isabella. To make assurance still more sure Fr. Persons proposed that she should marry one of the Farnese, the cardinal Oduardo who, it was hoped, would previously be

secularised by the accommodating Pope, in view of the
immense public interests the marriage would assist.[1]

Elizabeth was, of course, by no means dead yet, and gave
no sign of dying soon. Nor had these tireless schemers any
more concrete prospects of imposing their will on their
fellow-countrymen in the matter of the succession, than they
had had in the earlier matter of liberating Mary Stuart.
But against the day when the miraculous should begin to
happen, and lest the golden hour should find them without a
plan, they pushed on with their schemes, enlisted the
interest of the Holy See and, in 1594, what was in prospect
was publicly announced. The announcement took the shape
of an elaborate treatise : ' A Conference about the next
Succession to the crown of England. . . . Directed to the
Right Honourable the Earl of Essex . . . published by R.
Doleman,' which appeared in 1594 in two thick little volumes,
the second supplied with a large folding genealogical tree
to make it all clear.

The work caused an immense sensation. The question
it discussed was eminently topical and the book treated it
fully. Some two thousand copies are said to have been sold,
and this in spite of strong action by the authorities, who
went so far as to procure an act of parliament making it
treasonable to possess a copy. It is well known that Elizabeth's personal aversion from any mention of the succession
problem amounted, as she grew older, to mania, and this
book was the boldest of all the attempts to provoke a national
discussion and to satisfy a national anxiety.

But it was not only at the court that R. Doleman's book
provoked furious retaliation. By no means all the Catholic
leaders held these pro-Spanish views about the coming
sovereign. For years there had been a strong anti-Spanish
faction among those exiles whose activities were more
simply political than the activities of, say, Allen and Persons.
Two of the chief supporters and agents of the Queen of
Scots, Charles Paget and Thomas Morgan, had for a good
ten years before the appearance of this book waged a ceaseless feud with those exiles who were the King of Spain's

---

[1] Although this scheme never matured, this lady did, ultimately, marry a
secularised cardinal, her cousin the Archduke Albert, Archbishop of Toledo
and Primate of Spain (though not a priest), and commander-in-chief for
Philip II in the Low Countries. The period of the joint reign of Albert and
Isabella in the Spanish Netherlands (1598–1621) is one of the golden ages of
Belgian prosperity.

own. Nor had the disappearance of Mary in 1587 reconciled them. Now they had their opportunity.

It was an opportunity also for those of the exiles and those of the Catholics at home—clerical and lay—who had no real interest in any of these political activities, whose one desire was that the government should forget their very existence, and leave them to eke out their lives in the peaceful practice of their religion. The appearance of the book on the succession caused resentment everywhere outside the group whence it had come, and as the months went by it became a matter of general suspicion and then of knowledge that ' R. Doleman ' was no other than ' R. Persons.' And then the feud blazed indeed.

It is possible that the publication of this book—which, though others had a hand in it, was Persons' book, and published by him—was the rashest act of which this famous man was ever guilty. His General, hearing what was afoot, wrote, in great dismay, to prevent its publication.[1] But he was too late. The Scottish Jesuit, Fr. William Crichton,[2] Persons' colleague in the plots of 1583, was now his opponent and denounced him mercilessly. ' I cannot see,' he wrote, ' that this book has done the least good though its disastrous consequences are manifest.' Even so it has to be borne in mind that Persons was not pro-Spaniard for the sake of the Spaniard. He had only one aim, to secure that the next ruler of England should be a Catholic. This alone was important, but it was all-important. The King of the Scots would obviously never be a Catholic, and here Persons judged much more surely than his Catholic opponents. Failing the King of the Scots, and there being no English heirs who were also Catholic, the Jesuit turned to Philip II, and strove to make him likeable in advance by telling the tale of his English ancestry.

' The importance of the book,' says Meyer, ' lay in its being not a private venture, but the programme of a party.' That party was not the Society of Jesus but, unfortunately for the Society's chance of peace in the England of the next twenty-five years, the leader of the party was the ablest and the best known of the English Jesuits, and their superior, now, as he approached his fiftieth year, attaining the maxi-

---

[1] *Cf.* PASTOR, Vol. 24, p. 43, quoting the General's letter to Persons.
[2] *Ibid.*, p. 44. Pastor follows Fr. Pollen's article in *The Month*, Vol. 101 (1903), pp. 516–532.

mum of his active apostolic zeal. As the man was great
in his mental stature so were the consequences great of
what limitations had circumscribed his life. The one-time
bursar of Balliol had lived for far too long in an alien world.
When he wrote his part of the book about the succession,
Persons had been, for seven years continuously, rector of the
English seminary that he had founded at Valladolid, and
busy about the court in that capital and at Madrid. Here
in that abnormal life is part of the secret of what Meyer
sums up in a single sentence, commenting on the blunder
of 1594. ' It is as if Persons had not lived to see 1588.'
Persons had, indeed, lived to see 1588, but he had seen it
through Spanish eyes and through the eyes, not of Spaniards
like Alva, but of patriots of a more *exalté* kind. Meyer's
words are a final damning sentence on Persons as a practical
statesman. It is, in fact, incredible that, six years after the
great English demonstration of national anti-Spanish
solidarity, there can have been found, anywhere, an Englishman so ignorant of England and the English as to busy
himself with plans for placing a Spaniard on the English
throne. Who else, indeed, could, in such circumstances,
have put out such a scheme, but one habituated to impose
his ideas on novices or seminarists, bound, by rule or by
vow, to assent silently and to accept as practically wise
whatever was decided to be for their good ? To be employed
for years in ruling subjects thus voluntarily passive, is rarely
good training for those who later are faced with the task of
governing subjects whose judgement is free. When Persons
came to grips with the missionaries of the secular clergy, and
this was the next misery that awaited the *Ecclesia Anglicana*,
he was to show himself still possessed of but a 'prentice
hand, and, a man turned fifty, he was for the first time in
his life to find himself betrayed into sudden, undiplomatic,
and most unseemly violence of speech and of action.

It is hardly possible to exaggerate the mistrust and
indeed the hatred (both of the author and, still more
unfairly, of the Society to which he belonged) stirred up
by this untimely publication. One of his critics speaks of
Persons much as the Protestants of Queen Mary's time spoke
of their rash and violent co-religionists in Germany : ' We
at home are paying the penalty for his sinning abroad.'
It had, in fact, been in England a felony punishable by death
—since 1581—to discuss the question of the queen's successor

and here was a Catholic, a priest and—for the secret was speedily betrayed—the reputed leader of the whole Catholic movement, not only writing a most elaborate treatise on the forbidden question, but suggesting as the queen's successor the King of Spain's own daughter. Is it really unnatural that there were henceforth Catholics who thought of Fr. Persons as an incendiary ?

One scene where the new bitterness began to show was the English College at Rome. In 1596 ' stirrs ' once more disturbed the academic round, ' stirrs ' caused by grievances that were real enough (as anyone can read for himself in the report of the subsequent visitation),[1] and caused also by letters to the students from anti-Jesuit clergy in England. This time the students were as eager to have their Jesuit superiors removed as their predecessors, sixteen years before, were to have them brought in. So hostile were the students, so the rector wrote to Persons, ' that I fear that they would be ready to join hands with the heretics in order to fight [the Jesuits], as the French have done to resist the Spaniards.'[2] The crisis was serious ; the Jesuit General was on the point of withdrawing his men from the college, and perhaps from England too. Clement VIII was never too generous in his judgement of Jesuit mistakes, and this new crisis in a Jesuit-directed college was likely to be a more serious matter for the Society than the chance which produced it warranted. It was Persons who saved the situation, and he did so by the simple influence of his presence, his patience, and his speech. ' He whom we most feared,' wrote one of the students to a friend, ' and whom we accounted for our greatest enemy had been our greatest friend.' Even if we discount somewhat Persons' own estimate of the seriousness of the crisis which he had charmed away, no one can doubt that he had wrought a great service

[1] Printed in MEYER, pp. 492–519. The college had had half a dozen rectors in as many years—none of them Englishmen. The Italian cardinal who made the visitation—that same Filippo Sega who makes such a figure in the history of Elizabethan plots—could not see, what leaps immediately to the English eye, that an immense part of the discontent was due to mere methods of discipline. None of these Italians in fact understood that the methods of supervision employed were, to these English, simple espionage, nor that, to the English, this is the unforgiveable sin, stamping the superior with an ignominy nothing will ever remove. Persons, of course, saw it at once. ' And for spyeries and sentinels . . . [that] is the waye to mar all,' he had written, some years before to his colleague, Fr. Creswell. (MEYER, p. 400, quoting Fr. Pollen, The Month, Oct. 1899, p. 359.)

[2] W.A., Vol. 215, quoted MEYER, p. 396.

to the college and to the Society, and that at this moment his credit stood high with the somewhat distant Pope whom now he met, as Pope, for the first time. The Robert Persons who now began a new chapter of his life as rector of the English College,[1] was the man who had restored all when all was about to fail. It was this *deus ex machina* who, seeing the origins of the new upheaval in the chronic formlessness of the *Ecclesia Anglicana*, now cast about for a means to remedy that first cause of all trouble.

Barely three years had gone by since Allen's death. They had been years filled with strife, and now, as Persons reached to a more fundamental solution for the problem of England, the quarrels suddenly moved to their bitterest intensity. The archpriest controversy begins to rise above the horizon.

§ iv. DIVISION ABOUT THE APPOINTMENT OF AN ARCHPRIEST

To go through the story of these quarrels, in which personal animosities play so large a part, is a dreary business, and difficult, too. For the contending parties wrote voluminously, and in some stages of the fight they printed and published their charges and defences and—what it is still harder to sift—their recollections. Much of what they wrote has not come down to us, or still awaits discovery in some archives or library. It is the easiest thing in the world, in such circumstances, unwittingly to omit points which must make a difference in any ultimate judgement on the actions of the rival parties. There can be few historical questions which bring so little pleasure to whoever must toil through them. And yet the examination of these questions is, for us, all-important,[2] for it is from the troubled closing years of Elizabeth's reign that there derives that rooted antagonism which, for generations, was to split the Catholic effort in England.

One feature of the trouble, to which attention has hardly been given, is that the number of Jesuits actually working in

---

[1] He remained in this post until his death thirteen years later (1597–1610).

[2] Not because it enables us to saddle X or Y with the blame for what went wrong—that, I believe, can never be done now ; nor would it matter —but because by an examination we may hope to discover the causes of later losses, the kind of mistakes that were made, and to understand the subsequent general collapse of Catholicism in England.

England during these critical years was remarkably small
—fourteen is the number given for 1598.[1] The vast majority
of the secular clergy—a body then four hundred strong—can
never even have seen a Jesuit since they came home from
their Flemish, Italian, or Spanish seminary life. Where the
total numbers were so small the action of three or four of the
members was bound to commit the whole body far more
easily, and it was the tragedy of these foundation years of
the great Jesuit work in England that the Society was so
committed. Long before the Jesuits were at all numerically
noticeable in England they were suspect as such to very
many of the secular clergy, suspected that is to say of a
design to control the secular clergy and to run that great
body as a mere instrument of Jesuit policy, and particularly
as an instrument to assist the daughter of Philip II to the
English throne.[2] The expansion of the Society in England,
once Elizabeth's reign was over, was exceedingly rapid. In
1598 there were but fourteen fathers at work in England ;
by the time the first bishop was appointed, 1623, the fourteen
had increased to 125. In these same twenty-five years the
feud had not only become a quasi-permanent feature of
Catholic life, but, because of the very different proportion
Jesuits were beginning to bear to seculars, the division was
bound to reach through the whole Catholic body.

It is indeed extraordinary what a control of the fortunes
of the *Ecclesia Anglicana* the small body of Elizabethan
Jesuits had already acquired by, say, 1599. Their superior,
Fr. Robert Persons, was the most trusted adviser of the Holy
See on English affairs. If any man had succeeded to
Allen's place it was he. The secular seminaries of Seville,

---

[1] Foley, *General Statistics*, I, lxvi.
[2] *Cf.* PASTOR, Vol. 19, p. 419. ' Most unfortunately . . . it was especially
the Jesuits, priests, and religious, who . . . mixed themselves up in matters
which were indeed at that time closely allied to religion, but nevertheless far
removed from their real mission.' The author notes the strong feeling
within the Society against this use of its members, and the strongly worded
prohibition of the general congregation of 1593. Pastor is, I think, unfair to
Persons when he writes (*ibid.*, p. 426) : ' he gradually gave up his pastoral
labours for politics.' Not even so strong an individuality as that of Robert
Persons could become a politician overnight of its own volition. When,
within six months of Campion's execution, we find Persons sitting in conference with ambassadors and nuncios at Paris, discussing schemes to
invade England and depose the queen, the presumption is that he was there
because he was ordered to be there, and that the order came from higher
authority than Father General. Would even Robert Persons' ' nerve ' have
enabled him to achieve alone, such superb ' gate-crashing ' as this ?

Valladolid, and of Rome itself, were ruled by Jesuits. At Douay, always since Allen's foundation strongly Jesuit in the tendency of its spiritual formation, the confessor was a Jesuit and the new president, Dr. Thomas Worthington, was —we know it now—bound to Fr. Persons by a secret vow of obedience. Finally, the new recently appointed superior of all the secular clergy, the archpriest, had been bidden in all affairs of importance not to act without consulting the resident English Jesuit superior.

The Jesuits, throughout the period, had in their favour this great point that they were themselves well-organised. Whatever was the state of things outside their body, within was law and order, life in defined subordination to unmistakable authority, and all the fruits of order. Here at least was a department of the *Ecclesia Anglicana* whence all that was slipshod was rigorously excluded, here were the reassuring signs of efficiency in administration, of competence in government. One natural result of this was a growing tendency among the shepherdless secular clergy to look to the tiny Jesuit nucleus for a lead, and to follow the guidance of the fathers generally. We know from Bl. Edmund Campion [1] how much of the success of his mission was due to the enthusiasm with which the secular clergy received him, and to the way in which, before his coming, they had sung the praises of the new order to their people.

To this fact of the natural expansion of Jesuit leadership we have explicit testimony from a far from friendly witness of it, that John Bennett who, as the agent of the clergy, was ultimately, in the teeth of Jesuit opposition, to win a bishop for England from Gregory XV. ' The secular priests were without a superior, and as each one was his own leader and law, many of them thought it safer to cling to the body of the fathers and to direct their ways by their advice rather than by their own private opinion. By this means they increased the power of the Jesuits, and won for them no common authority amongst Catholics. . . .' [2] There were secular priests whom this development alarmed, as the most evident sign of all that the future of English Catholicism lay with the great Society and, the Society being associated popularly with Spain, and an anti-national cause, that

---

[1] Letter quoted SIMPSON, p. 248.
[2] *Narratio historica* printed, with English translation, in Catholic Record Society, Vol. 22, pp. 133–146 : the quotation is from p. 140.

future hardly promised to such secular priests any likelihood of the real re-establishment of Catholicism among the English. Allowing all that can be said for the real abilities of Fr. Persons—who at this moment (1599) can easily seem a kind of vice-pope for England—allowing (as his critics never allowed) his great services to the colleges, and discounting all his unfortunate ventures into politics ; ignoring the Jesuits' somewhat naïve view of themselves as guardians and tutors of the more simple seculars which shows at times in their correspondence ; ignoring also Fr. Persons' expressed belief that the fathers were the salt of the earth, the very sun of our afflicted English Church,[1] the secular clergy would have been a body unique in history had all of them gone on indefinitely without sometimes wondering how far the state of pupillage yet remained to be extended, and without, sometime, kicking against the system that seemed to be threatening.

It is with some recollections of these facts as the background of the scene, that we must now look upon the controversies that centred round the appointment, in 1598, of an archpriest to rule the secular clergy, one of their own number, George Blackwell. Here we approach the least explicable of all the anomalous problems presented by the Counter-Reformation in England, the way in which the *Ecclesia Anglicana* was left, for generations, without any bishops.

The episcopal hierarchy, so the Catholic Church teaches as part of the Catholic faith, is not just a good means of ruling the Church, nor even the best means. It is the means divinely provided. It is of the very nature of the Catholic religion that it is a society ruled by bishops. To be ruled by bishops, to be a bishop-ruled institution is an essential part of what God did in calling the Church into existence. Deprived of its hierarchy the Church would cease to live. The bishops are to it as a vital, natural organ. To suppress the episcopate would be as though we deprived a man of lungs or heart and just as, if the whole Church could be deprived of bishops it would perish, so if in any part of it the local hierarchy is suppressed, Catholic life will inevitably wither away. Without bishops no part of the Church can live healthily. Suppress the

[1] *Cf.* TIERNEY, III, p. 45, note, quoting Persons' *Story of Domestical Difficulties*, pp. 166–169 : ' Certe, quisquis, infelicissimo illi regno societatis operam. . . .'

BONVM · FACIENTES · NON · DEFICIAMVS

TEMPORE · ENIM · SVO · METEMVS · NON · DEFICIENTES.

Father Robert Persons, S.J.
(1546–1610)

hierarchy in any locality, muzzle it, fetter its activity—or let this be fettered by the incapacity or the indifference of those who compose the hierarchy—and Catholicism rapidly declines. So it has always been, so it must be. For it is the very nature of the Church that demands episcopal rule.

There may be grave difficulties in the way of establishing episcopal rule ; there may be grave difficulties in the way of providing the right kind of men—as there was perhaps in France during the eighteenth century and in England on the eve of the Reformation. But the law of the Church's nature holds true. And unless God changed the nature of the Church—made it a different kind of thing from what it has hitherto been—then, whatever the circumstances, the episcopate must be sustained and fostered and, if need be, reformed and brought to a healthier life. For ultimately episcopal action is indispensable to the Church's continued existence.

This truth cannot be too much insisted upon here [1] because if the first turning-point of Catholic history in this country is the failure to overthrow the régime established by William Cecil, the second is the extraordinary fact that for almost 125 years [2] there were no bishops at work in England. The deprivation of the bishops was the result of the Reformation crisis, and Rome's inability to replace them was a leading cause in the Counter-Reformation's failure. As the lack of real disinterestedness in Philip II of Spain wrecked the political side of the Counter-Reformation, so did the failure

[1] The plea was made three hundred years ago, by those who strove to prevent the restoration of the episcopate in England, that no country really stood in need of bishops so long as there was a Pope ; that, so long as there continued to be a Pope, and priests in England received their faculties directly from Rome, England was really episcopally governed and could not be said to lack any of the benefits conferred by the rule of bishops; and in our own time the astonishing suggestion that underlies this way of putting the matter has not lacked patronage among the historians of the quarrel. It is the not uncommon fate of the historian who turns advocate while he is supposedly writing history, that sooner or later he trips. It may, evidently, be impossible in a given place, at a given time, through a given period, to maintain the local hierarchy in being. But the abnormal system temporarily established in its place cannot ever become what the hierarchy is, namely the natural system. Nor can we envisage such an abnormal system extended to the logical finality of the argument, so that there would be but one bishop (*i.e.* the Pope) ruling the whole church by direct communication with all its priests. Fr. Pesch, S.J., writes, very pertinently : ' Non posset summus pontifex per se solum totam ecclesiam gubernare sine episcopis ordinariam iurisdictionem habentibus, quia hoc esset contra Christi institutionem.' (*Prælectiones Dogmaticæ*, edition of 1915, Vol. I, § 363.)

[2] *I.e.* from 1559 to 1623 and from 1631 to 1685.

to maintain the English episcopate wreck the best efforts
of its spiritual side and bring almost to naught an infinity
of high aspiration, gallant sacrifice, and heroic living and
dying.

The local episcopate ceased to be effective in the *Ecclesia
Anglicana* from the moment when, in 1559, the civil authority
which had deprived the bishops of their legal standing, took
away their liberty also.

The last survivors of Pole's hierarchy were the bishops of
Lincoln (Thomas Watson) and St. Asaph (Thomas Goldwell). Watson died in 1584 and Goldwell in 1585. Twelve
years later the energy of Fr. Persons forced upon the Curia
the question of consecrating some bishop in their place.
The outcome of these negotiations was the appointment, in
1598, of an archpriest, an important step, because the first,
in the slow process of restoring its hierarchy to the English
Church, and, as it proved, a step in the wrong direction.

If we recall, as we so continuously must recall, the Jesuit
General's review of the prospects in England in 1580, we
find that already a practical mind understood what must
ensue from the absence of resident bishops. There were
still alive, at that date, the two last survivors of Pole's
hierarchy. Rome now determined that the Bishop of St.
Asaph should return to England as ordinary for the whole
country,[1] to avoid those evils of which the Jesuit had warned
the Holy See. It was an incredible appointment. To send
an old man, well past his seventieth year and broken in
health, to govern the whole English Church, in the height
of a persecution ! And long before he came within sight of
England the bishop broke down, to the disgust of the
Roman officials who made no scruple of jeering at him for
a coward afraid of the torments that lay ahead.

How much these suggestions worried the old man or
provoked him we do not know, but there survives a letter
written from him to Gregory XIII [2] in which he roundly
declares to the Pope what the responsibility is and where it
lies : ' . . . It would be impossible for me alone,' the bishop
writes, ' to supply the wants of the Catholics, who are more

[1] SIMPSON, p. 139, quoting THEINER, *Annals*, III, pp. 219, 700, 701 : a
reference I have not had the chance to control : the phrase ' as ordinary '
should be noted, for it was a like general commission to Bishop Richard
Smith that was the cause of much of his troubles forty years and more later.
[2] July 13, 1580, in SIMPSON, p. 148.

by many thousands than I thought, and scattered over the whole kingdom. The most that I can hope to do is to supply for the city of London and some miles round. And therefore, in my ignorance, I cannot but marvel how it is that, after God has given your Holiness grace, as it were, to plant anew and support the Catholic faith in that kingdom, you make so many difficulties about creating three or four titular Bishops to preserve and propagate it—a thing that might be done with as little expense as your Holiness pleases ; for God has so inclined the minds of the priests to spend their lives in promoting the reduction of that kingdom to the Catholic faith, that, after being made Bishops, they would be contented to live as poorly as they do now, like the Bishops of the primitive Church. God inspire your Holiness to do that which shall be most to His honour, and prosper you many years. I humbly kiss your feet.'

But so long as the hope continued at Rome that the military conquest of England was only a matter of time, the question of sending bishops into England could hardly arise as an immediate, practical necessity. Once the allied army of the Pope and the King of Spain had landed, the papal legate who went with them—Allen, as Bishop of Durham first and then as Archbishop of Canterbury and Lord Chancellor [1]—would see to the restoration of the hier-archy as to all else. But the defeat of this great scheme in 1588, and the death of Allen six years later, brought the matter of a bishop for the English to the very forefront of the complex English problem. The chances of another 1554 were now, in the Curia, recognised as ended, and no Eliseus had come forward to take up Allen's mantle. There were suggestions indeed that Owen Lewis should be given his place in the Sacred College, and, when Lewis died (October, 1595), that the honour should go to Stapleton. But even had either of these plans been carried out, there would still have remained the difficulty, which not even Allen's gifts could permanently have overcome, of ruling at a distance of several months' journeying, priests scattered throughout England, who lived under constantly changing names, and in hiding-places which it was a matter of life and death to keep secret.

[1] *Cf.* Memorandum drawn up by Count de Olivares and Cardinal Allen regarding future appointments to offices in England, 1588 ; text (Spanish) in *L.A.*, p. 302, translation, *ibid.*, pp. cvi–cviii.

The first practical plan was due to Persons, and, looking back over the centuries, it is not hard to see that, at this moment, the association of Persons with the genesis of any plan was enough to wreck its chances of success with many of the secular clergy. To recall how some of these felt in the twelve months that followed the reconciliation at Wisbeach, in the very months when Persons was patching up the dissensions which once again had disturbed the college at Rome, and was about to arrange for the better government of the secular clergy, we may quote a few words from a luridly titled petition some of these made in 1597 against the Fathers. ' So holie, so godly, so religious would they seem to be, as nothing is holie that they have not sanctified, no doctrine catholick and sound that cometh not from them, no dispensation available that is not graunted by them, and, which is worse, they have beaten into the heads of the most, that the masse is not rightly and orderly celebrated of any but a Jesuite.' To impose on men bitter to such a degree against the Society—whether the foundation of their bitterness was reality or mere misunderstanding—a superior who had any connection whatever with the Jesuits was surely to throw oil on the flames. Yet this is what was now done.

If we add that, so far as all our knowledge goes, no one of the four hundred secular priests was taken into consultation by the Roman officials, that not only were Jesuits associated with the scheme from the beginning, but the only English opinion asked for was a Jesuit opinion, we find ourselves wondering how anyone can have hoped that the scheme would go uncriticised, if not unopposed.

Once again it is hardly fair to put all the blame on Persons. It may well be true that he had all the opportunities. But to whom was that owing ? ' It was not difficult for Persons and the Jesuits, owing to the recent increase in the strength of their position in the Curia, to get the better of the wholly unorganised seculars in distant England.' So Meyer,[1] and he is doubtless right, but he is not so right when he goes on to say that : ' This accounts for the fact that the organisation of the English secular clergy took shape under the preponderating influence of the Jesuits instead of at the motion and with the co-operation of the seculars themselves.' The Roman officials were under no obligation to allow ' the preponderating influence of the

[1] Pp. 411–412.

Jesuits ' to carry all before it. It surely is not Persons who must be blamed because at Rome they chose to act on his sole advice and to act without hearing the other parties ? It may well have been a ' walk over ' for the Jesuits, but whose doing was that ?

The first plan which Fr. Persons proposed to Clement VIII, in 1597, was that two bishops should be appointed, one to live in England itself and the other, his superior, to live in Flanders. The reasons he gives in his terse memorandum [1] are those which will be repeated by every memorialist on the subject for the next ninety years. They are the obvious need of someone to administer the sacrament of confirmation, to consecrate the holy oils, to settle authoritatively delicate points of conscience, to be a source of true information about English affairs for the Holy See, to end the dissensions among the clergy, and to fix the places where the different priests shall work and live. This last point has a special importance for the Jesuits, says Persons, because up to now, as far as they can manage it, it is they who have seen to the placing of the priests ; an act of charity that has brought them much labour and much bitter criticism. The bishop should have seven or eight assistants, dispersed through different parts of the country. The bishop (or archbishop) in Belgium would exercise that external jurisdiction [2] which the fear of an appeal to the persecutors would often sterilise in the case of the bishop in England. This archbishop would grant all permissions to those offering to serve the English mission, deciding who were suitable for the work, [3] and he would rule the colony of the exiles.

This scheme went no further, but in the following year the tireless Jesuit had produced another which, this time, he saw realised. The plan to appoint a local ruler of the *Ecclesia Anglicana* was now abandoned. In its place was something quite different, a device to provide a resident English superior for the secular clergy. He was to be one of their own number, and a priest, who was to bear the title of archpriest. Without any vows of obedience, and without

---

[1] Printed in TIERNEY, III, App., p. cxvii.

[2] Jurisdiction whose object is the *public* order of the faithful, *e.g.* the infliction of such penalties as excommunication, the concession of such favours as marriage dispensations.

[3] We are here introduced to the problem of the unsuitable missionary that is to cause such trouble thirty years later. Fr. Persons' solution is to make the bishop the judge of suitability.

any rule to which subjects and superior will, alike, be bound, the secular clergy would, like the Jesuits, be ruled by one of themselves. Whatever the fruits hoped for by those ¡who drafted and sanctioned this novelty, it carried within it the seeds of much future dissension. For it definitely divided the missionaries into two sections, those governed by the archpriest and those who worked in complete independence of his government. When the last archpriest was succeeded by the first bishops, the idea had already taken root that the superiors of the secular clergy could not be anything more, that the missionaries who were members of the religious orders remained entirely outside the limits of what jurisdiction they had. The first bishops, amongst other difficulties, had to fight the notion that they were no more than archpriests with episcopal orders.

There was another misfortune allied to this first. From now on (1598) the secular clergy never ceased to beg that the system of archpriests should give way to the more normal rule of bishops, and the question of bishop or no bishop rapidly became a party question between Jesuits and seculars, for from now on the Jesuits steadily fought all schemes to appoint a bishop. Inevitably the appointment of a bishop, if and when it came, must mark a Jesuit defeat, and it would be difficult indeed for the defeated party to see, with a detachment complete and devoid of all fears, a quondam leader of the other side elevated now, not to a mere superiority over his own, but to rule the whole English Church.

How far the archpriests were from being rulers of the whole English Church can be seen from a study of the faculties granted them by the Holy See.[1] They had no authority over the laity, nor over any priests except those educated in the seminaries. They had no power to inflict canonical censures (such as excommunication or suspension) nor any power of making laws. They could not deprive a priest of faculties given him by the Holy See, nor interfere with his use of them. At the most they could recall what faculties they themselves had given. They had no power to move their priests from one place to another. They could call meetings to which their priests were bound to come, and, ·

---

[1] *Cf.* the letter of March 7, 1598, constituting Blackwell archpriest (TIERNEY, III, App., p. cxix), the brief *Venerunt Nuper* of Oct. 5, 1602 (*ibid.* p. clxxxi), and William Harrison's faculties of July 23, 1615, (*ibid.*, V, App., p. clxxxi).

in consultation with the twelve assistants, they could make rules which the priests must obey. For the rest their faculties are mostly what any priest in a missionary country would need to have, and the third archpriest—William Harrison—is in fact given power to communicate any of these faculties to the other priests. There are some exceptional faculties, such as the power to dispense from the matrimonial impediment of consanguinity, to bless vestments, to consecrate chalices and altar stones, to dispense from fasting and abstinence during Lent, and to dispense priests from the recitation of the divine office (substituting some other prayers). This last power is—in Harrison's faculties—the sole reference to any kind of authority over the priests. Nowhere, in the last stage of the régime, is the archpriest given any power to suspend a delinquent priest, or authority to allot special work to particular individuals. He is definitely told he cannot confirm or ordain, and he is made little more than the local agent from whom the clergy may more easily obtain what extra spiritual powers any special occasion puts them in need of. Finally, the archpriest (*i.e.* in 1615) is told of the new decision whereby the nuncio at Paris is made the ' ordinary for the English and the Scottish with every power which ordinaries have in their dioceses.' [1]

The new régime lasted for twenty-three years (1598–1621). There were three archpriests in succession, and the history of the first is stormy reading. It was taken for granted by many of the secular clergy that the scheme emanated from the ingenuity of Fr. Persons. That the priest named now as their superior, George Blackwell, was a known intimate of the Jesuits,[2] made the matter more suspicious still. When they learnt, further, that Blackwell was commanded by his letters of appointment to take the advice of the Jesuit superior in England in all the more important matters that came before him, they reacted very strongly. Nor is this surprising. The archpriest was the superior of some four hundred clergy, and the Jesuit superior in England had but

---

[1] The actual wording of this is important, for it was afterwards repeated in the briefs to the first two bishops and was the subject of much controversy : ' quod R.P.D. nuncius apostolicus . . . sit ordinarius Anglorum et Scotorum, cum omni potestate quam habent ordinarii in eorum dioecesibus.' TIERNEY, *op. cit.*, V, p. clxxxiii.

[2] His position in the recent controversies can be divined from the phrase, quoted by MEYER (p. 415), in a letter he wrote (Dec. 10, 1597) to the Cardinal Protector : ' There can be no greater viciousness,' he says, ' that to be the enemy of the best,' these last being the fathers of the Society.

a bare dozen subjects at work under him. But while the archpriest was bidden to consult the Jesuit before taking action in any important matter, the Jesuit superior was not given any like instruction to consult the archpriest. It is not wonderful that a régime was resented which seemed not only to accept the alleged Jesuit theory of the inferiority of the seculars and to endorse it, but to make it indeed the very basis of ecclesiastical government in England. Add, as a final combustible ingredient, the high praise lavished on the Jesuits in the letter establishing the archpriest, the way in which they alone are commended for what they have done and suffered, and the reminder to the seculars that Jesuits have given their lives for the faith (while not a word is said of the ten times more numerous martyrs from the secular clergy), add all this and neither the fact of the reaction nor its violence can be a surprise.

'All Catholics must hereafter depend upn Blackwell,' wrote William Watson, the wildest and indeed the least reliable of the Jesuits' adversaries, 'and he upon Garnet and Garnet upon Persons, and Persons upon the Devil, who is the author of all rebellions, treasons, murders, disobedience, and all such designments as this wicked Jesuit hath hitherto designed against her majesty, her safety, her crown, and her life.' [1]

It was also an immense handicap to the secular priests' willing acceptance of the new system, that it was not only new to them, but something, so they considered, hitherto unheard of in the Church. The arrangement was without precedent, a system in fact devised *ad hoc*. How very novel the new institution was, how incredible, from its novelty, it appeared to the priests, and therefore how reasonable it appeared to them to ask if it could really have the Pope's authority behind it, we can judge from the recorded opinion of Dr. Humphrey Ely. We have met this priest twice already in this story. He was one of the band who accompanied Fr. Persons and Bl. Edmund Campion into England in 1580, and, later in that same year, we find him in Lisbon, consulting the nuncio about the lawfulness of a plot to take Elizabeth's life. Ely was a canonist, and after teaching

---

[1] *Cf.* the title of this work, *A Sparing discoverie of our English Iesuits, and of Fa. Parsons' proceedings under pretence of promoting the Catholick faith in England : For a caveat to all true Catholicks, our very louing brethren and friends, how they embrace such very uncatholicke, though Iesuiticall deseignments* (8vo, pp. 70, 1601).

first at Douay and then at Rheims he was given a chair
of canon law in the university of Pont-à-Mousson in Lorraine. He intervened in the controversy, in reply to Fr.
Persons' *Briefe Apologie* (500 pages, octavo), with his *Certaine
Briefe Notes* (312 pages) *upon A Briefe Apologie*. ' Marry,'
says Ely, ' if you can show me that a protector hath, without
bulls by the express commandment of his holiness, instituted
a new dignity which was never in England or in the Church
of Christ before, then will I burn my law books and quit
that profession, for it is against law, against custom, and
against the style of the court of Rome.' True there have
been archpriests already, and there are such in the Church.
But ' for an archpriest to have as great and ample and, yea,
greater jurisdiction over all the priests of two realms as had
all the bishops of those realms when they were Catholic,
is new and extraordinary . . . the question is not of the
ancientness of the dignity, but of this new and never-before-
heard-of jurisdiction, and authority. . . . None but the
Pope, and that by his bulls, can institute or erect a new
dignity or office in God's church.' [1]

John Bennett [2] describes the tense state of feeling among
the secular clergy. ' The archpriest himself, and the twelve
assistants assigned to him were men thought to be either
secret Jesuits or most devoted to the Society. . . . The
priests at first were stupefied and amazed at the novelty of
the arrangement : then they took it hardly and were
indignant : finally they came to loathe the cunning and
the sham ' [*i.e.* by which they thought it had been brought
about]. [3]

Cited LAW. *J. and S.*, lxvi–lxvii. Law's comment—after fifty years—
still holds. ' How so important a measure, involving the institution, as Ely
declares, of a jurisdiction unheard of in the previous annals of the church,
came to be promulgated without bull or brief or any papal document, by the
mere letters of a cardinal whose office of protector, as such, gave him no
canonical superiority, has had no sufficient explanation.' The Roman
official appointed to examine Bishop and Charnock declared, quoting the
Pope as his authority, that Clement VIII was doubtful how far the order
would be obeyed, and therefore preferred not to set his own hand to it and
thereby risk a serious defiance to his commands. So LAW, *ibid.*, note 2, quoting JOHN COLLETON, *A Just Defence of the Slandered Priestes* (1602), p. 34.

[2] *Op. cit.*, p. 135 : there is an error in Bennett's first sentence, for only six
assistants were assigned by name ; the other six were left to the archpriest's
choice.

[3] To understand much of the heat now generated it has to be remembered
that these priests believed that the whole archpriest scheme was a Jesuit
trick to perpetuate the hold of the Society on the English Catholic body.
Why did the Jesuits desire such control ? So that, said their opponents,

The Jesuits, so Bennett's account proceeds, had got wind
of a movement among the clergy to ask for bishops. They
knew well—the Jesuits that is—that Rome could not refuse
so just a request (what they—the Jesuits' critics—did not
know was that Rome had already the year before said ' No '
to a like request from . . . Persons himself). But, says
Bennett,[1] the fathers smelt out the secular clergy's scheme,
got in first and planted the archpriest on their opponents
before their movement had got as far as the resolution
stage. When the news came of the archpriest's appointment [2] the clergy saw new storms threatening, and so
' meeting together [the priests] besought both the Jesuits
and the new archpriest to carry themselves peaceably '
and to take care not to raise discussions, until the secular
clergy had had a chance to put their case before the Pope.
Neither Blackwell nor his Jesuit advisers would promise
anything. *Roma locuta est*—in their favour. Let the rest
show themselves obedient and bow their necks.

The clergy—that is to say a small but very active group
of them—deputed two of their number, William Bishop
and Robert Charnock, to make an appeal at Rome against
the scheme. But, whatever the rights and wrongs of this
action, the Jesuit was too strong for them. In all simplicity
they made their way, only to find themselves arrested at
Rome (December, 1598) and then imprisoned in the
English College with Fr. Persons himself as their jailer.

when the crucial moment came they (*i.e.* Fr. Persons) could swing the whole
weight of English Catholicism to the support of the Spanish claimant to the
English throne. Whether this were true or not, it is important to remember
that these men believed it. That extremely sober personage, Dr. Lingard,
also believed it, on the authority of ' a memorial in favour of the archpriest
in my possession.' Unfortunately he gives no information about the proven-
ance of this source, but proceeds to quote from it this passage which I
venture to translate (from the original Italian), ' the chief reason is not only
to preserve unity while the queen is alive, but much more to secure it once
she dies in order to bring about that her successor is a Catholic in accordance
with certain briefs which His Holiness has already most prudently written
to the Catholics.' LINGARD, VI, p. 313, note 1. Even were this the case,
the Spanish policy was not so much a Jesuit policy as a Robert Persons
policy. There were Jesuits on the Scottish side as well as seculars.

[1] Bennett is of course writing in 1621, twenty-three years after the event.
He is, however, writing apparently for the information of Rome and writing
at Rome, where all the documents of the affair were easily available for his
readers—the Pope and his cardinals of the Holy Office—to check what he
wrote.

[2] The letter of Cardinal Cajetan, protector of England, appointing the
archpriest is of Mar. 7, 1598 : text in TIERNEY, III, App., p. cxix.

The fate of the envoys—and Fr. Persons' association with it —inevitably added to the bitterness of the controversy. For the unfortunate priests never again left the college until, the whole matter having been decided against them, without a hearing from the Pope, without their ever even seeing the Pope, they were expelled by the Pope's orders and forbidden ever to return to England or to Italy, banished, the one to France, the other to Lorraine, and even forbidden to travel from Rome in one another's company. ' Posterity hereafter,' wrote a contemporary sympathiser,[1] ' will wonder to hear or read that two Catholic priests coming as appellants to Rome out of an heretical country, in which they maintained constantly, with danger of their lives, the honour and preservation of that See, and one of them had suffered some years' imprisonment, with banishment afterwards, for the article of St. Peter or his successor's supremacy over all other princes and prelates, that these priests (I say) should, before they were heard what they had to say, be cast into prison, yea and imprisoned in the house and under the custody of their adversaries.'

The main matter of the appeal to Rome had been a doubt whether it really was the Pope who had appointed the archpriest, for the nomination was made in the name of the Cardinal Protector of England only. This doubt was now settled,[2] and the clergy had to bow to the inevitable.

Blackwell, however, while the appeal was pending, had struck hard at the dissidents and had suspended two of the seniors, John Mush, once the intimate and confidential friend of Allen, the director of Margaret Clitherow, and the man who had brought peace to Wisbeach, and John Colleton, who had stood in the dock with Edmund Campion. Though he now removed the suspension, Blackwell declared that they had been guilty of schism and must acknowledge their sin and make satisfaction for it. As he continued to treat them as schismatics, Colleton laid the case before the theological faculty of the University of Paris. The reply was favourable. But Blackwell only noticed it to repudiate and condemn it, and he renewed the suspension. Where-

---

[1] Ely in *Briefe Notes*, p. 107 ; quoted Law, *J. S.*, p. 87, note 1.
[2] April 6, 1599 : the brief *Inter Gravissimas*, printed in Tierney, III., App., p. cxxviii.

upon seventeen of the clergy drew up a solemn protest [1] and appealed once more to Rome (November 17, 1600).

All seventeen appellants were prisoners in the castle of Wisbeach. Their appeal had been forwarded through the archpriest and now the most unlikely things began to happen. Some of the appellants got into touch with the government and the persecuting government came to their assistance. They strove to make the government understand that the Jesuits were indeed traitors, and necessarily so ; the secular clergy were anti-Jesuits, anti-Spain, and loyal subjects. It suited the government's game to accept this distinction between the Jesuits and the rest, and to treat the leaders of the appellants as, at any rate, less disloyal subjects. Some of the prisoners were now released and allowed to go about the country seeking monies to take them to Rome,[2] and the envoys were got out of the country by an arranged ' banishment.' [3] The government's reward would be increased distrust of one section for the other, ultimately hatred, and perhaps also the Pope's withdrawal of the Jesuits from England—not an impossible happening in a pontificate which had seen the credit of the Society suffer heavily in the *Curia*.[4] Had not the Pope himself asked the president of Douay : ' Do you think the whole world would perish if the Jesuits ceased to govern it ? ' [5] And there had been more serious incidents by far.[6]

The delegation had scarcely set out when the papal answer to their appeal arrived. This second brief [7] is a fairly

[1] Text in TIERNEY, III, App., p. cxxxiii–cxliv.

[2] See the explanation of all this made by Thomas Bluett (the first of the secular priests to treat with the common enemy) to the cardinals of the Holy Office in March, 1602 : printed in LAW, *J. and S.*, p. 153. They collected about £600 in money and some £400 in jewels ; enough to take five envoys and their servants to Rome and maintain them there for several months. Actually, as it happened, once they arrived at Rome the Pope saw to their maintenance. LAW, cxx.

[3] Bluett to John Mush, July 1, 1601, in LAW, *J. and S.*, p. xcvi, quoting Persons' *Apologie*, p. 108.

[4] For a temperate statement of this alliance with Beelzebub, *cf.* MEYER, pp. 425, 434–446 ; Meyer's summary of its effect, which of course needs qualification is that ' The secular priest looked upon the Jesuit as a traitor to his country, and the Jesuit looked upon the secular priest as a traitor to the church,' p. 428.

[5] Barrett to Persons, Sept. 26, 1596, in KNOX, p. 386.

[6] *Cf.* PASTOR, Vol. 24, pp. 14–15 : ' God resists the proud ' was the Pope's marginal comment on a Jesuit complaint, and on another he wrote about the ' need for the public humiliation of such people.'

[7] The brief *Cum Nobilissimum*, Aug. 17, 1601. TIERNEY, III, App., p. cxlix.

lengthy document and, like the first, it is addressed to Black-well. It tells the story of the institution of the new régime, of the first dissensions and the earlier decision, which is now confirmed. It then proceeds with a stiff lecture to Blackwell on the spirit in which he ought to exercise his powers. He is told that his authority is not given for any man's destruction. He is to be a father and a shepherd and not a tyrant. Nevertheless, the Pope has not entertained the appeal, and the appellants are paternally admonished not to forget the demands of charity. The archpriest is to forbid the publication of any further writings about this quarrel, and the whole affair is to be buried and forgotten. All are forbidden, under pain of excommunication, to preserve, much less to circulate, any of the ' literary memorials ' of the controversy, and the very word ' schism ' is not to be so much as mentioned henceforward. Finally the Pope reminds all of what they are prepared to suffer for the faith from the persecutors—of what indeed many of them have suffered and indeed are suffering—and he says, touchingly, *Cur igitur invicem non suffertis, qui tanta perferre parati estis* ?

This should have been the end of the trouble, but Blackwell suppressed the brief. For it forbade all further publications, and Persons' *Brief Apologie* (in support of the archpriest) was not yet out! Once this had made its appearance Blackwell published the brief, January, 1602. In the meantime the delegates—although the nuncio in Flanders showed them the brief—persisted in their intention. When they reached Rome they had so much to say that the Pope ordered the whole case to be re-examined. The case they presented for a bishop made indeed no headway, nor did the delegates gain the additional archpriest for whom they asked. Nor were the Jesuits withdrawn from England—if, indeed, the delegates asked for this. But in a final brief the Pope gave them the immense satisfaction not only of removing from the archpriest the obligation to consult the Jesuit superior in England, but of positively forbidding him to do so.[1] In the second brief Blackwell had been admonished, but now the appellants were cleared entirely, and it was not only said that the suspension of the appellants had been invalid, but that the priests concerned had never

---

[1] And indeed to consult any member of the Society about the business of his office, directly or indirectly, by word or by letter. Brief *Venerunt Nuper* Oct. 5, 1602, in TIERNEY, III, App., p. clxxxi.

lost their faculties. The archpriest was finally ordered to take three of the appellants into the council of his assistants.

The reign of Elizabeth had but a bare six months to run. The most striking move, on the part of the appellant secular clergy had yet to be played. The government, sure now of the real divisions among the missionaries, and aware that the Holy See was not going to recall the Jesuits from England, issued, just one month after the last brief, yet another proclamation banishing all priests. It was, however, a proclamation with a difference. Several of its features need to be noted, and it provoked a reply from some of the appellants.

This proclamation, of November 5, 1602,[1] opens by recalling that, in the hope of winning over the missionaries to greater loyalty, the persecution has recently been slackened. The late controversies between the missionaries have revealed that while some, ' the Jesuits and the secular priests their adherents,' [2] are inveterate plotters, others, ' the other secular priests,' protest against all this as ' most wicked, detestable and damnable,' and offer to be the first to reveal such plots and to resist them. Much as the queen would like to befriend this more loyal party, she is nevertheless compelled to treat them as enemies since they, too, ceaselessly endeavour to win over their fellow-subjects to the cause of the Pope—who, as a temporal prince, has lately been at open war with the queen.

The queen calls God to witness how innocent she has ever been of ' any purpose to grant a toleration of two religions within our realm.' The recent misunderstood and misrepresented, clemency is to cease. (1) All Jesuits and the seculars who are of their mind, are forthwith to depart the realm. (2) The other seculars are to leave by the coming January 1. (3) Excepting such as will present themselves to the council or the bishops, and acknowledging their allegiance, submit themselves to the queen's mercy ; with these last some special arrangement (not specified in the proclamation) will be made.

The full severity of the laws will operate against all priests of the first class who stay in the country after

---

[1] Text in TIERNEY, III, p. clxxxiv–clxxxviii.

[2] *I.e.* ' almost all the secular priests, by yielding their obedience to a new kind of subordination among them, have in effect subjected themselves to be wholly directed by the Jesuits,' Proclamation, *op. cit.*, p. clxxxv.

December 4, 1602, and of the second who linger after February 1, 1603.[1]

There has survived the joint reply [2] to this proclamation, of one group of the anti-Jesuit secular clergy. It is dated January 31, 1603, *i.e.* the last day on which, since they had not presented themselves to the authorities, these priests had leave to be in England. There are thirteen signatories, amongst whom are nine of the appellants, Bishop and Charnock, the two luckless envoys to Rome of 1598, and two of the martyrs of the next reign, Roger Cadwallader and Robert Drury.

The Protestation of the thirteen secular missionaries begins with a reference to the recent proclamation. The priests are grateful for it, and " most willing to give such assurance and satisfaction in this point [of allegiance and fidelity to the queen] as any Catholic priests can, or ought to give unto their sovereigns.'

Then, in detail, they state : (1) They acknowledge the queen to have as full authority over the realm and themselves as ever had any of her predecessors. This is God's will for all ; and so assured are they of this that no authority can warrant Catholics to disobey the queen in any civil or temporal matter, any more than it can warrant Protestants ; (2) As to the various conspiracies, schemes to invade the realm and the like, they note this ' intendment of restoring the Catholic religion by the sword ' as ' a course most strange in the world, and undertaken peculiarly and solely against ' Elizabeth out of all the princes who had given up the Catholic faith. Also, they say, these various enterprises have been the reason—not indeed for the laws against Catholics—but for the increasing severity of these, the union of faith between the Catholics and Rome creating a presumption that Catholics as such favoured these schemes. Where-

---

[1] This last proclamation of Elizabeth against priests of the old religion has a further interest for what it reveals of the persecutor's understanding that he is primarily persecuting, *i.e.* not punishing traitors : *e.g.* the laws under which priests have suffered, and with which they are again menaced, are laws ' established for the conservation of the true religion now professed in our kingdoms ' (Proclamation, *op. cit.*, p. clxxxiv) ; again the crime of the priests is that they ' seduce our people from their affection to religion, and so, *by consequence* [italics this writer's] from the constancy of their obedience to us ' (*ibid.*) ; finally, when the priests are reminded of the doom that continually hangs over them, the Act of 1585, it is explicitly declared of them ' by whose sole act of their very coming into this kingdom they are within the danger of our laws.'

[2] Text in TIERNEY, III, pp. clxxxviii–cxci.

fore, the thirteen priests solemnly protest that they will be the foremost to fight in defence of the queen in the event of attacks or an invasion, and the first to denounce to the government any news that comes to them of all such projects ; (3) More explicitly they pledge themselves to disregard any papal sentence of excommunication against the queen, even should it extend to all those who do not abandon her cause. ' In these, and all other like cases we do think ourselves, and all the lay Catholics born within her majesty's dominions, bound in conscience not to obey this or any suchlike censure.'

The signatories are aware that their action will be misconstrued by some Catholics, and carefully misrepresented to the Pope. To protect themselves in advance against such calumniators, they therefore beg the queen to allow them in this protestation of loyalty, ' to make known by like public act, that, by yielding her right unto her, we depart from no bond of that Christian duty, which we owe unto uor supreme spiritual pastor.' And they proceed to state explicitly their Catholic faith, that the Pope is St. Peter's successor and has all the authority (but not any more) ' over us and other Christians ' that the apostle had by Christ's commission and gift ; that they will obey him ' so far forth as we are bound by the laws of God to do.' This, they do not doubt, is fully compatible with their loyalty to the queen, and they end with the resounding declaration to the government ' as we are most ready to spend our blood in the defence of her majesty and our country, so we will rather lose our lives than infringe the lawful authority of Christ's catholic church.'

§ v. DIVISION ABOUT THE OATH OF ALLEGIANCE

The unhappy George Blackwell had begun his reign in storm, and it ended in a great personal catastrophe, after the experience of seeing two of his priests [1] hanged for their share in the Bye Plot, and the whole Catholic body involved in the obloquy of the still more mysterious catastrophe called Gunpowder Plot. The last of the gunpowder conspirators was scarcely executed when James and the parliament joined their wits to construct two new penal statutes, whose end was to cut the Catholic off from all possibility of sharing

[1] The appellants, Watson and Clerk.

the national life, and to bring him to speedy, and indeed immediate, financial ruin. So far searching were the provisions of the new acts, that a man at least as wise as the English ministers, Henry IV of France, protested in the common interest against such insane provocation.

What the new acts did was this. The first of them [1] began by laying upon Catholics already convicted of the offence of not attending service in the parish church— Recusants—the new obligation of once a year receiving there the sacrament. For a first omission a fine of £20 was imposed, for a second £40, for a third £60. The Crown had already a financial interest in the conviction of recusants, its share of the £20 per lunar month which was the fine they paid. Now, by the new act, the king could, if he preferred, instead of levying the fine take the whole of the convict's personal property and two-thirds of his real estate. The old law that made it treason to reconcile an Englishman to the Catholic Church, or for an Englishman to be so reconciled, was now extended to make reconciling and being reconciled treason even if this took place abroad. And, the most cruel provision of all, as it turned out, the head of the house was made liable to a fine of £10 per month for every visitor he lodged and every servant he employed who neglected to attend the services of the church. Immediately Catholic servants all over the country found themselves discharged, and so numerous were these victims that the French ambassador thought their despair something worth while reporting to his government.[2] Finally, this act imposed the new oath of allegiance. But before this is analysed it will simplify the narrative to describe, first of all, the second of the new penal laws now passed.

By this second law [3] Catholics were banished from the court and forbidden either to reside within ten miles of London or to move more than five miles from home, except with the written licence of four justices counter-signed by the bishop of the diocese or the Lord Lieutenant of the county or one of his deputies. They were forbidden to practice or to be employed as lawyers, physicians, apothecaries; they could not act as judges, clerks, stewards, or

---

[1] 3 & 4 Iac. I, c. 1.

[2] The act came into force June 26, 1606; the ambassador's letter, quoted TIERNEY, IV, p. 67, is dated a month later, July 30, 1606.

[3] 3 & 4 Iac. I, c. 5.

officers of any court or corporation ; they were barred
from commissions in the army or navy, from all public
offices of trust or emolument, disabled from acting as
executors, administrators, or guardians. Even though the
husband conformed (or though he were a Protestant) the
Catholic wife convicted of neglecting the new law to receive
the sacrament, was to lose two-thirds of her dower, two-
thirds of her jointure, and became incapable of acting as her
husband's executrix. Catholics married elsewhere than in
the Protestant Church, or by any but the Protestant minister,
lost what interest they might have in one another's property.
If they failed to call in the Protestant minister to baptise
their children they were fined £100, and if Catholics were
buried elsewhere than in the Protestant church or church-
yard the executors were fined £20. Upon the Catholic
who was a convicted recusant there also fell the new
disability of excommunication, with its consequence that
he was thereby disabled from maintaining or defending
any personal suit or action. His house might at any moment
be entered and searched, his books and furnishings be burnt
as superstitious, his arms put under sequestration.

But the most ingenious of the new trials was the new
Oath of Allegiance. This might be tendered to all recusants,
and also to all Catholics who had not twice within the past
year received the sacrament in the parish church. The
penalty for refusing the oath was stiff, loss of all property
and life imprisonment. And while the oath was such that
no Catholic could take it, only by an elaborate explanation
could the Catholic who refused it save his name as a loyal
subject. For while whoever took it swore acknowledgement
of James I as his lawful sovereign—and this was the case for
Catholics as for non-Catholics—he also proceeded to state
his belief that the Pope had no power or authority to
depose the king. Here was a first nice point ; for the oath
did not deny the papal power of excommunicating kings in
general, nor of declaring them deposed when excommunicated. It simply denied that the Pope had any power to
depose King James I, and to bring on him the *sequelæ*
that usually followed the excommunication of a reigning
prince, namely the transfer of his kingdom to another, the
discharging of the subjects from their duty of allegiance,
the permission to them to take up arms against the prince
excommunicated, ' or to offer any violence or hurt to his

majesty's royal person.' James I, the child of Mary Queen of Scots, was of course baptised by Catholic rites, but since before the age of twelve months he had been bred a heretic. The modern canon law would not consider him as its subject in purely disciplinary measures. But in these years when Catholics were hardly yet awake to the new fact of there being places where heresy had been so long in possession that there actually existed educated Christians who were heretics in good faith, our modern distinctions were not drawn. James I was as good material for excommunication as, not only the never really Catholic Elizabeth, but even her father Henry VIII, once undoubtedly a Catholic and so staunch indeed as to merit the papal title Defender of the Faith. Could the Pope excommunicate James I ? And if he were to do so, must not the sequel follow that Catholics, so far as possible, must no longer recognise him as king ? For the popes, excommunicating a sovereign prince, did not so much depose him as make public his inevitable incapacity to be any longer a lawful ruler of Christian people.

The Pope, then, so the oath began, has no authority to depose the king. The practical consequence of belief in this view of the matter is then set out in a pledge that ' notwithstanding any declaration or sentence of excommunication or deprivation made or granted . . . by the Pope . . . I will bear faith and true allegiance to his majesty . . . and . . . will defend [him] against all . . . attempts whatsoever . . . made . . . by reason or colour of any such sentence.' This is the pledge of the thirteen priests in their protestation made to Elizabeth just three years earlier. But now it is no volunteered offering : it is a promise made under oath, and at the bidding of the government. It is, by the way it is done, a public repudiation in advance of papal policy made at the behest of an heretical power. Who could expect any pope of this Counter-Reformation time, to allow his people, in a country where Catholicism was fighting for its life, so to defy his authority in advance ?

It might be that James I was beyond the reach of excommunication—a question, perhaps, of fact ; it might be that, privately, a Catholic would be safe in conscience if he disregarded such an excommunication were it decreed ; but the next clause of the oath destroyed all chance of its being an oath which any Catholic could take. ' I do further

swear,' the text proceeds, ' that I do, from my heart, abhor,
detest, and abjure, as impious and heretical, this damnable
doctrine and position—that princes, which be excommunicated by the Pope, may be deposed or murdered by their
subjects, or any other whatsoever.' Can anything seem more
damnable to decent men, or be more damnable, than
murder ? But to kill a justly excommunicated tyrant and
usurper is not necessarily murder.[1] And no doctrine ever
said that the excommunicated may be murdered. Thus to
swear one's rejection of a doctrine that the excommunicated
may be murdered is certainly to suggest that Catholicism
has authorised such a doctrine. The difference between
what is suggested and the common teaching and practice
of Catholics for five hundred years is evident, it may be, to
a student, and considerable; but yet, so far as words go,
the two positions are too nearly akin for a Catholic of 1606
not to be taken as here abjuring a recognised Catholic
position. But the text makes the oath impossible even for
a Catholic who is willing to take ' murder ' as meaning ' kill
on his own authority,' by coupling with murder the deposition of the excommunicated ruler. May subjects not
depose their excommunicated sovereign ? All Christendom
for a good six hundred years has held that they may, if not
indeed that they must. If the excommunication is valid,
then the deposition follows logically. But even though the
Catholic subject of King James were so ' advanced ' as to
protest that excommunicated sovereigns cannot be deposed,
the oath still held him. He must give up yet more of the
current Catholic practice. He must declare that this cen-
turies-old way of looking at the matter is ' damnable,'
' impious and heretical.' Whatever may be said of the
position which declares that excommunicated princes may
be deposed by their subjects, it is not impious and it is not
heretical. The difficulty here is one of fact, and no Catholic
can swear to the false statement which these words contain.

The Roman rejoinder to the new penal laws and the
oath was not long delayed. On September 22, 1606,
Paul V, by the brief *Magno animi mœrore* [2] reminded the
Catholics of England that it was sinful to frequent the
Protestant churches, to assist at services, to be present at
sermons. Moreover, they must not take the new oath,
which, as must be evident to them from its very text,

[1] *Cf. sup.*, pp. 216 *seq.*   [2] Text in TIERNEY, IV, App., p. cxl.

contains many things contrary to faith and salvation. When the authenticity of this decision was questioned a second, confirmatory brief was published, August 23, 1607.[1]

The oath of allegiance was destined to be a cause of much division for the next half-century, for there were always to be found Catholics who protested that to take it involved no repudiation of Catholic doctrine, but only of political practice. Very many took it, and there were never wanting, here and there, priests to approve their action; and this division of practice—despite the repeated papal condemnations of the oath—was perpetuated by the multitude of tracts and pamphlets which never ceased to appear defending, more or less elaborately, the lawfulness of the oath, and finding subtle explanations why the papal prohibitions lacked force. It was on June 25, 1606, that the act establishing the oath became law—barely six months after the execution of the last of the Powder Plot conspirators, at a time, that is to say, when any Catholic might, in desperation, risk anything, short of flagrant apostasy, to be believed a loyal subject. The Jesuits were unitedly resolute that the oath was unlawful. One of the most prominent of the Benedictines[2] became its steadfast champion. The archpriest was hostile, so violently hostile and so immoderate in his manner as to alarm his friends. But later on, in the next year, 1607, he fell into the hands of the pursuivants, and now he not only took the oath, but wrote a pastoral letter explaining with what reservations he had done so and that it was lawful to take it in this fashion. And now there came into his life—as there had already come into the controversy—the most celebrated of the theologians of the time, the Jesuit whom we honour today as a doctor of the Church, St. Robert Bellarmine.[3] But his exhortations failed entirely to move George Blackwell and on February 1, 1608, Paul V deposed him. In the same brief the Pope nominated his successor, George Birkhead.

[1] *Renuntiatum Nobis : ibid.*, p. cxlvi.
[2] Dom Thomas Preston, *alias* Roger Widdrington : never a monk of the English congregation.
[3] BRODRICK, II, pp. 139 foll.

CHAPTER II

THE SECULAR CLERGY AGITATE FOR BISHOPS IN ENGLAND, 1606–1624

DURING the ten years of Blackwell's term of office a new attempt had been made to persuade Rome to appoint a bishop, or bishops, for England, but without any success at all. Antony Champney and John Cecil [1] had arrived in Rome, in May, 1606, to present a petition signed by seventy priests. But Fr. Persons had had news of their coming, and he succeeded in persuading the Pope that the character and antecedents of the envoys were such, that their cause was not worth a hearing. He even suggested that the Pope would do well to have them arrested. Though he failed here, the envoys returned without achieving anything at all.

The new archpriest, George Birkhead, was, like his predecessor, known as a man on friendly terms with the Jesuits, and—what was worse still, no doubt, in the eyes of the more active of the secular clergy—known as a one-time intimate of Persons. For a moment it seemed as though the conflict of ten years earlier was to begin all over again. But Birkhead assured his brethren that he meant to govern in the spirit and letter of the last ruling of the Holy See, and presently he agreed to authorise a further attempt to win from the Pope something like a restoration of the hierarchy. The delegate he chose was Richard Smith, who thus, at forty years of age, now makes his first appearance in Catholic public life.

In Smith's commission he was bidden to consult with Fr. Persons at every step, and to be guided by the Jesuit's experience. At the same time the archpriest wrote to Persons telling him of what was proposed and asking his assistance.

---

[1] For the sinister dealings of this personage with the English government ; cf. POLLEN, *Archpriest Blackwell*, pp. 67–70.

Once more the Jesuit's moves were more rapid than anything his unconscious opponents could counter. He replied immediately to Birkhead, May 31, 1608, that the mission was useless, as the Pope would never receive it. Others wrote from Rome in the same sense, and in September, before Smith had set out, Paul V issued an order forbidding any petitions for a bishop (and also any recommendations of particular individuals) which had not the unanimous support of all the secular clergy. This was indeed strong confirmation of Fr. Persons' warning, and Tierney is not slow to suggest, and offer evidence in proof, that it was the Jesuit who inspired the decree. Smith, however, came on to Rome where he arrived in May, 1609, for the new archpriest had a most important personal matter to refer to the Holy See. Did the prohibition to his predecessor, about consulting Jesuits in what related to his duties as archpriest, bind Blackwell alone, or did it refer to the archpriest as such? Birkhead had felt a strong desire to take the advice of Jesuits on various points, as he had been used to consult them all his life. He had written to ask what Persons thought and Persons had reported that his own opinion was that the prohibition was personal to Blackwell, that he would ask the Pope about it, and that meanwhile Birkhead need have no scruple in following this opinion. So Smith came out to Rome and, as a man rather less informed if not less wise, began to consult with the Jesuit at every step in a matter where Persons was hoping and working against him.

After a certain amount of hedging on the part of the Jesuit, the intervention of the General of the Society forced his hand. He consented to the great question about the binding force of Clement VIII's brief being put, and at Smith's audience, on May 24, 1609, Paul V declared that the prohibition did indeed bind Birkhead, as it was meant to bind all Blackwell's successors. This was the only point on which Smith received any satisfaction, for now Persons definitely turned against him and he never again saw the Pope. His petitions and memorials remained unnoticed, while Persons—though Smith probably did not know this— poured in counter-memorials, in which he painted Birkhead as the unwilling tool of a dominant clique among his clergy and described Smith's mission to Rome as a thing which the archpriest had only allowed against his real judgement.

In September, 1610, Smith, outwearied, resigned his commission and came home.

The archpriest meanwhile had set himself to the immensely dangerous task of collecting the signatures of the clergy, and soon (by July, 1610) he had in his possession a collection of documents that would have rejoiced any pursuivant's heart, letters from no fewer than two hundred of the missionaries. By December, 1611, he had managed to smuggle this dangerous package out of the country to his new agent at Rome. The Jesuits in Rome—not Persons, for he died in April, 1610—drafted a petition in the contrary sense, and upon this second effort of the archpriest there fell a silence never broken. He wrote repeatedly to ask for news, he sent memorials and petitions, and twice at least he offered his resignation, but all to no end. No reply of any kind was given either to him or to his agent, and Birkhead died, April 5, 1614, with matters still in the same unsatisfactory position as six years before.

After a long interregnum of fifteen months the third archpriest was appointed,[1] Dr. William Harrison, 1615. Once again the nomination had gone to a priest who, in the long controversies, had shown himself hostile to the party of the appellants. Harrison, indeed, as Blackwell's agent in the Roman Curia, had striven actively, and with Persons' help, against their influence, even after the settlement of 1602 between them and the archpriest, and he had gone so far as to declare to Paul V that the oath of allegiance lately condemned (1606) simply embodied the theology of the appellants, and ideas which they had long been disseminating. It says much for the readiness of both sides to forget the past that Harrison's short reign (1615–1621) was peaceful and without any notable events. True, at Douay, the new president, Matthew Kellison, was finding the liquidation of his predecessor's[2] reign a none too easy task. Kellison had Harrison's sympathy and, as far as the archpriest could render any, his assistance too. But at home the chief feature of the time was the silence with which the Curia continued to meet not only petitions for an improved system of government, but the whole correspond-

---

[1] For the story of this appointment cf. the documents printed in TIERNEY V, App., pp. clxii–clxxxvi.

[2] Dr. Thomas Worthington, under whose administration the studies, discipline, and general well-being of the college had suffered extraordinarily.

ence of the archpriest. For the unfortunate man never wrote without drawing attention to the many ills he was powerless to cure, and without hinting at the need for a bishop even when he did not state it outright.

Then, after six years nearly, came a great revolution in the political world, and a new opportunity for the Church in England. James I, who had already long since abandoned the policy of hostility to Spain, now, in 1619, so far reversed the Elizabethan situation as to plan to marry the Prince of Wales to the daughter of Philip III. Philip II, the legendary enemy, had once been King of England, now his grand-daughter was to be its queen. The proposal raised a host of delicate problems, but none so delicate, or so import-ant, as that of the attitude of Rome. The Spanish princess could never give up her religion, nor could the Prince of Wales become a Catholic. A papal dispensation would be needed before the marriage could take place. Would Rome grant it ? and if so on what terms ? The needs of diplomacy led the king to deal more gently with his Catholic subjects. Soon there were to be drafts of marriage treaties, and in all of these provision would be made that the Princess of Wales should have full liberty to practise her religion, a public chapel in London and indeed wherever she went. Catholi-cism was to be, as it were, inlawed in her person, and the persecution was to cease, no more laws being enacted against Catholics and the old laws being allowed to fall into desuetude.

The story of these involved negotiations must be read elsewhere.[1] For this present narrative they are important because of the new opportunity they gave to the archpriest and the new Roman atmosphere they promised for his patient petitions should he continue them.

Moreover, on January 28, 1621, the long reign of Paul V (1605–1621) came to an end. A new pope might mean a new policy for England. So indeed it fell out, for in what followed, the personality of the new Pope, Gregory XV, proved to be the most important factor of all. It was in May, 1621, that Harrison chose John Bennett, one of his assistants, as his envoy, and commissioned him to ask the Pope in the name of the English Catholics and for the sake of preserving the faith, to grant the dispensation and, at the same time, to beg that the system of the archpriests should

---

[1] PASTOR, Vol. 27, pp. 159–196, gives a useful, documented, summary.

be replaced by the more normal régime of episcopal rule.
But before the matter could go any further Harrison
suddenly died, May 11, 1621. It was some months before
his assistants could come together, to renew Bennett's
commission, and it was not until November that Bennett
arrived in Rome.

He reached Rome to find, as always, that his coming had
been anticipated by those opposed to the scheme he came
to plead for. The line they took was simple. Paul V
had forbidden all mention of the matter unless the secular
clergy unanimously petitioned it. But Bennett acted with
great shrewdness. He made no confidants. He kept his
plans and the desires he came to speak for, to himself. Not
until he had his first audience with Gregory XV did he
declare his commission, and he then began by asking the
Pope to allow him to speak of it despite the prohibition of
Paul V.[1] The first sign of favour was the new Pope's reversal
of his predecessor's ruling. This was in February, 1622, and
the Pope appointed a commission of cardinals to discuss
whether a bishop should be sent into England. For four
months the debate continued before these cardinals of the
Holy Office, and especially between the two who stood
henceforward as champions of the rival parties, two of the
leading personalities of the Sacred College, Ottaviano
Bandini,[2] Cardinal Bishop of Palestrina and Giangarzia
Millini,[3] the Cardinal-Vicar. Finally, in June, 1622, the
Pope's decision was announced. There would be no more
archpriests ; Harrison's successor would be a bishop. The
hopes of thirty years were to be realised at last, and whatever
else there might be, the sacrament of confirmation, after

[1] *Cf.* Bennett's letters to Kellison, Bishop, and Edward Bennett in
TIERNEY, V, App., p. ccxxxii and fol.

[2] Ottaviano Bandini (1558–1629), a close friend of Clement VIII, who
gave him the red hat in the consistory (June 5, 1596) which saw also the
elevation of Camillo Borghese (Paul V, 1605–1621), Tarugi, and Baronius :
' a prelate of very great authority here,' writes Bennett to Bishop, ' and our
special patron.' The cardinal was one of the most influential personages in
Rome during Gregory XV's short reign (1621–1623). In the conclave which
followed he was a very strong opponent of the cardinal ultimately elected—
Urban VIII, and thenceforward his influence declined.

[3] Giangarzia Millini (1572–1629) was a nephew of the strongly Hispano-
phil Pope, Urban VII, who reigned for just ten days in the autumn of 1590.
He was greatly in favour with the Pope whose reign had, in 1621, just
ended. Paul V, who employed him as nuncio in Germany and in Spain, gave
him the red hat and named him his vicar for Rome. In the conclave which
followed the death of Paul V, Millini was for a time the candidate of the late
Pope's powerful nephew. He had been vice-protector of England since 1612.

sixty years and more, would once again be given to the persecuted Catholics of England.

Tierney [1] prints a most instructive memorandum of the speeches or opinions of the two cardinals, Bandini and Millini, drawn up apparently by an opponent of what was ultimately accomplished. Bandini's speech, except for the remark that the only opposition to the plan came from the Jesuits who, in this matter, need not be seriously noticed, merely repeats the commonplaces of the clergy's habitual argument. He remarks that the hopes of the marriage with Spain have brought the king to an unusual clemency towards Catholics which argues well, but adds that even were times as bad as previously, persecution should be no argument against giving bishops to rule the Church. Had the line of bishops in England never been broken, religion there would be in a healthier condition and scandals fewer. Millini's speech,[2] for the opposition, is weaker than anyone would believe who had not read it. It dwells largely on the new inconveniences which the sending of a bishop would produce. There is an unfortunate reference to the Vandal persecution in Africa (c. A.D. 500) as a precedent, to the fact that for twenty-seven years the sees there were left without bishops. Confirmation, it is pointed out (and truly), is not a sacrament necessary for salvation. The state of England is witness that Catholicism can survive without it. If it is really necessary some bishops can come over from Ireland and run round administering it with more safety (*festinanter transeuntem administrari*) or—a solution which, curiously enough, was never until this suggested and never adopted— the missionaries might be given power to confirm. The one solid reason for the creation of bishops is to ordain priests, and so long as ordinations can be held abroad there is no need for a bishop in England. A bishop in England might mean ordinations in England, even clergy trained in England, and under what conditions! What wretched priests these would necessarily be! As things are, the English Catholics are well supplied with priests, who visit them regularly in their homes, so that no one, save through his own supine neglect, lacks means for full instruction in

[1] Vol. V, App., pp. ccxxxix–ccxlv (from Gradwell MS. 299). The MS. (in the archives of the English College, Rome) is endorsed in a later hand ' a good piece.'

[2] It occupies four and a half pages, against the single page allotted to Bandini.

his faith, or to receive the sacraments every month.[1] There was no danger, or even difficulty, from the system by which the holy oils were obtained from the Continent, as one would expect seeing that once upon a time all the Oriental churches procured theirs from the one source, viz. the Patriarch of Constantinople.(!) Priests could be given power to consecrate altars, chalices, and the like. Even were there ten bishops in England, priests would still have to do this or go without, such are the difficulties of communication and the dangers on every side from heretics. As to the government of the clergy, it is not necessary that their ruler should be consecrated, for jurisdiction does not depend on the orders of the ruler. The present system by which the Pope himself rules the Church in England through a cardinal protector and subordinate officials is so good that nothing so good can be hoped for from the rule of any bishop. Were there a bishop in England, he would never be able to make a public appearance. He would spend his life in hiding, and need to dress as a layman. None of his flock would dare to give him shelter ; none would dare to approach him. His efforts to enforce discipline would cover him with ridicule, for at his first threats the guilty would simply denounce him to the State. One proof that, in this respect, a bishop would be useless, is that no one of the Catholic bishops who survived Elizabeth's change of religion ever exercised, thereafter, his public jurisdiction.(!) A bishop's authority must be cheapened if he has not at his disposal, a jail, handcuffs, and the power to make the wrongdoer infamous. The whole business of a bishop's jurisdiction *in foro externo* will be impossible. As to the hopes built on the Spanish marriage—the marriage is yet but a project ; and King James, all the world knows, is thoroughly unreliable, as witness his duplicity in the years before he gained the English throne and in the first years that followed it. The ambassadors of France and Spain in London who are now so zealous for the appointment of a bishop, are not really interested in Catholicism ; their sole thought is the welfare of their own nation. Their opinions

---

[1] This roseate picture of Catholic life in England is in such flat contradiction with every other report, from whichever side of the controversy, that it can only be understood in the light of the complaint made later by Propaganda that the Holy Office never realised that there was a régime of persecution in England.

can be set aside. A bishop, it has been said, will keep the
Catholics from sedition and treason. How unlikely this is !
In Ireland there are many bishops ; is there no sedition,
no rebellion in Ireland ? [1] The feud between the seculars
and regulars will be increased rather than healed, by the
appointment of a bishop ; his dignity and office will give
fresh pretexts and there will be yet more ' stirrs.' Especially
is this true because of the close connection between many of
the secular clergy and the Sorbonne, and the extent to
which the opinions of the Gallican bishops of France infect
them. No Pope will dare to correct an English bishop who
can call to his aid the whole body of the Church in France.
And suppose the bishop falls, as Blackwell fell ?   Blackwell
was not the only secular priest to take the oath, and what
about the thirteen who signed the protestation of 1602
' against the Pope's authority and in favour of Queen
Elizabeth ? ' Whatever the merits of the clergy now petitioning, it ought to be borne in mind that the great men of that
body in the past, Allen, Sander, Bristow, and all the great
martyrs and confessors, never dreamed of such a thing as is
now asked for.[2] The petitioners of to-day count among
their number some of those who in 1587 [*i.e.* thirty-five years
before], with Owen Lewis, the Bishop of Cassano, already
dared to set up a quasi-episcopal régime in England. The
risks and dangers to religion which must follow from the
nomination of a bishop in England are, then, too great
for the thing to be done at present. The petition should be
dismissed or put off until a better time.

Cardinal Millini's argument has been given at length

[1] Even anno Dni. 1622, English Catholics and Irish Catholics are as
one. . . .

[2] But Allen was well aware both that in his own time there were scandals,
and that these were due to the lack of proper government, *e.g.* his letter to
Chauncey of Sept. 10, 1577 : '. . . scandals and defects will be and appear
to be. The cause whereof this is specially (which many one seeth not that
reprehendeth it) that in this state of things our Catholic Church, or the relics
and seeds thereof in England hath no form of external common wealth, no
discipline or censures neither to drive the priests nor people into order, no
man subject to his fellow, no way to call disorders to account, no common
conference, no sovereignty nor subjection ; but everyone living severally
and secretly by himself, and often far from any fellows, is ruled only by his
own skill and conscience ; which even among the Apostles had bred disturbance. . . .' (*L.A.*, p. 35.) It may be noted that this letter describes an
England in which the only clergy at work were seculars ; there are not yet
in the vineyard those Jesuit and Benedictine labourers, whose coming
(whatever it added to the complexity of the troubles) cannot be represented
as the troubles' first beginning.

because it is the fullest statement so far discovered of what one may term the official case against the appointment of bishops. It is by no means accurate in its historical references, and it is not the work of one familiar with the actual conditions of Catholic life in England, but it is important to bear it in mind because, although in 1622 the cardinal was overruled—and apparently the whole force of the Holy Office with him [1]—the episcopal restoration lasted less than ten years. There followed yet another fifty years (1631–1685) in which the policy of the Holy Office prevailed once more, and there are signs that the inadequacies of Cardinal Millini's speech hardened—for the officials of the Holy Office—into a kind of traditional view of the English situation, a legend against whose power nothing could prevail.

In 1622, however, it was the case for a bishop that won the day, and John Bennett found the new Pope so amenable that he could write to his brother : ' Had I cared to be importunate I might have had more.'

It was in June, 1622, that the Pope made his decision, and then followed those three summer months in which no man will look for unnecessary activities on the party of any civil service. But Bennett grew anxious. Not until the bishop was named, and indeed consecrated, could he feel sure that, even yet, he might not lose what he had gained. By October he was pressing the Pope anxiously, and then came news that seemed likely to put an end to the affair altogether for another generation.[2] The opposition laid a petition before the Pope in which they told him that James I had heard of the scheme, that he was transported with rage, and that he had sworn that the bishop should never set foot in England. Bennett was sent for and the Pope promised to have the matter investigated. Letters were sent to the ambassadors of the Catholic powers in London asking for information, and Bennett, too, wrote to London, urging the clergy there to use all diligence in ferreting out what had happened.

Soon the matter was clear. It was true indeed that the king had sent to the Spanish ambassador the blood-curdling

[1] Cf. Ingoli : Consideratione del secretario circa lo stato di cattolici e missioni d'Inghilterra rappresentato dal signor agente del vescovo Chalcedonense e del clero anglicano. Die Feb. 28, 1633, A.P., Anglia, 347, f. 363 seq.

[2] Cf. TIERNEY, V, App., No. XXXIX, for the sources, viz. text of the memorandum, Del Risentimento del Re d'Inghilterra, intorno alla concessione di fare Vescovi Inglesi, Bennett's letters, Heynes' Memorandum of his interview with the Lord Keeper, Carandolet's letter of Dec. 27, 1622, to Millini, and the Spanish ambassador in London to the same.

threats which had been reported, and that he had bidden the ambassador transmit these to Rome. But what had been reported to the king was that the Pope was planning to send into England not a single titular bishop, but a whole score of bishops bearing the titles of one-time Catholic sees. There were to be once more a Catholic archbishop of Canterbury, bishops of London, Durham, Lincoln, and the rest. A priest, John Heynes, who was a near kinsman of Bennett, was, so it chanced, personally known to the king's principal minister, John Williams, Lord Keeper of the Great Seal and Bishop of Lincoln. In an interview, Heynes discovered from the statesman what it was that had so enraged the king, and received as much of an assurance as could be given that to the plan actually in contemplation there would be no objection. The further intervention of a cleric [1] in the service of the Spanish ambassador completed the king's enlightenment. The news of what had been attempted in London was passed on to Rome, and now the way was clear. One question alone remained to be settled, who was to be the new bishop ?

In their petition of August, 1621, the assistants to the arch-priest had asked for the appointment of a Spanish Dominican, Diego de la Fuente, one of the Spanish ambassador's chaplains. He was a man with long experience of the affairs of the Church in England and, possibly, it was thought that his foreign nationality would save him from the harassing interference of the pursuivants. But the more any man knew of the affairs of the English Catholics the less likely he must be to desire to carry the whole burden of them. The Spaniard made his excuses and, on December 18, 1621,[2] begged for his name to be taken out of the petition. Three men, apparently, were in men's minds generally as likely subjects, Dr. William Bishop, Dr. Matthew Kellison, and Dr. Richard Smith. The Pope chose Bishop, and his bulls were made out March 15, 1623.[3] As had been explained to King James, he was given a titular see, and Chalcedon being at the moment vacant by the recent translation of Charles Louis de Sales to succeed, as Bishop of Geneva, his

---

[1] Carandolet, Archdeacon of Cambrai.

[2] Letter in TIERNEY, V, App., p. ccclxvii.

[3] Printed TIERNEY, IV, App., p. cclxx. He gives the date, wrongly, as 1622 : not having noticed, apparently, that the reckoning is *Anno Incarnationis* (in which the last day of the year is not Dec. 31, but Mar. 24) and not *Anno Domini*.

cousin, St. Francis de Sales, the first of the new line of bishops in England was styled Bishop of Chalcedon.

The appointment of William Bishop was proof to all the clergy, to seculars and to Regulars alike, that at Rome a wholly different spirit was now inspiring the policy towards English affairs. All three archpriests had been taken from that section of the clergy who were on terms of intimacy with the Society of Jesus : they were, all of them, men who, at any rate, had taken no active share against the Fathers in the controversies of the last twenty-five years, and also they were not, any of them, men of any notable personal quality. But now, for the first bishop, there had been chosen one of the most outstanding of all the Jesuits' opponents, that envoy of 1598, in fact, whom Fr. Persons had had imprisoned in the English College, an unwavering leader of the party of the appellants—though untouched by the excesses which had disgraced more than one of these—and the priest whose signature stood first among the thirteen names on the protestation of loyalty to Elizabeth, which was at the same time so direct a repudiation of the policies of St. Pius V and Gregory XIII.[1]

In the first excitement over the new oath of allegiance, in 1606, Bishop had been of the opinion that it could lawfully be taken, and although he had never taken it himself, nor condoned the taking of it, nor in any way failed in his acceptance of Paul V's condemnation of it, the accusation that he favoured the oath had been too easy for his opponents not to make it, and at one time it actually had been reported to Rome that he had had a share in drafting the oath. Like Newman, nearly three hundred years later, Bishop had lived to see Rome disregard alike his Catholic opponents and his Catholic calumniators. He had given long service in England as a missioner. He had suffered imprisonment and had twice been banished. One period of exile he had used to gain a doctor's degree from the Sorbonne and for some years now he had been one of the chief figures in the little colony of writers who made up the Collège d'Arras. How far would his merits and his gifts outweigh the

---

[1] Law goes so far as to speak of the appointment as ' a triumph for the appellants ' ; it was one of the miseries of the situation that any episcopal appointment must have seemed such, for those who opposed the bishop-schemes had also opposed the appellants. But to name William Bishop as the first bishop was, inevitably, an underlining of what triumph there was.

Dr. William Bishop
(1553–1624)
Bishop of Chalcedon

prejudices that must await him, the inevitable prejudices of the parties with whom he had for so long fought, and the impersonal prejudice of those who thought the new policy of sending a bishop to England wholly inopportune ? Time alone could tell, and, as it happened, Bishop's time was to run out all too shortly. Those who recommended Bishop, and those who appointed him, took a most extraordinary course when they brought about the nomination, for it was a man already seventy years of age that they set to the herculean task, for William Bishop was born, at Brailes in Warwickshire, in 1553.

The new bishop was consecrated, at Paris, on Whit Sunday, June 4, 1623 He arrived in England towards the end of July, and eight months later he died, April 14, 1624. Of that short, but in one respect very fruitful, episcopate we have a valuable account in the report drawn up by the bishops' officials for the information of propaganda.[1]

The bishop's first care, seemingly, before he left France, was to work out some system by which he could govern the vast territory for which he was now responsible, England, Wales, and Scotland. After much consultation of bishops and canonists he mapped out England into a score of districts, over each of which he proposed to set an archdeacon, and over every county of each archdeaconry he set a rural dean. Finally, the most momentous of all his acts, in the light of the history of the next fifty years, he set up a chapter of canons—with some hesitation apparently.

After his consecration he went first from Paris to Douay, and here he discussed with Kellison his plan for a permanent understanding with the Regulars. The scheme was shown to the Douay Benedictines, and they spoke enthusiastically about it. The nuncio at Brussels in whose sphere of observation England had lain since 1622,[2] Bishop did not venture to visit personally, fearing the publicity which a journey to the Belgian capital would involve. Instead he sent John Bennett, to report not only what he was planning in the way of organisation and for the reconciliation of the clergy, but also the history of the long negotiations in the Curia which had preceded his appointment.

The bishop landed near Dover at midnight, and to avoid

[1] Breviarium rerum gestarum p.m. Rmi Dni. Gulielmi Bishopi Epi. Chalcedonen, primi post schisma Angliæ et Scotiæ Ordinarii. A.P., *Anglia*, 347, ff. 11–14 : printed C.R.S., Vol. 10, pp. 224 *seq.* : translation, *ibid.*, 401.
[2] *Acta* S.C.P.F., VI, f. 3, 5⁰.

traps and spies, he walked twelve miles through the storm
to the house of Sir William Roper who was to be his first
host. A few days later he reached London, and here ' a
certain widow who had done much to shelter priests, but
whose name the iniquity of the times forbids us to reveal,'
gave him a home. After a conference with the assistants of
the late archpriest, he took possession of his jurisdiction,
and named the twenty archdeacons (five of whom were
also appointed vicars-general) and the rural deans, and the
notaries attached to each. Finally he announced his
nominations to the chapter and of all this he sent an account
to the Holy See.[1]

The bishop's main anxiety, however, was to administer
the sacrament of confirmation. This he did for the first
time at Cowdray in Sussex, where he confirmed four hundred
people, and among them his host, Viscount Montague.
Wherever he went he was received, as we can readily
believe, with the utmost joy, and in the two months of
September and October, 1623, he confirmed another two
thousand. Then he returned to London, to discuss with the
Regulars his plan for an understanding. The Benedictines
and most other religious accepted the proposals willingly,
but the Jesuits—though very amicably—appear to have
objected that they were not in a position to agree to anything without consulting their General. It was explained
that the whole affair was ultimately to go to Rome for
ratification, and that it would be submitted to the General
as well as to Propaganda. And here the matter seems to
have ended, so far as the Jesuits were concerned. The
pact with the Benedictines bears the date November 29,
1623, There would hardly be time for the Jesuits to consult
their superiors in Rome, for these to discuss the matter and
reply before the bishop's last illness and death some four
months later.

Dr. Bishop had to steer very carefully between exposing
himself rashly to the pursuivants and seeming to fear
the pains that lay in wait for him. As the opponents of the

[1] This letter I have never found. It is not in the archives of Propaganda,
but there is a reference to it in the *Acta* of the congregation under the date
Jan. 10, 1624. The letter is noted as read and it is also noted that the Pope
was very pleased but, on the advice of the cardinals, referred the matter of
the chapter to the Holy Office for its consideration, ' since it was by a decree
of the said Congregation of the Holy Office that this bishop of Chalcedon
was first given to England.' *Acta*, S.C.P.F. t. 3, fol. 81, 4º.

scheme had foretold, there was a great outcry from the
Puritans once it was known that a bishop was at work in
England, and an increased activity generally amongst the
magistrates and pursuivants. The Catholics, on the other
hand, were apparently greatly stimulated, and from all
parts of the country, men and women, of all grades of
society, made their way to the bishop to be confirmed.
The government does not appear to have been at all hostile,
and when anti-Catholic zeal began really to stir up public
feeling, privately advised the bishop to go overseas until
the excitement had died down. This, of course, he refused
to do, replying to the friendly minister, that he was as
ready to go to prison a third time for Christ as he had been
twice already.

We have little information about the bishop's last days.[1]
Apparently he died simply worn out by his work and by
exposure, after a week's illness, at Bishopshall in Essex,[2]
April 14, 1624. As he lay dying, prayers were asked for him,
and particularly the bishop turned to those whom he had
confirmed. His patrimony, twelve hundred a year, he had
long ago made over to his younger brother. What money
he had in his possession at death was to go to the use of the
clergy. William Bishop passed from life as simply as he had
passed through it, and when they came to prepare his body
for burial, the secret of a lifetime was revealed in the hair-
shirt that he had retained even during his last illness.[3]

The old charges against the bishop's orthodoxy did not,
of course, die with him, and the nuncio in France,
announcing his death to Propaganda, says : ' People speak
very diversely about his faith. There are some will have it
he was imbued with Edmund Richier's anti-papal theories,
and that he was one of those who subscribed to the English
oath.' [4] Such charges, indeed, hung permanently over the
secular clergy until in the next generation, it became more
profitable to their enemies to suggest that they were all
Jansenists.

The details of William Bishop's treaty of peace with the

[1] ' I hear that the Bishop of Chalcedon is acting with prudence and is
doing his duty, but I have nothing particular to report to Your Illustrious
Lordship.' The nuncio in Flanders (di Bagno) to Cardinal Ludovisi, Mar. 2,
1624. A.P., *Anglia*, 347, f. 216.
[2] *Southcott's Diary*, C.R.S., Vol. I, p. 100.
[3] *De Morte R. D. G. Bishopi Epi. Cal. Ordin. Angliæ & Scotiæ* in A.P.
Anglia, 347, ff. 19–20.
[4] Letter of May 23, 1624 : A.P., *Anglia*, 347, f. 276.

English Benedictines have been preserved.[1] The main consideration, on the bishop's part, is to find a means of knowing what priests are actually at work in England, which of them are seculars, which Regulars (and therefore who in England is responsible for their conduct), what faculties they possess, and where they live and work. The Benedictines have to maintain their traditional exemption from episcopal authority and whatever other rights and privileges the order possesses. The eleven canons cover the whole field where the two jurisdictions—that of the bishop and that of the superiors of the order—may seem to overlap. It is, then, agreed as follows : (1) To satisfy the bishop's conscience in the matter, the Benedictine superiors agree to tell him the number and names of all the monks now at work in England. For the future they will notify him of all new arrivals, and of their sufficiency, and the local superior, once the new man has taken up his residence, will notify this to the vicar-general of the district ; (2) As to delinquent monks (*i.e.* those guilty of a notorious offence that gives public scandal), the bishop, hearing of such, shall inform the Benedictine superior, and it is for him to see to the correction of the offender. He will also certify the bishop or district vicar-general what has been done. If nothing is done, then the bishop, or vicar-general, will, according to his discretion, punish the offender as the Council of Trent lays down ; (3) provides for an exchange of hospitality between the two groups ; (4) the monks undertake to use their influence with their own benefactors to obtain alms towards the bishop's maintenance : contributions thus obtained to be sent to the bishop by the Benedictine provincials ; (5) neither monks nor the clergy will take for their respective group any church property except what they know to be expressly the property of the group ; (6) the Benedictines, as an exempt order, are not bound to attend the bishop's synod as are the secular clergy. But, for the sake of peace and to help on the good work of order and discipline, as well as to give the benefit of their knowledge and experience, the president of the English Benedictines and the two provincials will attend the synod. The president is to have the next place after the bishop, the

---

[1] *Canones Ecclesiastici ad pacem et disciplinam inter clerum secularem et monachos Benedictinos conservandas a Rmo in Xto Patre et Dno. Dno. Gulielmo epo. Chalcedonen. propositi.* A.P., *Anglia*, 347, ff. 15–17.

provincials after the vicars-general, and other prelates of
the order after the archdeacons. Graduates are to sit in the
order of their promotion, and other priests according to the
date of ordination *nisi quid venerabilis aetas aut mutua dilectio
aut alia iusta ratio suaserit* ; (7) the Roman Ritual is to be
used by all in the administration of the sacraments, *with what
change the Synod shall think fit.*[1] Secular priests are not to
change penances imposed by Regulars—and vice versa.
No secular shall confess penitents whose usual confessor is
a monk (and vice versa) unless it is certain that they have
not left their usual confessor for a wrong reason, *e.g.* because
they find their usual confessor too strict in such matters as
expenditure on pleasure, gaming, dress, feasts, and the like ;
(8) lest scandal be given to non-Catholics by our legal
decisions, it is ordained that no priest or monk shall grant
any dispensation, or in any way interfere in any grave case
of doubt or controversy, especially in what concerns marriages to be contracted, in disputes about restitution where
transfers of patrimony or an inheritance may bring serious
loss to one of the parties, and in cases where a suit in the
civil courts can be foreseen—unless the priest or monk has
first discussed the matter with the bishop. It shall then be
lawful, for those (monks included) who enjoy such a papal
power, to proceed to the dispensation or decision without
awaiting any further permission from the bishop. So that
the monks may not feel that in this they are being fettered
by the seculars, the bishop will admit some of them to what
meetings are necessary to discuss such cases ; (9) by the
Canon Law, the ancient custom of the English Church,
and the Council of Trent, the bishop is the custodian of
charitable bequests. Monks, as well as priests, will, therefore,
see to it that all such pious bequests are made known to
the bishop so that he may satisfy himself that the wishes of
the testator have been faithfully carried out ; (10) all
disputes between monks and secular priests are to be
settled by arbitrators appointed by the bishop and the
president of the Congregation ; (11) finally, it is forbidden,
both to monks and to priests, to attack in conversations or
in sermons the customs or actions of any order, state, or
individual. No one is to seek, under any pretext, to drive

[1] Against the phrase here underlined there is a note in the handwriting of
Mgr Francis Ingoli, secretary of Propaganda, ' Non semper sustineri posse
quod hic statuit cum ad papam mutatio rituum pertinet.'

another from his residence. No one is to put obstacles to the collection of alms from the willing faithful, whether the alms are meant for their own group or for any other : abuses in this are to be corrected by the respective superiors.

The pact is dated November 29, 1623, and to it the following signatures are attached : Fr. Joseph of St. Martin,[1] Canterbury Provincial ; Fr. Leander of St. Martin,[2] prior of St. Gregory's [3] [Douay], in the name of the Very Reverend Father M. Rudesind Barlow, President General of the Benedictine Order in England ; William, Bishop of Chalcedon, Ordinary of England and Scotland. A few weeks later, January 15, 1624, Fr. Barlow wrote to the bishop gladly accepting the agreement and canons, and, supposing a permanent commission of arbitrators, he named six of his monks, three for England and three for the Low Countries : naming, for the first, Fr. Benedict Jones and the two English provincials ; for abroad, Fr. Leander, Fr. Thomas, and Fr. Edward Mayhew.[4]

This happy event is the more noteworthy because the Benedictines had had a grievance all their own against William Bishop. When Fr. Rudesind Barlow wrote, in 1622, to the Clergy Agent at Rome in support of the petition for a bishop, he urged that either Smith or Kellison should be nominated. Bishop he passed over, because, asked if he would respect the privileges of the Benedictines, he had answered, ominously, that would be seen when the time came to discuss what their privileges were. Apparently it was not prejudice which had prompted the reply, but the lawyer's sense of order which, in the event, the pact with the monks proved Bishop to possess in such large measure.

[1] I.e. Joseph Prater, cf. C.R.S., Vol. 33, pp. 197–198.
[2] I.e. John Jones, the first president (1619–1621) of the restored congregation, cf. ibid., p. 199.
[3] Actually the text has ' George ' here, but it is ' Gregory ' that is meant.
[4] A.P., Anglia, 347, f. 18.

CHAPTER III

RICHARD SMITH, BISHOP OF CHALCEDON, 1625–1627

ROME learnt of William Bishop's death from letters [1] sent by Colleton, as dean of the chapter lately set up. The chapter asked that another bishop be sent in William Bishop's place, but made no suggestion as to whom Rome should appoint. Meanwhile the confirmation of the chapter and the grant to its dean of the faculties once given to the arch-priest, would be useful during the interregnum. The letter spoke of the immense work that lay before the bishop, and urged that not one but three bishops should be appointed. From the anti-episcopal camp in England, came a letter in the contrary sense.[2] The writer criticised the late bishop's activities and argued that the experiment should now cease. If a bishop were sent his jurisdiction should be severely limited.

The Roman authorities were hardly likely to hurry over an appointment that was bound to meet with opposition, but they had probably made up their minds to appoint a bishop, and to appoint Richard Smith when, in December, 1624, they received a letter recommending Smith or Kellison from the President of the English Benedictines.[3] On January 2, 1625, Smith was appointed, and a month later the brief was made out [4] delegating to him for England and

---

[1] (1) April 15, 1624, to Ludovico Ludovisi, the Cardinal Protector of England, A.P., *Anglia*, 347, f. 219.

(2) April 21, 1624, to the Cardinals of Propaganda, *ibid.*, f. 220.

[2] *Exemplar litterarum ex Anglia . . . de conditionibus in creando epo. requisitis.* Archives of the English College, Rome; no signature; dated May 6, 1624, o.s., inc. *Accepistis ut opiner.*

[3] Rudesind Barlow, O.S.B., to S.C.P.F., Douay, Dec. 12, 1624, A.P., *Anglia*, 347, ff. 135–136. PANZANI states that the Jesuits opposed the nomination of Smith because he was a partisan of France. *Relatione*, f. 5.

[4] *Ecclesia Romana Sollicita*, Feb. 4, 1625; this is word for word the same as the brief of Mar. 23, 1623, to William Bishop, except for one additional paragraph, 'teque ad præmissa omnia et singula auctoritate et tenore

Scotland all the faculties of an ordinary. It is important to notice that the new bishop was not the nominee of Propaganda, as were the vicars-apostolic later and all the bishops of England down to 1908 when this country ceased to be ranked as a missionary country. The congregation of Propaganda was as yet hardly organised. The prestige of the older congregation of the Holy Office still overshadowed all else in the Curia. It was here that all grants of faculties to bishops were made, and when Colleton's petition of April, 1624, came before Propaganda, July 7, 1624, the Pope [1] ordered that the appointment be delayed until the resolution of the Holy Office was taken ' in which congregation the business of the demand for a bishop in England is dealt with.' [2] The Holy Office, this time, was favourable to the demand, and it was by a decree of the Holy Office that Smith was appointed. [3]

Somewhere towards the end of April, [4] 1625, the new bishop, styled Bishop of Chalcedon like his predecessor, crossed into England. Richard Smith, at this great moment in his life, was a man in his fifty-eighth year. He was born at Hanworth, a few miles from Lincoln, in 1567, and his parents were either Protestants, or else Catholics who had conformed since Elizabeth's accession. While at Trinity College, Oxford, Smith was converted to the old faith (1586) [5] and left England for the English College at Rome. Here he began his personal experience of the religious with whom his whole life was to be so bound up, for both this college (where he remained until 1588) and Valladolid

prædictis delegamus. Causarum tamen in secunda instantia cognitionem et terminationem, omnemque a quocumque gravamine recursum nostro apud charissimum filium Ludovicum Francorum regem christianissimum nunc et pro tempore existenti nuntio reservamus et reservata esse volumus ; cui non intendimus per præsentes ullatenus præjudicare,' *i.e.* the nuncio at Paris is constituted the judge of any appeals from decisions of the English bishop's tribunal. DODD (III, p. 7) prints both briefs in parallel columns. TIERNEY prints the brief to William Bishop with the bull appointing him to the see of Chalcedon and a decree giving him power to name a vicar-general (Vol. III, App., No. LVII).

[1] Urban VIII, elected Aug. 6, 1623 ;   Gregory XV had died July 8 previously.
[2] Endorsement by the Secretary of Propaganda (Mgr Francis Ingoli) on Colleton's letter, A.P., *Anglia*, 347, f. 220. *Cf.* also *Acta*, S.C.P.F., July 7, 1624.
[3] Decree in MAZIERE BRADY, III, p. 74.
[4] *Southcott's Diary*, in C.R.S., I, p. 100.
[5] The bald statement in PASTOR (Vol. 27, p. 304), ' Smith was a convert,' though true, hardly conveys the truth that Smith had been a Catholic nearly forty years at the moment of which Pastor is writing.

(where he spent the next six years) and Seville (where he
taught from 1598 to 1602) were under the management of
Jesuit superiors. The future opponent of Fr. Persons and of
Fr. Persons' successors had thus his first experience of
Catholicism as a pupil of the Society, when through sixteen
years together, the adolescent of eighteen grew into the man
of thirty-four in Jesuit-directed colleges. At Valladolid he
taught philosophy for a time and, with some unusual éclat,
took his doctorate in theology. He left for England in 1602
and, family business delaying him, he spent some months
teaching at Douay. Then, after an absence of seventeen
years, he took up the work of a missionary in Sussex, as
assistant, for that county, to the archpriest. He served as
chaplain to Viscountess Montague and for the next six years
lived in her household at Battle Abbey. Smith's Latin life
of this saintly woman was one of his earliest publications.

It was shortly after her death that archpriest Birkhead
sent him to Rome in 1609, as has been told, and here he
won from Fr. Persons the commendation of being the most
stubborn man the Jesuit had ever had to deal with.

The Roman mission over, Smith returned to the scholastic
life and became the senior of the newly founded English
house of studies at Paris, the Collège d'Arras. This very
modest establishment was one of the most interesting of all
the Catholic ventures of the penal times, for it was a college
where all were priests, and its aim was ' to associate some of
the ripest and most quiet, sociable men to write,' and to
lodge and maintain those reading for degrees at the Sorbonne ; also ' to procure some relief for learned ministers
converted, and other such like scholars.' Allen had long
had in mind such a foundation, but had never had either
the means or the men to spare for it.[1] Now in 1612, stimulated by James I's charter establishing just such a college
at Chelsea, a group of secular priests founded the Collège
d'Arras, with the financial support of ' Mr. T. S.'[2] The
English Benedictines assisted the enterprise nobly by
introducing it to the notice of that abbey of St. Vaast at
Arras which had already sponsored so much of the effort
to save the faith in England. It was, indeed, in a property of the abbey now made over to its use that the new
community was housed. There were no more than five

[1] *Cf.* Fitzherbert's Vita Alani in *L.A.*, p. 17.
[2] Thomas Sackville ; so TIERNEY, IV, pp. 136–137 ; cclxix.

priests to make a beginning—Dr. Bishop, Dr. Kellison, Dr. Smith, Dr. Champney, ' and Mr. William Smith, a grave and ancient priest, and a very good linguist ' [1]—but all of them, to judge from what they produced, were learned and able publicists, and the standard they set up was steadily maintained by their successors for the next seventy years. Richard Smith was the most prolific of this first group of writers, and his many books cover a very varied field.[2]

It was from ten years' work among such studies that the first bishop of Chalcedon proposed to call Smith when, in 1623, he named him one of the canons of his chapter, but Smith was still in Paris when he was nominated to succeed William Bishop. When was he consecrated ? Mazière Brady [3] says on January 12, 1625, but this would seem doubtful, since the brief dated three weeks later still styles him bishop-elect.' His predecessor had been consecrated by the nuncio, now Cardinal Spada, and it was Spada, too, who consecrated Richard Smith. One would like to think it might well have been a personage still more famous, the Cardinal de Richelieu. For to Richelieu, now in the first flush of his power as Louis XIII's minister,[4] Richard Smith was very well known indeed. Richelieu had become Bishop of Luçon at the early age of twenty-one, and his first anxiety had been to fit himself for the work he proposed to do by acquiring the necessary professional knowledge. He needed to know some theology, and Richard Smith was recommended to him as a tutor. So for a space of time, somewhere between 1605 and 1608, that was to be much more important in Smith's career than many much longer periods of work, he daily tutored in theology the juvenile prelate who was one day to be France's greatest minister. If Richelieu, twenty years later, did not himself consecrate his one-time tutor, he certainly had not forgotten him for

---

[1] Cf. Regulations for the Establishment at Arras College, April 28, 1612, printed by TIERNEY, IV, App., p. cclxix, from Dr. Smith's copy.

[2] GILLOW gives a list of some seventeen published works, and states that there are (or were) other works never published. The earliest is An Answer to Thomas Bell's late Challenge named . . . the Downfall of Popery, published at Douay in 1605, 466 pp., 8vo ; the last, published in the bishop's eighty-seventh year, is the Florum Historiæ Ecclesiasticæ gentis Anglorum. . . . Paris, 1654 ; this also runs to over four hundred pages.

[3] This is the date given also by John Southcott, who was later Smith's secretary ; cf. Diary, in C.R.S., Vol. 1, p. 100.

[4] Richelieu took up his office April 29, 1624, cf. Lettres du C- de Richelieu, I, p. 788.

French ambassador in London to
...s he could.

...ichard Smith's rule were peaceful.
...e visitation of the huge province
...he administration of confirmation.
...ng so eagerly,' he wrote to Propa-
...t,' and he describes how they came,
...s of them, from all over England
... So many requests had come in to
...e country that he doubted whether
...y them.[1] By the date of this letter
... two months in progress. It was
...ear and a half, and in February,
...eport that he had visited every part

...n England had coincided with the
...reign.[2] Charles I was king, young,
...tractive, and, what was all important
...ed to a Catholic princess, the sister
... The marriage took place in May,
...lic queen at Whitehall and the new
...there should be no more persecution,
...olics must have run high indeed.
Smith wrote to Rome that orders from the king had slackened
the activities of the pursuivants, but as the opening of
Parliament came nearer the bishop grew anxious, and spoke
of the Catholics as kept in continued suspense.[4] They had
now, working for them at Court, the French ambassador,
and Henrietta Maria's two chief almoners, the Bishop of
Mende and Fr. de Bérulle. But what would this influence
achieve once Parliament met ' breathing out threats ? '[5]

The anxieties were, of course, fully justified. Before the
year 1625 was out the marriage treaty was disregarded,
the machinery of the law once again in active employment,
Catholics everywhere were suffering and many priests were
thrown into prison.[6] The storm, so Smith reported, was

[1] Smith to S.C.P.F. ; Winton, Sept. 7, 1625. A.P. *Lettre Antiche*,101,
f. 10.   [2] James I died Mar. 27, 1625.
[3] May 10, before the great door of Notre Dame, Paris. The queen arrived
in England on June 12.
[4] Parliament met June 28, 1625.
[5] Letters of April 28 and June 28, 1625 ; A.P., *Anglia*, 347, ff. 242,
190–193.
[6] Letters of Fr. Simon Stock, Carm. Disc., to S.C.P.F. ; London, Dec.
5 and 15, 1625. For Fr. Simon (*vere* Thomas Doughty), *cf.* ZIMMERMAN,
pp. 23–40.

greater than any within living memory, and since the chief
form it took was the confiscation of property, the whole
Catholic body seemed menaced with utter ruin. What
slight resources the bishop himself possessed had all gone in
helping the victims of the great plague which had raged in
London during the previous autumn. The poorer Catholics,
he writes, are already in a state of great poverty, and he
does not know where to find means to help them.[1] Everywhere, he explains to his agent, Catholics are being rounded
up and prosecuted for recusancy—the first legal step to the
confiscation of their goods. In Buckinghamshire, at the
Lenten assizes, 208 were brought into court : in London
close on a thousand.[2] More than five thousand Catholics
have been driven from their homes.[3]

The bishop reports [4] that the young queen—she was only
seventeen—is standing firm in the domestic persecution to
which she has been subjected. If many of the weaker sort
are falling away, driven by the fear they will lose all their
goods, many others of the wealthy Catholics are constant.
In September, 1626, it was rumoured that warrants were
out for the bishop's arrest also.

It was then through a community deeply troubled that
Smith journeyed to make the first visitation which the
Catholic Church in England had known for nearly seventy
years. No report of it survives, nor any itinerary. That
many irregularities in procedure would be found may—
in the light of what we know of the history of the previous
thirty years—be taken for granted. We might also guess
that not everywhere was the bishop's arrival welcomed.
Not only the froward would look askance at his coming,
and the authority it implied, but also those good men who
sincerely believed they were altogether exempt from his
authority. Here was a situation of novel delicacy, the
presence, within the geographical frontiers of a bishop's
jurisdiction, of priests belonging to orders that were exempt
from episcopal jurisdiction, but who were yet not living the
normal lives of the exempt religious orders, religious who
had no monasteries or common life, and who were engaged

[1] Smith to Ludovisi, Mar. 31, 1626 ; A.P., *Lett. Ant.*, 101, f. 3.
[2] London, Mar. 18–29, 1626 ; A.P., *Lett. Ant.*, 101, f. 3.
[3] Excerpt from Smith's letter in *Acta*, S.C.P.F., Vol. 4, Cong. 38, No. 17,
Mar. 31, 1626.
[4] Smith-Agent, July 13, 1626, in A.P., *Anglia*, 347, f. 195.

in exactly the same work as the bishop's own secular clergy, the pastoral work of preaching, and administering the sacraments.

For the innumerable difficulties that might be expected to arise from such an unprecedented state of things the Roman authorities had not made any explicit provision— nor is it easy to see how they could have done so. The bishop was given a very generous jurisdiction, expressed, however, not in any list of faculties such as the archpriest had had, but in the general terms of the brief that deputed him.[1] The terms of the brief were definite, and they were general, and very soon they became the subject of keen controversy. '. . . 'tis a very intricate controversy,' said Dodd, who was a pioneer in the attempt to unravel it, ' and in no way diverting.' [2] The part Richard Smith played in it, as the story has usually been told, is far from creditable.[3] He is given credit for honesty of purpose, for learning, for general uprightness, but is described as acting with such lack of tact, such rash imprudence, that he appears a very bull in the china shop. No attempt will be made here to describe the controversy as a whole, nor to write its history. But the bishop's own account of it has never really been set out, and it seems more than worth while to perform this act of justice to the memory of a very great champion of the faith, and a man who deserved a better fate than befell him, if only because he wrote the little book that was the spiritual vade-mecum [4] of generations of secular clergy in the dreary years that lay between Richard Smith's death and the Catholic renaissance of the nineteenth century. And no

[1] The words of the brief (*Ecclesia Romana Sollicita*, Feb. 4, 1625) are : ' Tibi . . . ad nostrum et sedis apostolicæ beneplacitum, omnibus et singulis facultatibus olim archipresbyteris . . . concessis, nec non quibus ordinarii in suis civitatibus et dioecesibus utuntur, fruuntur et gaudent, ac uti, frui, et gaudere possunt, similiter uti frui et gaudere libere et licite possis et valeas, apostolica auctoritate, tenore præsentium [concedimus et indulgemus ac] licentiam et facultatem impertimur ' (Dodd, III, p. 7), *i.e.* a specific grant of whatever had been granted to the archpriests, and also the permission and power to use, enjoy, and freely exercise whatever faculties diocesan bishops use, enjoy, and exercise in their cities and dioceses.

[2] *History of Douay College*, 1714, p. 24.

[3] For the latest repetition of what may be called the legend, *cf.* PASTOR, Vol. 29, p. 303 and following (London, 1938).

[4] *Monita quædam utilia pro acerdotibus seminaristis missionariis Angliæ. Una cum methodo agendi cum Hereticis, Schismaticis, et Catholicis Anglis.* Authore R. Smitheo, Epo. Chalcedonensi, Angliæ and Scotiæ Ordinario. Paris, 1647. 18mo, pp. 154 ; reprinted Douay, 1680 (?) ; London, 1695, 12mo ; London, 1741, small 8vo.

one familiar with Challoner's *Missionary Priests* will fail to recall the continual reference in it to the *Bishop of Chalcedon's Catalogue*, the first official act in the process of the canonisation of the English martyrs, a most important document which we owe to Richard Smith's theological skill and practical gift of organisation.

Richard Smith, as we have seen, came to England as bishop for the English Catholics in April, 1625. He left England for France in August, 1631, and though he lived for another twenty-five years nearly, he never saw England again. The Regulars, so he contended, were from the beginning determined to get him out, not because he was Richard Smith, but because they meant not to have a bishop in England. His attempt to lay the foundations of order in the formless chaos of the Church in England gave them their opportunity. It was used unscrupulously, and successfully. From August, 1631, until September, 1685, Catholic England was delivered from any such regularity as the rule of bishops. The troublesome parties, from the bishop's point of view, were the superiors of the two orders to which, after the secular clergy, most of the priests belonged, the Jesuits and the newly restored English Benedictines.[1] With these last, Richard Smith's predecessor had recently made a concordat. But it was around a point not touched by that agreement that the new trouble centred, the question, namely, whether the missionaries in England who belonged to the religious orders needed the bishop's ' approbation ' before they could validly hear confessions, and from this the dispute passed to the more fundamental question of the nature of Smith's authority. Was he a bishop with the same powers over England which diocesan bishops enjoyed with regard to their dioceses ? Or was he no more than the superior of just the secular clergy ? The new controversy, then, had to do with intricate questions of Canon Law, but its issue, for the ordinary man, seemed to be the very practical point whether the absolutions he was receiving were really valid or not.

While Richard Smith's appointment was still under consideration there broke out in the English College at Rome

---

[1] The Jesuits numbered a total of 133 priests in England in 1625, 164 in 1632 (FOLEY, *Gen.* I, p. lxxiii–lxxv) ; the Benedictines of the English Congregation had sixty-three priests in England in 1633 (C.R.S., Vol. 33, p. 265). There were, perhaps, 400 secular priests.

yet another of the periodic disturbances between the students and their Jesuit superiors. This time the cause was the alleged undue influence brought to bear by the superiors to persuade the students to enter the Society. The disturbance was settled by a papal decree forbidding any seminarist of any of the colleges to be accepted by any religious order until the question of his vocation had been decided by an outside commission. So ended the last of these great ' stirrs,' and it is only mentioned here to recall that the new bishop began his work in an atmosphere still warm from recent conflict.

One of Richard Smith's earliest letters as bishop is written to thank Propaganda for the decree that had brought peace to the college, and to suggest with all possible force that the mission in England has the first claim on the seminaries, and that the secular clergy of England have a special claim to the Holy See's consideration if only because, in recent years, 130 of them have given their lives in defence of its primacy.[1] In June, 1625, he writes of his resolve to give himself to the work of reconciling the divers labourers in the vineyard,[2] and in September Propaganda is asked about a scheme in which Henrietta Maria's almoner, the Bishop of Mende, shall arbitrate between the contending parties.[3] Why this scheme did not come into operation does not seem to be known. The cardinals did not reject it out of hand, but ordered that it should be submitted to the nuncios at Paris and Brussels, who would make enquiries and forward the results with their own opinions. Their replies do not seem to have survived, at any rate in the Propaganda archives.

The first inharmonious note about the Regulars is a letter from the bishop [4] in which he complains that the

[1] It was this reference to the martyrs which led to the composition of the bishop's Catalogue of Martyrs, for on receipt of this letter, dated Sept. 7, 1625, the cardinals ordered the bishop to send to Rome a note of all the martyrs, giving their names, surnames, birth-places, date of death, and the way they were put to death (endorsement on the letter), A. P., *Lett. Ant.*, 101, f. 10 *seq.*; *cf.* also, *Acta*, S.C.P.F., of Feb. 6, 1626. The bishop's acknowledgment of this command and his promise to do all he can to carry it out is in his letter of Mar. 29, 1626, to his agent. If he had been able to find helpers as keen as himself, he says—none too hopefully—something would already have been done about it. The letter is in A.P., *Lett. Ant.*, 101, f. 3.

[2] Smith to S.C.P.F., London, June 28, 1625 ; A.P., *Anglia*, 347, ff. 190–193.

[3] A. P., *Acta*, S.C.P.F., Vol. 3, Cong. 262, No. 10, Sept. 19, 1625

[4] Read in the Congregation of Mar. 31, 1625 ; A. P., *Acta*, of that date, Vol. 4, Cong. 38, No. 17.

Jesuits did not do their duty by the plague-stricken Catholics in the previous autumn (1625). In June, 1626, his agent is drawing the notice of the Sacred Congregation to the interference of fathers of the same Society in the affairs of the new secular college at Lisbon, and to their alleged mismanagement of the secular college at Madrid.[1] The question of the distribution of alms also brought the bishop, if not into conflict, into close contact with the different orders. For he wrote very urgently to Rome explaining the great needs of his people, and asking that moneys collected should be sent rather to the various archdeacons for distribution at home. Propaganda was agreeable, and promised to write to the generals of the orders to instruct the regular missionaries to fall in with the scheme. To judge from the several later complaints on the subject the trouble seems not to have been cured.[2]

In July, 1626, the bishop again consults Rome about a problem where Jesuits are concerned. Within the last three or four years, he says, six or seven Jesuits have been expelled from the Society, some of them for scandalous misconduct. These ex-religious have, none the less, not been deprived of their faculties. If their faculties are taken away, they must starve, for their priesthood is their living. But to allow such men to go on ministering to souls is obviously dangerous. Moreover, if the secular clergy are to be bound to take in such *eiecti*, what will the position be like in a few years ?[3] The bishop's doubts are resolved by a decision given September 7, 1626. Regulars, he is told, who are sent into England by the generals, by virtue of apostolic privileges, with faculties to administer the sacraments, may not make use of these faculties if, expelled from their order, they enter the ranks of the secular clergy. Nor can rectors of pontifical seminaries grant to dismissed Regulars who are now secular priests the same faculties which they grant to their own students, supposing these Regulars have not previously received such faculties from their own generals. Nor, again, can Regulars who have such faculties for England, from the rector of a pontifical college, use them once they have been dismissed from the order in which they

---

[1] Congregation of June 1, 1626 ; A. P., *Acta*, S.C.P.F., Vol. 4, Cong. 63, No. 25 and 24.

[2] Congregation of 16 June, 1626 ; A.P., *Acta*, S.C.P.F., 4–70–12.

[3] Letter of July 13, 1626 ; A. P., *Anglia*, 347, f. 195 ; decision in *Acta*, 4–117–16.

were professed. So much for the general principles of the matter. As to the particular case of the ex-Jesuits, it is left to the bishop's prudence to decide in each case what is best to be done. This incident is not, perhaps, of any general importance, but it does show Smith—as indeed it seems to me, his whole correspondence shows him—as anxious not to try any innovation, and as desirous, at every step, of guidance from higher authority.

Smith touched a far more delicate matter when he wrote to suggest to the cardinals of Propaganda that it would be well, until the present factions among Catholics were ended, to suspend the sodality of the Immaculate Conception. Here is one of those occasions on which a Catholic's familiarity with the Catholic practice of to-day can be an obstacle to his immediate understanding of the practice of the Catholic past. Nothing could sound more strange than such a request from a bishop. But the famous Jesuit sodality had apparently become in England a source of trouble. It divided the laity into sodality Catholics and non-sodality Catholics, and the fathers were stated to oblige their sodalists to confess only to Jesuits. Cases were cited of sodalists dying without the sacraments rather than confess to the only available, non-Jesuit, priest. And at a time when—it was one of the major ills—a priest's priesthood was, only too literally, his living, the extension of the sodality meant, under these circumstances, the gradual extension of the Jesuit hold on Catholic resources, and the starving out of the other clergy.[1]

The bishop is not extravagant in his language, nor in his demand. He speaks of the sodality question as one of the ' inconveniences ' (*incommoda*) that have come to his notice during the visitation. He leaves it to the cardinals to make the decision, and he does not press the matter unduly. What he asks is either a suspension of the sodality, or that all priests should be given power to admit to it whoever wills to become a member. This would destroy all chance of its being a special clique.[2]

So far we see the bishop confidentially putting his difficulties before the Roman authorities. At the same time,

---

[1] And especially the starving out of the secular clergy, so they complained, because while the Jesuits had their sodality, the other religious had each some like association to bind the laymen especially to them.

[2] Letter of Sept. 20, 1626 ; A. P., *Lett. Ant.*, 129, f. 199 *seq.*

as the months went by, his activities began to arouse criticism. ' The fathers of the Society begin to speak openly against my visitation,' he wrote to his agent,[1] ' and they are spreading unbelievable calumnies about me.' The subject of these calumnies was the bishop's attitude to the Oath of Allegiance, that had so fatally divided the Catholics since the days of Blackwell's fall and continued still to divide them. ' Some of them have written to my illustrious protector, saying that when I am consulted about the oath I answer in a lukewarm way and ambiguously.' The bishop has, therefore, sent to the cardinal, what he sends now to his agent also, a copy of the letter that he wrote to the nobles who asked his opinion. This letter is a simple reminder that the question of the lawfulness of the oath has been decided once and for all by the Holy See. To this the bishop can add nothing, except to remind them of the number of martyrs who have given their lives rather than take it. The nobles had asked if they could not take the oath with a mental reservation ; but the bishop points out that this would be no more lawful than to assist at heretical services with a like reservation. That suffering will follow on refusal of the oath must not, he says, daunt any of us. We must not shrink from following where others have gone before us, and the bishop cites the classic confessor Francis Tregian, who lost all his wealth for his association with Bl. Cuthbert Mayne and lay in an Elizabethan prison for the next twenty-five years.[2]

The answer is, of course, all that one would expect from a man of Smith's antecedents. It is the charge that is incredible, and, just as incredible to us, the fact that the charge was made. But the atmosphere in which all these men lived, in which they were born and had their whole being, was an unnatural, strained, and deforming atmosphere, and the charges so frequently met with are perhaps more important as testimony to the unhealthy life that is the lot of the persecuted, than to the possibilities of wickedness either in the accuser or the accused.

Smith ends his letter to his agent with a request. ' Beg their lordships to keep their ears fast closed against such charges as these. Otherwise they shall never know rest,

[1] Sept. 6, 1626 ; A. P., *Anglia*, 347, f. 197.
[2] Smith's letter to his agent is in A. P., *Anglia*, 347, f. 197 ; the letter to the nobles in *Lett. Ant.*, 101, f. 12, endorsed as read on Dec. 16, 1626.

nor I have ever any heart to carry out their commands. Moreover, it is disgraceful that a bishop's good name should be jeopardised by tales to which no one witnesses, set round without any proof.' And this same letter witnesses that Smith has, in the course of his visitation, published the brief condemning the oath.

The first complaint [1] made against the bishop, so far as the archives of Propaganda provide a record, is the letter of a missionary of the Cassinese Congregation of the Benedictines, Dom David Codner, dated January 10, 1627.[2] Apparently the writer has not been long in England, and he complains to the secretary of the Sacred Congregation, Mgr. Francis Ingoli, that the Bishop of Chalcedon had hidden himself away so well that he has failed so far to find him, though he has searched and searched. The London vicar-general, George Muscott, has been just as inaccessible. The monk's faculties are given conditionally on the bishop's accepting him. What is he to do ? Is he to stand idle all the day ? He explains that the persecution has greatly slackened in the last few weeks, except in the case of the bishop and his vicar-general. Special orders, it is said for certain, have been given for their arrest. The letter goes on to describe how dangerous it is to write to correspondents abroad, but the writer will brave the risk and not leave Rome without news of his activities. Meanwhile he is watching most keenly for a chance of presenting himself to the bishop. Ingoli answered the letter on March 8 and told the monk that as far as regarded the point of the bishop's consent, he would be advised in due time how he should act.

This interchange of letters is interesting, because Dom David Codner was to be one of the most active of Richard Smith's critics for the next six years or so, and the charges he makes were to be one basis of the Roman case against the bishop. It is impossible to find this bishop ; the exercise of episcopal authority is impossible in the present circumstances of English life ; to make missionaries dependent on him for the exercise of their duties is to sterilise their power of action ; the bishop is an object of special hatred to the

---

[1] The *Acta*, S.C.P.F., under date of Feb. 22, 1627, record a petition of the Prefect of the Scottish Mission, Fr. Silvanus, O.S.B., that he and his companions be released from the obligation of seeking the Bishop of Chalcedon's consent before using the faculties granted them by the Holy Office. The petition is granted, but in lieu of the bishop's consent they are to ask that of the nuncio at Paris. *Acta*, 4–189–17.   [2] A.P., *Lett. Ant.*, 129, f. 210.

government ; even though the rest of us are no longer persecuted the chase is still hot after the bishop.

How far it is true that Muscott was not to be found cannot be ascertained. The bishop, we know, was still engaged on the immense task of his visitation,[1] and a regular missionary who had been at work in England for years, a very trusted correspondent of the Roman authorities, Fr. Simon Stock of the Discalced Carmelites, was at this moment writing for permission to live under obedience to the bishop as the only means by which he could continue to work in England with any fruit.[2] However, a month or so after the receipt of Dom David's letter the Cardinal Protector—Ludovisi—handed on to Ingoli a letter from the nuncio at Brussels [3] with a similar complaint. The missionaries in England and Scotland, he wrote, were asking that the clause ' with the consent of the ordinary ' should be struck out of their faculties, seeing that the Bishop of Chalcedon in this time of persecution did not allow himself to be found.

The nuncio thought it would be a good thing if the bishop were instructed to allow the heads of the religious orders to come to him—no more than four or five persons in all, and probably of sufficient discretion, and not likely to use their knowledge of the bishop's hiding-place in such a way as to endanger him or themselves. The bishop should, within limits, give power to these superiors to give the missionaries subject to them whatever faculties they needed. If the bishop thought it too risky to receive the superiors, powers should be sent them through the nuncios at Paris or Brussels, which the superiors might give to their subjects for one or two years. By that time circumstances might change and suggest a new scheme. For the present this would seem to safeguard the bishop's authority and also to remove the difficulty of which the missionaries were complaining. Ingoli notes [4] that the two nuncios are to be asked to consult and arrange the matter. The cardinals of Propaganda [6] decided that the nuncio's proposal was to be sent

[1] From another letter of Dom David we learn that the bishop believed him to be a spy ; if this be so, Smith's unwillingness to meet this particular missionary is not, in the circumstances, unnatural.

[2] Letter to S.C.P.F., Feb. 12, 1627 ; A.P., *Lett. Ant.*, 129, f. 108.

[3] Guidi del Bagno ; letter of Mar. 13, 1627 ; *ibid.*, f. 163.

[4] Endorsement on the letter.

[6] April 16, 1627, Congregation, 74-.

on to Smith and that he was to be asked to suggest an alternative, if this did not strike him as useful.

Before making any comment on this letter from Brussels we may consider the reply which the nuncio at Paris [1] sent to Propaganda's enquiry. He gave it as his opinion that priests who, owing to the persecution, could not get into touch with 'their ordinary the bishop of Chalcedon,' [2] should apply for faculties to him, the nuncio at Paris, by letter. As the bishop had an agent at Paris it would be an easy matter for the nuncio to get advice on each case. The best plan, so he thought, would be for the bishop to delegate one, two, or more priests up and down England to examine faculties and grant these authorisations. The cardinals decided [3] that Smith should be told to do this.

The nuncio for Paris had been made ordinary for England as far back as 1615. Whether he ever acted as such, or how, does not appear. Upon the appointment of the first bishop, as with the faculties of an ordinary, the nuncio was given authority as a court of second instance to hear appeals from the bishop. There is a letter, of later date than this, from the nuncio to Propaganda asking whether he was still ordinary. This nuncio was, then, a personage with ecclesiastical jurisdiction over England. His colleague at Brussels was no less intimately connected with this country, for, ever since March, 1622,[4] it was part of the duties of his post to watch all that happened in England and to keep Propaganda well informed. Here we have a charge that Smith has made himself inaccessible, and that the priests cannot get the visa (so to call it) for their ecclesiastical papers. He is told to delegate his authority in this matter to others. But, in the first months of his administration, he had set up a whole corps of officials, deans, archdeacons, and vicars-general, placed in various parts of the country, and to whom he had already delegated these very powers. In fact, one of the many contradictions in this involved dispute is that this very multiplication of officials was actually urged

---

[1] Bernadino Spada (1593–1661), cardinal priest of Sto. Stefano in Monte Coelio since Jan. 19, 1626. Letter of May 1, 1627, *ibid.*, f. 4.

[2] A phrase to be noted. Later it would be urged that Smith was not an ordinary.' Part of his case in reply to this was that he had always been addressed as such and spoken of as such by his superiors. Here is an instance of this.

[3] Congregation of June 5, 1627, *cf.* endorsement of Spada's letter.

[4] *Acta*, S.C.P.F., Vol. 1, f. 3, No. 5.

against the bishop as one proof of his ecclesiastical ambition. But of all this constitution of officials and delegation of authority neither of the nuncios, evidently, knows anything at all !

Smith was away from London when, in the last weeks of July, 1627, the letter from Propaganda arrived, bidding him delegate his authority to inspect the letters patent and faculties of the missionaries. The letter was, therefore, acknowledged by three of his vicars-general, John Colleton, Edward Bennett, and John Jackson.[1] The vicars-general, with a certain note of satisfaction, report that ' the bishop, in his pastoral care and watchfulness, has himself already, long ago, by himself and without any admonition, made full provision for these cases.' Their illustrious and most reverend lordships will see how devoid of all substance are the complaints of this kind made by the Regulars against the bishop. For at the very beginning of his coming, that is more than two years ago, the bishop appointed several officials for this very purpose. The trouble is not that Regulars are unable to find the bishop and so obtain ' recognition ' of their faculties, but that, many of them, are refusing all recognition to his authority.

There is in this reply a certain note of satisfaction. The other side has succeeded in getting a hearing for a complaint, and not only does the grievance complained of prove to be non-existent, but authority prescribes for a remedy the very means already adopted in order to prevent the grievance arising—a means which the complainants have refused to make use of. These are occasions when even good men go cock-a-hoop. Life being what it is the crowing is, frequently, premature.

The remainder of the long letter of the vicars-general is taken up with the first events of the main controversy, soon to be explained. Before we come to that, however, let us note that, in the summer of 1627, a first complaint from the bishop reached Rome, sent off from England, apparently, before Smith had received Propaganda's instructions about his duty of examining the faculties of Regulars. Again it is not fanciful, I think, to see in the informal way Smith makes his complaint the action of a man who is feeling his way and wants solutions rather than victories. For he sent the complaint verbally (by a priest passing through Brussels)

[1] Letter of Aug. 1, 1627, to S.C.P.F., A.P., *Lett. Ant.*, Vol. 102, ff. 7–8.

to the nuncio there, and the nuncio sent it on to Cardinal Ludovisi for his advice.[1]   Smith's message was that many Regulars were betaking themselves to England as missionaries, some of whom were unwilling to present themselves to the bishop as the ordinary and to make known to him what faculties they possessed. The bishop is therefore unable to satisfy himself that these missionaries are not apostates, *i.e.* religious who have run away from their order. What he would like is that none of these religious administer the sacraments before presenting themselves to him. Evidently the bishop asks nothing better than to see the Regulars pouring in with their demands for ' recognition.' This is a very different picture from that of the bishop withdrawing himself from all chance of contact and yet keeping all power in his own hands ! And, it is worth while noting, the bishop makes no reference to the point around which the new controversy has already begun—do Regulars need his ' approbation ' before hearing confessions ? are confessions made to a priest who lacks ' approbation ' invalid ? has the bishop any right to demand that the missionaries seek ' approbation ' ? Apparently it was not until his return to London, a few weeks later, that the bishop learnt of this new development.

Were there such Regulars as those of whom the bishop writes, Regulars, that is to say, who had the best of reasons for not showing him their papers ? We know only too well that there were many such, and this not in England only, but in Ireland, in Holland, and in Poland ;[2] living testimony, in their unfortunate predicament, to the moral chaos which always follows on religious revolution. In these very summer months of 1627 which saw the beginning of the new disputes that were to lengthen the time of chaos in England by another fifty years, we have a testimony to the mischief these apostates wrought from a missionary and a Regular, Fr. William Thompson of the order of Friars Minor Conventual.[3] He speaks of Franciscans—none of them, of course, of his own order—sent into this country by their superiors, without any authorisation from Rome, and

---

[1] Letter of July 31, 1627, A.P., *Lett. Ant.*, Vol. 129, f. 166.

[2] For Ireland and Holland, *cf.* the letters from David Rothe and Rovenius in C.R.S., Vol. 22 ; for Poland, *cf.* VON RANKE, *History of the Popes* (ed. 1856), Vol. II, p. 160.

[3] Thompson to Ingoli from Paris, Aug. 9, 1627, A.P., *Lett. Ant.*, vol. 129, f. 151.

without any faculties except what they presume themselves to possess through what is called the 'communication of privileges' between the different orders. The more scrupulous of such missionaries go the rounds of the other religious begging faculties. There is a good deal of anxiety as to how far the acts of such men are valid, whether the absolutions they give, or the dispensations they accord. Would the Sacred Congregation, therefore, declare whether superiors have power thus to send these missionaries, and whether such missionaries can use these faculties given them by other missionaries ? Or would it not be as well not to send any missionaries to England without an explicit mandate and defined faculties, and to see that they all present themselves to the nuncio in Flanders before passing into England, that he may judge how far they are suitable for this work ?

Thompson's letter was sent on to the Holy Office, whose business it was to deal with all questions of faculties. What the outcome was is not recorded, but the letter is yet another testimony that a real problem existed, and that it could only be solved by some kind of local supervision of the whole personnel of the mission, a supervision that called for the examination of the papers of the missionaries as a first requisite. Rome was declaring to the bishop that such supervision was part of his duty, and the bishop was, at the same time, reporting that the Regulars resisted his exercise of it. Nay, more, when this decree of June 5, 1627, reached him he declared he dared not even begin to put it into practice. Already, in a matter much more definitely in his province—to all seeming—than the examination of the faculties of Regulars, there was beginning to be violent resistance. To proclaim now this real innovation, brought about by the decree of June 5, 1627, would be to throw oil on the flames.

It is more than time to come to the crux of Richard Smith's career, the fight about 'approbation' and the nature of his episcopal jurisdiction, but this will not be the less understood for being set against the events and tendencies of the first, peaceful, two years of his rule.

CHAPTER IV

THE NEW WRECKING CONTROVERSIES, 1627-1631

THE first question around which the controversy raged which ' broke ' the Bishop of Chalcedon, the question about ' approbation,' can be stated very simply. The sacrament of penance can only be administered by priests. In addition to the power received through the sacrament of holy order priests also need, for the absolution of sins, what is called the power of jurisdiction. This power of jurisdiction some priests have because it is part of the office they hold, as is the case with parish-priests. Others possess it because it has been specially granted to them by those who hold it in the first way. In the first case the jurisdiction is technically called ' ordinary jurisdiction,' in the second case the jurisdiction is said to be ' delegated.' To-day any priest can give absolution within the limits of the jurisdiction attached to his office or set forth in the commission delegating him. No more than this is needed. But from the time of the Council of Trent down to the coming into operation of the present code of canon law in 1918, there was a further requirement. In the case of all priests but parish-priests it was further required that they be ' approved ' by the bishop, and this under pain of nullity in the absolutions. By ' bishop ' here there is meant the bishop to whom the person making the confession is spiritually subject.

According to the law in force from 1563 to 1918, then, a curate would need from the bishop of the diocese where he worked not only a grant of jurisdiction but a certificate of approbation before he could validly grant absolution. With such diocesan clergy who secured their ' approbation ' from the same source whence came their jurisdiction, no difficulty would be likely ever to arise. The one examination of the priest would serve both purposes, and jurisdiction and approbation be granted together. The possibilities of complications—and therefore of different views, of discussions, disputes, and of serious trouble—arose in the case of those religious orders whose members were not tied down to perpetual residence within the enclosure of their monastery and whose whole work lay precisely in the matter of preaching and hearing confessions. The first orders of this type were the two great institutes founded in the thirteenth century by St. Dominic and St. Francis of Assisi. Other orders were soon established with a like aim and a similar way of life, and in the last centuries of the Middle Ages the itinerant missionary friar was the popular confessor as he was the popular preacher. Now such friars might cross and recross the frontiers of half a dozen dioceses in the course of a twelve-month ; they passed and repassed, that is to say, the frontiers of several episcopal jurisdictions. And the jurisdiction, they themselves enjoyed, which enabled them to preach lawfully and to absolve validly, they derived not from any of the several bishops but from the Pope. And the jurisdiction, as it derived from the highest source of all, was of very generous dimensions. Regulars could, by virtue of this grant, hear the confessions of whoever came to them [1] anywhere, at any time, and, outside Italy, could absolve from all but the most reserved papal cases. But wide as these powers were, the Regular could not, after the Tridentine decree of 1563,[2] put them into operation until he had first secured from the local bishop ' approbation '; and he could not secure this unless formally presented to the bishop for ' approbation ' by his own lawful religious superior. The element of ' approbation ' provided a means by which the bishop's responsibility for seeing that only suitable priests heard confessions in his diocese could be harmonised with the suitability of giving itinerant confessors wide powers and jurisdiction independent of an authority geographically restricted. The system provided that so long as the Franciscan or Jesuit was living his religious life, and the local bishop had no reason to declare him unsuitable, he could hear confessions the world over. Now this episcopal ' approbation ' was, after the Council of Trent, as much a *sine qua non* for the Regular as for the secular who had not a parochial benefice. Absolutions given by an unapproved Regular (or

---

[1] Excepting other religions.
[2] Session 23, cap. 15, De Reformatione ; July 15, 1563.

unapproved secular who was not the parish priest of the parish) were henceforth null. This stringent decree of the Council of Trent, the Dominican Pope, St. Pius V, relaxed for a time, substituting a kind of ' approbation ' by the Regular's own superiors, but in 1570, by the bull *Romani Pontificis Providentia*, he restored the Tridentine Law.[1]

The law demanded that the priest be approved by the bishop ; but what if there were no bishops at all in the country to which the priest was officially commissioned and in which he had sacramental jurisdiction ? The law of approbation could only apply in countries where there were bishops, as the law annulling clandestine marriages could only apply where there were parishes.[2] In England, in 1563, when the new law about approbation was enacted, there were no bishops at liberty to exercise jurisdiction. By the time, sixty years later, when Richard Smith began first to plan how to bring some semblance of order into English ecclesiastical affairs, a way of life so altogether novel had developed, a system so completely *sui generis*, that not even the bishop seems to have had in mind that there was any need to correct it in this matter of confessors and the exercise of their powers. Smith came to England in April, 1625, and he seems to have begun his great visitation in the following January. It is not until eight months later still that there occurs what—so far as I have found—is his first reference to the matter, and that is almost an *obiter dictum*. The bishop is writing to the Cardinal Protector and putting before him some of the things which seem to call for remedy, as the visitation is making them known to him. He mentions the difficulties connected with the Jesuit sodality and then goes on to say : ' Certain Regulars, some who have fled their order and others expelled, have made their way into this vineyard, and after the fashion of the other priests sent here by authority of the Holy See, are administering the sacraments not having received (so far as my knowledge goes) any faculties, nor approbation lawfully had.' [3] Seven months

---

[1] *Cf.* PASTOR, Vol. 17, p. 270, and the *Bullarium Romanum*, VII, pp. 574 and 938.

[2] Because by the very terms of the law it binds in every parish thirty days after its publication in that parish.

[3] ' His accedit, quod quidam Regulares vel profugi vel eiecti in vineam istam se ingerunt, et sacramenta ad instar reliquorum Sacerdotum Apostolica authoritate missorum administrant, nullis (quod sciam) acceptis facultatibus, aut approbatione legitimé habitâ.' Sept. 20, 1626 ; A.P., *Lett. Ant.*, 129, f. 199 v.

later the three vicars-general are writing to Rome to defend
the bishop's ' recent ' demand that the Regulars shall receive
his ' approbation ' for the hearing of confessions.[1] What
had happened in the interval was this.

We have the oath of Richard Smith that it was as a case
of conscience, put to him as bishop by a Regular, that the
question first rose. This priest, a Benedictine, was chaplain
to a nobleman [2] who, alas, gave himself to turning over the
pages of the canon law. Here he found the bull of St. Pius V,
Romani Pontificis Providentia ; and from that he passed on
to the Tridentine Law about ' approbation ' which it
reaffirmed. Then came the layman's anxiety. Since
nowadays there is a bishop in England, do not confessors
need ' approbation ' in order to hear confessions ? And to
his chaplain he put the pertinent question : ' Are you
" approved " by the bishop ? ' The chaplain was not, but
straightway sought out the bishop, put the difficulty to
him and asked for ' approbation.' [3]

Now that it had been brought to the bishop's notice that
there were even the beginnings of anxiety as to the need of
' approbation ' for the validity of absolutions, he had no
choice but to go into the whole matter. He appears to
have done so with every care not to offend the susceptibilities
of the Regulars. Later Smith was to protest most solemnly
that in his moving the matter he had never had an eye to
their subjection, and certainly his way of acting now, gives
no ground for disbelieving him. He asked the provincials
of the Benedictines and the Jesuits to meet him. He told
them of the ' case ' put to him, and he showed them the
texts that set forth the law. The provincials were convinced
by the evidence, and one of them asked there and then for
approbation for himself, and the next day he sent his own
confessor to do the same. Both undertook to explain matters

[1] Visum est nuper praedicto Rmo . . . a Regularibus . . . exigere, ut
. . . approbationem ab eo acciperunt ad secularium confessiones excipien-
das. April 27, 1627, to Cardinal Protector, A.P., *Lett. Ant.*, 136, f. 211 v.
[2] Viscount Montague, says PANZANI, f. 6.
[3] *Cf. Southcott's Diary.* ' There began a controversy about approbation
between the Bishop and the Regulars, Jesuits and Benedictines chiefly, in
April ' [1627], C.R.S., Vol. 1, p. 103. PANZANI (f. 6) relates that Smith now
told the Benedictine that he had been worried by this matter ever since his
arrival in England. He could hardly believe that the Regulars would
willingly neglect so important a law, wondered if they knew of it. and finally
dreaded the storm that would ensue should he make a demand that
Regulars present themselves for approbation.

to the missionaries subject to them and to see that they also
became ' approved.'

There was never any trouble, on this score, between the
bishop and the other religious—Dominicans, Franciscans,
Carmelites—and not all the Benedictines or Jesuits were
involved in the controversy that now began. Many missionaries of both these orders agreed with the bishop's reading
of the law, but most of them did not, refused to ask ' approbation ' and soon were attacking the bishop with great bitterness. There was hardly any need to publish in the Catholic
body the disconcerting fact that bishop and priests were
disputing so vital a business. But for those of the Regulars
who had viewed the appointment of a bishop with mistrust
and who had laboured first to prevent it and, since then, to
have the appointment revoked, this serious difference of
opinion was an opportunity to be exploited. Through their,
no doubt confidential, speaking of it to their friends and
clients among the laity the differences soon became known
generally, and it became known as a grievance of the
Regulars against the bishop's attempt to usurp authority
in a matter where they were exempt—the thin end of a
general attempt on his part to reduce the Regulars to a
general obedience to him and to rule the laity also.

This was the condition of affairs when the bishop returned
to London from that visitation which had taken him ' into
the most remote provinces.' He met the situation by an
appeal to Rome to decide the question of ' Approbation '
and by a letter to the lay Catholics in which he explained
what he had done and why.[1]

The bishop writes very simply and very objectively, with
really astonishing forbearance of language—considering the
accusations and slanders which were already flying round,
and considering the fact that a section of the priests had not
merely disagreed with his view of their duty, but had gone
so far as to rouse the laity against him. Point by point he
shows the complainants that he had no designs to lessen the
powers of the Regulars, but simply to secure that they had
that ' approbation ' which secular priests too (unless they
are parish-priests) must have before they can hear confessions. To ask such ' approbation ' does no ill to the Regular
nor is it any hardship (especially as the bishop has offered
their superiors to approve the whole body *en bloc* if he is

[1] The text of this letter of Oct. 16, 1627, is in C.R.S., Vol. 22, pp. 148–158.

but given a list of their names). It is not destructive of any
privileges, for again the bishop has declared he would
waive his demand as soon as the Regulars showed him they
had any contrary privileges. Finally, the demand is not
unusual. All over the Church, since the Council of Trent,
this is the universal practice. Next the bishop passes to
explain that his authority is such that he has the right to
make the demand of the Regulars. The foundation of his
case here is the very text of the brief appointing him, which
gives him ' all and every faculty which ordinaries have or
can have in their cities and dioceses.' It has been objected
that ' faculty ' cannot mean jurisdiction or power, and the
bishop argues the point. He quotes St. Thomas, and the
legal definition of jurisdiction, and turns the argument back
on his critics. More decisively he points out that the nuncio
at Paris has been appointed to hear appeals from his tribunals. Is it not plain that he, the bishop, must then have
jurisdiction ? The legal subtlety that had been so successful
in turning the laity against him—namely that his authority
is but delegated, therefore he cannot be an ordinary—he
answers very neatly, saying that whether his authority be,
as to its origin, ordinary or delegated, matters little ' so
long as it is as ample as the authority of ordinaries. . . .
If I have this authority as an ordinary I can [examine and
approve Regulars] *iure communi* : if I have it as delegate of
his holiness I can do it *constitutione speciali.*' He then goes
on to give his own opinion that actually he is no delegate
but, from the terms of his appointment, ' a true ordinary
in England . . . an ordinary made *extraordinario modo* (as
the lawyers speak) as Legates, Nuncios, and such like are
ordinaries. . . .' He quotes in support of his claim the
practice of Propaganda, which addresses him as Ordinary
of England and Scotland, and in its grant of faculties to
Regulars in England inserts the clause ' with the consent
of the ordinaries.'

The bishop next relates how the question came to be
raised. It was in order to quieten consciences that he pursued
the matter, and the way in which he has acted since, ought
to show how far he is from any desire to make himself the
Regulars' superior. To none of the Regulars indeed has
he spoken, but to the two provincials, and he spoke to them
privately, none present but themselves. Nor did he make
any demands. He put the case before them as it had been

put before him, and they agreed with his reading of it. Later, when some of the Regulars demurred because their request for ' approbation ' might be quoted to the prejudice of the privileges of their order, the bishop offered to give a written assurance, signed and sealed, that he would not so use their request, and that, until Rome had decided the point, he would be content that they asked ' approbation ' ' not as a thing due to me,' but simply as a charity towards the peace of mind of those who come to confession to them.

In the last part of the long letter the bishop asks the laity to induce their confessors to apply for ' approbation ' ' to prevent scruples and doubts about the validity of your confessions.' He assures them that he has no intention of exercising any jurisdiction that will make their lot harder, bringing them into new dangers from the law. Nor does he plan to diminish the right of any religious order. He asks the laity not to believe all that is being said against him, and to put down this scandalous gossip ' for this were not well done towards any private man much less towards your spiritual father and pastor, whose honour and fame you are bound to maintain as much as in you lieth.'

The bishop's letter produced a speedy reply from three of the lay notables.[1] One point alone, they said, really troubled them—the bishop's claim to possess the authority of an ordinary. They wish to call in question the implication

---

[1] C.R.S., Vol. 22, p. 159. One of the three was Sir Toby Mathew, and it is significant of the chaos which Richard Smith hoped to reduce to order, that although the bishop knew it not, this gentleman was a priest and had been a priest for some thirteen years. There were, indeed, rumours that he was ordained, and—because of his close friendship with the Jesuits—rumours that he was a Jesuit. Toby Mathew was one of the bishop's most persistent opponents, and in 1631 we find Smith going to the trouble of seeking sworn attestations from people who declared they had seen the knight saying Mass (cf. DODD, III, p. 155–156, for several such sworn statements). Sir Toby was the son of Toby Mathew, Archbishop of York. Oxford, Grays' Inn, and the House of Commons (1601–1604) had educated him—and the intimate friendship of Francis Bacon. He became a Catholic in the course of a long stay in Italy—and Fr. Persons had a great share in his conversion. On his return to England he was imprisoned for refusing the new Oath of Allegiance, and then banished. This time he remained abroad nine years (1608–1617), familiarising himself with Catholic notables in Brussels, Madrid, and Rome. It was now that he was ordained (1614) at Rome, and by no less a personage than St. Robert Bellarmine. James I made use of him as an agent in the negotiations for the Spanish Marriage, and it was his services during the hare-brained trip to Spain of the Prince of Wales and Buckingham (1623) that won the priest his knighthood (cf. GILLOW, IV, pp. 531–543). Even in 1637 Panzani knew no more about the mysterious Sir Toby than that he was reputed to be a Jesuit, although he has accepted a knighthood and lives in very noble style (Relazione, f. 713).

that he has over them, the laity, that same authority which the Catholic bishops exercised in Catholic times. For an ordinary has authority to prove wills and to grant letters of administration, to settle disputes about titles, contracts, marriages, divorces, alimony, and bastardy, slanders and many other things. But, in England, the civil authority now claims power in these matters. For the bishop to set up a tribunal distinct from—worse still, contrary to—the king's courts will be treasonable, and lo, here is a new trap for the unhappy Catholic. And such cases are so numerous that there is no chance of any episcopal court working secretly. Had Rome understood the position in England ' no such authority would have been imposed on us. Neither can we be persuaded that there is a necessity of conforming ourselves thereunto as to a matter of faith or yet that we can be obliged to lose our states and ruin our posterities where the necessity of profession of faith doth not oblige us.' Will the bishop make this known in Rome, and believe that it is the general opinion of the laity? Finally, the three gentlemen ' humbly beseech ' the bishop that the controversy with the Regulars may be conducted with ' charity, sweetness, candour, and without noise.'

To this protestation the bishop replied [1] with unwearied patience, and with even a touch of humour. He does not write to the three directly ' because whatsoever I write is carried to the state and increaseth my danger.' The laymen, he says, need have no fears. He has no intention to act for the future otherwise than he has acted during the two years he has already been their bishop. ' The authority itself can bring trouble to none but myself.' As to the quarrel about ' approbation ' he has lately made a further offer to the superiors of the Regulars. If they are not willing—pending a decision by Rome—to ask ' approbation as a charity done to their penitents and not as a thing done to me ' let them propose some other reasonable course. If the peace of consciences can be had ' by any reasonable way I have my desire.'

From the day on which Smith first met the two provincials he never again succeeded in his attempt to discuss matters privately and peaceably with them. It had been a complaint to Rome that the bishop was nowhere to be found,

---

[1] Dec. 2 1627, printed in C.R.S., Vol. 22, pp. 157–158 (from Old Brotherhood MSS., I, 92), and wrongly dated Oct. 2.

and now he makes the complaint that the regular superiors carefully kept out of his way. While they were spreading the news of the episcopal tyranny that was preparing, and working up the beginnings of that agitation among the laity that was, in the end, to produce the impression at Rome that the bishop's claims were so hated that episcopal jurisdiction had best be suspended,[1] there came to the bishop Propaganda's decree of June 5, 1627, by which he was ordered to inspect the letters of appointment and faculties of all missionaries henceforth arriving in England. If the Regulars protested so strongly when the bishop asked what, to all appearances, the universal practice of the Church (alike in Catholic countries and missionary countries) demanded, it may be guessed what would have been their opposition to such an innovation as this new decree. So the bishop reasoned, as he tells us, and he decided to say nothing about this decree of Propaganda until the Holy See had decided the question of ' approbation.'

This decision lay not with Propaganda, but with the Holy Office, and in December, 1627, it was announced.[2] The Regulars were not to be urged to ask for ' approbation ' so long as the heat of persecution endured. They must, however, ask the bishop's approbation for the administration of the three parochial sacraments, namely baptism, extreme unction, and matrimony. Finally, the bishop is bidden not to insist any longer on his title of ordinary, but to be content with his ordinary's jurisdiction. The decree has all the weaknesses which make an administrative ruling so much less satisfactory than the sentence of a court of law. It has peace in view and the satisfaction of all the contending parties. It gives something to each and is dumb about the principle which divides them. In the end it really settled nothing. Regulars who feared that Smith's demand in the

---

[1] Already, six years before this, use had been made at Rome of the layman's alleged repugnance to bishops (if we are to believe John Bennett) in order to prevent the nomination of the first bishop. ' The Jesuits here,' so he wrote from Rome to Kellison, Nov. 26, 1621, ' are making catalogues of lay people's names, who forsooth would have no bishops ; and this as a great weapon, they purpose to use, and adding, that never a catholic in England desireth bishops but my lord Dormer.' TIERNEY, V, App., p. ccxxxii.

[2] Text of the second message sent to the bishop by the nuncio in France in 1629 is in DODD, III, pp. 17-18: with it is what appears to be a memorandum of the points of the decision of 1627, called by Dodd a ' decree,' and said to be copied in the bishop's own hand, though from the last sentence—Monitus pluries fuit, nec tamen acquiescit—this appears most unlikely.

matter of approbation was the first move in a scheme to dominate them entirely, would hardly possess their souls peacefully when, absolved from the need to ask ' approbation ' for hearing confessions, they found themselves saddled with a new similar restriction for baptism, extreme unction, and marriage. The bishop had found it difficult to secure observance of the law about confessions ; would he find it easier—and after six months of strife and controversy— to secure obedience regarding these three parochial sacraments ?

Actually the decree was taken as a victory for the bishop's opponents. They made known that it freed them from the yoke the bishop had sought to impose. They evaded the new obligations imposed by the decree, and they interpreted the decision about Smith's use of the title ' ordinary ' to mean that the bishop had no other jurisdiction than what the archpriests had enjoyed. For which reason, so Smith's agent reported to Propaganda, the bishop had ever since become really concerned about this style and title, outward signs of an inward power.

The bishop's attitude to the decree was one of simple acceptance. Before it actually reached him he had news of it in private letters from Rome, and immediately had abandoned his fashion of styling himself Ordinary. So he wrote to Propaganda,[1] promising to follow that congregation's admonition to obey the decree of the Holy Office once it appeared. In the same letter he warns Propaganda that new troubles are preparing and that the Regulars opposed to him have shifted their ground. There will be no peace, so far as they are concerned, unless the bishop is prepared to divest himself of all the authority which ordinaries have whether over Regulars or the laity, and reduce himself to the condition of the archpriest, and he gives the cardinals news of the appearance of the first printed book the controversy has produced.

The new year, 1628, then, which brought to England the decree of the Holy Office, was filled with fresh troubles, a new controversy about the nature of the bishop's jurisdiction and the passing of the controversy into print. Once books began to be published—and this was the experience of the controversy about the archpriest thirty years earlier— bitterness was increased tenfold and hates of incredible

[1] May 25, 1628, A.P., *Anglia*, 347, ff. 501, 502.

strength were speedily generated. About the books which
now appeared I do not propose to say anything in detail,
for the very good reason that none of them has come my
way. The first of them was the work of Fr. Rudesind
Barlow,[1] the president of the English Benedictines. The
most effective if, to speak dispassionately, we measure
this by the subsequent commotion, were the work of Jesuit
writers. But more famous names than these were soon
engaged.[2] Whoever was attacked by Jesuits would not lack
defenders, in that fatal ten years or so when Jansenism was
slowly crystallising. French theologians hastened, some to
defend episcopal rights considered to be menaced and in
danger, others to chastise the presumptuous Jesuits. Works
by English Jesuits were condemned by the University of
Paris and by the French hierarchy. The French Jesuits
disavowed their anonymous English brother. Then,
presently, there appeared a succession of works by one
Peter Aurelius. 'This is suspected to be a pseudonym,'
wrote an English correspondent from Paris. Pseudonym
indeed, and it hid no less a personage than the abbé de St.
Cyran, the father of Jansenism himself. The fire that
threatened the little outhouse of Catholicism which was
what the *Ecclesia Anglicana* had become, was growing into a
conflagration that threatened France too ; once it developed
where would it stop ?

It is, then, against a much more lurid background than the
petty rivalries of the morbid, persecution-ridden enclosure

---

[1] *Epistola R.A.P. Præsidis Generalis et Regimini totius Congregationis
Anglicanæ Ordinis Sancti Benedicti* ; 12mo. It was addressed to the Provincials and Definitors of the Congregation, and printed for private circulation within that body, the members of which were forbidden to show it to
others. However, the book soon began to be more generally known. The
preface is dated Oct. 1, 1627, and from its first word, this work received the
title *Mandatum*, by which it is usually named, *cf.* C.R.S., Vol. 33, pp. 214–
215. Another of the English Benedictines—and Fr. Barlow's immediate
successor as President—was one of Richard Smith's staunchest defenders.
This was Fr. William Benedict Price, who published, in 1631, his *Mani-
festatio circa Declarationem Jesuitarum Anglorum, etc.* The *Mandatum* was
delated to Rome by the bishop, and was condemned ; *cf.* letter from nuncio
at Paris, ordering Smith to suppress the work, in DODD, III, p. 157. For
Fr. Barlow, ' accustomed to have his word accepted as law . . . a dour
opponent ' and his jealous elimination of Fr. Baker, *cf.* McCANN, xxxiv–vi.
[2] The chief work, written by a secular priest, was Dr. Matthew Kellison's
book, *A Treatise of the Hierarchy and Divers Orders of the Church against
the anarchie of Calvin*, 8vo, pp. 420, Doway, 1629. Kellison, no less prudent
than dutiful, submitted his book to Rome for censorship. Despite his
opponents it was licensed.

of English Catholicism that the next, and final, act of the
tragedy of Richard Smith is played ; and, if a continental
background, a background no less political than theological.
For, yet once again, there crosses the path of nascent
Catholic hopes in England, the blighting rivalry of Spain and
France and the intricate game of both in the Curia Romana,
which had been a more or less permanent feature of the
drama since the first months of Mary's reign, now three-
quarters of a century ago. By the time of Richard Smith's
début in the bureaux of the Holy Office, the Thirty Years'
War was beginning to be more and more evidently a struggle
in which France would, at all costs, intervene directly, and
it would intervene, of course, on the anti-Spanish side, the
anti-imperialist side, the side of the almost annihilated
Protestant States. That the French minister responsible for
this was a cardinal, hardly made French policy any more
palatable at Rome. And what of Richard Smith, reputed
Richelieu's protégé ?   Only lately, in fact, denounced as
Richelieu's secret agent in London ? Without risking the
blunders that come of guesswork, we know that the Spanish
ambassador in London now worked for the Regulars as
strongly as the French ambassador worked for the bishop.
The names of these diplomats, and their charges or defences,
cross and re-cross in all the papers that deal with this complex
business. A detailed and documented history of the *affaire*
Smith would be a cross-section of European history at a
critical moment in which all the tendencies, and most of the
personages, of the day would sometime appear.

It was now nearly four years since the opening of this sad
episcopate, and time for the bishop to make his quadrennial
report to Rome. He determined to do this through a special
agent and for this deputed one of his vicars-general, John
Bosvile, a priest who had had personal experience of every
phase of the long controversy, for he had been one of the appel-
ants against Blackwell thirty years before.[1] Bosvile is described
in the bishop's letter as a very old man and in poor health.
The bishop could, at any rate, rely on his loyalty and on his
enthusiasm for the interests committed to him. Bosvile left
England August 12, 1628.[2] He was not to make his entry

---

[1] Letter of Credence to S.C.P.F., dated July 14, 1628, in A.P., *Lett. Ant.*,
Vol. 131, f. 183.
[2] *Southcott's Diary*, C.R.S., Vol. I, p. 104.

Dr. Richard Smith
(1567–1655)
Bishop of Chalcedon

on the Roman scene for some months yet.[1] When he did appear there, a shower of serious accusations followed. He was immoral ; he was an alchemist ; if he did not actually defend the oath of allegiance, he was not so enthusiastic about the rights of the Holy See as became a good priest.[2] Meanwhile others were active on the bishop's behalf. The London Carmelite, Simon Stock, remained his staunch supporter, and continued to press Propaganda to support him. 'The regular clergy have lived here so many years without bishops, and with such freedom that all do as they please—and the very words " bishop " and " subordination," little as this may be, are unwelcome to them.' From Douay came a letter signed by the President and all his staff. They beg for an explicit declaration that the bishop's jurisdiction is that of an ordinary, and that the Regulars should seek ' approbation.' Like the theologians they were, they pointed out that this would be the beginning of an introduction of the Council of Trent's reforms into England. They thought it must mean an increase of the Holy See's prestige, even among those outside the Church, and the fact of there being a bishop resident in the country with power to suspend the clergy's faculties and, if need be, to excommunicate the laity would keep the whole Catholic community in better order. The Douay letter strongly denied that the laity as a body were opposed to the idea of episcopal authority. Apart from a few penitents of certain Regulars, most of the laity desired the bishop's jurisdiction as something essential to well-being. If the bishop is not supported by the Holy See it will be a cause of great uneasiness to his flock, whom his presence comforts and maintains. As it is, the tumult in England is most serious. Were it not for the heroic charity of the bishop there is no saying what might happen, for these Regulars are so inflated with wild hopes, even before they have gained their suit. Finally, they beg for a formal condemnation of Fr. Barlow's Mandatum.[3] A letter from a Conventual Franciscan, Fr. Francis Maitland, tells a like tale of scandalous dissensions no longer hidden.

[1] Note of reception of the letter of credence in Acta, S.C.P.F., for Jan. 12, 1629 ; his business on the bishop's behalf is to work ' contra molestias Regularium,' A.P., Acta, Vol. 6, f. 199, 32°.

[2] Codner, O.S.B., to Ingoli, Mar. 7, 1629, in A.P., Lett. Ant., Vol. 131, f. 185.

[3] A.P., Lett. Ant., Vol. 131, f. 177 ; letter is of July 17, 1628, received Jan. 12, 1629.

A A

Richard Smith had sought advice outside England, from countries where bishops had to face difficulties of like kind with his own. Of this correspondence there has survived a reply from the famous Bishop of Ossory, David Rothe,[1] and a letter that is still more to the point from the Vicar-Apostolic of Holland, Philip Rovenius,[2] titular Archbishop of Philippi. Evidently the Bishop of Chalcedon had put to these two missionary bishops, who both had to labour like Smith himself, under the dark menace of a penal code, the question whether his demands about ' approbation ' were actual or not. The Bishop of Ossory answers that this is a frequent subject of discussion among the Irish bishops. The law is a stumbling-block against which many in their blindness are brought up. In Ireland the law is enforced, and in his own diocese the Regulars all present themselves for ' approbation ' and he takes care to examine those about whose suitability he is doubtful. The diocese is divided into parishes and the Regulars do not concern themselves with the parochial sacraments. Once upon a time it was a serious difficulty in Ireland that the Regulars had wider faculties than the bishops ! But Rome, at the petition of the bishops, curtailed these, and at the same time amplified the bishops' powers. The letter of Rovenius deserves quoting in full, for in many respects the domestic history of Catholicism in the United Provinces tallied with that of the *Ecclesia Anglicana*. What the bishop has to say about the spirit of his opponents, and about the attitude of the Roman officials is curiously similar to what, from Smith's letters, we can gather were the Englishman's opinions on these matters.

' I easily gather that your differences with the Regulars are not unlike my own, that it is with reluctance that they show that obedience which they profess, and not only to the ordinaries to whose assistance they are sent, but also to the Apostolic See. Only lately a certain prelate at Rome said to the Minister General of one of the orders that it seemed to him that Regulars only obey the commands of His Holiness as far as the Pope is able to force them through the ministry of justice. It is our experience here that, notwithstanding the decision of the Holy Father in 1623—by which the Regulars, among other things,

[1] Dec. 6, 1628, printed C.R.S., Vol. 22, pp. 165–170.
[2] *Ibid.*, pp. 158–161.

are commanded to obey the Vicar-Apostolic as the special
delegate of the Holy See in all that concerns the *cura
animarum* in this country—the Regulars nevertheless,
according to their custom, subvert all order ; nay, they
do this eagerly, so that, order being overturned, they may
themselves act as they please and make piety a traffic.
His Holiness has more than once commanded in his own
person, and still more often through the Apostolic
Nuncios, that the concordat between us and the Regulars,
which the intervention of the bishops of Belgium brought
about in 1624, be carefully obeyed. . . .

' I also note that at Rome so many and so serious
complaints are made, from all parts, about the unruliness
of the Regulars that the necessary remedies ought to be
applied and the power of the bishops strengthened,
unless they wish to see their own in peril.

' I am not surprised that they do not ask approbation
from Your Lordship for hearing confessions because they
almost persuade themselves that it is a crime to entertain
doubts about their own sufficiency, whereas, often, they
are by no means fit. Others think that once admitted,
by any bishop and in any place whatsover, they are
to be admitted everywhere. . . . The practice of the
bishops in Belgium is that each bishop takes care to
re-examine and approve confessors even when [already]
admitted elsewhere. Nor can I see that it is unlawful
for Your Lordship to require this of the Regulars sent
[to England], unless they declare themselves to have
been specially examined at Rome and found fit for the
hearing of confessions in any part of the world. . . .

' I consider it mere silliness to say that we are not
ordinaries, for whatever the case may be, we at least
have the power of ordinaries and to this there is added
the Vicariate Apostolic. As to the calumnies and dishonour we suffer when we do not assent in everything
to the wishes of the Regulars, we are already hardened
to that, nor do I think detractors are so easily believed
now as they used to be. . . . To say what I think, so
slowly is any decision got from Rome, occupied as they
are with business from all over the world, and our affairs
seem to be so little taken to heart or (if I may say it) so
little reliance is placed on our reports (although these
are most true) that I become weary of frequently com-

plaining and choose rather to lament in silence very often
and to commend matters to God, than uselessly to strive
for human support.   But the charity of Christ urges us
to make a stand for good order as far as we can, and to
help each other by our mutual prayers.'

UTRECHT,
   26 *July*, 1628.

The letter of Rovenius bears the date July 26, 1628.
Eleven days later Viscount Montague [1] was writing to the
General of the Jesuits a letter that is no less important.
Lord Montague was, if we consider active labours for the
faith and generosity in suffering for it, the leading layman
in England.   His great mansion at Cowdray, in Sussex,
had been the home and headquarters of the archpriests
first and then of the two bishops.   In the security of his
chapel the fullness of the ancient liturgy had come to
life again after seventy years of proscription, and the congregations had seen the bishop confirming and pontifically
singing Mass.   In this letter to the supreme command of the
Society Lord Montague carefully avoids any judgement on
the point in debate between the bishop and the Regulars.
He writes simply to protest against the way in which some
of the fathers are conducting the controversy, and he names
as offenders the Provincial, Fr. Richard Blount, and Fr.
Laurence Anderton.   He charges them with insulting
language about the bishop, in their conversations and in
writing.   The Jesuits engaged in the controversy have
treated the bishop shamefully, and their defence is altogether
lacking in moderation and humility.   But the most serious
charge of all is that, by a not incredible transition from
attacking an unwelcome official to attacking his functions,
Jesuits, to lessen the bishop's chances of attracting to himself
their clientele, are openly depreciating confirmation, the
special sacrament he administers, and influencing their
flock to neglect it.

In December, 1628, came a sudden and unexpected stroke
from without.   A proclamation was issued for the bishop's
arrest.   About its preparation a most sensational story has

been told. But before this is recalled it may be well to set out the way in which the disturbances in England were, by this time, appearing to the officials at Propaganda—or at any rate to the secretary, Mgr. Francis Ingoli—and to consider how the bishop was represented to the cardinals of the Holy Office. Ingoli, whose long tenure of this office, in the very foundation years of the new congregation [1] fashioned its procedure, we now know, for centuries, was, after all, in his own day, no more than an official. His business was to see that the policies of his chiefs, the cardinals of the congregation, were carried out. But the secretary, too, had his ideas, and when the occasion presented itself he urged them on the cardinal prefect. Occasionally a scribbled note—and in what a hand!—on the back of a letter lets us into the secret place of his mind. So it is with a letter of June 27, 1628, from that untiring correspondent of Propaganda, Fr. Simon Stock. From making, on the back of the letter, his usual brief précis of the contents the secretary has expanded into comment, and at the end is the note, ' for Cardinal Antonio Barberini,[2] for the next [meeting of the congregation] in the presence of the Holy Father ; would Your Illustrious lordship deign to read and to consider well what is written here. It is of great importance.' That meeting took place November 24, 1628. Ingoli's notes then are written somewhere about that time.[3] The secretary was, later on, to show himself, in so far as such notes as these reveal his mind, a strong advocate for the policy of sending bishops to England and also for the upholding of Richard Smith. Here, however, his subject is the general question of the relations of bishops and Regulars in missionary countries. The note is worth giving in full.[4] ' Whoever studies carefully the business of the missions knows this truth, that the exemption of Regulars [i.e. from episcopal jurisdiction] in the missions gives rise to scandals, for one notices that it is the fat, rich places that the religious frequent, and the poor places that they leave abandoned ; this is to

From 1622 to 1649.

[2] The Pope's Capuchin brother (1569–1646), an excellent religious and a most enthusiastic supporter of the missionary movement ; Prefect of the Congregation of Propaganda in 1632, on the death of Ludovisi.

[3] We can note once more the immense delays arising from the difficulty of getting letters to the Holy See out of England. This letter is written on June 27, and only comes before Propaganda, to whom it is sent, five months later.

[4] A.P., *Lett. Ant.*, 102, f. 12 v.

be seen in the mountains of Scotland, where everyone is
poor, and where no Catholic priests have ever gone, nor
heretical preachers, because there is nothing to get but a
little barley bread, and where men are to be found almost
pagan, men seventy years of age and not yet baptised, as
the four missionaries told us whom the Sacred Congregation
sent to those parts with a provision of 60 scudi each upon
the Holy Father's [1] report made when he was yet a cardinal.

' The Regulars in England were accustomed to the liberty
which the archpriest gave them,[2] and nevertheless there
were always disputes : now they are unable to endure the
authority of the bishop. Your lordship, who is the protector
of that kingdom, will deign to make provision for these
present discords and divisions, because instead of gaining
ground we are losing. Remember that golden saying of
Aristotle in the Metaphysics, *Entia nolunt male gubernari,
unus ergo princeps*. This is most true with regard to missions,
where there needs to be a single chief, who can place the
workers in the places that need them, and not allow the
poor to die without the sacraments.

' The same wrong state of things, and on an even greater
scale, is to be seen in Scotland. Because not only do the
Regulars hold on to the rich places and neglect the poor, but
not having there any superior they do as they like and no
one is ever able to find out what actually is going on there.
As the duty of my office I recall all this to your lordship
with my humble respect, leaving it to your authority and
patronage to seek out some remedy. In the Holy Office
there has always been (upheld ?) this principle of ecclesiastical government, namely, to support the Regulars, for the
reasons which were discussed at the Council of Trent and
in the time of Pius IV : but these reasons hold for churches
already organised, with Regulars who live in monasteries
and not in the missions. Experience shows that what is
wanted in the missions is a director for the religious who
live in freedom outside their monasteries and at a great
distance from their superiors, who, for the most part, remain
in Flanders or in places in England where they can do little
to provide against this unseemly style of things.

[1] Urban VIII (elected Aug. 6, 1623).
[2] One of those astonishing instances of official ignorance that not infrequently astound whoever studies, even indolently, these documents. The
archpriest did not ' give ' the Regulars liberty : he had, of course, nothing
whatever to do with their life or conduct.

' I add that, for lack of such a director, many runaway friars, and friars of bad life, come into England, nor is there any one to choose them out or to make other arrangements for them : we have the recent example of Father Brown,[1] of the order of Minims, who stays on in England, without any authority and under obedience to no one, and the harm he is doing it would take more than these few words to describe.'

To one point only of this document do I wish to draw attention, namely, to the hint it gives of an important difference of opinion as to policy, between the Secretary of Propaganda and the officials of the Holy Office. I believe this difference to have gone very deep, and in fact that it is here that we must look for the real source of the struggles over the body of English Catholicism in the sixty years after 1620. For the Holy Office in the 1620's was as pro-Regular as Propaganda was pro-episcopal. And if the struggle of that first decade, the struggle that filled Richard Smith's episcopate, ended in a victory for the Regulars, it ended in victory no less for the view of the English situation held by the Holy Office. Henceforward, until another revolution dislodged its hold, the ' legend ' of the Holy Office was Rome's official view of the English imbroglio and, I suggest, the ultimate reason why, despite continuing efforts, nothing was ever done. John Leybourne's appointment as vicar-apostolic in 1685 was the sign that Propaganda was now really in control and it was marked, appropriately, by the Holy Office cancelling its decree of 1627 which exempted the Regulars from the bishop's control in the matter of approbation. But this is to anticipate events.

To us who, three hundred years after the event, strive to reconstruct the story of Richard Smith, the contest must at times appear vague and uncertain, for nowhere—save in the inaccessible archives of the Holy Office—is there a dossier that comes at all near to being complete. And even to the contending parties the whole affair seems to have partaken somewhat of the nature of a fight in a fog, so difficult were either communications with allies or contacts with foes. Rome acts, and it is months before the news of the action can reach those it most concerns, and longer still before they get the news in such form that

---

[1] This gentleman was to prove a trouble for years yet to come. His name crops up continually in the correspondence of nuncios and other officials.

they can safely give it credence. Given the decree of the Holy Office of December, 1627,[1] it is as enlightening, as it is disconcerting, to find no less a personage than the President of the English Benedictines writing, at least nine months later,[2] in a complaining tone that the Bishop of Chalcedon in his visitations claims that the Regulars cannot administer the parochial sacraments without his authority, and that he has the right to nominate who shall administer them. And eight months later still—in May, 1629—an unknown correspondent of Fr. Henry Sillesden, S.J.,[3] quotes Smith's secretary, John Southcott, as saying with certainty that Rome has made no order about the parochial sacraments. That rumours, under such conditions, were endless, and that they were as wild and as contradictory as they were numerous, is not surprising. They clouded the issue for the contestants then, as they still obscure it for the historian.

Continually, in the minutes of the meetings of the Propaganda cardinals, one reads that the letter, or memorial, or a copy of it, was ordered to be sent to the Holy Office, since it is there that the dispute is being dealt with. And at a later date the Holy Office descended on Propaganda and made a clean sweep of the papers still there which related to this case. It is not easy, therefore, to make out the actual formality of the charges against the bishop on which the final decision actually turned. But there still remain in the archives of Propaganda sundry defences put in by the bishop and his agent, and there remains at any rate one formal statement of the case against him. But this is not from the parties regarded as his chief opponents. It is not the work of any Jesuit or Benedictine of the English Congregation, but (reputedly) of Dom David Codner, a Benedictine of the Cassinese Congregation, professed monk of the monastery of the order at Ravenna.[4]

---

[1] Cf., p. 355 sup.

[2] Letter in C.R.S., Vol. 22, pp. 173–174 ; the reference in it to the Lancaster martyrs (Bl. Edmund Arrowsmith and V. Richard Herst) gives a clue to the date, for they were put to death Aug. 28 and 29, 1628.

[3] Letter of May 28, n.s., in C.R.S., Vol. 22, pp. 172–173.

[4] Compendio di una lettera scritta in Inghilterra per il Rev. P. Don David Inglese, monaco della Congregatione Cassinese sopra le controversie tra il Revmo. Vescovo Calcedonense e li Regolari et laici d'Inghilterra per essere insinuato all'Illmi Signori Cardinali della S. Congregatione del Santo Officio. A.P., Anglia, 347, f. 198 seq. I say ' reputedly ' because it was alleged that Dom Thomas Preston made use, at times, of his confrère's name to cover his own productions.

This is a lengthy document, which, abbreviation or
compendium as it is, runs to more than nine pages of
typescript. From it we learn one very important fact,
namely that in the case before the Roman authorities the
bishop was not the defendant but the plaintiff. He is thus,
urges the monk, the assailant of those in possession, the
Regulars and the laity who have, since the schism began,
enjoyed all these rights of action and freedom from interference of which he is now doing his best to deprive them.
They are possessors in good faith. His authority is, at best,
only doubtful. How can they be bound to submit and to
surrender ? The bishop is truly an ordinary—but of the
diocese of Chalcedon. Nor can he show that the Holy
See had delegated to him, in the extraordinary manner
necessary, the authority he claims to be his. Are Regulars,
to whom, because of the peculiar circumstances obtaining
in England, faculties of unwonted scope have been granted,
bound to seek approbation from a bishop of this sort, who
has to admit that he is not an ordinary in the usual sense of
the term ?

The bishop, it is true, has arguments to bring forward.
What of them ? His own doubts are evident, from the way
in which he has written to Rome asking leave to ' reserve '
certain cases, and for Rome's opinion whether Regulars
need seek ' approbation ' from him. If the bishop's brief
gives him ' all the faculties which ordinaries enjoy,'
' faculty,' nevertheless, never means jurisdiction in any
sense outside that of sacramental absolution. All that the
brief does is to give the bishop leave to administer the
sacrament of confirmation and to bless the Holy Oils.
When the bishop cites, in proof of his contention that
the Regulars need his ' approbation,' the decree of Trent, the
bull of St. Pius V and a decision of the Congregation of the
Council, and the universal practice of Catholic countries,
it is to be borne in mind first, that the Council of Trent
has no binding force in England in so far as its decrees
about the reformation of Christian life are concerned. Even
were this not the case, and were the council ' received ' in
England, the decree on ' approbation ' leaves the Regulars
untouched for they are despatched to England as ' extraordinary parish-priests,' [1] and have the same status and
rights there as the secular clergy. The Holy See has already

---

[1] Mandati la come parochi estraordinarii.

found them suitable, and admitted them to a cure of souls and to [perform] parochial offices.[1]

So far the memorial is answering the bishop's arguments. It now passes to the attack. The subjects of complaint are the way in which he has conducted the business of urging ' approbation,' his creation of so many officials and dignitaries bound to him by an unusual kind of oath, and his exercise of jurisdiction outside [2] the sacrament of penance.

1. The bishop and his officials declare to the laity that all the confessions they make, or have made, to ' unapproved ' Regulars are null and void, and must be made over again. If this were the case, it would also hold good of confessions made to the secular priests. Here we have an instance of the bishop's lack of prudence and discretion, tormenting consciences and throwing them into confusion ; and this for an inaccurate, or at any rate doubtful, reading of the law, for the bishop has written to Rome to ask whether it is the Pope's intention that the Regulars shall ask ' approbation,' and, without awaiting the reply (which seems itself a lack of discretion), he is going about declaring that all confessions made to Regulars who have not, as they ought, received ' approbation,' are invalid.

2. The bishop has created all sorts of new dignitaries in England, vicars-general, archdeacons, deans, the chapter. He has obliged all those whom he has appointed to these offices to swear an oath of obedience to himself and his successors such as was never seen before in the Church, as though his authority was not merely ' at the goodwill of the Holy See,' but enjoyed a perpetuity of succession.[3] Likewise he has divided the kingdom into many new dioceses and districts, and to these officials he has given canonical authority for these districts of his. They are exercising this authority, and we may well fear that in a short time this dean and chapter will be claiming the right to elect the bishop, when the see is vacant, without reference to Rome. If the Regulars, exasperated by these attacks against them, were to declare that the said bishop and his said official, had fallen under a censure for this abuse of

[1] Essendo già per autorita della Santa Sede trovasi idonei, et admessi ad curam animarum, et functioni parrochiali.

[2] Essercitio di giurisdittione in foro externo.

[3] Come sua autorita fosse con successione perpetua ancora chi sia solamente ad beneplacitum Sanctæ Sedis.

authority, what a great scandal would result among the faithful.

The writer then gives the text of the oath complained of and notes that its terms are revealed only to those it concerns. ' I, A. B., a priest, swear and promise on my priestly word, that from this hour I will be faithful and obedient to the Rt. Rev. the Bishop of Chalcedon, Ordinary of England and Scotland, and that I will give obedience to his commands and to those of his successors. I profess myself to be a genuine member of the English secular clergy ; I shall ever be loyal to this body and defend its dignity ; to the best of my power I shall work efficaciously for its spiritual and temporal welfare. I shall not, knowingly and willingly, work any harm or prejudice to the said clerical body, nor shall I allow anything of the kind to be done or attempted by others ; nor shall I know anything which I will not reveal to the said Lord my ordinary and to his successors, at least through some one who can, without fraud or guile, bring it to their notice as soon as possible.'

The oath, so the criticism runs, is intended to keep all possible sources of alms for the profit of the secular clergy, and thus binds those who take it to a breach of the divine and natural law. More, the oath makes for divisions, and the end of the friendships there should be between priests. The clause ' nor shall I know . . .' has caused much unfavourable comment among the laity of quality. It has the appearance of appointing officials to act as spies on the general body.

3. As for the bishop's claim to exercise jurisdiction *in foro externo*, the laity already, last July, sent a memorial to him on this matter. The present writer encloses a copy, and for his own part is content to recall the great scandals that ensued when the archpriest George Blackwell, thirty years before this, attempted similar proceedings. Rome decided that he had gone beyond his powers, and forbade him ever to do the like again. ' For this reason we can well imagine that the present Holy Father has not meant to make the bishop who is now in England either bishop of all England or of Canterbury or of any other see in England, but only of some place *in partibus infidelium,* giving him some faculties, as has been explained, which he can exercise in England.'

The long letter ends with a statement in the writer's own defence, against the bishop's charge that he is the associate of spies. If he guesses rightly whom the bishop means by 'spy,' this person is one recommended to his attention by the bishop himself, the writer's superiors and also certain cardinals 'there in Rome.'

There are two proclamations [1] against 'Richard Smith, a Popish priest ; styled, and calling himself Bishop of Chalcedon.' To read carefully the language of horror at his activities which fills them, and to know the familiarity with the queen which the bishop never ceased to enjoy, is itself a good lesson in the business of never taking official statements at their face value. The first proclamation, of December 11, 1628, notes that by his writings in print and otherwise, the bishop persuades the king's subjects from their allegiance ; he is exercising in England an episcopal jurisdiction usurped from the see of Rome ; he is in constant correspondence with the king's enemies ; therefore he is guilty of high treason ; and yet divers of the king's subjects harbour him, and become thereby liable to the death penalty. Whence this order for Smith's discovery and arrest, and a command to all and sundry to deliver him up. The second proclamation is dated nearly four months later, March 24, 1629 : 'The said Smith being still hidden and harboured.' It lays special emphasis on his correspondence with the king's enemies, and unites, in its menace of penalties, harbourers of any other priest or Jesuit. As to the bishop, £100 reward is offered to whoever brings about his arrest, and also whatever property is forfeited by the conviction of his host.

There is a somewhat Gilbertian atmosphere about these proceedings. We have, in the State Paper office, complaints of pursuivants that their information about the bishop's hiding-place was disregarded, and at least one application for the reward. The king, to soothe the scrupulous mind of Henrietta Maria, then with child, and ordered meat on fasting days, sent to the proscribed bishop to ask a dispensation for her.[2] Then, so the nuncio in Flanders [3] reported to Rome, in order to please the queen he held up the proclamation altogether. Richard Smith did not leave

---

[1] Text in DODD, III, pp. 143–144.
[2] PANZANI, *Relazione*, f. 11.
[3] *Acta*, S.C.P.F., Mar. 3, 1629.

England because of these proclamations—though this has been asserted. He remained in England, in defiance of whatever menace they contained, for another two years and a half. But his movements were henceforth necessarily circumscribed. A proclaimed traitor, with such a reward offered to his captor, would hardly be long abroad without a host of informations being sworn before magistrates all over the country, to the embarrassment of the friendly court no less than to his own inconvenience. Now, more than ever, Richard Smith lay hid and kept his rooms—in the palace of the French ambassador. Four years later when the question arose whether he should be reinstated in his English post or another bishop sent, Smith cited this fact of his being a publicly proclaimed traitor, with a price on his head, as one very good reason for appointing some other bishop.[1]

If the court was so friendly to Smith how came it that he was singled out for this uniquely ingenious [2] piece of persecution ? The dossier of the *affaire Smith*—and indeed of all this long tale of the woes of Troy—would not be complete did we not give the bishop's own account of it, the account he sent to Rome by his agent.[3]

' When the news reached England that the bishop of Chalcedon's vicar [4] had arrived safely in Rome, straightway a marvellous anxiety seized on the spirits of the Regulars. Jesuits went about saying that he would be sent back immediately with the answer that the bishop was not an ordinary. Benedictines asserted that the Holy See had sent him a severe warning. So they gave out, but their

[1] Chalcedon to Fitton, Mar. 11, 1633, in C.R.S., Vol. 21, p. 179.

[2] The unique feature is the offer of a good reward in cash to whoever takes him. So far no reward had ever existed to tempt whoever was needy enough to turn priest-catcher. This last ingenuity was to be systematised seventy years later by the Act of William III, which, introducing the new and milder penalty of life imprisonment for the captured priest, offered now £100 for whoever took him. Readers of Bishop Challoner's life will recall how a new menace hung over priests in England thence onward until, in 1771, Lord Mansfield stopped the trial of a priest under this statute by requiring from the informer proof of the ordination of the accused.

[3] A.P., *Lett. Ant., Anglia*, 347, f. 171 *seq.* : endorsed *Relatione del bando dato al vescovo Chalcedonense* : *Die* 8 *Martii* 1629. *Congregatio* 106.

[4] John Bosvile (*cf.* p. 358 *supra*). We do not know the date of Bosvile's arrival. His credentials are dated July 7, 1628 ; they are officially acknowledged in the *Acta*, S.C.P.F., for Jan. 12, 1629 : the first proclamation is just a month earlier than this last date, *i.e.* Dec. 1, 1628, and almost three months before the date of this *Relatione* which, presumably, is Bosvile's work.

friends, to whom they revealed their true feelings, whispered that they were in desperation about their case and expecting a decision in favour of the bishop. Nor did the Regulars themselves hide their feelings sufficiently. They spread evil sayings about the nuncios, the cardinals, and even about the Pope himself. They spread sarcasms, Roman in origin, and they held little meetings in which the principal question discussed was how to disregard the papal edict (if the Roman decision were given for the bishop). It seemed the best plan (as the event showed it) to fill the minds of the Catholics with fear, so that by some means either they who, in all the hundreds and all the counties, were showing themselves supporters of the bishop, should desert him or, the persecution being increased, the Pope could be persuaded to recall the bishop. They [*i.e.* these Regulars] were much worried—not indeed by the letter they had forged in the name of the laymen (although this was shown to the king), not by the *Mandatum* of the Benedictines (although this was praised by the pseudo-archbishop of Canterbury), not by the letter of the three Regulars to the bishop, nor, finally, by the published letter of Dom David, otherwise Preston, to the abbot of St. Paul's [1] (in which they called down, undeniably, the hatred of the king and his council on the bishop)—they were much worried until somehow it had been brought about that the king would take action against the bishop. For although the ruling authorities rejoiced at the sight of all this, and perhaps greatly hoped that the bishop would commit himself in some way against the king, nevertheless they were unwilling to meddle in the matter, both because they knew that these charges were calumnies and because nothing was more pleasing to them than these divisions among the Catholics.

'Therefore a certain nobleman, a man skilled in affairs (except for his own conceit of his powers), but always a most factious partisan of the Jesuits, drew up a kind of petition or rather declaration in which he explained to the King's council, professing himself to speak for the whole Catholic body, that the Catholics were the king's faithful

---

[1] *I.e.* St. Paul's-outside-the-walls, Rome, at which famous Benedictine monastery both Dom Thomas Preston and Dom David Codner had, at one time, resided. Panzani also states that Preston was the real author of this treatise on the bishop's authority—for such the letter was—and that he made use of his ellow monk's name ; *cf. Relazione*, f. 7.

subjects and were not willing to allow the present bishop of
Chalcedon to exercise his episcopal jurisdiction upon them.
This petition was presented to the council by its author,
and two days later, at a council held in the king's presence,
the secretary produced nine probates of wills—forged—
which were said to have been granted by the bishop of
Chalcedon. The secretary, the Lord Keeper and the
pseudo-primate of Canterbury, urged the matter violently
against the bishop, nor did anyone dare to open his mouth
to excuse him. And so it was achieved that a proclamation
was issued against the bishop. Truly enough this was more
terrifying than actually harmful. For while the charge
was being most warmly urged against the bishop, the council
was advised where he lay, and how he could be taken.
But the council was not willing to send to take him, and a
peer in whose house he was known often to stay was warned,
by order of the king, to go cautiously. No order was ever
given to any officer to search for the bishop—and unless
this is done there is no danger to be feared from any
proclamation. Whence, notwithstanding [the proclama-
tion], the Catholics invite the bishop to their homes, and a
certain statesman of experience, asked why there was this
discrimination against a member of the clergy, answered
that it was intended to foster in this way the existing quarrels
between them and the Regulars.

   ' This is the story as the agents of the English clergy had
it from friends worthy of credence who assert that they speak
from certain knowledge, and they add that if the Pope now
decrees anything against the bishop, it will wholly destroy
his authority and the clergy : nor does there seem any other
way of restoring peace than to create, at least two other
bishops. For as long as the Regulars have any hope of
being able to overturn episcopal authority, they will never
be quiet.'

   This, it will be agreed, is a most extraordinary story, and
were it not presented to us as the explanation given officially
by the bishop's agent in the Curia we should be tempted to
ignore it as we ignore the extravagances of the anonymous
letter-writer. How regrettable that whoever drafted the
report suppressed the name of the nobleman ! Is this
really how it all happened ? We shall probably never
know. But we do know that what roused opposition to the
bishop among the laity was precisely this report that he was

claiming that wills should be submitted to him for probate. We know this charge was made against him at Rome, and we know—from the bishop's own denial of it to Henrietta Maria [1]—that the charge was also made against him to the king. The accusation had been made, and was denied by the bishop, as early as his letter to the lay-Catholics of October, 1627. But, despite the denials, it continued to be made, and it has survived as a proved count in the indictment against him down to our own times. Yet the bishop not only denied it, to the end, but repeatedly, in his letters to Rome—whither, as he must have known, all the evidence that would secure his disgrace was being sent—he challenged his opponents to bring even a hint of proof. Actually the only explicit reference to any particular wills alleged to have been proved in his court, is this in the bishop's counter-charge against those who were opposing him.

Whatever the origins of the two proclamations the fact that they were issued was, by the bishop's opponents, speedily turned into an argument for their case against him. So Fr. Rudesind Barlow writes to Rome to Fr. Henry Sillesden, S.J., of the bishop as one ' now proclaimed traitor twice for things that concerned not his religion.' [2] This letter, and another written [3] about the same time to the same correspondent, throw some light on the organisation of the case against the bishop. ' It is hard to procure particulars well proved against Mr. Harvie,' [4] says the un-identified writer of the second letter, ' seeing that he lieth to us and our friends inaccessible and unknown ; the brags and continuance of former claims are made by his adherents.' It is now made a complaint that the bishop has sent to the

---

[1] Letter (undated), Latin version, in A.P., *Anglia*, 347, f. 171 *seq.* ' Fourthly, that I set up a court and prove wills. This is a pure invention of certain Regulars. They cannot bring forward a single instance that I have ever attempted this, nor did I ever intend [to use] any other tribunal than what St. Paul used for the excommunication of the incestuous Corinthians, and which the superiors of the Regulars use for the correction of their own subjects, nor in all these years have I ever exercised any jurisdiction at all over any laymen. . . . These are all the reasons so far as I have heard, why the king's mind is turned against me . . . wherefore I beseech your Majesty to deign to inform the King of the truth. . . .'

[2] Letter of April 9, 1629, C.R.S., 22, p. 174.

[3] Letter of May 28, 1629, n.s. ; *ibid.*, pp. 172–173.

[4] *I.e.* the bishop ; *cf.* the next paragraph of the letter where he is said to have issued an order about the conditions for gaining the jubilee.

Benedictines and the Jesuits, as well as to the seculars, an instruction to insert a special collect in the Mass for the queen's safe delivery. Then the Benedictine president has heard that the Jesuits in Rome are thought to be hostile to his book against the bishop. At any rate the bishop's Roman agent, Peter Fitton, is said to have this impression. This piece of information moves the monk to exhort the Jesuit not to desert the common cause : ' The cause is not ours only,' writes the Benedictine, ' neither are we so far off the hooks but that we could come on again with such conditions as you would hardly believe.' There is an open reference to the bishop's ' violence and indiscretion,' which should be made clear to the nuncio at Paris, and Fr. Barlow goes on to say that although the secular clergy think himself ' only a hair-brained fellow . . . if you there [i.e. at Rome] and Mr. Foster at Paris, I here [i.e. at Brussels] and ours at Paris and such as I can find in France cry out with open mouth as we have occasion given to do, something would be got from the Nuntio without whom they at Rome will do nothing because he indeed is ordinary.'

Meanwhile the case dragged on before the cardinals of the Holy Office. In November, 1629, it was rumoured in London that a decision had been given, and Simon Stock, writing to Propaganda, joyously because at last some decision had been come to, seems to assume that the case has gone in the bishop's favour. Four months later he speaks of the rumours as still flourishing, and says that they were so constant that they took him in. So it was to be for yet another eighteen months, and, because it was always difficult to secure definite publication of Roman news under a régime where to be in possession of a Roman document was itself treasonable, it was inevitable that there should continue to be rumours, even after the decision had been given. In this matter the bishop was as much at the mercy of circumstances as the rest. In December, 1630, for example, he was writing to Rome that he had heard that the case was settled, but that no authentic copy of the sentence had reached him. In this letter there is not a hint that the bishop expected anything less than a complete vindication of his authority. The Pope's brief, six months later, was to fall like a thunderbolt.

In this letter of December, 1630, the bishop officially brings to the notice of Propaganda some of the literature of the controversy. Particularly he denounces a work [1] written by a Jesuit (under a pseudonym) and published, without leave, of course, either of any bishop or of his own superiors. In this work it is stated that ' the Pope is not of the essence of the Church,' which Smith notes to be the very heresy of Richier.[2] Then, he quotes from the book, it is stated that ' There is no need of bishops except for ordaining priests and ministers of the Church ; a body of Catholics which is ready to receive a bishop when one is lawfully sent to it possesses all that is essential to the Church ; the episcopate as a state binds, under pain of damnation, to actions which, morally speaking, are impossible, and therefore it is not so much a state of perfection, as a state to be deplored. There is no necessity for the Sacrament of Confirmation, the anointing with Chrism at baptism by the priest was instituted to supply the effect of Confirmation by a bishop. The *status* of the religious life is higher than the *status* of bishops.' With regard to Smith himself, the book states that he is but a judge on paper,[3] and has no jurisdiction over the Catholics of England, unless these themselves wish for it. Moreover, unless he is the ordinary of the Catholics they are not bound, in justice, to give him so much as a penny.

Once more the bishop begs the Congregation to bring about the execution of its decree [4] ordering the Regulars to present their letters and faculties to the bishop for his inspection, and he then passes to make two very serious charges against two Jesuits whom he names. One of these charges has long ago been shown to be without any foundation.[5] The other is as likely to be just as true. The accusation has an incredible air about it, and the bishop evidently believes it.[6] ' I also beg that Your Eminences will procure

[1] *An Apology of the Holy See Apostolick's Proceedings for the Government of the Catholicks of England during the tyme of persecution.*

[2] The senseless calumny that Smith was tainted with the heretical theories of this Frenchman, which he is here denouncing, was recently repeated in Pastor's far from informed account of this controversy ; *cf.* Pastor, Vol. 29, p. 305. Smith's letter is in A.P., *Lett. Ant.*, Vol. 100, f. 134 *seq.*

[3] *Iudex Chartularius.*   [4] *I.e.* of June 5, 1627.

[5] The accusation against Fr. Gerard is noted and discussed by Lingard in note HHH of his *History of England* (edition of 1855, Vol. VII, p. 277).

[6] The accusation was, says Lingard, laid before the bishop by affidavit. He had no choice but to send on the matter to Rome, and the Jesuit authorities immediately summoned Fr. Gerard to defend himself. He swore his innocence, upon the Blessed Sacrament—and we can agree with Lingard that the accuser (a secular priest, Antony Smith) ' unintentionally attributed to him what he had heard him say of some other person.'

the removal from the English College, Rome, of Fr. Tompson, *alias* Gerard, who is the confessor there, and from the English College at Valladolid of George Champion, a Jesuit lay-brother who serves as doorkeeper. For I have before me the testimony of a priest worthy of credence that the first named (apart from the fact that he was condemned by name by the public authority in England on account of the Powder Plot) said in this priest's hearing that " digging with the others under the houses of parliament, his shirt was as wet with sweat as though he had dived into the river." I have like testimony from another priest that the second of the two named has said that " he was to have put fire to the powder, had the man appointed for the task defaulted." ' It is to be feared, says the bishop, that heretics will take occasion of the presence of such men in the pontifical seminaries to suspect the Holy See of sympathy with the Plot.

This letter—of December, 1630—reached Propaganda in time to be discussed at the congregation of April 12, 1631. The only points in it which attracted attention were the extracts from the anonymous Jesuit publication, but since ' the business is pending in the Congregation of the Holy Office, the decision is to be awaited from thence ' and a copy of the letter was sent to the other congregation for its information.[1]

A month later the decision was published—the brief *Britannia*,[2] and it was, apparently, a complete justification of the bishop's opponents.

[1] *Acta*, Cong. 139, No. 8.
[2] May 9, 1631.

CHAPTER V

THE BRIEF *BRITANNIA* ; PROPAGANDA AND RICHARD SMITH

THE brief *Britannia* of Pope Urban VIII is a lengthy document that runs, in the English translation, to five and a half of Dodd's folio columns. It is a noteworthy specimen of the baroque humanism now beginning to be fashionable at the court of the Pope who was Bernini's first great patron.[1] In florid, complimentary phrases the glory that was the medieval church in England is described at length, and the still greater glory of the later Church resisting the persecutor's snares. 'But the devil could no longer endure, that the cruelty of his power should serve for an exercise of your valour.' So he tempted the English Catholics in another way, and through their faults and vices he was not altogether unsuccessful. The story of the opposition to the archpriest is referred to as a first instance of the devil's success in securing a following. And now the very establishment of a bishop in England has proved the occasion of new divisions, 'those remedies which were prepared for your salvation, are changed into means of perdition.' No doubt all the contendants think themselves fighting for what is right. But there cannot be any discord that does not come from the fraud of the devil. The very heretics are now mocking at the dissensions of people who boast of their unity as of nothing else.

Wherefore the Pope decides (1) 'that all and every one of these controversies, or any other, which have arisen and been moved and canvassed, upon what pretext soever, between the Bishop of Chalcedon, the Regular priests of the mission, and the lay Catholicks of England . . . be appeased, suppressed, and extinguished.' The decision of these, and of any new controversies arising out of this brief,

---

[1] And the contemporary translation printed by DODD (VIII, pp. 158–160), which is the work of an anonymous Benedictine, is a fine piece of English writing.

belongs to Rome alone, and it is forbidden to take such controversies for decision to any other tribunal. They are not further to be prosecuted, defended, or continued in any manner whatsoever, under penalty of excommunication. The second matter is the printed literature of the controversy. So far no pontifical censure has been passed on any of the books, says the brief, but no other authority is to presume to anticipate Rome's judgement. The Holy See reserves the judgement to itself, and it now decides that ' all of the books, which belong to this present dissension, are to be taken from the hands of the faithful.' Catholics are forbidden, under penalty of excommunication, to read these books, or to keep them, and whoever writes, prints, or publishes any further matters dealing with the controversy, is to be similarly punished. ' Let it not be irksome to you learned men, to offer up this most acceptable sacrifice unto God, by killing these issues of your wits.'

Thirdly, the brief announces that ' the confessions which have hitherto been heard by regular priests were valid and so shall be hereafter.' As to ' approbation,' ' since they did hear [confessions] hitherto, and so shall do hereafter, by apostolical authority, ordinary leave, or approbation, neither was, nor is hereafter needful unto them.' The missionaries are to continue to enjoy all the privileges that have been theirs since the beginning of the century.

If any of this seems not too clear, the further decisions of Rome are to be awaited.

The last paragraphs of the brief are a public rebuke of the bishop as one who stirs up disagreement and quenches love and charity, a man so learned that his gifts have become a stumbling-block over which the weaker brethren trip into perdition. Nevertheless his undoubted great gifts will, of themselves, no doubt win him reverence if only he will rejoice in the cross of Christ and the new reconciliation. The faithful are to reverence and respect their clergy, and if they spy faults in their shepherds to give themselves to prayer and not to reproaches.

A letter from the Cassinese Benedictine, David Codner,[1] gives an idea of the joy with which the Regulars received the brief. ' The brief of the Holy Father has at last arrived, countersigned authentically by the apostolic notaries and sealed with the seal of Cardinal Ginetti, the Pope's vicar.

[1] To Ingoli, Sept. 15, 1631 ; A.P., *Lett. Ant.*, 100, f. 162.

It has given infinite satisfaction to the Catholic laylords, who have considered themselves to be parties most interested. . . . The Pope's orders about the suppression of the books are being carried out, and, so far as I can do it, I have secured the surrender of many. The brief has done much to increase the loyalty of the lay Catholics who consider themselves as saved by the prudence of the Holy See—especially when they consider the mischievous opposition of the French intriguers. Those whom it has displeased are only a tiny minority. There are rumours—which both the French and Spanish ambassadors confirmed to me—that the Bishop of Chalcedon has left for France. Some say he has gone that he may personally stir up new troubles and make new claims.'

The brief *Britannia* is dated May 9, 1631. It did not reach the bishop until, perhaps, three months later. Before we examine how he took it, we can consider these three letters which he wrote during this interval.[1] The brief had not yet arrived, but rumours of the truth were beginning to leak out.

1. *The Bishop of Chalcedon to the Cardinals of Propaganda, London, June 14 (o.s.), 1631. (Reported at Congregation of August 26, 1631.)*

MOST EMINENT AND MOST ILLUSTRIOUS LORDS,

I have received Your Eminences' letter of the 26 April, and I have greatly regretted that the matter of the controversy between myself and certain Regulars has been entirely transferred from your tribunal, where, I make no doubt, it would long before this have been decided. Nevertheless I still cling to the belief that there will be nothing to forbid your defence of the two decrees made by Your Eminences, in one of which you order me to inspect the faculties of missionaries to be sent into England or already sent there, and in the other state that the Jesuits are to suspend the exercise of their Sodality of the Conception of the Blessed Virgin until God sends happier times to the English.

It certainly concerns greatly your own standing that you should defend your own decrees and not allow them to be scorned by Regulars of whom some are not ashamed to say that your congregation has no jurisdiction over them. It also concerns the needs and the poverty of this

---

[1] A.P., *Lett. Ant.*, Vol. 100, fols. 142–146.

afflicted church and its clergy. For if Regulars are not bound to show me their testimonials, they can hear confessions without having any faculties at all, and deceive souls damnably—as five of them have already done and one still continues to do.

It is also, very certainly, to the interest of the clergy that the Jesuits shall not be allowed, under the pretext of the said sodality, to take away the laity in order themselves to hear their confessions. In Catholic countries the clergy are maintained either by private patrimony or benefices, and are promoted to sacred orders on these; in no way, therefore, do the secular clergy depend for their living on those who come to confession to them. But the secular clergy in England are not ordained on any title but that of their mission, nor are they maintained by any other resources than come from their penitents, and therefore to take these away from the clergy, for any reason whatsoever, is to deprive them of maintenance and of food. Your Eminences will know that the English secular clergy were the first of all the missionaries to be sent into this vineyard by the Apostolic See; that they have expended more of sweat, and of blood, in its cultivation than all the Regulars put together; and that nowhere, except in England, have they any place they can call their home. The Regulars maintain, outside England, monasteries to which they can betake themselves, and therefore it is a wicked thing that the laity are drawn away from the secular clergy by the greater faculties and favours which the Regulars obtain from the Apostolic See.

I therefore beseech Your Eminences to defend the decrees you have enacted; that our Regulars may realise that your congregation has authority over them; that the English Catholics may have security that the Regulars to whom they make their confessions really hold faculties for the hearing of confessions; that the children whom the secular clergy have borne to Christ may be preserved to them, and not allowed to be drawn away by pedagogues; that the title by which the clergy are promoted to holy orders may not be unfruitful, and the clergy, after such a service of labour and of blood to the Church, may not be reduced to a shameful life of begging that is a disgrace to their priestly condition.

The Jesuits, I know it well enough, allege that in this

matter they are not promoting their own interests, but the
honour of God and the good of souls, and would that they
did not just allege this, and that we did not by actual
experience know that, in the creation of the said sodality,
they were looking after themselves, drawing away disciples
and fostering a faction hostile to the clergy. Let Your
Eminences be the judges whether this, however insigni-
ficant it be, which they allege to be for God's honour
and the good of souls, is of such moment that it is to be
carried out, entailing as it does such heavy loss to the
clergy, such vexation to them, and such a loss of charity—
especially in a time so filled with calamity, and with
minds so sore. Would it not rather work for the honour
of God and the good of souls to suspend the practice of
this sodality until it could be renewed without this serious
injury to the body of the clergy ?

I most earnestly beseech Your Eminences in no way
to believe that those English notables form one-third of the
Catholics of England, whom Don Carlo Coloma—the late
Spanish ambassador here—asserts, in his testimony, which
the Jesuits have printed and scattered broadcast, to have
approached him stating that they cannot subject themselves
to any episcopal authority.[1] For—to say nothing of the
fact that all the notables who have refused me recognition are the penitents of Regulars, and of this fact also
that for a whole two years I met with no opposition from
any Catholic at all, until the time when I took up with
the Regulars the question of ' approbation '—exactly
seven, or eight at most, English notables came to see
the French ambassador about this matter, nor could
others have been to see his Spanish colleague. Two of
these, namely, Somerset and Baltimore, are not English,
but Irish notables; a third, Herbert, is not a peer of the
English parliament, and a fourth who is their leader,
when afterwards he was rightly informed about the
authority I claim over the laity, immediately sent his
brother to the French ambassador to protest that he was
not opposed to my jurisdiction. Since therefore there are
now in England twenty-four catholic notables,[2] how small

---

[1] The reference is to Coloma's support of the declaration of the lay
Catholics of England against the bishop's claims, published (with signatures)
in the previous March (1631) ; *Southcott's Diary* in C.R.S., Vol. I, p. 106
[2] The twenty-four Catholic peers.

is the number of those whom the said Don Carlo can adduce as declaring themselves opposed to my authority, in comparison with the whole body of Catholic notables ?

If, however, I were willing,[1] at the risk it would entail to the signatories, to collect the votes of those other Catholics who most gladly accept the bishop's authority and who are highly indignant at this opposition made against it in the name of the Catholics of England, surely my opponents would blush at their shameful imposture.

But, relying on the justice of my cause, and the prudence of the Apostolic See, I have never been willing to subject a bishop's authority to the judgement of laymen.

Moreover, these laymen who oppose me have never been willing to meet me—although I have frequently invited them—in order to inform themselves rightly about my jurisdiction and my intentions, but will only listen to my adversaries. Certainly they showed themselves far from rightly informed when they alleged that the reason for their opposition was that I was planning to set up a court—and this in opposition to the courts of England

[1] A letter from the French ambassador in London to his colleague in Rome—undated, but written much later this same year 1631, after the appearance in England of the brief *Britannia*—testifies to the bishop's reluctance to anything like an organisation of the laity who were faithful to him in a counter, anti-Regular petition. ' L'evesque ne voulut pas alors agir avec la mesme addresse ; ni faire parler à cinque ou six de ses partisans seulement, sous le nom du général des Catholiques ; comme avait fait les autres.' The bishop, handicapped by his sense of what was due to his office, was out-manœuvred, and when he began to make enquiries through his vicars-general as to the general sentiment of the leading Catholics, it was too late. ' Les reguliers ayant, pendant cela, soigneusement poursuivis leur affaire, ils ont obtenu le bref . . . lequel estant grandement prejudiciable à l'évesque, et donné sur un fondement qui n'est pas véritable. . . .' Whence the ambassador begs his colleague to enlighten the Pope and the congregation concerned, and to insist that the bishop and his clergy are not so lacking in support as has been represented.

As the letter states that the bishop is still lodged with the ambassador, it must have been written before Aug. 24, 1631, the date on which the bishop left England according to Southcott (C.R.S., Vol. I, p. 107). The text of the ambassador's letter, given as from a 'copy in *Doway* college,' is in DODD, III, p. 143. In this same volume are also printed some of the letters from the bishop's officials concerning the feelings of the laity about the bishop's authority (pp. 149–150) ; two letters from the queen, Henrietta Maria, one (Aug. 10, 1631), asking the help of the French ambassador at Rome for the bishop, and the upholding of his authority and commending to him the bishop's new agent, Peter Fitton, the other (Nov. 23, 1631) supporting the letter enclosed, *viz.* a memorial of the clergy and laity asking (i) for a declaration in support of the authority of the bishop ; (ii) that the bishop be sent back with full, well-defined powers ; (iii) that additional bishops be appointed, whom (iv) the petitioners pledge themselves to maintain (*ibid.*, pp. 141–142).

—in order to prove wills, to collect tithes, to move priests wherever I chose, to declare null confessions made without my ' approbation,' and other things of this same kind, all of which are most foreign to the truth of the matter, and to my own mind, so that what they are in fact opposing and refusing to submit to, is not myself, but a figment of the Regulars.

To this it must be added that the testimony of Don Carlo against me should be considerably discounted for this reason that he openly admits that he suspects me not to be well disposed to Spain because I was so long in the household of the Cardinal de Richelieu, who he persuades himself is a most bitter enemy of Spain.[1] The ambassador was also most annoyed because, when he was leaving England, I did not personally pay him a farewell visit. This, without a certain and serious risk of being arrested, I could not do, but a few days before he left I sent two of the principal priests to pay him my respects. Moreover, in a letter which he recently wrote to the president of Douay College he openly asserted that he favoured my opponents because he knew them to be more favourable to his master's sovereignty than to any other foreigners.

I put these things forward, and much else of the like sort, that Your Eminence may bring it to the notice of His Holiness. It is not indeed that I am longing to keep my position as bishop here, for I live shut up perpetually in one small bedroom, and can never allow myself to breathe fresh air ; I am at the mercy of the plots of the heretics and of the harassing Regulars, without any consolation from elsewhere ; my life is in danger. It is a state of things that I would gladly exchange for freedom in France. But [I urge these considerations] because I am wholly convinced that for me to be deprived of my authority because of the empty and imaginary pretexts of a few laymen, stirred up by Regulars, could not but entail infamy to the Apostolic See, dishonour to the episcopal dignity, danger and scandal to other bishops, and finally the most serious loss to the whole body of the secular clergy in England and to by far the greater part of the laity.

[1] Cf. the letter of George Leybourne to the bishop, written three months later than this (Sept. 6, 1631), in which the Spanish ' case ' is given in detail: ' These points the agent did utter with great passion and bitterness ' : text in C.R.S., Vol. 22, p. 176.

May Jesus Christ the bishop of bishops inspire his vicar with counsel for this matter which may be truly fruitful for this most afflicted church.

Along with this letter I send to Your Eminences the censure of a blasphemous book which the Jesuits have had published and have arranged to be publicly sold by the heretics, so that Your Eminences may understand, from this and at the same time from the other book they have poured forth, what need there is here to set up a bishop's authority as a bulwark to deaden their unbridled attacks. May God bless, etc. etc.

(Signed) R. BISHOP OF CHALCEDON.
LONDON, 14 *June*, (O.S.), 1631.

The secretary's note of the Congregation's discussion of this letter [1] gives us the information that the object of the Spanish ambassador's letter was to bring about the bishop's withdrawal from England. The cardinals ordered a copy of the bishop's letter to be sent to the Holy Office ' although the case of the bishop and the Regulars is at an end.'

On the same day that he wrote this long official letter to the cardinals of Propaganda, the bishop wrote privately to Mgr Ingoli.

2. *The Bishop of Chalcedon to Monsignor Francis Ingoli. June* 14, 1631 (O.S.).

I have received your Lordship's two letters dated for Easter, through the agent of the Grand Duke.[2] They were a great consolation to me amidst the enormous heap of troubles which, partly from heretics and still more from Jesuits, almost overwhelms me. I thank your lordship from my heart, and as I thank you, so shall I ever be mindful of my debt to you.

Certain difficulties which I was not able to overcome brought it about that, until now, I have not been able to send an agent to Rome.[3] Nevertheless now I shall send someone as soon as possible.

---

[1] A.P., *Acta*, Aug. 26, 1631, Cong. 146, No. 33 : ' Pro exclusione episcopi in Anglia.'
[2] *I.e.* of Tuscany.
[3] The importance of a bishop's maintaining a permanent agent in the *Curia Romana* is self-evident. Once the Congregation of Propaganda was fully organised it became part of every missionary bishop's duty to have a

I would gladly forward letters through the agent of
the Grand Duke, except that his ardent enthusiasm for the
Jesuits forces me to suspect him somewhat, for he has,
hereabouts, taken their part against me bitterly. If,
however, this notwithstanding, your lordship continues
to advise me to do this I shall willingly follow your advice.

I have no doubt whatever, if the issue could be decided
by a vote of the Catholics of England, whether it would
be the bishop or the Jesuits who would be called forth
out of that country.

As it is, some Catholics, of their own motion, are
speaking of a petition to the Pope to recall the Jesuits.

If there should come into your hand a book entitled,
Apology of the Jesuits for the Bishop of Chalcedon, you may
see in it our Jesuits playing the part of gods, and, as
though it were their own special business, now arranging
that bishops and episcopal authority are suitable for
England and now denying it ; now they argue that the
laws of England stand in the way of this, and now that
they are no obstacles ; and so with regard to many
other things, which shows openly that, in the name of the
laity, the Jesuits are furthering their own interests and
patronising or attacking episcopal authority just according
as it responds to their nod or not. Whether in the present
circumstances of England episcopal authority is expedient,
this at any rate is surely not to be borne that these men
should stir up the laity of their party to work for its
extirpation, and this upon the false pretext of the laws

Roman agent (*cf.* the instructions to the newly appointed vicars-apostolic
for China in PASTOR, 31, p. 151). This need was at its maximum for bishops
in whose dioceses or districts the regular clergy were engaged in a quasi-
parochial apostolate. Whenever a real crisis arose in such administrations,
the bishop without a permanent Roman agent was badly handicapped ; for
the Regulars are, corporally, ever present to the curial officials, given that
Rome is, normally, the G.H.Q. of the orders. Readers of Cardinal Vaughan's
life will recall how, in the last battle of the long war that opened with
Richard Smith's defeat, it was necessary for the Bishop of Salford (as
Vaughan then was) to leave his diocese for three years to the care of
neighbouring bishops, while at Rome he manœuvred and counter-
manœuvred against his well-organised opponents. When Bosvile went to
Rome in the autumn of 1628 as Richard Smith's agent, the bishop had been
without an agent since the death of More in April, 1625 (*Southcott's Diary,*
C.R.S., Vol. I, p. 101). Bosvile was back in England by February, 1630,
and in the surely critical year that preceded the issue of the brief *Britannia,*
the bishop and his case were once again unrepresented in Rome. It was
only in August, 1631, that Smith was able to find the means—always the
great trouble with these unendowed bishops—to send a successor to
Bosvile. This was Peter Fitton (*alias* Biddulph).

(whereas no law has so far been enacted against a bishop's authority) and of losses and dangers, concerning which last, in all these eight years since that authority was restored, no one has been at the loss of a penny on account of it. And even more, they have striven to compel the consent of His Holiness to their plans by means of the importunity of these laymen, in which (as others have noted) they keep up the old custom to win princes to their opinion through fear of the people, and the people through fear of the princes, so that they may dominate both.

I write to you only a short letter, because I am sending to you, unsealed, the letters which I have written to the Sacred Congregation of Propaganda and to his eminence Cardinal del Bagno,[1] which letters I beg Your Lordship to read and then to convey to their destination. God keep your lordship ever safe from harm.

(Signed) R. BISHOP OF CHALCEDON.

14 *June*, 1631.

3. *The Bishop of Chalcedon to Monsignor Francis Ingoli.
July* 20, 1631.

MY LORD,
What your lordship advised me to do when you wrote, I now perform, having overcome the obstacles which hitherto have stood in the way of it, sending the bearer of this letter, the Reverend Peter Bidulph, *alias* Fitton, to plead at Rome my cause and the cause of the English secular clergy. He is a priest of noble birth and of tried prudence, and as I think, already known to your lordship. I commend him as much as I am able to your lordship and I earnestly ask for him from you whatever aid of counsel or favour he may stand in need.

Our Regulars are now boasting everywhere that His Holiness, by a recent decree, has stripped me of all episcopal power and has reduced me to the rank of an archpriest. If he has done this, I am afraid he has brought shame to himself more than to me. For that a bishop

---

[1] Gianfranceso de' Conti Guidi di Bagno (1578 1641), one of the best-informed officials of the Curia so far as English affairs were concerned. He was nuncio at Brussels from 1621 to 1627, and at Paris from 1627 to 1630 ; *cf.* CARDELLA, VI, p. 285, BIAUDET, p. 269.

has been overthrown, not for any deserts of his, but solely because of the clamour and the impositions of certain Regulars and the factious behaviour of a few laymen, cannot be disgraceful, for punishment where there is no fault cannot entail disgrace. But that the Supreme Pontiff should strip of his episcopal dignity a bishop chosen and established by himself—who for the Catholic faith has been twice put to the ban by his own king—and all merely because of the tricks of certain Regulars, tricks that have taken in His Holiness, the suggestion, for example, that all or most of the Catholics in England are resolved not to endure a bishop, and tricks that have roused these laity against the bishop, such as the suggesting that he was planning to set up a court and to prove wills, collect tithes and other like actions—all of which is not only not true but as far removed from any kind of truth as may be—I fear that this will be to the Pope himself somewhat inglorious, and dangerous in the extreme to the whole episcopal body.

For what bishop will have any trust in the Apostolic See as his defence against the efforts of such Regulars, when it is seen that a bishop specially chosen and appointed by that see itself, who has suffered so often and so heavily for the faith, is deprived of his dignity, without any demerit on his part, and exposed to the mockery of the Regulars, and that the Regulars not only are not punished for their intrigues and their raising of factions against the bishop, but, as it were, rewarded and allowed a triumph ? And what will not Regulars in the future dare against bishops, when they see that bishops whom they do not want are not allowed by the Holy See either to be appointed or to survive ? Nay, by the very fact, they think it matters not at all whether the liberty and government of the church is handed over either to laity or to Regulars, so long as this is done by those whom the Holy Ghost has placed to rule the Church of God.

I whisper these things into Your Lordship's ear, fearing that, unless some remedy is found, there will not be wanting others who will cry them out loud in the open.

(Signed) R. BISHOP OF CHALCEDON.

LONDON, 20 *July.*

This letter seems to have stirred the secretary deeply, for he sent it on to the Cardinal Prefect with the following note :

' This was written to me in confidence. Your Eminence can see it in order to learn with what feelings the Bishop of Chalcedon must have received the news of the decision arrived at by the Holy Office in favour of the Regulars, and although he may not have yet received the Brief—whose context is not so displeasing—nevertheless the way in which it is written has changed very greatly the spirit of this bishop, it seeming to him that he is blamed where he ought to be praised and defended.'

This note, scribbled by Ingoli on the back of the bishop's letter, bears the date November 11, 1631. By this time Richard Smith had left England.[1] Many guesses have been made as to what moved him to this act, and as to what he had in mind. I have not met any explanation of it among what papers of his have come my way. Certainly it was not, in the bishop's mind, the preliminary to any abdication. From the two letters written to him from London, immediately after his departure, by the priest, George Leybourne,[2] who had been his companion as far as Calais, we get the impression that Smith was preparing some new intervention at Rome.[3] And in a letter to Ingoli,[4] written in the first few weeks after his arrival in Paris, he speaks of the pleasure it would be if ' during my absence from England ' some (unnamed) abbot should be consecrated and sent there. Also the bishop states that in his latest letters to the Pope he has asked (and not for the first time apparently) that several bishops be appointed and the country divided between them.

From this letter to Ingoli of October 10, 1631, we learn that the bishop had not, before leaving England, made any official communication of the brief to his flock, and this

[1] Southcott gives the date of his departure as Aug. 24, 1631, C.R.S., I, p. 107.
[2] (1593–1677.) Later, as President of Douay College (1652–1670), a most strenuous champion of orthodox thought and traditional ways in the later disputes that divided the leaderless secular clergy. He was the nephew of James Leybourne, executed in 1583 for refusing to acknowledge Elizabeth as queen because of her excommunication, and the uncle of Dr. John Leybourne, his own successor at Douay, and then (1685) Bishop of Adrumetum and the first of the vicars-apostolic.
[3] C.R.S., Vol. 22, p. 176.
[4] Letter of Oct. 10, 1631, A.P., *Lett. Ant.*, 100, f. 147.

in spite of Ingoli's advice. He has not published it, he writes, because to have done so would have wholly alienated his clergy, and for a fuller explanation of this he refers the secretary to his new agent, Peter Fitton, now in Rome. No doubt the bishop, at this moment, had hopes of persuading the Pope to reverse the decision. His mind may have recalled Clement VIII's reversal of the first adverse sentence in the case of the Appellants.

But the decision—in so far as it can be called a decision— of the brief *Britannia* was not reversed, and the Bishop of Chalcedon lived the rest of his life abroad, and in a curiously ambiguous position. The Pope had not deposed him, nor had he resigned. But the Pope appears, for reasons so far not discovered, to have considered that he had resigned, and to have treated him as a bishop who has resigned and to whom other employment has not been given. In later years there seems to have been some kind of prohibition against his returning to England, for we meet references to his willingness to go back to England if he is allowed, and when, with the Civil War, the persecution is renewed and blood begins to flow once more, the bishop, now an old man well past seventy, begs the Pope to allow him to return for if he can do nothing else he can at least testify with his life to the faith.[1] None of these petitions was granted. For a time the Pope seems to have had it in mind to give Smith a benefice in Rome itself, and though the bishop would have obeyed, he did not like the idea of living in Italy.[2] Nor did his patron Richelieu. He it was who ultimately provided for his old tutor, giving him *in commendam* the abbey of Chelles for his support. When Richelieu died, in 1642, Smith lost his abbey, and shared in the general rout of Richelieu's friends that followed the rise of Mazarin. In his prosperous days the bishop had greatly helped the foundation in Paris of an abbey of English Canonesses of St. Augustine. To them he turned in his need, and for the last thirteen years of his life he lived with them, acting as their chaplain, an informal head of the English Catholic community in Paris, busy to the last with the care of the nuns, his books, the instruction of converts, and until a

---

[1] *Cf.* the nuncio at Paris to S.C.P.F., Jan. 20 and Mar. 17, 1645 ; A.P., *Lett. Ant.*, Vol. 143, f. 5, 50 ; the nuncio speaks of him as ' a prelate of great holiness.'

[2] Richard Smith to Fitton, March 11, 1633, in C.R.S., Vol. 21, p. 179.

general Roman decree interfered with this, ordaining and confirming as an auxiliary to the archbishop of Paris and his coadjutor, the Cardinal de Retz. Unlike the famous cardinal, Richard Smith left no memoirs behind him. But we do possess the memorandum he sent to Rome on the brief which—as he conceived it—ended his usefulness to the Church in England, and we know of his strenuous efforts to secure the appointment of a successor. When he came to die, a patriarch of eighty-eight, on March 12, 1655, Richard Smith was buried in the church of the convent where he lived. On his tombstone it was written that 'he was proscribed for the faith,' and also that ' he was sold by false brethren.' It was the nuns for whom he had cared who now cared for his memory, and, as it were, had the last word, on his behalf, in the long controversy. When, two hundred years and more after the death of the bishop, this community returned to England,[1] it took with it, among other treasures, a portrait of its venerated patron and his rosary, which by a pious custom each religious, week by week, uses in turn to pray for the conversion of England.

Was Richard Smith indeed ' sold by false brethren ? ' It is more than, at this time of day, any man can safely assert, and it is more important for the historian to turn from the construction of verdicts against ' persons unknown,' to the consideration of the bishop's criticism of the *mens* that was to preside over the destinies of the faith in England for the next fifty years after the brief *Britannia* (1631–1685), and to a consideration of those persistent—if less pleasing— features of Catholic life which, all through the century, drove the chief of the secular clergy to their incessant appeals to Rome for the creation of bishops in England.

The Bishop of Chalcedon, deeply though he felt the brief *Britannia*, gave no public sign of his attitude. But the archives of Propaganda still conserve the protest which he instructed his agent, Peter Fitton, to make in his name.[2] The bishop begins by reviewing the history of the con- troversies, from his own appointment down to the issue of the brief. His objections are rather to the language of the

---

[1] It is now established at Hill Crest Road, Ealing, London, W.5.

[2] A lengthy document, in *Anglia*, 347, ff. 346–352 v. ; this appears to be Fitton's own copy. It is not written in the hand of the professional scrivener, and two writers have shared the labour. The paper begins : ' Dispersis per Angliam et Scotiam Christi fidelibus,' and it is addressed to the Cardinal Prefect of Propaganda.

brief and to the way in which the decision is given, than to
that decision itself. The Pope has peremptorily announced
in the brief that there must be no more discussion on the
controverted subjects, and that all the confessions made to
Regulars have always been valid, are valid now and always
will be. Of the accusations made, so generally, against the
bishop the brief says not a word. There is no word to
reprove those who make these accusations nor any word to
reprove the bishop, supposing the accusations were justified.
Had the bishop indeed exceeded his authority ? Had the
Regulars acted lawfully in their proceedings against him,
in England and in Rome ? About these central facts of
the controversy—questions in which lay the seeds of inevitable future trouble—the brief was silent. The bishop has
found his jurisdiction opposed and denied in certain quarters.
He has appealed to Rome, and the Roman answer is a
simple declaration that these quarrels must utterly cease
and not be renewed.

Such is the introduction to the paper. The protest
proper opens with a reference to the clause of the brief
which states that all the confessions made to the Regulars
were valid. This the bishop quotes in order to say that,
of course, he has never thought otherwise. It is the common
teaching of all authorities, and more than once he has said
this quite openly to quieten scrupulous consciences, and has
done his best to persuade all concerned that confessions
made in good faith are not to be called in question.

But when the brief goes on to say that such confessions
(*i.e.* those made to a Regular who has not obtained any kind
of recognition of his faculties from the bishop) will be valid
also for the future, it in effect deprives the bishop of a power
which, by the law, the councils, and a papal constitution,
belongs to him as to all ordinaries. The bishop does not,
of course, question the power of the Holy See to do this,
and he declares that had this change been demanded in the
spirit in which it has been granted, *i.e.* to promote the
interests of religion—he should rejoice. As it is, the Regulars
are joyously announcing the news as proof that the bishop
has been in the wrong, and in speech and in writing are so
holding him up to mockery that not only these powers of
his are lost, but his very reputation is destroyed.

To correct this interpretation of the brief as a condemnation of the bishop, Smith would like to see certain modifica-

tions in its language, so that the office in which the Holy
See has placed him may be given support, and himself not
seem to have been asking something unreasonable of the
Regulars. He asks for changes that will make it clear that
a bishop's authority is not something that can be ignored
and, as it were, given only a second place, and, finally—
most importantly, one would say—the changes should be
made so that it will not seem that he, the Bishop of Chalcedon, has so abused his power that he is now put aside in
punishment and the Regulars allowed to hear confessions
without paying him any further attention.

In this spirit, and with these objects in view, the bishop
makes some concrete suggestions. A phrase might be added
to the clause which deals with the Regulars' power to hear
confessions, saying that confessions heard by an 'unapproved'
Regular would be valid supposing it had been too serious
an inconvenience for him to have sought 'approbation,'
the responsibility in the matter being left to the Regular's
conscience. As the Regulars interpret the 'extinction of
controversies' clause to mean that Chalcedon is stripped
now of all episcopal authority, and that the decree about
submitting their faculties for his inspection and about asking
his approbation for the administration of the three parochial
sacraments is a dead letter, and as they state that he is a
bishop in name only [1]—so that there is not a single episcopal
right which they do not deny him—since this is their present
state of mind, if the Holy See allows nothing more to be said,
the brief leaves the case of the Regulars in possession.
There are to be, henceforward, two parties in England, those
who think like this about bishops and the rest.

The brief, then, as things are, works implicitly not only
against the Bishop of Chalcedon, but against the rights of
bishops everywhere. This anti-episcopal interpretation is
given credit all the more readily in England because, while
the brief says not a word in support of episcopal jurisdiction,
it expressly notes that the Regulars retain all their privileges
and declares explicitly that they can make as full use of these
as before the bishop was appointed. At the same time the
brief contains much which seems to make it doubtful if the
Regulars owe any duty of subordination at all to the bishop.
The brief states, in fact, that the Regulars are exempt from

---

[1] ' That he has the keys to open indeed, but not to close ; the mitre, but
not the crozier ; is a bishop sent just to bless the Holy Oils and such like.'

any duty to ask ' approbation ' because they are missionaries, and the Regulars proceed to enlarge on this and to declare that, by the same title, they are exempt from all subordination to the bishop, and that this would be true even if he really were an ordinary.

It must also be said that the brief contains passages which ' the said Regulars ' can have no difficulty in interpreting as such a condemnation of this bishop that Catholics, for the future, are likely to shun rather than reverence him. The Pope says, for example : ' As for the rest, venerable brother, we beseech you to remember in what country and what stormy days you are living, and to make it your ambition to be held there as an extinguisher of factions and as one who excites love.' In a second place the Pope says, again : ' And through your learning, brother, the weak will perish, for whom Christ laid down his life.' These passages cannot but suggest that, in the judgement of the Holy See, all these dissensions arose from the bishop's imprudence, and that the Holy See is approving all that the clamour of these Regulars has effected against the bishop.

The bishop ends with six specific requests :

1. A declaration that the brief which appointed him keeps all its force, that he retains all his jurisdiction as an ordinary and that he is not a mere ' bishop on paper,' [1] and that this is the law of the matter.
2. A declaration that it is his duty to inspect the letters patent and faculties of all missionaries—as Propaganda has already decreed.[2]
3. A declaration that the bishop has the right to appoint parish priests, i.e. priests who will be bound in conscience, ex officio, to give the sacraments and to undertake the cure of souls.
4. A warning to the Regulars to observe the law about the administration of the three parochial sacraments,[3] to refrain from public criticism of the bishop, and from giving absolution in cases reserved to the bishop.
5. A declaration that Regulars are not to absolve from excommunications imposed by the bishop.

[1] Episcopus chartularius, a phrase coined by one of his Regular opponents.
[2] By decree of June 5, 1627.
[3] The bishop notes that twice already, through the nuncio in Paris, he has been admonished by the Holy Office to see to this.

6. Some modification of the language of the brief *Britannia* (in the passage that deals with the Regulars' power to hear confessions independently of the bishop's ' approbation ') in order that the bishop's reputation may be safeguarded. The modification suggested is that already explained in the petition.

Whether this petition ever got beyond the drafting stage, whether it was presented, and what kind of a reception it received, we do not know. Nothing was done ; and the brief *Britannia* remained Rome's last word on the intricate question of the Bishop of Chalcedon's jurisdiction.

There is also in this same volume *Anglia*, at p. 347, a short summary headed *Præcipua quædam puncta proposita ab Epo. Calcedonen. Circa iurisdictionem ipsius in Anglia sustentandam.* It is not dated and bears no endorsement, but it was apparently drawn up about the same time as the longer protest just analysed. It calls for notice because it expresses the bishop's mind on matters not touched on by the longer protest, and affords further evidence of the spirit that moved Richard Smith throughout this delicate business. The bishop here asks, in fact, for a declaration (1) that he is not bound to give the Regulars faculties to administer the three parochial sacraments unless there is no parish priest within two miles of their residence ; (2) that he has power to deprive of their faculties to administer these sacraments Regulars who are notoriously guilty of offences in administering them ; (3) that if any Regular falls into a notorious crime and his superiors, notified by the bishop, neglect to correct or remove him, the bishop may punish the offender according to his discretion, as the canons of Trent direct. Then follows a detailed passage about the needed—or desired—authority over the laity, a passage of great importance in view of the eternal repetition, in what we may call the anti-Smith dossier, that the bishop had endeavoured to rule the laity, with laws and tribunals, as though England were a Catholic country ; in view, also, of the bishop's charge that the laity were stirred up against him by stories that he proposed to tyrannise over them ; and in view, finally, of the decisive effects of these fictions in the Curia. The bishop, with the laity in mind, begs a declaration (*a*) that he has the same power of binding and loosing—for the removal of scandals—which other bishops possess for their respective dioceses ; (b) that he is the lawful judge in England for ecclesiastical causes and that the Catholics of England must take their cases to him, especially marriage cases, cases concerning pious legacies, calumnies, and all suits which cannot be brought before a heretical tribunal either because of the scandal or because they involve priests ; (c) that pious bequests are to be referred to the bishop ' for confirmation,' [1] or, at any rate, that executors must make known such bequests to the bishop, so that he may know whether the dispositions of the testator have been carried out. Here the bishop takes the opportunity of once more denying that he has ever desired to exercise any jurisdiction over Catholic laymen, or to levy tithes, and he invites, in the public declaration for which he is petitioning, an explicit exception of these several matters ; he asks (4) that he may erect a chapter to function so long as England remains separated from the Holy See and to be *ad beneplacitum S. Sedis* ; and (5) authority to nominate parish priests.

Finally the bishop asks that he be granted a title that will be in keeping with the authority which he enjoys. This last request touches on one of the weakest points in Richard Smith's position and one of the most important of the many curious administrative shortcomings in which his case, as far as we know it, abounds. For no one seems really to have known what status in the hierarchy Richard Smith possessed. He was the titular Bishop of Chalcedon in Asia Minor, and the brief that appoints him carefully safeguards the rights of his metropolitan the Patriarch of Constantinople. He was not a vicar-apostolic, although he is always classed as such to-day in what official lists we publish. Nowhere in all the correspondence and papers of this controversy, does that title ever occur. There were, at this very time, vicars-apostolic abroad, as there were, later, to be vicars-apostolic in England. The Archbishop of Philippi, whose letter to Richard Smith has been noted, was vicar-apostolic of Holland, and there were, from time to time, in the seventeenth century, vicars-apostolic appointed in Ireland. But Richard Smith was the Bishop of Chalcedon and, for so long as it pleased the Holy See, he enjoyed in England the faculties which all ordinaries enjoy and possess. What

---

[1] *Ut ratificentur.*

the original cause of the vague and anomalous position remains one of the mysteries of the case.

Was the real source of the whole controversy Richard Smith's personality ? Or were the Regulars who, as it might be expressed, ' worked him out,' hostile in reality to the very idea of episcopal rule ? And if this last were not so, could not another have been appointed in the place of the Bishop of Chalcedon, or, better still, several bishops have been sent into England, and to make it evident to the Regulars that no attack on the orders was intended, some of these bishops be Regulars ? All these ideas we find actively circulating in the high places of ecclesiastical government during the years of the crisis and even after Smith's retirement to France. The nuncio at Paris, for example, was telling Smith, in March, 1633,[1] ' that it is *sub iudice* whether I or another be sent as bishop into England,' and the bishop thereupon sent to his agent in Rome the names of the four priests he thought most fit for the post. These were John Southcott, his one-time secretary ; George Muscott, his London vicar-general ; Antony Champney, an old colleague of the Collège d'Arras and now vice-president of Douay College ; Cuthbert Trollope, and Edward Bennett, both of whom are vicars-general. The bishop thought it would be better to choose any one of these rather than that he should go back, for he personally would be doubly handicapped by the proclamation still in force against him and the hostility of the Jesuits. The nuncio, however, was of the opinion that Chalcedon himself should be sent back to England : ' And I told him I thanked him for his good will, but not for the thing.'

Just a week later than the date of this letter Fitton was handing to Mgr Ingoli a petition [2] much in the sense of the bishop's letter but, to judge from the date and some of its details, prepared independently. From this petition we gather that Smith has not resigned his appointment, for the paper begins by saying that he is prepared to do this, for the sake of peace, whenever the Pope desires it, but in making this offer, he begs the Pope not to accept it until other bishops are chosen in his place, so that the *Ecclesia*

[1] Letter of Chalcedon to Fitton, Mar. 11, 1633, in C.R.S., Vol. 22, p. 179.
[2] *Quædam perpenda circa præsentem episcopum Chalcedonensem et alios pro episcopis in Anglia eligendos.* A.P., *Anglia,* 347, ff. 366 and following ; endorsed by Ingoli, ' Havuta dal signor agente di detto vescovo li 18 Marzo 1633.'

Anglicana may not be left without a head. The bishop also
asks that the change shall be so arranged that he shall
not seem to have been deposed for some fault of his own,
and also that the Pope will provide for his future
maintenance.

Next, the petition presents the desire of the clergy of
England for the appointment of three or four bishops, one
of the four to have jurisdiction, as archbishop, over the rest.
The clergy—this is given as their opinion and wish, and quite
independently of Smith's own views—think that the archbishop should be Richard Smith. No one of the clergy is in
greater favour with the queen—and the queen's support is
all-important. Besides, through his good relations with
Henrietta Maria the bishop has secured the good opinion
of the king, who knows him as a loyal and faithful subject.
Moreover, Smith, because of his powerful friends in France,
can do much more for his people than any other bishop could
achieve. Finally his merit has won him such a name
among all Catholics, and even among Protestants, that he is
truly a man apart.

It may be that the cardinals of Propaganda will think it
better, ' for the sake of peace,' to pass over all this merit.
In which case the clergy present as worthy of the honour and
as suitable for the burden of the episcopate, the following
fifteen priests, and beg that four or at least three may be
chosen and consecrated, for with less than three bishops
the work cannot be done. The priests presented are
Edward Bennett ; John Bosvile, a vicar-general, a one-
time appellant and recently (1629) the bishop's agent in
Rome ; Cuthbert Trollope ; Matthew Kellison, D.D., the
President of Douay College ; Antony Champney ; George
Muscott ; William Farrar ; Henry Mallard, D.D. ; Thomas
White, D.D., a one-time Roman agent of the bishop ; [1]
Edmund Stratford (*vere* Lechmere), S.T.B. ; William
Shelley ; John Southcott, D.D. ; Fr. Simon Stock, of the
Discalced Carmelites, and superior of the order in England ;
Dom Maurus Tayler, O.S.B., of the Cassinese Congregation ;

---

[1] He was also (for a time) president of the Lisbon seminary, and later the
author of some more than doubtfully orthodox theological works, and the
theorist of the attempted *rapprochement* with Cromwell. This theological
rationaliser, the friend of Hobbes, is the nearest approach to a heresiarch
that English Catholicism has produced since Cranmer. A study of his life
would throw light on many dark places. Needless to say that, at the time
of this petition, the future of Dr. White, *alias* Blacklow, was all unforeseen.

Fr. Bonaventure Johnson, O.S.F., one-time superior of his English brethren.

The inclusion of the three Regulars is interesting, as is the remark of the petitioners that they are ' men of peace.' But the clergy beg the Pope not to make more than one regular bishop at any one time, and not to choose a Regular as the bishop who is to have precedence over the other bishops. Also, bishops who are Regulars should be bidden not to choose other Regulars for their officials.

There are two significant omissions in this list, the English Benedictines and the Jesuits. As to the first the petition is silent, but about the Jesuits it becomes suddenly eloquent, with an almost embarrassing eagerness. No Jesuit is proposed because the clergy do not know a single one who is not, for just reasons, suspected as a partisan. Any Jesuit to any secular priest would be, as his bishop, *persona ingratissima*. They are, of course, in very bad odour with the king and the nation. There hangs about them still the suspicion that they had something to do with that Gunpowder Plot ' whose anniversary is annually kept with much solemnity.' Finally, did not Clement VIII in the brief ' *Venerunt Nuper* ' forbid Jesuits ever to mix themselves in the business of ruling the secular clergy ? And who that loves peace will abrogate such a rule, at any rate ' until the ' said fathers and the clergy agree better with each other.'

Although, five months later than this (August 26, 1633), the Bishop of Chalcedon was writing to Fitton his pleasure at the news that England was to have a bishop again, the scheme was never realised, nor any part of it. It was not, in 1633, a new scheme and it had already been, somewhat peremptorily, brushed out of the sphere of practical politics by the hand of the Pope himself, Urban VIII. What part the direct action of this augustan personage played in the *affaire* Smith it would be interesting to discover,[1] as it would

[1] Pastor may be quoted describing the vivid personality of this first of the baroque Popes :
'. . . a self-possessed and keenly observant man who brooked no contradiction. . . . His was a jovial disposition and like a true Florentine he loved to season his private conversation with clever and witty remarks. . . . His self-reliance was such that he disdained other people's opinions and would not even listen to them. Neither flattery, fear, nor interest could cause the Pope to swerve from a decision : he knew what he was and as such he wished to be treated in all things. . . .
'. . . He would not allow his nephews to influence his government in the

be interesting to know this same Pope's personal part in the suppression of Mary Ward's first Institute. Cardinal Ottaviano Bandini, who, ever since the contest about the nomination of Smith's predecessor, had been a firm friend to the idea of bishops for England, had fought strenuously in the conclave of 1623 against the forces that ultimately elected Maffeo Barberini who issued forth from it on August 6 of that year as Urban VIII. Richard Smith's Roman champion was far from being so friendly with the reigning Pope as he had been with his predecessor, Gregory XV. And on the other hand the champion of Smith's adversaries, the Cardinal Giangarzia Millini was, under Urban VIII, restored to favour. The critical reign, for future English history, was the short thirty months of Gregory XV (1621–1623). He it was who broke with the tradition and appointed the first bishop. And he did this ' off his own bat,' with the aid of Bandini, and in spite of the Holy Office, taking the matter out of their hands, says Ingoli.[2] In spite, also, of Cardinal Millini, who, in the Holy Office, had opposed the bishop-project as, a few months earlier, in the conclave that followed the death of Paul V, he, Giangarzia Millini, had been himself most successfully opposed by the friends of Alessandro Ludovisi, now Gregory XV. While Ludovisi was ruling the see of Bologna, Millini, the nephew of Urban VII, had been Paul V's cardinal-vicar. He was vice-protector of England also, a power in the Holy Office, Paul V's man of confidence indeed, and the candidate of Paul V's party in the conclave that ensued. Who shall say what part personal relations between the highest of all officials—relations which did not in any way originate from the facts of the English problem—played in the solutions of 1627 and 1631? Ingoli is again our informant—not in any memoir, or gossipy paragraph, but in a confidential note [3] recalling a known fact—that it was

slightest degree. Self-reliant and self-willed he kept the management of affairs entirely in his own hands. As early as 1626 one who knew the situation wrote that government had become absolute, for none among the cardinals dared to resist and none would offer advice without being asked. If ever a Pope was jealous of his authority it was the present Pope.' PASTOR, Vol. 28, pp. 35, 36, 48–49.

[2] *Considerationi del secretario circa lo stato de' cattolici e missioni d'Inghilterra rappresentato dal signor agente del vescovo Chalcedonense e del clero anglicano.* Die 28 Februarii 1633. Congregatio 174. A.P., *Anglia*, 347, f. 363 *seq.*

[3] *Parere del Secretario Ingoli nel negotio delle controversie fra il clero secolare e regolare d'Inghilterra.* A.P., *Anglia*, 347, f. 359 *seq.*

Pope Gregory XV
· (1621–1623)
(*Alessandro Ludovisi, born* 1554)

Millini who brought about the victory of the Regulars in the Holy Office.

Urban VIII, as Maffeo Barberini, had been one of the great papal diplomats of his time. He had been nuncio at Paris at a critical hour in the affairs of English Catholicism (1604–1607) and, in a certain sense, the English problem may be said to have been familiar to him. When the proposal for a kind of hierarchy came before him he blasted it with a single word. It was not that the scheme came from Richard Smith. The first notice of it is a letter from Fr. Simon Stock,[1] written July 25, 1630, while the controversies were still raging, suggesting that it would make for peace if two more bishops were appointed, a Benedictine and a Jesuit. Then, in August of that same year came a letter from the Bishop of Ferns.[2] He pointed out that since Rome had increased the number of bishops in Ireland, things had greatly improved there. Would it not be the same in England ? The news sent to Rome, that conditions in England were too dangerous for bishops to be able to live there, was false. And, along with this letter from Wexford, there came a more solemn appeal in the shape of a joint letter to the same effect from the Archbishop of Cashel and his suffragans.[3] ' But the Holy Father rejected the scheme.' All the troubles, he said, had come after the appointment of the Bishop of Chalcedon, and if now, instead of one bishop, three bishops were appointed ' the trouble would not be appeased, but rather increased, for there would be in addition the fights of the bishops one with another.' [4] And this reply was ordered to be sent back to England.

Two months later than this, even Dom David Codner, O.S.B., was asking for more bishops—not, of course, for the return of Richard Smith, but for additional bishops *who should be ordinaries*. For the brief *Britannia*, he says, has not ended the dispute. There are abuses in the administration

[1] A.P., *Lett. Ant.*, 132, f. 144.
[2] A.P., *Acta*, S.C.P.F., Vol. 7, f. 116, 50⁰ ; *cf.* also *Acta* for Jan. 10, 1623, ' quod discordiis Regularium cum secularibus in Hybernia creatione novorum episcoporum providebitur ' ; the bishop of Ferns, Dr. John Roche, was in London, as we know from *Southcott's Diary*, in the May of 1629 ; *cf.* C.R.S., I, 105.
[3] *Ibid.*, Vol. 7, f. 115, 45⁰.
[4] A.P., *Acta*, S.C.P.F., Vol. 7, f. 180, 41⁰. Nov. 22, 1631 *i.e.* six months after the publication of *Britannia*.

of the sacrament of Penance and disorders of usury and simony among his own brethren.[1]

There were, I venture to suggest, rival policies about English problems, in the Rome of 1622-1640. In the brief *Britannia* and the refusal of bishops in 1633 the Holy Office policy triumphed. What was the other policy, the policy of Propaganda ?[2] Let Ingoli tell us, who strove for it as manfully as he strove unsuccessfully. Ingoli's life story has never yet been told. Francis Ingoli was the first of the long line of Secretaries to the Congregation *de Propaganda Fide*. It was his organising ability and his grasp of the essentials of the missionary task[3] that really made the Congregation of Propaganda a working institution, and his importance for this history is that he was, in intention, the most clear-sighted patron the *Ecclesia Anglicana* knew in Rome in a century and a half.[4]

Ingoli, it must be borne in mind, when he spoke of the problems presented by the state of Catholicism in England and suggested a means of solving them, had before him the experience of like troubles in other countries too. He knows

---

[1] A.P., *Acta* (Feb. 3, 1632), Vol. 8, f. 14, 18⁰.

[2] PASTOR, Vol. 30, p. 190, writes of Ingoli as ' the quickening spirit ' of the new Congregation of Propaganda. It was his plan (*ibid.*) ' to place all the missions under the immediate direction of Propaganda, to render them independent of the Colonial Powers, to employ only secular priests, and to create a native clergy.' It was only gradually, after much experimenting and many crises, that the two main difficulties were solved, viz. the status and power of the bishops in missionary countries and the relations of the bishops to missionaries belonging to the exempt religious orders who worked in their districts or dioceses. The troubles which from now on (1623) we know to have affected England down as far as the last Homeric struggle of 1873-1880, that ended in the bull *Romanos Pontifices* (*cf.* SNEAD COX, *Life of Cardinal Vaughan*, for an account which is a model of the way a controversy should be recorded), are all to be found recurring in various parts of the missionary world. The three last-published volumes of Pastor (30, 31, and 32 : 1644-1700) are most instructive in this respect.

[3] The interested reader will note that we have now parted company with ' Jesuit plots (!), suspicions of, and proffered proofs.'

[4] Ingoli's view of what should have been done can be found set out very clearly in four papers preserved at Propaganda; (1) *Parere del Secretario Ingoli nel negotio delle controversie fra il clero secolare e regolare d'Inghilterra* (*Anglia*, 347, f. 359) ; (2) *Che la missione dei Vescovi sia la piu importante, che possa far la Sacra Cong. de Propaganda fide etiando ove è piu fervente la persecutione* (*ibid.*, f. 465) ; (3) *Considerationi del secretario circa lo stato de' Cattolici e missioni d'Inghilterra rappresentato dal signor agente del vescovo Chalcedonense e del clero anglicano* (*ibid.*, f. 362 and fol.) ; this paper is dated Congregatio 174, Die 28 Februarii, 1633 ; (4) *Discorso del Secretario Ingoli circa le provisioni da farsi in Inghilterra per servitio della Religione Cattolica all'Emin* : *Sig. Card. Barberini Padrone* ; this is of later date ; from its reference to Mgr Rosetti as then in London it must belong to 1639 or 1640.

there were similar troubles in Holland,[1] which he had been largely responsible for ending. He knows what remedy had served there, the appointment of a bishop[2] with a certain jurisdiction even over the Regular missionaries. He knows what a power the bishops have been in Ireland. He can contrast the flourishing state of the mission in Bosnia and in Albania—where there are bishops—with the decay of the Church in Servia, which lacks bishops. He can point to Hungary, bishopless, as another warning and distinguish between the different islands of the Aegean Sea. He can even go so far as India and see the beneficent results to the mission of there being at its head what God everywhere meant to be at the head, a hierarchy of bishops with real power to rule the churches committed to them. Still more widely informed, he can point to the fact that the patriarchs of the schismatic churches of the East—the Nestorians, the Jacobites, the Copts, the Syrians, the Greeks—have never ceased to appoint bishops, despite the Mahometan persecution. And the result is to be seen in the fact that all those parts are full of Christians still loyal to their bishops. Whereas in the Latin sees the Faith has disappeared : the Popes having failed to provide a succession of bishops.[3]

Here then is the considered opinion of the Secretary of Propaganda.[4] It has never, so far, been so much as mentioned among us, and as an official view that directly contradicts what for centuries has passed as the official view of the *affaire* Smith, it calls for publication in this first attempt to set out Richard Smith's own case.

1. I take it to be the case that the Regulars in England

[1] *Cf.* the letter of the vicar-apostolic, Rovenius, to Smith, already cited, *sup.*, pp. 360–2.

[2] ' Qui cum potestate delegata munia ordinariorum illis in provinciis obeat,' so a memorial of the clergy of Utrecht describes his powers : it is an exact description, it seems to me, of what was granted Richard Smith, and of what, in him, the Regulars who opposed him denied. *Cf.* PASTOR, Vol. 32, p. 484, note 7.

[3] *Che la missione,* etc., MS. cit. It is not without interest to note this first secretary of Propaganda stating, in terms that might have been borrowed from Pius XI, the advantages of a native clergy, ' si vede in fatto che la più importante missione è quella che fa colli vescovi e la ragione è evidente, perche li missionarii, senza vescovo con poca scientia fanno più per l'affetto naturale che hanno alli loro compatrioti et il credito che hanno presso di quelli col special impulso dello Spirito Santo.'

[4] What follows, to the end of the chapter, is as literal a translation as I can accomplish of the whole of the paper headed, ' *Parere del Secretario Ingoli,* etc.,' from A.P., *Anglia,* 347, f. 359 and fol.

have always felt badly the decision to create a bishop in
that island, not only because with the archpriest formerly
established there they enjoyed great freedom, but also
because they were certain that with the coming of a bishop
their influence would decline. Perhaps, too, they believed
that they would come to lose the assistance that came to
them in return for their services to the Catholics of that
country. For the Catholics would easily cling to the
bishop as a personage of greater distinction and more
necessary for their spiritual needs. By this means the
faithful would give themselves entirely to the secular
clergy.

2. I take it to be the case that, for the reasons just
stated, it was very likely that the Regulars would use all
their best endeavours to take away episcopal authority
from that island, and because they could not do this
directly—not being able with a priori reasons, to persuade
the Holy See not to make bishops, since even in the
bitterest persecutions the said see has never failed to
nominate these most important of all the servants of the
Church of God—they set themselves to dispute with the
Bishop of Chalcedon, so that the Holy See, because of
the anxieties which he suffers and will suffer, would decide
to put England back to its former state with only an
archpriest. And that this is likely to be the truth about the
matter can be learnt manifestly from the origin of this
dispute of the Regulars. For it had no other foundation
than the hair-splitting subtlety,[1] invented by the Regulars,
of the difference between the Bishop of Chalcedon's
being the ordinary in that island or a delegate with the
faculties of an ordinary. I call this, the foundation of
their case, ' a hair-splitting subtlety ' because every day
the Holy See establishes as administrators for the various
sees in those countries where the Turks are masters, many
bishops whose titles are taken from other places, and
in every case these administrators have all the preroga-
tives of ordinaries, although, in fact, they are delegates
with the faculties of an ordinary, and with this for their
title they give ' approbation ' to the Regulars for hearing
confessions, and they do not allow Regulars to administer
the parochial sacraments without their leave, i.e. Baptism,
Matrimony, Easter Communion, Holy Viaticum, and

_____
[1] *Sottigliezza.*

Extreme Unction. They do this, basing their action on the sacred Councils of Vienne and Trent and the age-long practice of the church. For these sacraments have always been reserved to bishops and parish priests, for one reason to avoid confusion in the ecclesiastical hierarchy, and also to prevent such promiscuous administration of these sacraments as would hinder the shepherds from keeping count of the souls committed to their keeping.

Now, the foregoing being presupposed, both as to the facts and as to the law, I deduce and set out the following conclusions :

1. That from the beginning it was necessary to stabilise episcopal authority in England by granting the aforesaid powers which are given to administrators and to ordinaries and that in this way the said disputes would have straightway died down. *This would have been done by the Sacred Congregation of Propaganda, for such was its judgement in the matter,*[1] had it not been opposed by Cardinal Mellino, who was in favour of the Regulars. That what I say here would have succeeded in England the example of the pact in Holland has proved. By this pact the immediate jurisdiction (as a court of first instance) of the vicar-apostolic, the Archbishop of Philippi, was greatly strengthened, even to cover delinquent Regulars, and, as it were immediately, all those conflicts died down which, for years and years, kept coming before the Sacred Congregation of Propaganda from the various provinces subject to the orders in Holland.

2. I conclude that it is not possible now to make the like arrangement in England because men's spirits are grown embittered, and this is especially true of the two most powerful bodies, the Benedictines and the Jesuits. We must look for some other way. This other way, in my judgement and in that of others, in England, disinterested persons, who have written to the Sacred Congregation of Propaganda—and it is the best way that can be found for the good of that island, circumstances being as they are, and even absolutely speaking—this other way is to create two additional bishops, one a Benedictine,

---

[1] This deserves italics, I think, from anyone interested to restore Richard Smith's good name. It is as near to an official apology and justification as may be.

the other a Jesuit, dividing England into three clearly defined parts. The reasons for this are (1) this plan will effectively remove from the minds of the Regulars any hope that the régime of the archpriest will ever return, and so they will peacefully accommodate themselves to the rule of bishops ; (2) these two new bishops will smooth down the Benedictines and the Jesuits from whom derive all the present differences, through their being great and powerful bodies and accustomed to freedom ; (3) the Catholics of England will be better provided for, their pastors always being closer to them and certainly there will be greater progress in the spread of the faith. Nor need there be any fear of greater disputes, especially of disputes between the new bishops and the old, for the division of dioceses will remove all occasion for this.

3. When these bishops are created, it will be necessary to give them the authority which ordinaries enjoy, and even greater authority still, because it is understood that the Regulars live with so much freedom that in many cases, perhaps, they do not make such progress in spreading the faith as they should. It is certain that the system of [the bishop as a court of] first instance should be adopted as in Holland, because only the fear that they can be punished by the bishops will keep the Regulars within due limits.

4 and lastly. Supposing that this plan of new bishops is not found suitable, some rumour of it should be allowed to reach the ears of the Regulars, so that, by this means they will abandon their hope of an archpriest. It appears necessary to preserve, in every way, for the Bishop of Chalcedon, the aforesaid parochial sacraments, and to give orders to the superiors of the religious orders that they do not send any more of their religious into England without the leave of the Holy See, to be given in each case by a special patent, and that in this patent the clause shall be inserted ' de licentia tamen episcopi Chalcedonensis,' as has been already decreed by the congregation of Propaganda ; this should be in writing and petitioned for by the missionary or his agent. The bishop will readily fall in with this arrangement, for the hope he will have that, in the end, there will not be any Regular who does not depend on the bishop or who does not recognise him as his superior.

There need be no fear that what is suggested in the third and fourth paragraphs will provoke Regulars to any act to the prejudice of the Apostolic See or the Catholic faith, for the two new bishops will be sufficient to keep the Regulars in their place, being taken from the ranks of the two most powerful orders. And the last remedy is so reasonable in what relates to the parochial sacraments that it will give no excuse to the Regulars to rebel, and the arrangement about letters patent does not apply to those already in England, but only to those to be sent there in the future.

CHAPTER VI

VINEA FACTA AMARA

WE know that the views of Mgr. Francis Ingoli did not prevail, and although we are not in a position to say confidently why it was that another fifty years passed before the local episcopate was restored in England, it may lessen the mystery somewhat if some other events are recalled which had their beginning about this time. For it was in this very summer of 1633, when Richard Smith was congratulating himself that Rome had decided to send a bishop into England, that there arrived in Rome from England, and, by a devious diplomatic detour, from the English court itself, the mysterious mission of George Douglas.[1]

From this mission whose object was the creation of an English (or Scots) cardinal, and whose, alleged, motive was the likelihood of the conversion of Charles I, there came, ultimately, the re-establishment of quasi-diplomatic relations between Rome and the English court. Three papal envoys in succession took up their residence in London, Gregorio Panzani (1634–1637), George Conn (1637–1639), and Carlo Rosetti (1639–1641). One of the stated reasons for Panzani's going, which bore about it a distinct air of preparation, was to report on the condition of Catholicism in England, and his famous report, made on his return to Rome in 1637, is for the most part devoted to nothing else. That Rome, from the moment this new state of things came into being, could not act so freely as before, in the matter of naming a bishop, is evident. Also, whatever progress the ideas set forth in Ingoli's memoranda might have made during the seven years of this diplomatic interlude, in which Ingoli's Congregation of Propaganda had to yield the *pas* to the Secretariate of State, as ten years earlier it had been forced to bow to the Holy Office, the sudden violence of the bitterly anti-Catholic civil war, the expulsion of the royal house and the establishment of a republic, ended all

[1] *Cf. The Conversion of Charles I*, by the present author, in *The Clergy Review*, August, 1934.

Catholic hopes for a generation. When the son of Henrietta Maria regained his kingdom in 1660, the world of the Counter-Reformation had finally passed away—in continental Europe with the Treaties of Westphalia, in England with the last security of the absolute monarchy. The summer months preceding the arrival of George Douglas in Rome were then—though no man could know it—the Holy See's last chance, for a generation, of effectively restoring the episcopate to the English Church. With the history of Charles I and the court of Rome we need not concern ourselves here. It has recently been described admirably.[1] But something needs to be said of what those disorders actually were which, so the leading members of the secular clergy never ceased to urge, only the nomination of bishops could correct, disorders to whose existence the correspondence, during the first thirty years of the seventeenth century, of all manner of authorities bears unanimous witness. Whether it be the Carmelite Simon Stock, the Benedictine David Codner, the Bishop of Chalcedon, the French or Spanish ambassadors, that mysterious Capuchin agent of the emperor, Fr. Alexander of Hales, or the envoy of the duke of Mantua, all join to say that the condition of things in England is such that no man will believe it who has not seen it. I propose to describe it as the agent of Richard Smith set it before the cardinals of Propaganda in 1632.[2]

His report opens with a statement that occurs again and again in its hundred pages, namely that the whole fabric of Catholicism in England is threatened with utter ruin for lack of bishops to restore and repair ecclesiastical discipline. This, it declares, will be proved by this survey of conditions, set out under eight heads.

In the first chapter [3] the evil is described that there is no system of any kind by which the priests, on their arrival in England, are placed. There are no churches, no clergy houses, no monasteries, and the clergy live wherever they can find hospitality. Almost one-fifth of the peerage is

---

[1] GORDON ALBION, *Charles I and the Court of Rome.*

[2] Breve raguaglio di alcuni abusi introdotti nella Chiesa anglicana, delle Cause di essi e del modo estirparli dal quale si raccoglie il miserissimo stato de Cattolici in Inghilterra, sinche saranno senza Vescovi. A.P., Scritture Referite nei Congressi. *Anglia, I*, ff. 99–143 v ; the document runs to ninety sheets, but the last pages are missing.

[3] Ff. 99v–101. Del mancamento che nasce dal non osservarsi ordine alcuno circa la distribuzione de Missionarii, secondo la necessita delle Provincie in Inghilterra.

D D 2

still Catholic (twenty-four lords out of 130), and there are many Gentlemen, perhaps seventy-five or so (described as ' of the lesser nobility ') who are no less rich than the peers and no less liberal to the missionaries. Priests lodged in the households of these lords and gentlemen not only live in safety, but very comfortably, with pensions that are as good as really rich benefices. Other priests live in the houses of the less wealthy and are as rich, or as poor, as their hosts are rich or poor.

But in all this there is no system whatever. The missionaries can wander about as they choose, changing their residence as it pleases them, so that 'almost all' of them, seculars as well as Regulars, desire and are eternally on the look-out for a place in the house of some wealthy man or noble. Most of these desirable patrons live in London or its neighbourhood, and so it comes about that the most of the priests are to be found in those parts, and that they do their best to remain there for the better chance it offers of introducing themselves into such noble families. The more distant counties go wanting priests, which is yet another hindrance to the spread of the faith, for the population in the counties remote from London is much less attached to heresy. Far from there being priests to take advantage of this favourable circumstance, they are so few in these districts that the Catholics—who though many are poor—very often die without the sacraments. In London there are far more priests than are needed, and they are really in each other's way.

Again it is in London that all the superiors of the religious live. It is their aim to plant their men in the best places possible, so that, once again, the provinces are neglected.

The trouble is, then, that there is no one in England with power to oblige any particular priest to live in these more distant and less agreeable provinces, and there is no priest who is bound *ex officio* to do so. The best remedy would be to divide England into three or four districts, and set a bishop over each, one bishop only to live in London. Each bishop would see to it that his priests resided with their flocks.[1]

The present lack of system gives rise to the fantastic state

---

[1] This matter of assigning definite districts to the priests had presented itself, fifty years before the date of this report, at the meeting of the pioneer Jesuit missionaries with the London clergy, the so-called ' Synod of Southwark ' (? July), 1580 ; *cf.* POLLEN, p. 337.

of things described in the second chapter of the report,[1] the fights and intrigues among the clergy to get into better houses and to oust the present possessor (ff. 101–107 v.). While there are only about 100 of these 'first-class' posts, the total number of clergy is nearly 600 ; whence competition, open, undisguised, as one of the common features of every-day Catholic life.[2] Each of the religious orders now represented in England is ambitious to increase its numbers, and it happens that all take in more recruits than they can afford to maintain. They are thus forced to send some into England, not so much as missionaries to spread the faith, but rather as collectors of urgently needed funds. Such missionaries have a great desire for good places, whence they can collect more generous alms for their monastery.

Another unhappy consequence of the lack of system in the matter of residence, is that it is, in practice, left to the laity to choose what priest they will have for pastor, to dismiss him when it suits them, and to take another in his place. The whole business of where the priests shall live and work is thus in the hands of the laity. So it comes about that the best places go to those who know best the art of capturing the goodwill of the wealthy Catholics, and of putting these under an obligation to themselves. From this arises one of the most serious abuses of all, that missionaries are more anxious about the favour of the laity than about the spread of the faith, or the exercise of their spiritual functions. To keep the favour of their patrons they follow the laxer way in directing them, and allow many things, which are against the common practice of the Church, without any just reason. They are far from anxious to reprove patrons when their life gives public scandal, for should they strive to bind their patrons to a stricter way of life there is always handy some other missionary, ready to seize this opportunity to 'get the chaplain in bad' with the patron and insinuate himself into the place. This is the reason why so many Catholics in England can be found who have taken the Oath of Allegiance, for if one priest refuses the sacraments to such, others are soon found who, for the sake of an appointment, will admit them.

[1] Ff. 101–107 v. Gli abusi, che commettono i Missionarii nel contrastare sopra le residenze e nel supplantarsi l'un 'l'altro.
[2] This competition to live in a nobleman's house as his chaplain is, seemingly, a thing of the past. Regulars and seculars no longer destroy one another's reputation for the sake of such luxuries.

In this desire to supplant their better-placed brethren, missionaries are to be found who make an ill use of their faculties, showing the patron that they have wider powers than the priest he has taken in, or special privileges, faculties to dispense from abstinence and fasting, for example, or from matrimonial impediments. The priests in possession, on the other hand, do all in their power to prejudice their patron against all other priests not of their own order.

Others, in London, to keep a hold on more than one family, do not hesitate to say Mass, twice or even three times on Sundays.

Then there are the missionaries who induce those who come to confession to them—especially the women—to swear a vow not to confess to any other priest. Sometimes the inducement is some indulgence which they alone can grant, or ' an especially solemn absolution which fathers of our order are able to give,' and which they give with so much ceremony, of magnificent gesture and grandiloquent phrase, that their uninstructed penitents think that any other kind of absolution, if not invalid, is at any rate not nearly so efficacious.

Finally these missionaries, all belonging to different orders, fight between themselves with marvellous keenness in order to capture other residences for their own institute. Whence an infinity of discord, of calumny, and detraction. It is only by such means that a priest can arrive at these desirable posts, or, having obtained such a place, maintain himself against rivals.

In this competition the secular clergy are at a disadvantage, for they have no affiliations to offer, no confraternities, indulgences, or other special spiritual favours, nor the same generous faculties which the Regulars possess. The prestige of the secular priests, with the laity, naturally suffers. They are looked down on as second-rate fellows indeed.

The writer now proceeds to give some specific examples of priests manœuvred out of their residences by such ignoble brethren, and a letter from a secular priest—one of many sent to him—that shows the system in actual operation. The writer [1] is Thomas Longueville, and his complaint is chiefly of Jesuits. It was a father of the Society, he states, who, by telling a tale of his expulsion, as a student, from the English College at Rome for insubordination, and by

[1] Letter dated April 25, 1632 : f. 104.

working on the women-folk of the family where he lived, strove to bring about his dismissal. They were finally successful, once Fr. Mountford, S.J., had offered Longueville's patroness to pay something towards her chaplain's keep if she would engage a Jesuit. The same stratagem, says Longueville, has been used elsewhere against him. The Jesuits are, in fact, a greater anxiety than the heretics, especially since the bishop's departure. The writer has been thinking seriously of leaving England altogether, as many have done before him, and passing over to France or to Ireland. So he begs the clergy agent to intervene with the Jesuit General, to bring about a more charitable spirit in the English members of the order.

Next, in evidence, there is given an extract from a petition made by a group of clergy in this same year 1632 (in which, once more, it is the Jesuits who are accused of using the spiritual prestige of their order to attract penitents and supporters), and then comes a list of twenty-nine households from which Regulars are said to have secured the ejection of the secular clergy. Without prejudice, in any way, to the facts of the case, the list is worth printing for the names it contains of families supporting a priest and for its evidence as to the distribution of the regular clergy in a century about which so little is yet known.

KENT	Antony Roper, Esq.	Carmelite
	Thomas Pordagio,[1] Esq.	Jesuit
	Lady Mallory, a widowed noblewoman	Franciscan
SUSSEX	John Carell, Knight	Jesuit
	The widow of Sir Thomas Carell, Kt.	Benedictine
SURREY	John Southcott, Esq.	Jesuit
	William Copley, Esq.	Jesuit
	Richard Weston, Esq.	Jesuit
BERKSHIRE	Lady More	Jesuit
	The widow of D. Derkin, Esq.	Franciscan
OXFORDSHIRE	Sir Henry Brown, Kt	Benedictine
	Countess of Banbury	Jesuit
WARWICKSHIRE	William Sheldon, Esq.	Benedictine
	—— Throgmorton, Esq.	Jesuit

[1] *Sic!*

HUNTINGDONSHIRE	William Price	Jesuit
LINCOLNSHIRE	Sir John Thimble	Jesuit
HAMPSHIRE	Mrs. Wells, widow	Jesuit
YORKSHIRE	—— Trollop. Esq.	Jesuit
AND DURHAM	—— Foster, Esq.	Jesuit
	—— Constable, Esq.	Jesuit
	—— ?	Jesuit
	—— Gascoigne, Esq.	Benedictine
	—— Thomson, Esq.	Benedictine
	—— Tunstall, noble-woman	
HEXAM TOWN		Benedictine
STAFFORDSHIRE	Richard Rodulph, Esq.	Jesuit
FLINTSHIRE	In the city of St. Wine-fred	Jesuit

Once more, says the writer of the report, bishops with a jurisdiction that covers every priest in their district and extends to the creation of quasi-parish-priests, are the only remedy for this state of things. If this is done, and the rules about the parochial sacraments are kept, there will always be a priest at hand to see to the sick and dying and the competition for places (with its abominable consequences) will cease. There are enough Catholics to keep all the priests busy and to maintain all the priests, for while there are something more than 600 priests in all, the total Catholic population is 200,000, for the most part well-to-do people.[1]

A system of this kind would also prevent what so often happens, namely, that priests coming to England and not finding a fixed residence are forced to wander from inn to inn and to live in lodgings where it is necessary to pretend to be other than what they are. Such priests dare not ever say Mass nor recite their office, and it is not unknown that they fall away into evil lives.

There is literally no general system of control of any kind in England to certify that a man is a lawful missionary or even a priest at all.[2] Missionaries arrive from overseas with-

---

[1] ' This does not include the " schismatics," i.e. Catholics who make an appearance of conforming, who are very numerous and who mostly, by the grace of God, die reconciled to the Church,' f. 106 v.

[2] Here begins the third section of the report, ff. 107 v–113 v. Come operari discoli sono mandati in Inghilterra e come sacerdoti fuggitivi, ed Apostati, tanto Regolari, quanto secolari vanno la sotto pretesto della missione, et ingannano dannabilmente i Cattolici.

out any written commission or papers of any kind. The Catholics have to take their word that they are what they say they are, and once they are seen to be familiar with the ceremonies of Mass and to know how to use the breviary, the Catholics ask no more questions. Two serious abuses arise in this connection.

(1) England becomes a convenient dumping ground for the discontented religious who encumber the convents of their order beyond the seas. The English Regulars are so anxious to increase their numbers that they take in far more than they have means to support, and subjects of more than doubtful vocation and no capability. These last soon become a nuisance to their communities, and the English mission provides an easy way out of the difficulty. A third reason for the presence of many Regulars is the desire of their superiors to increase the fighting-power of the order in the English arena. The slacker the religious, the more eager are his demands to be sent to England, and once in England no power on earth can get such men back to their monastery.

(2) The way is easy for runaway religious, bad men, and heretics also, to pass into England as missionaries and damnably deceive the Catholics there. Many villains of this kind have been discovered, some only after a long period of mischief-making. These runaway religious change their names, pretend to be of other orders than their own (to escape any chance of control by English superiors of their order) and pretend, at times, to be secular priests. As the number of Englishmen entering religious orders is yearly increasing, and the number of Catholics in England steadily declining, the chances are that the numbers of these miserable refugees will grow. Since the coming of the Catholic queen [1] not Regulars only but secular priests also have begun to be attracted by the freedom which missionaries enjoy in that island. And as evidence of this a list is appended of delinquent clergy—six in all—who have been discovered. To these must be added seven priests expelled for evil conduct from the Society of Jesus, but who have continued, in various places, to act as priests.

The writer recalls the decree of Propaganda [2] ordering the

[1] Henrietta Maria, married to Charles I, in May, 1625.

[2] Of June 5, 1627 : this, it will be remembered, is one of the decrees which the Bishop of Chalcedon declared he dared not attempt to enforce, so fierce already was the spirit of the Regulars against his rule.

bishop to inspect all letters of missionaries on their arrival. This should be enforced, and Catholics forbidden, under penalty of excommunication, to have recourse to the ministry of any priest who cannot show a recommendatio either from the bishop or one of his vicars-general. The local English religious superiors should give the bishop a list of their men with the faculties allotted to them. Regulars in England who have no English superior should be made to show their faculties to the bishop or his vicar-general. The difficulty that many Catholics have been so taken in by the specious piety of these clerical scoundrels that they will not leave them, might be met by a power to the bishop to excommunicate all who assist at their Mass or use them for confession.

We come now to what is by far the longest section of the report.[1] It opens with a vivid picture of the contrast between the way of life for a religious in his monastery abroad and as a missionary in England. All the safeguards which his rule has devised to protect him in his calling are now absent. There is no community life. The missionary may go for years and never see his superior, never even see any of his religious brethren. He is dispensed from the fasts and other mortifications. He dresses, of course, like a layman and in the course of his work he has to mix freely in the world like any ordinary citizen using and retaining money, and to none accountable for the way it is spent. The change from the austerity of monastic restrictions to this régime of liberty and autonomy is not gradual, but made ' in one leap,' and in this circumstance, so the report suggests, is to be found the reason why so many of the Regulars have ended badly. There is so often the necessity to behave in such a way that one is taken for an ordinary man of the world, so many valid excuses for laying aside whatever habits might betray one's priestly character, so frequent a need to ' return to the world ' in ways which, though not sinful, are, for a religious, luxurious, that the monastic-trained missionary is handicapped from the start. Few of them grow holier after they come to England, so it is said, even by laymen. Any who are already discontented and restless, speedily become more relaxed than the other priests. The English monks of the

---

[1] Cap. 4. Dei Scandali che i Regolari commettono in Inghilterra, e dei loro abusi intorno all' amministrazione dei Sacramenti in gran pregiudizio della Religione Cattolica, ff. 113 v–125 v.

Cassinese Congregation are an example of this. Out of the six now in England four are men who give scandal by their way of life—for all that they lived for years abroad under the austere rule of their order.[1]

What does the writer understand by ' scandalous life ? ' It is necessary to ask this question for the censors of clerical life three hundred years ago had grimly narrow standards by which to measure, not decorum alone, but clerical decency. There exists among these papers a whole dossier about one unfortunate man, a Franciscan Conventual, whose offences, as ultimately proved by the nuncio at Paris, go no further than a habit of smoking and an ability to entertain Henrietta Maria with his stories. The mere general label ' scandalous ' must not induce us to hasty conclusions that the worst of all crimes are the man's habitual employment.[2] Of these Cassinese, and of others, it is said, for example, that they spend too much of their time in inns, chatting with the serving maids, drinking, and joking and the like. Nothing worse is noted of their personal behaviour, but serious complaint is made of laxity in the administration of sacraments.

There follows a list of twenty priests with particulars of their offences. Ten are Benedictines, eight Jesuits, one an ex-Jesuit, and one is of an order not named. In four cases only are the names of those accused recorded. The charges, this time, are serious. Three are alleged to have married, and to continue nevertheless to act as priests—one of the three has two wives ! Others have tricked Catholics into altering wills in their favour, or made such alteration a condition of absolution to dying penitents. Some give leave to have children baptised in the parish church by the minister, or admit to the sacraments parents who allow their children to attend heretical services. One man drinks before Mass ; another says Mass sitting down, under the excuse that he is not able to stand. A monk, who openly lives as a trader, induced a noble lady to pledge herself by deed never to dispose of her property without his consent. When she made a will in favour of a cousin, the monk wrung 2400 scudi out of the heir as the price of his consent.

---

[1] One of the four named is Dom David, who has been noted as a prominent opponent of the bishop ; another is Dom Thomas Preston, generally credited with the works in favour of the Oath of Allegiance written under the name of Roger Widdrington.   [2] *Cf.* here McCANN, pp. 41–42.

Another monk—this is the high light of the whole picture—
kidnapped a girl on the eve of her wedding, and held her to
ransom. Nor did he surrender her until the father paid
400 scudi.

How much truth is there in all this ? We shall never know.
The writer of the report makes no secret of his hostility to
the Regulars. On the other hand this is not any anonymous
denunciation, or letter sent to Rome from a distant mission.
The writer is the agent of the bishop, has composed the report
in Rome, is on the spot, and offers to prove each case—in
England if necessary and if the Holy See will make arrangements for the evidence to be taken there. Obviously if even
it is all true, it is true only of the individuals mentioned—
a very small proportion of the total of the Regulars at work.
Were there no delinquents among the secular clergy ?
The fact that a report on the sins of the Regulars is silent
here, is by no means proof of the Seculars' freedom from
defect. But such accusations—whether true in particular or
not—could never have been made, were there not much
gravely wrong among the clergy of the *Ecclesia Anglicana*.
Some such iniquities there must have been, and not in
isolated cases only, to have produced the phenomenon that
in every letter Rome received about English affairs, disorders
in the life of the clergy is always a prominent theme. This
document is evidence because it is a charge made by a
responsible official. Shall the student who discovers it
destroy it, because it embarrasses him to have to deal with
it, and not be able to disprove it or label it calumny ? Or
shall he omit the more embarrassing passages ? He must
surely—if he cannot print the whole [1]—give at any rate a
substantially faithful account of it.

Many Benedictines are said to take too lax a view of the
papal prohibitions to take the Oath of Allegiance. There is
quite a group of these Catholics who have taken the Oath
and yet have not abjured their faith by going to the
Protestant services.

The most scandalous of all the abuses are those connected
with the sacrament of matrimony, for the results here are
evident to the whole kingdom. No missionary, Regular
or secular, it must first be said, has any power to grant

---

[1] Cardinal Ehrle's golden advice, on this very subject, ' Print all the
documents, every word of every letter,' war-time restrictions at present put
out of possibility.

dispensations for marriage with a non-Catholic nor for the impediment of consanguinity or affinity in the second degree (unless the marriage has already been contracted). But many missionaries do ' grant ' such dispensations, usurping rights they do not possess. There is no one to say them nay. If another priest contradicts them it is a matter of the word of the one against the other. Once again the report gives specific examples, and the names of the missionaries (who again are all Regulars). Cases are mentioned of marriages with Protestants, of marriages of those already married,[1] and of marriages of minors without the consent of the parents. We hear of advice given to contract an unlawful marriage in order to qualify for the priest's power of dispensing the impediment once the marriage has been contracted, of advice given to withhold consent (in the mind, by a mental reservation) at the moment the words contracting the marriage were spoken, so as to be free to break the ' marriage ' should it not be found to go smoothly. There is a melodramatic story about Lord Baltimore's chaplain persuading a girl against her will to accept his patron's offer of marriage. Once the marriage was consummated the husband repented of his choice, and the compliant chaplain thereupon explained to the girl that the objection which she had first raised—and which he had then persuaded her was mere scruple—really existed, namely that she, being spiritually related to the man, could not be married to him at all.

The sole remedy for all this—so the report, in its never-changing refrain—is to put all Regulars who thus live outside their monasteries, under the rule of a bishop. At least it should be made obligatory for them to make known to him what powers they have, and for the bishop to examine if indeed they really possess such powers. If superiors neglect their duty of correction this should fall to the bishop, who, in whatever relates to the administration of the sacraments and the preaching of Christian Doctrine, should have the power of a visitor over all Regulars. Had a bishop such authority over the missionaries belonging to the religious orders, the superiors would be more careful in choosing whom to send to England, and those sent would

---

[1] At this time there was, of course, no means of divorce in England. The first person to have his valid, consummated marriage broken was Lord Roos in 1668—nearly forty years later than the date of this report. Even Henry VIII never sought a divorce, though several of his marriages were declared to have been null.

watch their ways more carefully. Missionaries should be
forbidden to give decisions that affect ownership, or permissions that may give rise to lawsuits, unless the bishop has
been first consulted.

We are next asked to consider, in the fifth section,[1] some
of the ways in which the anarchy affects the layman.
There is no lack of disputes between the English Catholics
and their clergy, as might be guessed from what has been
said already. Sometimes the cause is some matter of ecclesiastical law, marriage cases, contracts of marriage, divorces,
pious bequests, distribution of alms ; at other times some
matter of civil law, money debts, for example, or calumnies,
injuries, and the like. One curious circumstance is noted
as the cause of contention in civil matters, namely that many
of the chaplains act as their patron's steward, and manage
his estates for him.

It is by no means always possible to refer these matters
to Rome. In the first place any such use of the Roman
jurisdiction is high treason. Then, the expenses are
enormous of conducting lawsuits at such a distance from
England, by means of procurators. Nor is it possible, often,
for justice to be done except without a personal knowledge
of the circumstances nor for witnesses to be really examined
except by native advocates.

Some of the Regulars have always striven to the best of
their ability to hinder the appointment of bishops who would
have powers to hear and decide such cases of litigation
between Catholics. Catholics who feel unjustly burdened
must then either go without justice being done them, or
take what is perhaps an ecclesiastical case to the English
courts. More and more they are choosing the second alternative, priests as well as laymen, and the report proceeds to
give seven examples of ecclesiastical business brought before
the King's courts in the last two years. It is a new scandal
for the heretic to see the missionaries going to prison not,
this time, for the faith, but at the suit of some of their flock.
And, of course, to bring a priest into court, whatever the
reason, was to bring him into proximate danger of a sentence
of death for his mere presence in the country. Likewise
it was a serious offence to be married by any but the

[1] Ff. 126–130. Che i Cattolici per mancanza de Vescovi sono forzati
introdurre le cause Ecclesiastiche nel foro secolare, e litigare contro i
Missionari avanti i Giudici Eretici.

Protestant clergy, hence to bring Catholic marriage cases into the civil courts was to expose husband and wife and the priest who had married them to a rigorous sentence.

There are other abuses that arise from Catholics not having any bishop to settle their disputes and ecclesiastical lawsuits.[1] Since there is no Catholic authority with power to decide disputes about pious bequests, or the distribution of alms, many injustices are perpetuated. For it is courting certain loss to take such matters into the king's courts, since all such Catholic pious bequests are confiscated to the treasury. Next it is shown what chaos arises from the absence of any matrimonial tribunal in England. Sometimes Catholics will take their differences—demands for nullity decrees or for separations—to the court of the Protestant bishops. But these bishops have now no power to compel Catholics to appear in their courts, nor to enforce their sentences on Catholics, since the King has exempted Catholics from their jurisdiction in spiritual matters. This privilege has been used by many Catholics to justify their taking the law into their own hands. Catholics are often met with who, on their own authority, and without sufficient reason, live permanently separated from their wives or husbands. There are in fact actually more Catholics living like this than Protestants, for all that the Protestants are twenty times more numerous. There are perhaps more such unlawful separations among the English Catholics than in France, Spain, and Italy put together. From this well-known fact alone, Catholicism has a very bad name in England, and once again the report gives some outstanding examples of Catholics thus unlawfully separated, eleven in all, two of them peers and four knights. These examples are taken from London alone and its neighbourhood. It can be easily guessed, says the report, how many there are in the whole country. The greater part of these separations are due to the unchecked growth of family disputes. With a definitely established episcopal régime and the known fact that the separations are not to be obtained for the asking, Catholics would be attentive to the growth of such disputes, and quarrels would be made up and not

[1] Cap. 6⁰, ff. 130–134. Altri Abusi, che nascono tra i Cattolici per la mancanza de' Vescovi, che conoschino le loro liti, et controversie nelle materie Spirituali, ed Ecclesiastiche.

allowed to develop into feuds that only a separation can remedy.

One of the erroneous ideas spread among the laity by certain Regulars, at the time of the Chalcedon controversy, was that the bishop's jurisdiction in their regard was a power of favours only, namely of granting dispensations, indulgences, blessings, and such-like.[1] He had not, they asserted, any power to punish or correct. Catholics have nothing to restrain them from a bad life but their own conscience. Whatever they do, in this matter, there is no authority to call them to account. Not a few have become notorious for drunkenness and lust, beyond anything that is seen among the heretics. There are even, so it is said, heretics who embrace the Catholic faith in order to lead a bad life with greater security, for while they were heretics the threat of the Protestant bishops' authority was always before them. Once converted they are free of this, and there is no Catholic bishop.[2] The matter of women of bad life who use Catholicism as a means to ply their trade more securely is notorious.

The absence, for generations, of any local and evident ecclesiastical jurisdiction has bred a general habit, among the laity, of a certain disregard of the commandments of the Church and the Canon Law. Especially is this to be seen in the matter of marriages. They marry heretics, they marry without the assistance of the priest, they marry within the forbidden degrees of kinship and they withdraw from their clandestine marriages and contract new alliances, living with another henceforward in perpetual adultery, marry and 'dismarrying' at their pleasure. The heretics have a saying—and perhaps they believe it to be true—that Catholics can marry as often as they please and dissolve any marriage already contracted. Once again

---

[1] Here begins Cap. 7º. Degli abusi, che nascono per mancamento della Giurisdizione Vescovile cœrcitiva per raffrenare i Laici con censure, e pene Ecclesiastiche, ff. 134–137.

[2] What fifty years of persecution and proscription can effect in the ordinary Christian is shown if we compare the picture drawn here with that in Bl. Edmund Campion's letter to his general of Nov., 1580, written on the eve of the new era of extermination. 'Here, even among the Protestants themselves that are of a milder nature, it is turned into a proverb, that he must be a Catholic that payeth faithfully what he oweth, insomuch that if any Catholic do injury, everybody expostulateth with him as for an act unworthy of that calling.' SIMPSON, p. 248.

Catholic malpractice in this matter is safe from all interference, for Catholics are exempt from the jurisdiction of the
Protestant bishops.[1] Such evil-living Catholics can only be
corrected by the possibility of excommunication by a resident
Catholic bishop.

The clerical body, the conclusion of the report[2] declares,
is by no means homogeneous. The vast majority of the
priests—easily more than all the rest together—are seculars.
The Regulars are taken from no fewer than ten different
orders, and each of these ten sections has its own head,
independent of all other authority in England. The lack of
some single general directing authority is evident. In this
multitude of equally important chiefs, none of whom owes
any consideration to the rest, lies the real cause of all the
troubles and factions. There is no one responsible for the
mission as a whole, and no kind of subordination among
these many leaders. The fact that each superior, among the
Regulars, has an obvious duty to look after the interests of
his order as such, is an additional complication, from which
a factious spirit can speedily derive, the aims of each order
being by no means identical with the aims of the rest.

Even in their criticism of the Bishop of Chalcedon, and
in their conflict with him, the orders who fought were not
agreed. The Jesuits opposed every claim he made, and stood
out for an entire and absolute independence of his authority.
The Benedictines were willing that new-comers among them
should submit their papers to the bishop's inspection, but
not to ask for approbation in regard to the administration
of the sacraments. For the Jesuits have so many members
who lived disguised as laymen or as secular priests (only
known to be Jesuits to their superiors) and whose business
it is to keep an eye on all that passes, that they were not
willing that the bishop should know anything at all about
their affairs.[3] The Benedictine objections have a wholly

[1] With whom, at this time, lay the responsibility for the preservation of
public decency.

[2] Della divisione delli Missionari tra di loro, e come i Cattolici sono tirati
in diverse fattione, ff. 137–143v.

[3] This belief went to extraordinary lengths with some of the secular clergy
in these times. There exists in the archives at Archbishop's House, Westminster—but I am unable at the moment to lay my hands on it—an amazing testimony (in a letter of about 1696 from Dr. John Betham, I think) of
credulity in this matter, in the shape of an account given of the solemn
' swearing in ' of such Jesuit ' specials,' and all told on the (hearsay)
evidence of quite reputable persons.

different end in view. So many of their men are below standard in the matter' of professional attainments, that if permission to administer the sacraments depended on any episcopal judgement of their fitness few would be chosen out of all those called. The Dominicans, it is explained, had objections all their own—what they are is not, alas, revealed. The Franciscans and the other orders—Carmelites and Minims—made no objections whatever, but acted towards the bishop as religious always do in Catholic countries.

It is not possible that such diversity of practice—to say nothing of the open rivalry of these widely differing regiments of the Catholic army—can be without the most serious effects upon the laity. The fact is, of course, notorious that every faction among the priests has its following among the laymen. One unhappy result of the recent controversies has been that Regulars have indoctrinated many of the laity with the opinion that the bishop has no authority where they are concerned. On all hands one sees the laity violently divided, some pro-Jesuit, other pro-Benedictine and others again pro-seculars, and all these parties despising and scorning the rest. When the bishop published the brief announcing the Jubilee the laity attached to the Regulars ignored it, until the Regulars, some months later, had their own news of the event from abroad and communicated it to them. How is it possible for a bishop to keep such a flock in order, when insubordination is made a matter of religious principle ? A case is cited of one of the bishop's vicars-general threatening with excommunication a couple who had married in clandestine fashion, in order to compel them to regularise their position. This they refused to do and he excommunicated them. And immediately, without any reference to the vicar-general, a Regular absolved them. How, under such conditions, can there ever be a united Catholic effort for the good of religion ?

The first condition of any better state of things among the laity is peace among the clergy. The best means of all is to appoint bishops with a certain jurisdiction—as a court of first instance—over all the missionaries. This would end the present practice of the secular clergy forming themselves into leagues or brotherhoods to defend themselves against the Regulars. Nor, if the point of jurisdiction were made clear, would the bishop any longer suspect Regulars as men hostile to episcopal authority as such. If the bishop were the common superior of the whole body of the missionaries in his district, peace between the two bodies of clergy would be the first aim of all his government. On the other hand, if there is not to be some such system of subordination and hierarchical arrangement, then let all the Regulars be withdrawn out of England, and the mission be handed over to the secular clergy and the bishops, or else withdraw the secular clergy and leave the English mission to be the work of some single united order of Regulars. Under the present régime, of a dozen independent chiefs in the same territory, feuds and faction fights there must always be, as there have been until now.

With this paragraph the survey proper finishes. How the document ended it is impossible to say for the last pages are missing. But in the last sentences of what remains, the agent offers to prove all his assertions, either in Rome or, should it be so decided, before a competent tribunal in England. ' Meanwhile he is ready to show letters such that . . .' [1] and these are the report's last words.

To confirm the substantial truth of what this long report details, we can cite the contemporary testimony of a witness who was neither a secular priest nor a francophile : of that active diplomatic agent of the Emperor Ferdinand II, Fr. Alessandro of Hales, of the order of Capuchins. This order, as it is slowly beginning to be recognised, played an increasingly important part in the transaction of international affairs as the seventeenth century went by. What Fr. Joseph was to Richelieu, others of his order were, in lesser degree, to other princes. And wherever one tracks the less public diplomatic action of Ferdinand II, one finds, sooner or later, the able and experienced Capuchin, Fr. Alessandro. He had visited the court of James I, in the early years of the Thirty Years War, and he had been in England again in 1628, to judge from a letter he then wrote to Cardinal Barberini about the prospects of Catholicism.[2]

In 1632 the friar was once more *en route* in the service of the Catholic cause, now traversing a crisis in Germany. He visited Spain and he visited England, and on his return to Vienna he sent a long letter to the Cardinal Secretary of

---

[1] Folio. 143 v.
[2] June 2, 1628, V.L., *Barb. Lat.*, 7048, f. 58.

State, in which he analysed the meaning of all he had seen
in England, reported what he had heard and what remedies
thoughtful men considered necessary to meet the case.[1]

Fr. Alessandro reports that the brief *Britannia* is everywhere ignored : that the forbidden books are kept, read
and passed on, and that the trouble they caused is thus
really on the increase. Things said in the controversy have
done much harm to the prestige of authority. Quite
respectable people give proof that they hold the most amazing
ideas. Bishops, they say, are really a hindrance rather than
a help to the progress of religion—such ideas they get from
their confessors.

It is to the wretched absence of any system in placing and
maintaining the missionaries that he attributes all the
trouble. Since confessors depend on their penitents for
food and for clothing even, they are all too easily blind to
their penitents' faults. Hence many of the laity, preferring
to live under the rule of confessors chosen where they will and
fashioned to their liking, hate the very notion of episcopal
authority.

At present there is almost no persecution in England.
Hatred of Catholicism—so far as the government is concerned—has gone. In its place is the desire to make out of
Catholics all the financial profit that the recusancy laws
allow. It is the laity, rather than the priests, who are now
the object of attention, the laity who have property to be
confiscated. As far as the priests are concerned the imprisonment is now a real and evident farce. It is simply a matter of
payment, and the priest is free to go out whenever he chooses
—and wherever he chooses—according to the amount he
can pay. There are priests actually sentenced to death to
be found roaming about all over the country.

The Capuchin seems to think there are too many priests
in England, and that the opportunities of a comfortable,
relaxed life which the present situation holds out, attracts
far too many slack characters to the English mission, would-
be dandies, empty-headed, idle and sensual, ignorant and
the cause of ignorance in the laity who affect them. In
far too many cases it is beginning to be the fashion to hold
that all that is necessary is to declare oneself a Catholic. The
rules and warnings of ecclesiastical authority are system-

---

[1] There are two reports, one dated 1632 and the other sent with a covering letter of Jan. 15, 1633 ; V.L., *Barb. Lat.*, 7048, ff. 1–7 and 62 *seq.*

atically ignored, and whatever the decision that comes from
Rome every man has his private gloss to justify his evasion
of what it commands. In many cases it can be said that the
Catholics are worse in their way of living than the heretics,
and that the priests are worse than the laymen.

There are nevertheless many most saintly missionaries,
among the Regulars as well as among the secular clergy.
Of the two bodies Fr. Alessandro seems to complain less of
the seculars. Not only because they have been longest in the
field, and not only because they are by far the most numerous
but also because they are more generally men of holy life—
so he argues—the Holy See should give them more support
and encouragement.

The only remedy for the troubles is the appointment,
as soon as possible, of some really strong character to govern
the whole English mission. Who is this to be, and what shall
be the nature of his powers ?

First of all, the number of ordinations should be reduced,
and no Englishman (or Irishman or Scotsman) be allowed
to take vows in any religious order, except such as the Holy
See knows to have its affairs in England well managed. Too
many join these orders in the hope of coming to England and
there enjoying an easy life. All missionaries should be
obliged to swear that they will observe the decrees of Trent
and will see also that others observe them. Those orders
with subjects in England should hold annual chapters to
enforce discipline, and where the religious are too few for
this they should be aggregated for the purpose of discipline
to some other order. But the main reform—and on this all
else depends—is the presence in England of some capable
local ruler. All the best people in England agree about this.
Where they differ is as to the breadth of the powers he should
have.

Some would like to see the authority limited to the secular
clergy ; others would like to see at least the laity exempted.
But if the prelate is to be a delegate of the Pope there appears
to be no reason for exempting the regulars from his control.
After all it is from the Holy See that they receive their
faculties. How can they complain if they are subjected, in
their exercise of them, to the Holy See's delegate ? Others
say it would be wiser to send diocesan bishops, because while
there is no law against bishops as such, there is a most
stringent law against any such recognition of the Pope's

authority as would be implied in obedience to a papal delegate. A more novel suggestion is to appoint two chiefs, a bishop for the secular clergy, and a religious to act as prefect for all the orders in England : the two would be instructed to act together as a single authority.

Whatever is to be done ultimately, the Holy See should send someone over at least as a temporary measure, and here Fr. Alessandro makes a very interesting suggestion. This personage—who may remain as the permanent head of the mission—should not be one of the king's subjects. This will make it easier for him to move about the country, and his freedom from the penal laws will make it possible for the king and the government to do business with him. He must not be a Frenchman nor a Spaniard, for very obvious reasons. He should be an Italian ; a man of distinction ; cultivated, learned, and, as well as of really good life, a man well born. Let him be such that all who meet him will be impressed by the fact that the Pope has consented to deprive himself of so valuable a servant. Where can this paragon be found ? The Capuchin suggests, not for the office indeed, but as a specimen of the type he has in mind, a certain Fr. Valerian of Milan. The recipient of the letter [1] has added a word to say it is practically a description of the Capuchin who was once duke of Modena.

If this history ends somewhat abruptly, on a note of interrogation as it were, it does but in this respect copy life. History may confirm the truth of a thesis known to us by surer means, it rarely proves a thesis ; and it is never so much to be suspected as when it rounds off happily with a *quod erat demonstrandum*. That the Counter-Reformation failed in England was as well known to the reader of this book, before he began to read it, as it was to the writer. The book has been an examination of facts very often known already, undertaken in order to set out the story of that—as I must hold—tragic failure. If in the course of that narration, any of the reasons for the failure are revealed, so much the more useful is the examination. The event left the unsuccessful minority paying an impossibly heavy price for the failure. How heavy that price was, has not always been realised, and my concern to show what history costs the average man must be in large part my justification for

---

[1] ? Cardinal Francis Barberini.

insisting at such length on the conditions under which the garrison lived through the last stages of the war. We know much of the glory of the martyrs, and we are beginning to know more of the proud history of the confessors. There were others—who fell by the wayside. It is only right that we should know how they came to fall, and if we cannot exactly pay a tribute to the memory of these victims of the defeat—the average, unheroic, *homme moyen sensuel*—we may perhaps at least relieve it of some of the ignominy too easily heaped on it by later and more comfortable ages.

Vinea nimis amara. True indeed, but let it not be thought that every vine was soured. A history whose subject was wider than the subject of this book, would recall—what indeed is already far better known than the *historia amari-tudinis*—the triumphs of grace to be met in every corner of that vineyard. It is, for example, in these very years that such saintly Jesuits as Edmund Arrowsmith and Henry Morse, such Benedictines as John Roberts and Ambrose Barlow, such seculars as William Ward and John South-worth, and truly seraphic Franciscans like Henry Heath and Arthur Bell, prepare for the martyr's crown by lives of heroic sanctity. These are the years when, hidden from sight, Fr. Augustine Baker put together one of the master-pieces of English spiritual theology. And lesser men, but men no less devoted, produced, in these same thirty and forty years, those spiritual works and translations of the classic masters whose mere listing would fill pages. These books Catholics, somewhere in England, read and continued to read. Catholic girls went over the seas in a steady, increasing stream to fill the new convents of Benedictines, Poor Clares, Carmelites, and Dominicans of the Second Order, while Mary Ward, in the face of opposition darker and more mysterious even than what her contemporary Richard Smith had to face, founded that great Institute of teaching nuns which, for its government no less than for its extra-claustral way of life, has become the pattern of almost every order of women founded since. It was in 1645 that this heroic and saintly pioneer, in whose courageous heart and cheerful wit Thomas More lived anew, died in a Yorkshire village. Already a new storm was upon the much-tried English Church and its clergy, and already priests, both secular and regular, were testifying as their forerunners of Elizabeth's reign had testified, while the nobles and the gentry, with a sure intuitive discernment of where the greatest menace to religion lay, rallied to the standard of the king.

It was much more than picturesque coincidence that the ast of the royal strongholds was manned by a Catholic arrison ; that the Mass was being said within as the Puritan annon roared to the last stages of their victory ; it was of the nature of what was done that the sign of that victory was a butchery of the defenders, of their women, and of their priests.

WALTON,
June, 1939.
SIDLEY,
June, 1940.

BIBLIOGRAPHICAL NOTE

Containing the full titles of all works referred to in the text.

ALLEN. A True Sincere and Modest Defence of English Catholics that suffer for their Faith both at Home and Abroad . . . by William Allen. 1584. (Reprinted London, 1914, 2 vols. ; this is the edition used here.)

ANCEL. DOM R. ANCEL, O.S.B. La Réconciliation de l'Angleterre avec le St. Siège sous Marie Tudor. Legation du Cardinal Polus en Angleterre (1553–1554) in *Revue d'Histoire Ecclésiastique* (1909). Tom. 10, pp. 521–536, 744–798.

A.P. Archives of the Sacred Congregation for the Propagation of the Faith, preserved in the College of the Propagation of the Faith, Rome.

BECCATELLI. LUDOVICUS BECCATELLI. Vita Reginaldi Poli, in QUIRINI, *Epistolae Reginaldi Poli*. Brixen, 1744. Tom. I, pp. 1–65.

BENNET. JOHN BENNETT. Narratio Historica, C.R.S. 22, 133–46.

BIAUDET. H. BIAUDET. Les Nonciatures Apostoliques permanentes jusqu'en 1648. Helsinki, 1910.

BIRON. DOM REGINALD BIRON, O.S.B., et JEAN BARENNES. Un Prince Anglais, Cardinal-Légat au XVIᵉ siècle, Réginald Pole. Paris, s.d.

BIRT. DOM HENRY NORBERT BIRT, O.S.B. The Elizabethan Religious Settlement. London, 1907.

BLACK. J. B. BLACK. The Reign of Elizabeth. 1936.

BRADY. WILLIAM MAZIERE BRADY. Annals of the Catholic Hierarchy in England and Scotland, 1585–1876. London, 1883.

BRODRICK. JAMES BRODRICK, S.J. Blessed Robert Bellarmine. 2 vols. London, 1928.

BURTON and POLLEN. Lives of the English Martyrs. Second Series. Vol. I. 1583–1588. Edited by Edwin H. Burton, D.D., and J. H. Pollen, S.J. London, 1914.

CAMM. Lives of the English Martyrs declared blessed by Pope Leo XIII. Vol. II. Martyrs under Queen Elizabeth. Edited by Dom Bede Camm, O.S.B. London, 1905.

CARDELLA. Memorie Storiche de' Cardinali. 9 vols. 1792–7.

CARDON. GEORGES CARDON. La Fondation de l'Université de Douai. Paris, 1892.

CHALLONER. Memoirs of Missionary Priests as well Secular as Regular and of other Catholics of both sexes that have suffered death in England on religious accounts from the year of Our Lord 1577 to 1681, by Richard Challoner, D.D., Bishop of Debra and Vicar-Apostolic. London, 1741 : many times reprinted. Edition used here that of 1924.

C.R.S. Publications of the Catholic Record Society. London, 1905, and onwards.

DODD. The Church History of England, 1500–1688. Vol. III, by Charles Dodd (vere Hugh Tootell). Brussels (vere Wolverhampton), 1742.

E.M. The English Martyrs : Papers from the Summer School of Catholic Studies held at Cambridge, 1928. Edited by Dom Bede Camm, O.S.B. Cambridge, 1929.

FOLEY. Records of the English Province of the Society of Jesus. Edited by Henry Foley, S.J. 1877–83.

FRERE. W. H. FRERE. The Marian Reaction. London, 1896.

FRERE and KENNEDY. Visitation Articles and Injunctions of the Period of the Reformation. Vol. II. 1536–1558. Edited by W. H. Frere and W. P. M. Kennedy. Alcuin Club Collections XV. London, 1910.

G. and H. Documents Illustrative of English Church History, compiled by Henry Gee and William John Hardy. London, 1896.

GAIRDNER. JAMES GAIRDNER, C.B. The English Church in the Sixteenth Century, from the Accession of Henry VIII to the Death of Mary. London, 1903.

GAIRDNER LOLLARDY. JAMES GAIRDNER, C.B. Lollardy and the Reformation in England. 4 vols. London, 1908–1913.

GARRETT. CHRISTINA HALLOWELL GARRETT, M.A. The Marian Exiles. A Study in the Origins of Elizabethan Puritanism. Cambridge, 1938.

GASQUET. AIDAN, CARDINAL GASQUET. Cardinal Pole and his early friends. London, 1927.

GILLOW. JOSEPH GILLOW. A Bibliographical Dictionary of the English Catholics from the Breach with Rome in 1534 to the Present Time. 5 vols. 1885–1903.

HAILE. MARTIN HAILE. The Life of Reginald Pole. London, 1910.

KENNEDY. W. P. M. KENNEDY. Parish Life under Queen Elizabeth. London, 1914.

KNOX. The First and Second Diaries of the English College, Douay, and an Appendix of unpublished documents . . . with a historical introduction by Thomas Francis Knox, D.D., London, 1878.

L.A.   Letters and Memorials of Cardinal Allen. Edited by Thomas Francis Knox, D.D., of the London Oratory. London, 1882.

LAW.   THOMAS GRAVES LAW. A Historical Sketch of the Conflicts between Jesuits and Seculars in the reign of Queen Elizabeth. London, 1889.

LINGARD.   JOHN LINGARD. History of England. London, 1855. (6th Edition.)

MAGEE.   BRIAN MAGEE. The English Recusants. A Study of the Post-Reformation Catholic survival and the operation of the Recusancy Laws. London, 1938.

McCANN.   The Life of Father Augustine Baker, O.S.B. (1575–1641), by Fr. Peter Salvin and Fr. Serenus Cressy. Edited by Dom Justin McCann, O.S.B. London, 1933.

MEYER.   ARNOLD OSCAR MEYER. England and the Catholic Church under Queen Elizabeth, translated by J. R. McKee, M.A., of the London Oratory. London, 1916.

PANZANI.   Relazione dello stato della Religione Cattolica nel regno d'Inghilterra data alla santita di N.S. Urbano VIII da Gregorio Panzani doppo il suo ritorno da quel regno che fu nel anno 1637. Vatican Library. Barb. Lat. 5222 (fol. 1–46B).

PASTOR.   LUDWIG VON PASTOR. History of the Popes. English translation. Vols. 13–32. London, 1891–1940.

POLE.   Reformatio Angliæ, ex decretis Reginaldi Poli Cardinalis, Sedis Apostolicæ Legati, Anno MDLVI. Romæ MDLXII apud Paulum Manutium Aldi F.

POLLARD.   A. F. POLLARD, M.A. The History of England from the Accession of Edward VI to the Death of Elizabeth (1547–1603). Third Impression. London, 1915.

POLLEN.   JOHN HUNGERFORD POLLEN, S.J. The English Catholics in the reign of Queen Elizabeth. A study of their politics, civil life, and government. 1558–1580. From the Fall of the old Church to the Advent of the Counter-Reformation. London, 1920.

POLLEN Archpriest.   JOHN HUNGERFORD POLLEN. The Institution of the Archpriest Blackwell. London. s.d.

PROTHERO.   Select Statutes and other Constitutional Documents illustrative of the reigns of Elizabeth and James I. Edited by G. W. Prothero, Litt.D. 3rd Edition. Oxford, 1906.

QUIRINI.   Epistolæ Reginaldi Poli. Brixen, 1744. 5 vols.

RICHARD.   P. RICHARD, Docteur ès Lettres, Le Concile de Trente, being Tome IX of the Historie des Conciles, published by Letouzey et Ané. Paris, 1930.

RONAN.   MILES V. RONAN. The Reformation in Ireland under Queen Elizabeth, 1558–1580. London, 1930.

SANDER. The Rise and Growth of the Anglican Schism, by Nicholas Sander, D.D. Published A.D. 1585. With a continuation of the history by the Rev. Edward Rishton, B.A., of Brasenose College, Oxford. Translated, with Introduction and Notes by David Lewis, M.A. London, 1877.

SIMPSON. RICHARD SIMPSON. Life of Edmund Campion. New edition. London, 1896.

STONE. J. M. STONE. The History of Mary I, Queen of England. London, 1901.

STURGE. CHARLES STURGE. Cuthbert Tunstal. London, 1938.

TIERNEY. Dodd's Church History of England from the commencement of the 16th century to the Revolution of 1688, with Notes, Additions, and a Continuation by the Rev. M. A. Tierney, F.S.A. 5 vols. London, 1839–1843.

V.L. Vatican Library.

W.A. Archives in the possession of the Archbishop of Westminster, preserved at Archbishop's House, Westminster.

ZIMMERMAN. BENEDICT ZIMMERMAN, O.C.D. Carmel in England. London, 1899.

INDEX OF PROPER NAMES

Julius III–Pole	*Post nuntium nobis*	Aug. 5, 1553	61
	Cum nos hodie	id.	63
	Superioribus Mensis	June 28, 1554	62
Pius IV–Eliz.		May 5, 1560	154
Pius V–Eliz.	*Regnans in Excelsis*	Feb. 25, 1570	187
Gregory XIII–Irish Nation		Feb. 25, 1577	199
Clement VIII–Blackwell	*Inter Gravissimum*	Apr. 6, 1599	301
	Cum Nobilissimum	Aug. 17, 1601	302
	Venerunt Nuper	Oct. 5, 1602	303
Paul V–English Catholics	*Magno animi mœrore*	Sept. 22, 1606	308
	Renuntiatum Nobis	Aug. 23, 1606	308
Gregory XV–William Bishop	*Apostolatus Officium*	Mar. 15, 1623	321
	Ecclesia Romana	Mar. 23, 1623	321 329 n.
Urban VIII–Richard Smith	*Ecclesia Romana* *Britannia*	Feb. 4, 1625 May 9, 1631	329 n. 378–80

proclamations against him 1628–9, 370–5 ; Codner, O.S.B., states the case against him, 366–70 ; he denounces an anonymous Jesuit book to Rome, 376 ; is publicly rebuked by the Brief *Britannia* May 1631, 378 ; his strong letters to Rome June, July 1631 (text), 380–88 ; does not publish the Brief, 389 ; makes no public comment, 391 ; his protest to Propaganda, 391–7 ; share in new scheme for bishops 1633, 397–9 ; petitions to return to England 1645, 390 ; apostolate in Paris 1642–55, *ib.* ; death, 391 ; otherwise mentioned, 3, 5, 276

Smith, Sir Thomas, 94, 103, 134

Somerset, Edward Seymour, duke of, Protector, 20, 26, 96, 128

St. Cyran, Jean Duverger, abbé de, 355

Stapleton, Thomas, 162, 293

Statutes :

Against revilers of the Sacrament	Ed. VI	1547	21
Appeals	Hy. VIII	1533	12
Chantries, dissolution of	Ed. VI	1547	21
Clergy's children, legitimation of	Ed. VI	1552	23
Ecclesiastical Appointments	Hy. VIII	1534	13
Heresy, reviving laws against	Ph. & Mary	1554	97
Jesuits and seminary priests, against	Eliz.	1585	228–30, 252–4
Marriage of clergy, legalising	Ed. VI	1549	23
Obedience, to retain subjects in due, I	Eliz.	1581	246, 255
Obedience, to retain subjects in due, II	—	1587	230
Recusants, against Popish	—	1593	230–1
Recusants, for better repressing	James I	1606	307
Recusants, to prevent dangers from	—	—	307
Repeal of Reformation Laws I	Mary	1553	67
Repeal of Reformation Laws II	Ph. & Mary	1554	68–72
Roman bulls, etc., against bringing in	Eliz.	1571	255
Roman dispensations, etc., against	Hy. VIII	1534	14
Seditious words, against	Eliz.	1581	246, 255
Six Articles	Hy. VIII	1539	20
Submission of the Clergy	—	1534	12
Succession I	—	—	15
Succession II	—	—	—
Supremacy Act	—	—	14
Supremacy Act, I	Eliz.	1559	246, 254

Story, Bl. John, martyr, 247, 252
Stukely, Sir Thomas, 197, 198, 199
Supremacy, the Elizabethan, in religious matters, 138–42

Taylor, John, bishop of Lincoln, 68, 86
Taylor, Dr. Rowland, 106–8
Thirlby, Thomas, bishop of Ely, 86, 89, 90, 91
Thompson, William, Conventual Franciscan, 345
Throckmorton, Francis, 209
Topcliffe, 262
Trent, Council of, 6, 40, 41, 42, 75, 84, 93, 154, 348, 359, 364, 427
Tunstal, Cuthbert, bishop of Durham, 32, 33, 85, 86, 88, 89, 90, 91
Turberville, James, bishop of Exeter, 94
Tyrannicide, discussion on, 216–19

Uniformity, Acts of, Edward VI, Elizabeth, 138–142
Urban VIII, pope, 189, 330 n., 363, 399 n., 22–3, 400, 401

Vaast, St., abbey of, at Arras, 164, 165, 331
Vendeville, John, bishop of Tournai, 150, 160–2, 164
Veysey, John, bishop of Exeter, 85–7
Vimercato, Francesco, 55

Walsingham, Sir Francis, 131, 259, 260, 262, 263
Ward, Mary, 429
Warton, cf. Parfew
Warwick, Richard Neville, earl of, 'the Kingmaker,' 30
Warwick, Edward Plantagenet, earl of, 30, 31, 39
Warwick, John Dudley, earl of, cf. Northumberland
Watson, Thomas, bishop of Lincoln, 94, 278, 292
Watson, William, 273 n., 298, 306
Weston, William, S.J., 278, 279, 280 n.
White, John, bishop of Winchester, 94–5
White, Thomas (alias Blacklow), 398 n.
Whitehead, David, 126
Whitgift, John, archbishop of Canterbury, 262
Wolsey, Thomas, archbishop of York, Cardinal, 34, 79
Worthington, Dr. Thomas, 289, 314 n.
Wyatt, Sir Thomas, 59, 68

PRINTED IN GREAT BRITAIN BY THE WHITEFRIARS PRESS LTD.
LONDON AND TONBRIDGE